ADVANCES IN

EXPERIMENTAL
SOCIAL PSYCHOLOGY

VOLUME 13

CONTRIBUTORS TO VOLUME 13

John M. Darley

Edward L. Deci

Frank D. Fincham

George R. Goethals

Jon Hartwick

Joseph M. Jaspars

Howard Leventhal

Serge Moscovici

Richard M. Ryan

Robert S. Wyer, Jr.

ADVANCES IN

Experimental

Social Psychology

EDITED BY

Leonard Berkowitz

DEPARTMENT OF PSYCHOLOGY
UNIVERSITY OF WISCONSIN
MADISON, WISCONSIN

VOLUME 13

1980

 ACADEMIC PRESS
A Subsidiary of Harcourt Brace Jovanovich, Publishers
New York   London   Toronto   Sydney   San Francisco

ACADEMIC PRESS, INC.
111 Fifth Avenue, New York, New York 10003

United Kingdom Edition published by
ACADEMIC PRESS, INC. (LONDON) LTD.
24/28 Oval Road, London NW1 7DX

LIBRARY OF CONGRESS CATALOG CARD NUMBER: 64–23452

ISBN 0–12–015213–4

PRINTED IN THE UNITED STATES OF AMERICA

80 81 82 83   9 8 7 6 5 4 3 2 1

CONTENTS

People's Analyses of the Causes of Ability-Linked Performances

John M. Darley and George R. Goethals

The Empirical Exploration of Intrinsic Motivational Processes

Edward L. Deci and Richard M. Ryan

Attribution of Responsibility: From Man the Scientist to Man as Lawyer

Frank D. Fincham and Joseph M. Jaspars

Toward a Comprehensive Theory of Emotion

Howard Leventhal

Toward a Theory of Conversion Behavior

Serge Moscovici

The Role of Information Retrieval and Conditional Inference Processes in Belief Formation and Change

Robert S. Wyer, Jr. and Jon Hartwick

CONTRIBUTORS

Numbers in parentheses indicate the pages on which the authors' contributions begin.

John M. Darley, *Department of Psychology, Princeton University, Princeton, New Jersey 08544* (1)

Edward L. Deci, *Department of Psychology, University of Rochester, Rochester, New York 14627* (39)

Frank D. Fincham,[1] *Department of Experimental Psychology, University of Oxford, Oxford OX1 3UD, England* (81)

George R. Goethals, *Department of Psychology, Williams College, Williamstown, Massachusetts 01267* (1)

Jon Hartwick, *Department of Psychology, University of Illinois at Urbana-Champaign, Champaign, Illinois 61820* (241)

Joseph M. Jaspars, *Department of Experimental Psychology, University of Oxford, Oxford OX1 3UD, England* (81)

Howard Leventhal, *Department of Psychology, University of Wisconsin, Madison, Wisconsin 53706* (139)

Serge Moscovici, *École des Hautes Études en Sciences Sociales, Groupe de Psychologie Sociale, Paris, France* (209)

Richard M. Ryan, *Department of Psychology, University of Rochester, Rochester, New York 14627* (39)

Robert S. Wyer, Jr., *Department of Psychology, University of Illinois at Urbana-Champaign, Champaign, Illinois 61820* (241)

[1]Present address: Department of Psychology, State University of New York at Stony Brook, Stony Brook, New York 11794.

PEOPLE'S ANALYSES OF THE CAUSES OF ABILITY-LINKED PERFORMANCES[1]

John M. Darley

DEPARTMENT OF PSYCHOLOGY
PRINCETON UNIVERSITY
PRINCETON, NEW JERSEY

George R. Goethals

DEPARTMENT OF PSYCHOLOGY
WILLIAMS COLLEGE
WILLIAMSTOWN, MASSACHUSETTS

[1]Portions of this work were supported by NIMH grant MH 23527 to George Goethals. The authors are grateful to Rick Bender, Joel Cooper, Nancy Cantor, Amy Demorest, Susan Darley, Carol Dweck, Tim Elig, Nina Feldman, Irene Frieze, Kay Ferdinandsen, E. E. Jones, Diane Ruble, and Bernard Weiner for insightful comments and suggestions on various drafts of the article.

Since this article was written, we have seen an excellent article by Mel Snyder of Dartmouth College entitled "Attributional Ambiguity" that discusses many of the phenomena we put forward here. The two articles are complementary and the interested reader probably will want to obtain a copy of the Snyder work.

1

I. Introduction

A. THE NAIVE PSYCHOLOGICAL ANALYSIS OF ACTION

We live in a world in which a great deal of what we do is evaluated, both by other people and by ourselves. Performances on the tennis court, in the classroom, and in the concert hall are very frequently appraised, and for the most part such appraisals are undertaken with an eye toward evaluating the athletic, intellectual, or artistic ability that underlies the performances. The purpose of this contribution is to outline how ordinary people perceive these ability-linked performances and to explore the ways that they actively construct accounts of their own and other people's abilities in the service of both self-evaluative and self-presentational concerns.

Our discussion is in the tradition of Fritz Heider's (1958) "naive analysis of action." Heider's naive psychology outlines the commonsense assumptions about human beings that ordinary people use to understand behavior and to guide their interactions with others. The present approach reflects our sense of the value of the Heiderian approach in that its emphasis is clearly on how people understand performances in their own vocabulary.

One of our general themes will be that, even more than has been suggested in previous analyses, there is a complexity, richness, and imaginativeness in ordinary people's perceptions of the determinants of ability-linked performance. A second theme will be that this kind of complexity is used in extremely inventive ways, not only for people to evaluate their own and others' performances and abilities but also to present themselves favorably.

B. PLAN OF THIS CONTRIBUTION

The first section of this contribution presents a model for the ways in which people conceptualize the links between performances, the underlying abilities that those performances are thought to reflect, and the other factors that can raise or lower the level of a performance. We begin with a review of earlier attempts to conceptualize the relationship and then suggest what factors we see as present in ordinary people's conceptualization of the link between performance and ability.

Next, we suggest an equation that may represent the relationships between what turns out to be a rather large set of factors.

The next section considers how the analyses of performances are carried out in the everyday social contexts in which the need to do such analyses arises. Central to our argument is the idea that, as well as the concern for making accurate ability attributions, concerns for the saving of face and the maintenance of self-esteem also enter into the considerations of both the performer and the perceiver. (Sometimes, for instance, the performer who has given a poor performance will use his knowledge of the general performance equation to avoid having a low ability attributed to himself.) Next we indicate the role the performance equation plays in social comparison processes in which people learn about their own abilities. Finally we draw some implications for the general concept of ability.

II. The Perceived Causes of Task Performances

A. EARLIER APPROACHES

A person runs the hundred yard dash, takes an arithmetic quiz, or takes a college entrance examination board test. Since Heider, there has been a general recognition that more factors than the person's underlying ability determine his performance on these tasks. According to Heider (1958), the level at which a person accomplishes a task is a result of both *personal* and *environmental* forces. The environmental forces are those that contribute to the task's difficulty, while the personal forces are analyzable into two categories: *power* and *trying*. The power factor is most usually equated with the person's ability, while the trying factor (often referred to as the motivational factor in the context of ability-related tasks) tends to refer to the effort or exertion the individual is expending in order to accomplish the task.

Thus, Heider suggests:

$$P = [A \times M] \pm D$$

where P is performance, A ability, M motivation, and D task difficulty. It is assumed that theirs is a multiplicative relation between ability and motivation because if either is zero the personal force is zero. The relation between personal force and environmental force is additive because a given result, for example, getting a rowboat across a lake, could occur as a result of either force alone.

Many theoreticians accepted the validity of Heider's distinctions (Jones & Davis, 1965; Kelley, 1967). Also, some researchers found evidence that the distinctions were present in the judgments of perceivers. The first precise test of the mathematical forms of the relationship was conducted by Butzin and Anderson in 1974. They reported results that generally confirm Heider's hypothesis of a multiplicative relationship between the motivational and the power components of performance. For both a physical and an intellectual performance task they found that: First, judges did use motivational and ability information to predict the performances of hypothetical actors and, second, judges used a multiplicative rule for combining the ability and motivational information.

The evidence, then, for the role of motive and ability in the naive psychology of performance prediction is good. However, neither Heider, Butzin and Anderson, nor others suggest that these are the only two determinants of performance. In a landmark paper, Weiner, Frieze, Kukla, Reed, Rest, and Rosenbaum (1972) suggested that perceivers employ four general categories of causes in accounting for ability-linked performances. These categories were ability, effort, task difficulty, and luck. Weiner et al. further suggested that these categories could usefully be classified along two dimensions, one an internal vs. external dimension and the other a stable vs. variable dimension. For example, ability is classified as a stable, internal performance determinant and effort as a variable, internal determinant. Task difficulty is seen as external and stable, whereas luck is external and variable. This analysis essentially agrees with Heider, who discusses performance determinants in a similar manner.

There have been several studies that provide evidence that performers (Feather, 1969; Feather & Simon, 1971; Simon & Feather, 1973; McMahan, 1973; Weiner, Heckhausen, Meyer, & Cook, 1972) and people who observe the performance of others (Frieze & Weiner, 1971) do distinguish stable and unstable determinants of performance. However, these studies were not designed to show that naive observers use exactly the taxonomy of components suggested by the Weiner et al. (1971) paper. In fact, more recent theoretical and empirical papers by Weiner and others (Cooper & Burger, 1978; Elig & Frieze, 1975; Frieze, 1976; Rosenbaum, 1972; Weiner, 1974) have modified the Weiner et al. scheme and made it clear that there are more perceived causes than the four originally proposed. Most importantly, these papers recognize that the early classification of ability as a stable performance determinant and effort as a variable one was not entirely successful.

In the present contribution we suggest that the naive observer's attributions regarding success or failure can best be grouped under Heider's original three categories: power, motivation, and task difficulty. Therefore, although it owes a great deal to the work of Weiner and his associates, our analysis to some extent returns to the original formulation of Heider. Extending the recent modifications in the original Weiner scheme, we also suggest that each of these three loci can be considered to have both relatively stable and relatively variable components. Both Heider and Weiner discussed luck as an additional external locus of causality relevant to understanding success and failure. We will assign it multiple roles.

B. ELEMENTS IN THE PERFORMANCE ATTRIBUTION EQUATION

1. Power

One of the factors that determines the success or failure of a person's performances is the "power" he can concentrate on the tasks. Let us define power as a person's capacity to succeed at a set of related tasks at any given moment in time. Analysis suggests that ordinary people regard ability as the major, but by no means the only, component of power. This was recognized by Heider (1958), who states "that the power factor is often represented by ability; there are other characteristics of a person that affect his power, temperament for example, but ability is commonly felt to head the list" (p. 83).

"Ability" can be defined as the long-term upper limit that the person possesses to succeed at the set of tasks. Commonsense thinking does not completely equate ability with power for two reasons. First, it recognizes that without regard to other identifiable factors there can be short-term variations in the capacity a person has to do well in a specific endeavor. For example, athletes, writers, scientists, and musicians are often recognized to have "hot streaks" lasting various amounts of time and "bad days" as well. For a time their performances may be better than is generally the case. Later, their level of success may inexplicably drop; that is, there seem to be unexplained short-term fluctuations in their power.[2] Second, common sense identifies a set of short-term factors that affect power but do not affect the perception of ability. A runner who has pulled a muscle, or is not completely recovered from an illness that lowers his red blood cell count, temporarily runs a race more slowly than he normally does. Similarly, a person who takes a timed math test when he is out of practice with the symbols of mathematics will do less well than he

[2]Baseball provides a domain in which clear variations over time in levels of power are thought to exist and therefore it takes a long time to judge how much ability a player possesses. Assuming a player has managed to make it into the major leagues by the age of 25 it may take as long as 3 years to determine exactly where his ability lies. In gross terms, of course, ability level in baseball and probably almost every other activity can be determined rather quickly, at least in terms of a ceiling. It would take any judge of major league potential talent approximately 1 minute to determine whether most people have the minimal level of ability necessary to play big league ball. However, for a person who has established some basic level of talent a more precise estimate can be made only after an appraisal of a great many performances. It is recognized that a player may have good and bad days, good and bad weeks, good and bad months, and even good and bad years. Performance levels will vary over time in ways that seem for the most part determined by variations in the individual's power, rather than variations in effort, difficulty, or chance. Players report variations in their power level over time. When things are going well they talk in terms of how big or fat the ball looks coming up to the plate, and consequently how easily they can hit it. They feel that their swing is easy and powerful. They feel very strong. In short, over a short period of time, say a week, it is as if their level of power is very high. When things are going poorly they feel as if they have lost their timing, their strength, or their judgment. When such a thing happens there is nothing to do but persist until they "snap out of it" or "get everything together" again.

would if he were more in practice. In all of these cases, we judged (or could be convinced) that the person's motivation to do well on the task remained high: these factors are therefore not well assimilated to a motivational construct.[3] In commonsense terms, it makes poor sense to say that a sprain affects a person's motivation to run a race. In Heider's terms, they affect what a person can do rather than "how hard he tries"—the power he has available to him to expend on the task. Therefore, they are more similar to the ability term than they are to the motivational term. However, it also violates common sense to identify these factors with the relatively stable, long-term conceptualization of ability. They exist in common sense as relatively short-term influences on a person's power that cause his power to be less than perfectly reflective of his true underlying ability.

In general, these short-term power factors seem to operate in a single direction: to depress performance below what would be expected given a person's ability level. In other words, it is the multiple possible ability inferences that can be made after a person fails at a task that makes most clear the necessity for distinguishing power from ability. When a person fails at a task on which he has been trying to succeed, the conclusion is generally that the person does not, at least at present, have the power to cause a positive outcome. Does this mean that the person does not have the ability to perform the task? In naive psychology, not necessarily, because short-term power factors could have caused a person to perform "not up to" his true ability. Examples of this factor could be as short-term as a blister on a runner's heel, a 24-hour virus, or a cinder in the eye of a test taker. Other examples may be relatively longer term, such as a person's state of conditioning for a physical performance or level of practice in the case of intellectual performances. In all of these cases, in commonsense terms we would say that although his real underlying ability is high, there are other power factors operating that affected how able the performer was to give his best performance.

These examples reveal what is likely generally to be the case for power as well as for motivation and task difficulty—specific components of these factors are distributed along a temporal continuum, rather than perfectly dichotomizable into "short"- and "long"-term factors. Being "in practice" for a particular set of performances may involve years of time, and so is by no means a short-

---

[3]In a complex world, a single fact can provide evidence for several attributional characteristics. For instance, a person who does poorly because he is out of practice in the material covered in an exam avoids our concluding that his ability is low; if he knew about the exam in advance and did not bother to study, this causes us to conclude that his intrinsic motivation is low. This possibility we do not deny. However, we simply suggest that people can distinguish a power locus of effect of lack of practice from a motivational one. A case might be an arithmetic task given unannounced to a school child.

term power factor. Nonetheless, it is still not equated with the naive psychological concept of a person's "true underlying ability." Indeed, the ability construct, in naive psychological use is sometimes startlingly abstracted from empirically observable events. For instance, lacrosse is a sport that many people play for the first time in college, and coaches will occasionally judge from the good play of one of these people that he had the ability to be a top player if only he had practiced during that earlier period of his life when the basic skills were ingrained. Some aging faculty members, watching college athletic contests, believe that they have the ability to do as well as the players, were they only in practice, in condition, and had the benefit of good coaching. Ability then is not simply inferred from the level of an observed performance.

Furthermore, the connection of ability with a performance level is generally one sided; a person's ability level is usually at least as high as his performance level. Shorter term power factors usually act to hamper performance, causing a person to perform "not quite up to his true ability." This is probably true in general; however, one can think of a few instances in which some sort of short-term factors can cause a person to perform in ways that ordinary people might call "above his ability level." For instance, when a short-distance sprinter is in excellent physical condition the speed with which he is capable of sprinting is limited by the rate of oxygen exchanged between his blood and his lungs. Therefore, temporarily increasing the amount of blood circulating would increase this oxygen exchange and increase the speed of the runner. However, the difficulty of finding such cases probably is some confirmation of the idea that the short-term power factor usually lowers rather than raises performances.

The basic proposition is that naive psychological observers of their own and other performers distinguish between ability and shorter term power factors as determinants of those performances. Because the theory we are proposing is a naive psychological one, one line of evidence for the correctness of the distinction between ability and shorter term power components stems from its congruence with the intuition of the reader. However, more formal evidence that many people actually draw this distinction arises from a study by Elig and Frieze (1975). Those authors coded the responses of naive observers who listed the possible reasons for success or failure on an intellectual task, such as taking a test. The open-ended character of the task given to the judges enables us to estimate the causal categories commonly used by people, encued by the imposition of a limited number of scales by the experimenter. "Fatigue" and "illness" both appeared in the judges' open-ended lists, and both seem examples of short-term factors different from ability that nonetheless affect the actor's power to perform. In a study by Valle and Frieze (1976), in which observers gave predictions about the performance of a life insurance salesman, observers were influenced by the degree of knowledge that the salesman was described to have about life insurance, which is a factor equivalent to level of practice on an intellectual task. In sum, both long-term ability (A) and short-term factors related to ability (A') are perceived to affect performance.

2. Motivation

"Trying" is Heider's (1958) term for the motivational determinant of performances. It is often classified as internal and unstable (Weiner *et al.*, 1971). However, there is evidence both that there actually are relatively stable, long-term components of motivation relevant to performance and also that naive observers account for success or failure in terms of long-term motives. Evidence for a stable motivational component comes from research by McClelland and his associates. These studies show that a person's level of achievement motivation is relatively stable over time, and reliably measurable (McClelland, Atkinson, Clark, & Lowell, 1953). Related research has also shown that a person's level of achievement motivation is a powerful determinant of the effort he will expend on a wide variety of tasks that he perceives as achievement relevant (French & Thomas, 1958; McClelland *et al.*, 1953; Strodtbeck, 1958).

For present purposes the most important research is that showing that ordinary perceivers have a construct of people having stable dispositions to expend effort in order to perform well (Cooper & Burger, 1978; Frieze, 1976; Elig & Frieze, 1975). "These (intrinsic) motives are spontaneously mentioned in free response data rather consistently" (Elig & Frieze, 1975, p. 10). That is, in accounting for ability-related performances observers make extensive use of relevant long-term motives. Again, both long-term motivation (M) and short-term expenditures of effort (M') are perceived as factors affecting performance.

3. Task Difficulty

Difficulty is an attribute of a task or problem that Heider (1958) and Weiner *et al.* (1971) viewed as stable. However, it does seem reasonable to suggest that the concept of task difficulty can be thought of as having both a stable and a fluctuating component. First consider the stable component. For any particular ability, many tasks are thought of as "linked" to it in that these tasks are thought to require some level of that ability to perform. Intuitively, it seems reasonable to suggest that a naive observer can rank order these tasks in terms of their relative difficulties. In the simplest cases, this is because of the Guttman scale characteristics of some sets of ability-linked tasks. High jumping 7 feet is more difficult than high jumping 6.5 feet. Arithmetic tasks involving two-digit problems are more difficult than arithmetic tasks involving one-digit problems. However, even in cases in which this property does not apply, people still seem able to make task difficulty ratings. For example, observers are often able to calibrate the difficulty of playing one piece of music compared to another. Likewise it is seen as more difficult to run a mile than to run a half mile.

Even for a single task, ordinary observers seem generally capable of assigning a difficulty level. A likely way of determining the difficulty level that is indexed for these tasks is simply in terms of the relative degree of success that could be expected from a group of trained laymen or a group of experts. The naive observer may rank tasks on the basis of how many randomly selected people in a given population could successfully complete the task or how many of a group of experts could do it successfully. Ordinarily, these two measures are likely to give correlated results. In cases in which they do not, it can be expected that people will have some difficulty agreeing on the level of difficulty that should be assigned that task.

So there does seem to be a commonsense conceptualization of a task as having a fixed, stable component of difficulty. For any specific task, however, in the exact set of circumstances in which it is performed, there are a large number of highly transitory events that can momentarily vary its difficulty. For instance, a head wind may blow against the runner and make this particular mile on this particular day more difficult to run. The arithmetic test of one particular student may be the last one duplicated and therefore it may be blurred and hard to read. Or if the bowling alley is warped, it can be more difficult than it is normally to bowl a strike. When the pitcher applies saliva to a baseball, it is more than normally difficult to hit. Of course, such factors can be built into the definition of the task in the first place, but to list them all is tedious. The naive observer probably assigns an overall difficulty level to any particular task category, for instance, swimming a mile, and then recognizes that the difficulty of successfully completing the task on a particular occasion can vary because of any one of a number of other conditions as well. These momentary perturbations on task difficulty intuitively function as modifiers of the more stable and long-term components of task difficulty. In short, both long-term and short-term aspects of task difficulty (D and D', respectively) are used in analyzing performances.

4. Interactions

Interactive determinants of performance may arise from any particular combination of task and the individual's motivations and abilities. For instance, a test of math ability that may be given in any one of a number of formats happens to be given in a multiple-choice format and commonsense psychology firmly believes that some people have idiosyncratic difficulties with multiple-choice tasks—here, a task–ability interaction is being suggested. Likewise, one runner can have particularly acute difficulties running on a cold day. A child who learned her arithmetic test problems aligned vertically can have trouble when they are aligned horizontally. These sorts of possibilities are recognized by ordinary people as potential performance determinants (Elig & Frieze, 1975) and therefore need to be included in any naive psychological theory of performance determining components.

5. Luck

"Luck" is dealt with by Weiner *et al.* (1971) as an external, unstable determinant of performance. Our treatment of it is somewhat different. "Luck" seems to us to have multiple possible meanings and it is important to distinguish these meanings: (1) "Luck" can refer to the occurrence of one of the interactions discussed above. For instance, a friend might say to a runner "It was bad luck that it was so cold the day you ran," meaning roughly that it could not have gotten cold at a worse time, because this runner does particularly poorly in cold weather. (2) Some events are organized such that a chance as well as a skill component determines their outcome. That the child riding the old-fashioned carrousel was able to reach out and grab a ring as she went by is a matter of skill. That the ring was the brass one that won the prize was a matter of luck. (3) To suggest "luck" (good or bad) as the cause of a performance is sometimes to be proposing that it is not worth the effort to search for the exact set of personal or environmental causes of that performance. Instead, it is a proposition that we consider the performance an atypical one and do not search for its exact causes unless future performance outcomes prove that it was not atypical, does indicate something stable about the individual, and therefore is worth attributional analysis. The "luck" explanation, in this sense of being a suggestion to withhold analysis, is most likely to arise when the observer has detected some pattern in previous performances with which this particular performance is incongruent. Ordinary people, like psychologists, seem to have the conceptualization of error variance and recognize that no attributional pattern of abilities, motives, and tasks is going to predict performances perfectly (Frieze, 1973; Frieze & Weiner, 1971; Kelley, 1967).

The second sense of the word "luck" refers to a performance determinant that is external to the performing individual. In this usage, it is an external, unstable determinant of performance as Heider and Weiner suggest. In the first sense of the term, luck is normally an interaction between external and internal determinants rather than an external determinant. In the third sense of luck, it is a proposal not to assign a cause to a performance outcome, rather than the assignment of an external cause.

As Elig and Frieze (1975) discovered, there is yet a fourth use of the word "luck" in attributional processes. In their coding of the attributional statements made in response to open-ended questions, they found that judges would refer to an actor as being a lucky person, "with the implication that this is a stable, internal, unintentional trait of the person" (p. 9).

6. The Performance Equation Summarized

To summarize, we have argued that a commonsense analysis of the determinants of performance uses three broad classifications: power, motivation, and task difficulty. It recognizes a relatively stable and unstable component of each of those causes and suggests a role for interactional and "lucky" causes roughly equivalent to the roles of the interactional and error components in analysis of variance thinking.

An equation that expresses the ways in which these three classes of constructs are combined to predict performance is

$$P = [(A - A') \times (M \pm M')] \pm (D \pm D') \pm L$$

where, as noted above, P is performance, A ability, M motivation, D task difficulty, and L luck. A', M', and D', respectively, represent the short-term component affecting ability, motivation, and task difficulty.

For several reasons, this equation needs to be regarded rather tentatively. First, scaling procedures (Butzin & Anderson, 1974) are necessary to determine the weights each individual puts on the various components of the equation. Second, the precision it implies is somewhat illusory. A study by Kun and Weiner (1973) suggests that the relationship between ability and motivation is perceived to be multiplicative for difficult tasks but additive for easy ones. Also, a specific real-world event can trigger inferences about more than one of the theoretical constructs (e.g., a person's losing sleep by staying out late the night before an announced exam leads us to infer both low intrinsic motivation to do well and lowered power to do well). Finally, it must be remembered that the equation exists in "naive psychological space"—that is, it purports to describe how ordinary perceivers draw inferences, and the person perception process is well known to be a rapid, routinized process the rules for which can only be approximately characterized (Abelson, 1976). Still, even with these qualifications, the general concept that there are multiple determinants of a person's ability-linked performances is a useful analytic device in several domains. We now turn to the task of demonstrating this.

III. The Social Uses of the Performance Equation: Accuracy

Often the world is organized so that it is useful for people to know their own abilities. It is useful because it enables them to be able to predict the success or failure of their efforts. Knowing their own abilities keeps people from attempting tasks that are too difficult, which keeps them from the normally negative consequences of failure. Sometimes the failure is in the physical domain: A child, even when alone, may not attempt to jump over a brook if the jump is too difficult for him, because he will get wet if he fails. Other times it is a more social failure that is avoided: A college student who stays out of an intramural basketball game because the other players are above her ability level is avoiding the social cost of embarrassment. Generally, it seems useful for people to know that they do not possess enough of a requisite ability to perform a set of tasks at some defined level. Intuitively, much of what each individual has to learn seems of this sort, but successes convey useful information also. One avoids failure by knowing what one is "bad at" but achieves success by knowing what one is "good at." A child's choices of playground activities and of school lessons to take and a college student's choice of area of concentration and intended career normally represent an assessment of their own areas of strength, based on their experience of success in the past.

Trope and his colleagues have experimentally demonstrated that when it is useful for them to do so, people do choose tasks that will maximize the information they received about their abilities. Trope and Brickman (1975) defined the *diagnosticity* of a task as the degree to which performance outcomes vary on that task as a function of ability levels and demonstrated that subjects selected high- over low-diagnosticity tasks (see also Trope, 1975). Subjects are capable of quite sophisticated versions of this strategy; Trope (1979) caused subjects' ability uncertainties to lie on different points along an ability continuum and discovered that they then chose tasks that would be most diagnostic in their particular zone of uncertainty.

So, empirically, it is clear that people are sometimes motivated to determine their own ability levels. However, we suggest, people recognize that ability is not transparently revealed by performance. To determine their own abilities, or other stable dispositional properties that they possess, they need to make inferences that are guided by the performance equation. It is useful here to generalize our perspective and ask, "When a person observes either his own performance or the performance of another, what does he seek to infer and what strategies does he use to make the inferences?"

SEARCHING FOR STABLE COMPONENTS

As a fact in elementary algebra, any one of the variables in the performance equation can be made the one for which the equation is to be "solved." Paralleling this at the psychological level, changes in the question that the observer seeks to answer can cause him to attempt to solve the equation for different variables. For instance, the testers of a new running track surface want to determine whether that specific track surface is "fast" or "slow"; in other words, they want to determine the specific increase or decrease in the general task difficulty of running the mile that is caused by the new surface. Likewise, a guidance counselor who knows a high school student is generally scholastically able may use the student's pattern of grades to infer the pattern of the student's continuing interests. Therefore, our initial suggestion is that circumstantial pressures can shift the observer's strategic focus and cause any of the variables in the performance equation to be the one for which the equation is to be solved.

Having said that, we feel that it is still probably true that the "standard" performance-witnessing situation usually leads to a focus on a specific subset of the variables contained in the performance equation. It was Heider's insight that the process of person perception is an attempt to infer from observed actions the "dispositions" of the actor that led to those actions. These inferred dispositional constructs are those that are sufficiently stable to warrant the prediction of the actor's future performances in novel situations. It follows then that a person observing his own performance or the performance of others attempts to infer the stable determinants of that performance. It is knowing the stable, relatively long-term determinants of performance levels, rather than the short-term, unstable ones that enables one to predict the level of future performances. In the performance equation there are three such long-term determinants of performance: ability, motives, and stable task difficulty.

Heider goes on to suggest that ability is normally the first variable that a person attempts to infer when he observes a performance. This is because it is conceptualized as a long-term internal property of the performer. As such, commonsense psychology holds that it is causally implicated in determining the success or failure level of many related performances.

We suspect that ability is normally the variable that the observer seeks to infer. However, we would resist the suggestion that ability is always the automatic target of inference because our analysis claims that there is a long-term stable dispositional component that ordinary observers may infer about motivation as well; that is, there is a component of motivation that is thought of as a long-term internal property of the individual. Therefore, on commonsense psychological terms, this also ought to be a variable on which the observer would focus in determining performances. Intuitively, this seems correct. We observe the behavior of others to determine not only what they "are good at" but also what they are "interested in." Knowing this will enable us to predict what tasks they will choose to perform. If a person is constrained to give a performance, knowing whether he is motivated to do well at the task will enable an observer to predict whether he will "live up to" his ability level for that performance.

In addition, there are some instances in which the observer's interest is in identifying the contribution of the environment to the performance. When this occurs, it can be expected that the efforts of the observer will be to identify the long-term, stable difficulty components of the task, because this information will be generalizable. For instance, as a consequence of the metric system, there are several races in international meets that Americans cannot easily assess in terms of task difficulty. One way in which people will "calibrate" these races (e.g., figure out the task difficulty) is by getting a set of runners of known high ability to run these new distances. In this way, the typical difficulties of the new distances can be assessed.

To summarize, we have suggested that normally ability is the first performance component assessed, and there is generally a priority placed on assessing the long-term, stable performance determinants. However, this is by no means always the case. Sometimes the purposes for which the performance assessment is carried out will create a need to focus the assessment on a specific performance determinant. The day before the critical game, for instance, the coach may observe the performance of his injured star player for the purpose of determining the degree to which his injuries (short-term ability factors) will affect his performance.

1. The Importance of Multiple Observational Instances

As Kelley (1967) has most notably pointed out, people seem to seek to observe multiple performances of an actor before making confident attributions about his dispositions. Certainly, in the area of dispositional attributions, this strategy is sensible. In seeking dispositional attributions, by observing repeated performances, variation resulting from the various short-term determinants of performance can generally be minimized. Luck and short-term variations in task difficulty are generally thought to "even themselves out" within a few performances. Most short-term decrements in power or influences on motivation are not likely to have their influence over more than a few days, so observing performances over a several-day span is likely to minimize their efforts.

An alternative way of collecting multiple observations is to observe a variety of performances in a single situation (Kelley, 1967). If almost all people perform alike (consensus), then the attribution is to the "situation." In our terms, none of the performers has warranted an inference that he has either high or low ability or motivation. If attributions are made, they are likely to be made rather tentatively, and the observer is likely to adopt the conclusion that the observed individual is about "average." Likewise, as Kelley suggests, no person inferences may be made at all, which would be the equivalent of deciding that the performance situation was a "nondiscriminating test" in the sense of not creating a chance for the test takers to display the differential abilities or motivations they possess. One possible conclusion would be that the test situation was too easy on task difficulty terms.

2. The Consistency Dimension

Kelley also discussed the construct of consistency of performance on the part of one individual across "time and modality." In the area of ability attributions there is evidence that, in observing repeated performances, observers look for a pattern of consistency and make their attributions accordingly. For instance, Karaz and Perlman (1975) showed that judges who knew a horse consistently won or lost in a series of races made more extreme internal attributions to that horse than did observers for whom the horse behaved inconsistently. The same holds true for people judging the reasons for their own actions: Children receiving repeated successes or repeated failures at a task attributed a large percentage weight to ability as a determinant of their performance (Nicholls, 1975).

For a theory concerned with allocating the dispositional components of performance, it is possible to take Kelley's general construct of "consistency" and give it more precise meanings that are useful in this specific attributional context. The following set of principles is a first attempt at doing so. [Notice that they are generally consistent with the discounting and covariation principles of attribution theory (Kelley, 1967, 1971) and the studies supporting them (e.g., Jones, Davis, & Gergen, 1961; MacArthur, 1972; Orvis, Cummingham, & Kelley, 1975).]

Assume that a person has given a set of performances on a series of tasks that are all linked to a single ability but are given under a variety of situational circumstances. Several sets of distinctions between kinds of test circumstances are important to distinguish: First, some test situations hold out the promise of high extrinsic payoffs for doing well. These may be as simple as monetary or other rewards or may involve more complex social payoffs, such as group esteem or prestige. Other tasks, by contrast, have only whatever intrinsic satisfaction accrues to doing that task well.

Given these distinctions, the following principles of performance attribution can be suggested.

a. If a person does well at a family of tasks that the observer perceives are related to a unified underlying ability, then he will be perceived as possessing a high level of that ability. The larger the proportion of occasions sampled, and the wider the set of tests the sample ranges across, the more confident the observer will be in the high ability attribution.

b. If some of the tasks were given under conditions of low induced extrinsic motivation and if the actor's performance continued at a high level, then he will be perceived as having high intrinsic motives to perform well.

c. If a person does well only on tasks on which a situational motive was induced and performs poorly on nonrewarded performances, then he will be perceived as having high ability, and low intrinsic motives to do well on that family of tasks.

d. Generally, if variation in a person's performance can be associated with variance in the testing conditions, then the observer will determine the most plausible linkage for that variation with relatively short-term power, motivational, or task difficulty considerations and attribute ability and motivation accordingly. This principle is made clear only by examples. Suppose that the performer did well on tests whether or not prizes were given and did well when tests were handed out to each individual but did poorly when the tests were written on the blackboard; the most plausible linkage of this set of circumstances is to the short-term power construct, perhaps a difficulty in seeing the tests on the blackboard because of near sightedness. "Clutch hitters" have high abilities that they are extrinsically motivated to show in high-pressure situations. "Chokers," in contrast, have a power level that is reduced by pressure, and so on.

e. If a set of performances falls into an overall pattern that is explicable, but if one performance deviates from the pattern, then the explanation for the set pattern will be retained, with a short-term factor or luck added to account for the deviant case.

f. There is a one-sided character to the inference of ability such that a high level of performance tends to indicate a high ability, whereas a low performance does not uniquely indicate a low ability. In practice, this probably translates as follows: Any one high level performance can be discounted (e.g., attributed to luck, or some short-term power factor that temporarily facilitated performance). However, the observation of two or more high-level performances should make the observer believe that the performer possesses a high level of ability and attempt to account for any observed failures on other than ability terms.

3. On the Possibility of Disconfirming Evidence

Considerable research (e.g., Jones & Goethals, 1971) shows that the observer's inferences about the stable determinants of performances are likely to be arrived at early in the sequence of observations. Later performances that do not fit the attributional pattern are likely to be attributed to the atypical operation of short-term factors or luck. Because the performance equation we have suggested involves multiple intervening variables, and the states of all of these variables are necessarily inferred, a wide range of differing conclusions about the underlying ability or motivational dispositions of the actor can be sustained. One of the implications of the present analysis is that it is very difficult to conceive of a performance at any level of success or failure that conclusively disconfirms an already arrived at inference about the performer's underlying dispositions. An observer witnessing an actor try hard at a task is more likely to consider the possibility that there is a hidden payoff for doing well at the task than he is to overturn his previously assumed conclusion that the actor was not intrinsically motivated to do well at the task.

This inference perhaps creates an insight relevant to the research on interpersonal "self-confirming prophecies." It is frequently discovered (Meichenbaum, Bowers, & Ross, 1969; Rosenthal, 1976; Word, Zanna, & Cooper, 1974), for instance, that a teacher's initially randomly induced expectancies about the abilities of a student become confirmed during the course of a sustained interaction between the teacher and the student. The present analysis suggests that part of the reason for this lies in the difficulty of the student's performing any action that would disconfirm the teacher's expectancies. This difficulty in turn arises from the fact that a person's level of performance is genuinely recognized in commonsense psychology as being affected by a variety of determinants, only one of which is ability. The construct of a person's "level of ability" is a startlingly abstract one, reached only by a long chain of inferences on the part of the observer.

IV. The Role of Self-Esteem and Face-Saving Motives

So far, the discussion has generally assumed that an individual is motivated solely by a desire to determine accurately his own or another person's ability level or motivational profile. The reader may have noticed something spectacularly naive about this discussion, since, when abilities are at issue, the motivations of the perceiver or the performer are not always, or perhaps ever, so simple. Such complexity exists because abilities are societaly regarded as important and desirable for an individual to possess. (Exceptions would include the "ability" to make a fool of oneself, to hurt other people, etc.) Therefore, because an individual normally is socialized in the value system of his culture, performing poorly on an ability-linked performance task is potentially threatening to the self-esteem of the performer, and if his performance is observed, it is also potentially threatening in that it can cause the witnessing group to lower their regard for him. In other words, a performer can lower his own self-esteem and lose face by doing poorly on an ability-linked task.

A great deal of psychological research on the attribution of the causes of success and failure demonstrates this point in the case of self-attributions. In general, it had been suggested that actors, as opposed to observers, are more likely to attribute performance successes to internal dispositions, such as abilities, whereas they attribute failures to situational causes, such as high task difficulty. This effect is variously referred to as a "motivational" or "egoistic" one and has been defined by Stephan, Bernstein, Stephan, and Davis (1979) as a concern for self-esteem that motivates the actor to take credit for success and to avoid blame for failure.

Miller and Ross (1975) reviewed the pre-1975 evidence for this claim and found it not well supported; more specifically, they argued that one could not rule out the possibility that the obtained "motivational" effects actually resulted from nonmotivational factors (e.g., the differential focus of the attention of the actors and the observers). Bradley (1978), however, has reviewed the more recent evidence, including several impressive studies by Miller and by Ross, and concludes that a motivated, ego-defensive attribution pattern has been empirically demonstrated and is most likely to occur when the actor gives his performance in public, perceives himself as having had a choice about engaging in the performance task, or is otherwise ego involved in the situation, all of which are considerations quite closely tied with self-esteem and self-presentational ones.

Given the complexity of the inferences that we claimed were necessary to make when one was solely instructed to arrive at an accurate estimate of ability, the reader may feel that the addition of these two further motives creates insuperable analytic complexities. However, it is one of the major points of our argument that the recognition of the performer's complex motives, coupled with the complex and multivariate nature of the equation relating observed performances to inferred abilities, paradoxically make the performer's social task much simpler and more possible. Because the performer is concerned with preserving his self-esteem and saving face in front of others, and because he is aware of the performance equation and knows that others who observe his performance are aware of it also, having the occasion to perform creates a potential dilemma for him that is, essentially and starkly, self-preservational. The potential dilemma becomes an actual one when the initial performance he gives is poor. The performer attempts to convince himself and others that his poor performance occurred for reasons that do not reflect badly on himself. He attempts to give (Goffman, 1959; Mills, 1940; Scott & Lyman, 1968) some "account" of his failure that lessens or removes the possible negative inferences about himself that would usually follow. It is this multivariate nature of the performance equation which, from an accuracy perspective, makes the equation almost hopeless of solution, that creates the possibilities of the skillful self-presenter avoiding the normal attribution of low ability following a poor performance.

A. EXCUSES AND ACCOUNTS FOR POOR PERFORMANCES: MAINTAINING
    ATTRIBUTIONAL AMBIGUITY

The performance equation that we suggested had seven independent variables and therefore also the possibility of a large number of first and higher order interactions between them. For each independent variable, there is a long and open-ended list of instances that count as examples of it. Nonetheless, it is perhaps too simple a list to characterize adequately the kaleidoscopic and creative shifts in perspectives of which people are capable. Consider what a person who needs to excuse a poor performance can do.

B. SHORT-TERM EXCUSES FOR A SINGLE POOR PERFORMANCE

A person has given a performance that he knows, or has reason to believe, has been poor. To avoid a low-ability attribution, he can do several things: He can signal that his poor performance was caused by some unstable performance determinant, the occurrence of which was out of his control. A runner's careful examination of his spikes after losing a race, a basketball player's complaint about being fouled after missing an easy layup, and a test taker's comments about how little sleep he got the night before the test are all examples. For any one performance, a wide variety of causes may contribute to its outcome, and people are able to search among them with a great deal of ingenuity to select those that can be presented as plausible causes of the low performance but that also do not have self-image-damaging implications. For instance, staying out late is an adequate excuse for doing poorly on an exam if the exam was not announced in advance. If it was announced, however, questions arise about why the person took the exam so lightly. Therefore the offering of this excuse under these conditions may protect against an inference of low ability from the poor test score, but it does so only by supporting an inference of low motivation to do well, which may cause loss of face. One way of avoiding this situation would be for the excuser to claim that the loss of sleep was caused by anxiety about the test, thus at one stroke preserving the possibility that the underlying ability is high and using the evidence of the low score to "prove" that intrinsic motivation was high because it generated the anxiety that disrupted the performance. However, this reasoning too may be damaging, because it raises questions about the "psychological adjustment" of a person who is made so anxious by tests. Perhaps it would be better if the sleeplessness was caused by some irrelevant factor, such as a sick member of the household or some other family crisis.

People seem to know very well how to calculate the optimal excuse, so we need to remind ourselves that it is an extremely complex social process. The excuser must calculate the plausibility of various excuses, their power in explaining away the poor performance, and their possible negative implications for various aspects of his face or self-esteem before he decides which to put forward. Various audiences may have sharply differing reactions to the same excuse, and this needs to be considered as well. For instance, to excuse doing poorly on a task because of being out late the night before at a dance may be acceptable to a group of one's peers who have the same priority system but would be unacceptable to parents, exactly because of the priority system it signaled. The anxiety explanation might be more easily accepted by parents but might signal an unacceptable lack of toughness to peers.

Consider again the form of the performance equation:

$$P = [(A \pm A') \times (M \pm M')] \pm (D \pm D')$$

From this equation the general strategy of the person who seeks to avoid having a poor performance lead to an inference of low ability is clear. He must suggest a set of short-term power, motivational, or task difficulty factors that subtract from his power or motivation to perform the task, or that momentarily add to its difficulty. Also, he must consider which of these excuses is plausible and can be made to seem convincing to the audience. He must also be careful not to advance any excuses that, seen from some other perspective, would cast him in a bad light. A person who does poorly at a football game may avoid the inference of low ability by claiming that he was drunk the night before, but he certainly embraces the conclusion that he is the sort of person who lets his teammates down in this fashion.

These excuses, when entered into the performance equation, cause it to predict a lower level of performance even for a relatively high level of ability. If a person who uses these excuses later proves to do badly, his performance is judged as acceptable in light of the difficulties he faced. If he performs at even an average level, his observers who accepted his excuses will be led to conclude that his ability is high. These kinds of excuses can be called "performance-decreasing excuses," since they consistently shift downward the level of performances expected from a fixed level of ability.

Excuses for a poor performance are frequently more plausible if some sign of them is observable during the course of the performance. For instance, if a normally speedy football runner is hampered because of a pulled leg muscle, such a condition should be visible in his stride. Because performers are well aware of this rule of evidence, if they are concerned about the possibility of giving a future poor performance, or worse, if they are in the process of giving a poor performance, they may direct some of their attention to giving off cues that will support the performance excuses that they later may want to claim. Berglas and Jones (1978) demonstrated that males who achieved a prior success at a task that was unaccompanied by feelings of skill mastery were likely to choose a drug treatment that would provide a plausible excuse for a later poor performance. The authors call this phenomenon the "self-handicapping strategy," in which people "select the available environment best designed to protect their image of self-competence in the event of poor performance" (p. 416).

Clearly, the self-handicapping strategy achieves the central goal of the performance-decreasing excuse; it may also have other effects. The performer who imposes on himself the necessity of projecting the existence of factors handicapping his performance while also giving the performance naturally has his attention split and may give a less high-level performance than he would otherwise. Thus, he may miss the chance to prove to himself and others that he can actually do the task well. Also, absorbed in the process of generating "excusing cues," he may miss the chance to learn some critical elements of the task that would enable him to do it well in the future. Finally, he may develop habits of relying on excuses and habitual patterns of excuses that automatically are given in every performance situation, even ones in which they are unlikely to have been required. Jones and Berglas (1978) have pointed out that certain alcoholics may be using alcoholism as a habitual excuse of this sort, thereby defending their self-image of high ability. It seems clear that there are dangers for the performer in becoming facile at generating excuses, although the social pressures to generate them are frequently high.

Instead of decreasing the expected level of a performance, another kind of excuse simply "distances" a performance in that it makes a general claim that a performance should not be taken as directly indexing an ability level. These distancing tactics are generally used after it is clear or the probability is high that the performance was poor enough to require denying. However, they too have their dangers. If I distance a performance that later turns out to be acceptable (in the sense that it would ordinarily index a high level of ability), then I may not be able to reclaim it later. Drunk the night before, I say to a person whom I met at the party "I must have said some ridiculous things last night, I was pretty drunk." If, as I expect, my behavior had been boorish, then I may escape some of its normal consequences. However, if I had managed to be charming, and carried on what the other regarded as a meaningful and self-disclosing conversation, I may have just conclusively distanced what I now discover I could have embraced.

C. EXCUSES IN THE LONG TERM

People are usually able to select plausible and face-saving excuses for any single performance lapse. These have been outlined. However, providing suitable excuses for a series of failures poses extreme difficulties. "Excusing" or "accounting for" a poor performance means claiming that the performance is not a true reflection of the excusing individual's stable, underlying ability or of his level of intrinsic motivation. It ordinarily works by emphasizing the importance of some unstable and short-term cause (the emphasized cause may be drawn from the power realm, the motivational realm, or the realm of task difficulties or may simply be the assertion that the performance was unluckily low). One conclusion must follow this claim, and it is that once this atypical cause ceases to operate, better performances are to be expected. For each excuse, there is a likely time frame for its dissipation or for a set of circumstances that will lead to its removal. If I did poorly on a test because of emotional upset the hour before, then, in a few days, or at least in a few weeks, I should do well at similar tests. If I do poorly at a test because of anxiety, then there ought to be a set of circumstances that will reduce my anxiety and cause me to perform well. Exactly because excuses work by claiming that a performance was atypical, at least some future performances should be typical.

Consider what this means for an individual who is excusing a poor performance when he is aware that he must perform similar tasks in the future on which he suspects he may do poorly. Clearly his dilemma is more acute than an individual who knows that he need give only one performance relevant to an ability. Therefore, somebody who initially performs poorly at a task can be expected to attempt to avoid future performances, and particularly to avoid future performances in public if he can choose instead to perform in private. Insofar as he is constrained to perform in public, his strategy for choosing excuses is likely to shift. There is something implausible about a set of poor performances, each of which is excused by a different, unique, short-term cause. The person who first fails a test because "he lost sleep," next fails because "he forgot about it" and next because he "didn't study" soon is typed by others as a low-ability person who in addition has low ability at the social game of excusing. Facing this prospect at the beginning of what he recognizes might be a chain of poor performances, the performer is likely to search for an excuse that will more economically and plausibly span the entire series of constrained performances. Therefore, the repeating performer, unlike the individual who only has to explain away one poor performance, is likely to choose an explanation that spans the range of performances he fears it will need to cover. Because he seeks to preserve the perception that his ability is high, he will not choose low ability as his explanation. Because lacking motivation frequently reflects poorly on an individual, he also will not choose low long-term motivation as an explanation. Instead, he is most likely to choose his excuses from the middle range of explanation that will efficiently cover the range of performances that he feels he needs to cover. For instance, doing poorly because of becoming anxious through wanting to do well is a particularly apt choice because it applies to all future test situations.

Two kinds of costs are frequently paid when these middle-range excuses are adopted. First, there is frequently some loss of face incurred. To be a person who is test anxious is to be a person who is not "cool under pressure." This is partially so because the constructs that are middle-range power determinants for one ability, when seen from another perspective, are abilities themselves, e.g., the ability to "psych out a test," or the ability to "stay effective under pressure." Therefore excusing one's performance by citing one of these is to be defending the possibility of possessing one ability by asserting one does not have another ability. Yet from different perspectives and to different audiences, the ability so abandoned may be an important one.

Related to this, an excuse once given may have behavioral implications for other situations. "Test anxiety" or "being bad at multiple-choice tests" as an explanation for a poor math test seems to suggest that a person should do poorly at other than math tests. "The teacher hates me," as an excuse for a low grade on an English composition suggests that one should not care about that teacher's opinion, or take what he is teaching very seriously. These middle-range excuses, therefore, may commit the excuser to some future actions or stances that can have various consequences. For example, as we suggested earlier, he is also likely to avoid such tasks, thereby giving up opportunities for skill practice and discovery learning. The net results may be to make future performances poorer than they otherwise might be.

D. EXCUSES, INTERESTS, AND PERSONALITY

The kinds of excuses people give for their performances can have far-reaching consequences on what activities they regard as worthy and unworthy, on their developing interest patterns, and on what talents and skills they develop in their lives. For example, if a person continues to perform poorly at repeated instances of a task, he may then choose to present himself as having little intrinsic motivation to do that set of tasks, with the consequence that he actually may lose interest in performing well on those activities; that is, the person may be "taken in" by his own performance, as suggested by Goffman (1959), or may perceive himself as making valid self-descriptions (Bem, 1967). It is easy to understand in human terms how negative reactions build up as one repeatedly does poorly on a task and how they would generalize to the ability underlying that task. However, the excuses of such failures have an even more serious impact on the individual's future. He will not voluntarily choose to perform tasks that develop the ability in question, and limits on his future skills are thereby caused.

Other performance circumstances can lead to changes in an individual that are likely to be even more far reaching. If an individual is constrained to give a set of performances and does poorly on many of them, he may run out of excuses to give, or the excuses he has given may run out of coverage. Other people may conclude, and he himself may have to face the conclusion, that a particular ability is genuinely low. Two ways of minimizing the resulting loss of face and self-esteem are possible: First, the person can neutralize the value of possessing that ability, and second, he can negate it.

A person who becomes convinced that he does not possess an ability can minimize the effects this lack would normally have on his self-esteem by deciding that the possession of that ability is unimportant to him.[4] A person who is not good at mathematics can decide that he is essentially an artistic, intuitive, expressive type and that the possession of the step by step reasoning skills necessary to mathematics is irrelevant to his talents. (Whether "step by step reasoning" is an accurate picture of the talents involved in mathematics is a separate issue. The preceding is simply the picture likely to be adopted by the person doing the rationalizing that we are describing.) To do this, a person need argue not that a particular ability would be trivial for everybody to possess but merely that it would be trivial for him to possess, given the general directions of his talents and interests. Intuitively, something similar to this process seems to happen. A person asked to name an ability that he does not possess is able to do so, but is likely to include the descriptive reasons why the ability is not important for him.

A person can negate the possession of an ability as a continuation of the aforementioned process, by which we mean that he can come to believe that it would actually be bad to be "good at" some ability. The humanist can feel that

---

[4]As William James (1890) pointed out, self-esteem is a function not only of what one does well, but of what one cares about doing well. Therefore a self-esteem decrement can be solved by giving up caring about doing the offending task well. In his famous formulation, James states that success is the ratio of one's successes to one's pretensions.

being good at mathematics involves having an accountant's mentality that it would be bad to possess. A person who lacks self-presentational skills and is therefore "not able" to make cocktail party conversation may decide that those who are able to do so are essentially "phony." An academic poor at sports may decide the abilities involved are those that make man closest to lower animals and therefore may be pleased not to possess them, and so on.

These techniques may be satisfactory for reducing the impact of low ability on one's self-esteem; they can be expected to be less satisfactory in saving one's face in front of others. Society tends to regard abilities as important and is likely to regard less highly those people who do not possess them.[5] Because we are all influenced in our self-definition by the appraisals we get reflected from others, a person who performs poorly in public will not only lose face but, because he can take the perspective of the other, will be damaged in his self-esteem as well. All the more reason to avoid the performance of tasks at which one does poorly.

Protecting Esteem vs. Saving Face

The preceding discussion considers how people might use ambiguities about the causes of performance to protect esteem or save face. However, our last point indicates the two are not identical, and that they may not be equally well served by a single tactic. Is there any evidence that esteem-protecting and face-saving needs do lead to different interpretations? An interesting study by Gould, Brounstein, and Sigall (1977) suggests that there is. They showed that when subjects made public attributions about the success of another person with whom they were to compete, they attributed his success to high ability. This admission had advantages in terms of the subjects' public image. They could appear modest and also position themselves for great praise if they surpassed the other person in competition and for minimal loss of face if they lost in the competition. In private, the subjects attributed the other's success less to ability, perhaps to convince themselves that they could do well in competing with the other.

As many theorists have asserted, in the long term, one's self-esteem depends heavily on the esteem one receives from others. Despite this connection, it is possible in the short term that sharply differing considerations are involved in saving face and protecting esteem. In both cases there is the issue of the credibility of the account. However, making an account plausible to oneself involves

[5]Although it is less well known, William James discussed this also. After he presents his famous self-esteem formula (see footnote 4) he points out that society will not always let men do this. Stating the case in more modern terms, we can all take the perspective of another individual. Because abilities are normally regarded as good things to possess, when we take the role of the generalized other we are led to question our idiosyncratic conclusion that a specific ability is unimportant. As an academic I may genuinely be convinced that grace on the dance floor is not an important characteristic for me to possess. Nonetheless, if circumstances drag me to the dance floor, there is a "me" outside myself that regards my awkward gyrations and is diminished by them.

different contingencies than making it plausible to others. People probably have a prior concern with protecting face. In quite Machiavellian ways, they can give excuses to others that they do not believe themselves. For example, excuses about lack of sleep and not having tried hard cannot be checked by others and can be offered to save face but not self-esteem. At other times we can make excuses to ourselves about others having cheated, the task being too difficult, the deck being stacked against us, etc., that can assuage our own feelings but would have no currency with others. Saving face probably involves attributions about our own short-term effort or power, which cannot be checked by others. Such excuses can persuade them if not us. Protecting esteem probably involves making attributions about variations in task difficulty that persuade us, as we would never seriously test them, but would not persuade others, who might insist on examining the evidence for our claims. The person who was concerned both with saving face and esteem might have difficulty finding one set of explanations that does both simultaneously. It is possible, however, to protect self-esteem indirectly by accepting our own face-saving accounts of performance. As noted, we may often get taken in by our own claims.

V. Determining the Abilities and Motivations of Others

A person attempting to determine the abilities and motivation of others works with the same general equation as does the individual attempting to determine his own abilities but may do so with a different orientation.

A. THE "OBJECTIVE OBSERVER" CASE

In some cases an observer simply seeks to determine the motivational pattern and ability profile of an actor whose performance he witnesses, without having any particular investments in the outcome of his search. This observer can be said to have an "accuracy" set, and his procedures will be those mentioned in the previous discussion of accuracy-oriented uses of the equation. Still, the observer is likely to approach this task with certain biases: The first bias is the previously mentioned tendency of forming early impressions of ability and motivation and persevering in the face of later evidence that others might regard as disconfirming (Jones & Goethals, 1971). Second is the well-known tendency of the observer to make dispositional rather than situational inferences about the causes of others' behavior (Jones & Nisbett, 1971). In the ability-linked performance case, this tendency translates into a tendency toward making attributions about the actor's abilities and motivation, and away from attributing causal status to task parameters or to the various situational factors that have short-term effects on power or effective motivation.

B. THE "INVOLVED" OBSERVER

As in the case of the performer who was motivated solely to evaluate his performance in terms of accuracy, we find it hard to think of examples of the observer case in which the observer is not somehow involved with the performer and therefore disposed toward drawing certain conclusions from the performance data. A parent, for instance, generally hopes that his child's abilities will be high, and, more than other observers, will find evidence in the child's first faltering performance that these abilities are present. In contrast, as Heider's balance theory suggests, if we dislike an individual we may find it congenial to our view of the world to view his abilities as being low. Observing a moderately good performance on his part, we can nonetheless confirm our perceptions of his low ability by attributing the performance to compulsive overpracticing that makes the most of a mediocre talent. Certainly, we can avoid disconfirming our negative perceptions by attributing a disliked other's good performance to luck.

Category-based expectancies (Jones & McGillis, 1976), positive identification with ethnic groups, or stereotypes also create commitments in the observer to certain outcomes of the ability-determining process. A white racist expects a black to show low intellectual abilities and is biased toward extracting this conclusion from performance observations. A person hopes that his countrymen do well in international competition and may decide that they did so in the face of outcomes that others would interpret otherwise. ("Our basketball players are much better than the Russians even though they lost the game, because our team hadn't practiced together, and the Russians had.")

C. NEGOTIATED DEFINITIONS

Sometimes circumstances require two persons with different involvements to agree on the causes of a performance. The interactions that ensue take on a negotiated character that reveals both the complex and flexible character of the general performance equation and the fact that its application is governed by complex social motives. Consider two cases that arise in the educational setting: the conference between the teacher and the parent of the elementary school child, and the faculty member's conference with the undergraduate who failed the midterm.

Assume that a child has done consistently below-average work in arithmetic. The teacher is likely to regard this performance as a valid index of the child's low academic ability, whereas the parent is apt to regard it as a valid index of the teacher's low teaching ability. Both are likely to be aware that the first interpretation is unacceptable to the other, and both may be sufficiently open to consider other possible explanations. Their task, as they do so together, is partially conditioned by the evidence from the child's general school and home performance pattern, but also may be considerably conditioned by their needs to work out a mutually acceptable explanation. Lack of practice might be offered by the parent as an alternative explanation, as long as it can be documented by reference to days absent rather than to homework not done (which might be admitting that the child is not academically well motivated). The teacher also might not want to venture explanations of low intrinsic motivation, because it can be seen as part of the teacher's task to stimulate such motivation. Instead the teacher may suggest short-term motivational disturbances such as "tiredness" or "upset" on the part of the child. However, the parent may be resistant to these suggestions (although probably less resistant to these than to the suggestion that the child has low ability) because the "good" parent does not allow his child to become overtired or chronically upset. Moreover, perhaps the low performances to be explained have occurred over a sufficiently long time so that these explanations seem inadequate. If so, explanations of wider scope are needed, yet those emphasizing long-term stable components of ability and motivation may be resisted. Explanations that meet these multiple demands are available: For instance, the parent and the teacher might agree to regard the child as "developmentally immature," meaning that the child's physiological problem-solving apparatus somehow is not yet fully developed. This successfully accounts for repeated low performance in the past yet suggests that this low level of performance need not be expected to continue forever. In fact, performances can be expected to improve at some unspecified future time when this immature condition, for which neither teacher, parent, nor child can be held responsible, clears up.[6]

A faculty member's conferences with students who do poorly on tests or papers can also take on a negotiated, account-seeking character. As Jones and Nisbett (1971) point out, the faculty member may incline toward the view that the student is ill motivated, stupid, or both. The student's delicate task is to set forth a non-ability-linked explanation that also does not signal low motivation for the reasonably obvious cause of the poor performance—lack of study. What explanations are acceptable change over the years: Some are inward oriented ("identity crises," inability to get one's "head together"), whereas others rely on externally imposed pressures (priorities put on antiwar demonstrations or football team practices).

[6]The reader's thoughts may have turned to such recent discoveries as "hyperactivity," "minimal brain disfunction," "dyslexia," "learning disabilities," and "genetic damage." Without denying the nosological validity of such categories, it is important to point out that they function as acceptable accounts of chronic low performances. They are painful, last ditch accounts for parents to accept, because they are negative characteristics to impute to children and may imply negative things about the parents (e.g., genetic inadequacy); but they are perhaps less painful than the available options of low ability.

D. THE PAYOFF: CONSEQUENCES OF ATTRIBUTIONS ABOUT
    OTHERS' PERFORMANCES

Whether an attribution or definition of ability is made from an objective or involved stance, or as the result of negotiations, such an attribution or definition is likely to have consequences for how others are treated. Work on the self-fulfilling prophecy cited earlier (Rosenthal, 1976; Word *et al.*, 1974) and work on labeling (Rosenhan, 1973) suggest that our impressions and attributions regarding others have a sharp impact on how we act toward them and interpret later behavior. A diagnosis of a ''late-maturing'' child may cause the teacher to wait for the child to mature, instead of teaching him. Evidence of ability and improvement may not be taken seriously. Other labels, such as ''dyslexic,'' may have serious consequences as well.

One very important kind of consequence of attribution and labeling is future effects on the self. These effects are illustrated in studies by Dweck and her associates on children's generalized reactions to success and failure experiences. As Dweck and Goetz (1978) point out, there is an intriguing paradox to be found in the literature on sex differences in children's responses to failure. Empirically, girls are more academically successful in grade schools, and also are more highly regarded on ability and other dimensions by teachers, yet girls ''show far greater evidence of helplessness than boys when they receive failure feedback from adult evaluators'' (p. 164). Dweck, Davidson, Nelson, and Enna (1978) did a classroom observational study in which they discovered that teachers gave subtlely different kinds of failure feedback to boys and to girls. For instance, teachers attributed boys' performance failures to lack of motivation eight times more often than they did with girls. Girls received very little negative feedback couched in motivational terms. Instead, over 80% of the negative feedback they received referred to intellectual aspects of their work, a pattern that Dweck shows is likely to lead to low-ability attributions. (Of course, the ability domains in question may then be value neutralized or value reversed by the girls to cope with the negative self-esteem consequences of failure.)

Dweck further shows that children do systematically differ in the accounts they give for their own failures and successes, and that these differences are reflected in the children's behavior. Specifically, children who were prone to give motivational or effort-centered explanations for performance outcomes persisted in attempting problem-solving tasks more than did children who gave ability-centered explanations. Again, the attributional pattern was complex. Nonpersistent children were more likely to blame their own failures on largely uncontrollable external factors rather than on their own lack of effort; when they did attribute responsibility to personal characteristics, it was more likely to be ability-relevant internal factors than effort.

VI. Social Comparison Processes

As the reader will recall, social comparison theory (Festinger, 1954; Goethals & Darley, 1977) is concerned with how people evaluate various personal characteristics of their own, foremost among them, abilities. The theory recognizes that generally ability evaluation is social in nature in that people can only evaluate their own abilities by comparing them with the abilities of others.

Clearly, then, the naive psychological analysis of abilities that we have presented must be an analytic part of the social comparison process. One realization this generates is that ability evaluation is essentially indirect because abilities cannot be directly observed and compared. All that can be compared are ability-related performances, which reflect many factors other than ability. Ability evaluation through social comparison therefore is an exceedingly indirect and complex process. We have tried to outline the numerous interpretations that can be given for one person's performance. The number of interpretations that can be given for the outcome of a comparison between two people's performances more than doubles this number. Obviously, the possibilities for distortion, for deceiving oneself, and for attempting the same with others are many.

Because of ego-defensive motives, an individual considering his own performance is likely to make excuses for performances that fail to meet expectations in terms of short-term power factors, bad luck, etc. In general, the individual seeks to make the case that his performance was handicapped by nonability factors that had a negative effect on his performance. In various ways he argues that he was disadvantaged by these factors and hence was unable to perform "up to" his ability.

Because of the same motives, his interpretations of the roles of effort and task difficulty in a comparison person's performance are likely to be very different. Essentially, the person will be interested in making the outcome of performance comparison as favorable to himself as possible. Therefore, at the same time that he makes excuses for his own performance, e.g., suggests that it was hampered by nonability factors, he will tend to perceive the other's performance as having been facilitated by nonability factors. He may perceive the other as more invested in performing well for extrinsic reasons, as having performed under favorable conditions that have made the task somewhat easier, and so on. In attribution terms, he will seek to claim an augmenting effect for his performance, such that the perception of the plausible cause, ability, should be enhanced because the other causes were inhibitory. For the performance of the other, he will claim the discounting principle, suggesting that the attribution to the ability locus of causality of the other should be lessened by the facilitative nature of nonability factors. If a person is motivated to do so, therefore, the social comparison process is one that allows great scope for self-enhancing conclusions, in ways that are suggested by the present analysis.

VII.   Final Comments

A.   IMPLICATIONS FOR THE CONCEPT OF ABILITY

Naive psychological analysis seems to us to place a great deal of emphasis on the concept of "ability." Further, it seems to have adopted a particular definition of that construct. The paradigmatic cases of ability seem to be those involving physical performances, such as running or weight lifting. From these examples arises the connotation that ability is a fixed upper limit of a person that is set by his—in this case physical—machinery. We seem to think of all abilities in a similar fashion, i.e., involving a relatively fixed upper limit, even in cases such as mathematical ability, although there the machinery is mental rather than physiological. (Even here, however, there is a tendency for the physically imposed limit idea to creep back in. People do say "He just doesn't have enough brains for it.")

C. Dweck and J. G. Nicholls (personal communication, 1979) have suggested a developmental reason that our conceptualization of ability may be disproportionately influenced by the more physically based families of tasks. They point out that the first tasks the preschool child is concerned with mastering are in the physical domain or at least involve clear physical components. On these tasks, overt behaviors produce clear-cut, observable outcomes and task difficulty cues can be directly observed. In contrast, on more cognitive and intellectual tasks, it is more difficult to infer the success or failure of the underlying thought processes from their end product, and the task difficulty ones are also not easily observed. As Dweck and Nicholls say, on these typical tasks for the preschooler, "a ball is caught or not caught; a shoelace is tied or (k)not. In these cases children can infer ability from the fact of having executed the task. Further they are able to respond selectively to the concrete difficulty cues on such tasks (e.g., catching a ball thrown a greater or smaller distance)."

Again, these physical tasks occur developmentally prior, are easier to decode on ability terms, and therefore may form the paradigmatic cases by which people come to define the ability construct. As part of this paradigm, it is easy to see how a notion develops of an upper limit to a person's ability. However, is this a sensible concept to adopt for all of the hundreds of skills we refer to as abilities in everyday speech?

There are other ways of thinking about abilities than this fixed upper limit conceptualization. "Social abilities" seem more a matter of skill learning, and it is difficult even to give meaning to the idea of a fixed upper limit on them.

Mathematics has become incredibly more sophisticated in the last 200 years. Is this because there are suddenly many more people with high mathematical ability or because we have learned to think and teach about mathematics differently? Even in the realm of sports, in which the idea of fixed upper limits of ability probably has most validity, recent developments in training techniques have caused these limits to be revised upward. Records previously thought to reflect these upper limits are frequently broken. This way of regarding abilities is as much closer to a person's current typical good level of performance. If a person is motivated to do so, and training techniques are available and employed, a person can lift his "ability level" to some new height.[7]

We recognize that this alternate conceptualization of ability is one at variance with ordinary thinking and so will make one further point that may make it more plausible. If one thinks back on the tests taken that create the familiar bell-shaped distribution of scores and so provide the unexamined but apparently compelling evidence for the apparently creator-ordained existence of high and low abilities on every dimension measured, one notices that these largely have been rate tests. In more familiar terms, they were "timed" or "speed" tests. Of course, these create the score differentials to which we have alluded, and of course the children who perform their work more slowly soon come to feel the inferiority associated with having a "low ability." But why, as a matter of course, do we assume that a rate difference has anything to do with an absolute ceiling on the performances of either those working at a fast or a slow rate? The testing literature does not seem to us to warrant this assumption. In fact, one of the criticisms of untimed tests (sometimes called "power" tests) is that they frequently do not produce the normal distribution of scores. More specifically, too many people score "too high." What this conclusion means, however, is that we accept as a presupposition the "normal curve" theory of ability distribution, and demand tests that produce that distribution, without considering the possibility that the untimed, unstressed test situation that produces rather different patterns of results may also be producing evidence against these assumptions.

The present account of how one determines one's own or others' abilities from performances can explain why, even if the idea of an upper limit on ability is incorrect in some abstract sense, this idea comes to be true as a result of difficulties arising in the course of social interaction. The problem, clearly, is to explain why people think that they have low abilities in certain domains, and more pointedly why they act in ways that seem to confirm that they have low abilities and thereby cause poor outcomes. We suggest that the end result has its origin in a developmental sequence that begins when a person—normally a child—does poorly at a task that is thought to be ability linked. Recall that this

[7]For example, in testing vocabulary, most "ability" tests are achievement tests; "aptitude" tests measure things other than fixed upper ability limits.

failure can occur for any one of a number of reasons that have nothing to do with the performer's ability. The child may have been absent from school the day a critical bit of background information was given; an adolescent, transferring from a different high school, may never have had a chance to practice basketball, and so on. Two parallel processes are started by these poor performances. First, other people, who are not aware of the nonability factors that cause the performance to be low, may make attribution of low ability. To the extent that they have power over the performer, they may act in ways that cause him to continue performing at a low level, thus confirming their diagnosis of a low ability. The teacher will put the child in a lower reading group for instance, or the gym teacher will not suggest that the adolescent try out for the basketball team. In parallel, because he is embarrassed by his own poor performance, the performer will begin the excuse-giving process that we have described. Frequently, however, that process leads to avoiding practicing tasks relevant to the ability in question. Over time, then, because the person has had less opportunities to practice than have others of a comparable age and status, and because after a while this effect may not be apparent to others or even to himself, again a low-ability conclusion may seem warranted. Moreover, because the actor may go through the processes of neutralization that we have described, the actor himself may abet this process by announcing that he is not good at the task in question. (The other parts of his announcement, that it is not important to be good at the tasks in question, not surprisingly may be less attended to by the observer.) The point here is that it is conceivable that there are rarely upper limits on any person's abilities until socialization processes such as these come to set them. Once set, they are as real in their effects as if they were physical.

B. NOTES FOR A THEORY OF SELF-ESTEEM

"Self-esteem" is a construct that has been given multiple meanings in psychology. Still, based on the attributional and motivational factors put forth in this contribution, we can suggest the relationships between abilities and self-esteem and sketch a theory of self-esteem that flows from these considerations. First, people are normally motivated to think well of themselves (i.e., to have a high self-esteem). Because abilities are culturally regarded as desirable attributes to possess, people are therefore motivated to regard themselves as possessing high levels of all abilities—as, in the vernacular, "being good at anything they try." When they find themselves doing poorly at a set of ability-linked tasks, because they are motivated to maintain their self-esteem, their initial search is for a set of nonability variables within the performance equation that explain the poor performance while maintaining the perception of possessing a high level of the underlying ability. Initially this is done by rather superficial explanations, but pressures to give a series of performances, which go poorly, can cause the performer to give a deeper explanation for his failures; he can argue to himself and others that it is unimportant for him to possess that ability or that it would actually be negative for him to possess it. Initially a person's self-esteem is deployed to cover an ability; later it is withdrawn, so that performances on that task are no longer relevant to his self-esteem. An analogy comes to mind: The well-built medieval castle was constructed so that inner walls connected to outer walls. In this fashion the outer walls could be given up and new, less expanded defense perimeters could be maintained nearer the core of the castle. Similarly, all of us may cease to regard certain abilities as vital to our self-esteem because initial performances on tasks relevant to that ability go poorly. This idea will be particularly true, paradoxically, if initially the connection between that ability and one's underlying self-worth are made salient. A general "order of defenses" can also be suggested: First, the performer may offer a relatively low-cost (in terms of future self-presentational commitments) excuse. If circumstances force a continued set of performances, and those continue to go badly, then the performer may decide that his intrinsic motives to do well on those tasks are low. If pressures to perform continue and, as they often would, supply extrinsic motivations to do well, then the person may be forced to admit that he does not have the ability to do the tasks well and decouple that ability from his self-esteem.

Normally socialized people can routinely "take the role of the other" in interaction situations. Therefore, in situations, in which they are performing before an audience, they can "see" their own performance from the perspective of the audience. This ability is likely to have two effects: First, it is likely to make the ability–self-esteem connection more salient because the performer is likely to be aware of the observer's well-known tendency to make ability-centered dispositional attributions; second, it is likely to drive the performer more quickly to a low-ability attribution for his own behavior (although it is also likely in the initial stages of the performance sequence to cause the performer to be more motivated to find excuses for poor performances). Thus the presence of an audience, coupled with a set of poor performances given to that audience, may initially increase excuse-giving tendencies but finally may lead to a conclusion of low ability on these tasks, with the performer then concentrating on the critical task of convincing himself and others that his self-esteem should not be diminished by this low ability. (The well-known tactic of an individual to try to cause groups to engage in activities at which he excels can be seen as a remedial tactic to make up for previously incurred self-esteem deficits arising from the group's performing tasks in areas in which the individual did not excel.)

According to this deployment theory of self-esteem, a person's self-esteem normally should be high because he simply ceases to regard as important the possession of any ability that initial evidence suggests he does not possess. However, various self-esteem scales produce subjects who are "low on self-esteem,'' which seems to contradict our theory. We would argue that the contradiction may be more apparent than real. On inspection, many self-esteem scales contain questions that map the extensions of a person's self-esteem and assume that if the self-esteem does not extend into all the standard areas it is low. For instance, a person who answers ''false'' to a statement such as ''I am good at getting people to go along with what I want'' is making a ''low self-esteem'' response. However, imagine what that individual might say if he were asked why he was not good. He might be able to say that within his own character structure it was not necessary for him to get people to go along with what he wanted. It might be that his suggestions so often were correct and sensible that there was no need to convince people to go along with them; they spoke for themselves.

Our suggestion is that the self-esteem of normal individuals normally is high but is linked to different patterns of claimed abilities. Therefore it would be more important to map the scope of a person's ability claims rather than to measure some generalized notion of self-esteem. We argue that this is often what self-esteem measures prove to do, on inspection of their items, but this interesting scope of claims information is lost when the scores are summed into a global self-esteem score. A person with a low self-esteem score, in our terms, is one who has given up claims to possess many abilities—has retreated to the defensive core of his castle—but who we suspect retains and clings to the conclusion that there are performance areas in which he does very well indeed. This ''retreated'' person would be interesting to study, but we do not assume he has low esteem. Instead it would be interesting to determine how he maintains high self-esteem in the face of social pressures to think otherwise.

The last point should be amplified. Our theorizing does predict that all people will occasionally feel lowered self-esteem. This occurs because society generally does regard abilities as important things to possess and, being socialized into cultural norms, we all can be made to subscribe to that perspective. Therefore when circumstances force us to perform a task that we do poorly, because of this perspective-taking ability we will be momentarily diminished in our self-esteem. Moreover, if circumstances entrap a person into the continuing performance of a set of tasks he does poorly, he may suffer a continuing decrement in his self-esteem, not exactly because he independently regards possessing the underlying ability as important—he may have neutralized or negated that—but because he is forced continually to perform in front of others, sees himself as ineffectual from their perspective, and at some level shares their perspective.

C. SUMMARY

The present contribution has had two purposes: first, to present an analysis of the schemes ordinary people use to make sense of the ability-linked performances of themselves and others; and second, to suggest some of the psychological uses these people make of the analysis. Following Heider, we suggested that the perceiver's central task was to infer the stable dimensions underlying the actor's set of performances, and that the construct inferred was normally the ability of the actor; secondarily his motivational patterns, and occasionally the long-term difficulty level that accrues to the task.

Our analyses also suggested a wide set of possible short-term influences on performance, a classification of these short-term influences, and even a decision equation for combining them. Whether the list is complete, or the suggested combinational rule an accurate description of the way ordinary people combine information, remains to be seen; the second theme of the analysis is independent from this determination.

More than previous authors, we have attempted to specify the psychological uses people make of the general performance equation. If we have a novel theme, it is that people use the equation, and other people's knowledge of the equation, not only to "discover" abilities, but to maintain or enhance their own self-esteem and to protect or even to enhance the regard other people have for them. In this rather demanding social task, people generally find useful exactly the ambiguities that make the analysis of the naive psychology of abilities so complex. For instance, that human ingenuity seems near infinitely capable of discovering yet more short-term factors negatively affecting the potential power a person has available to expend on a task is as distressing to us as theorists as it is useful to us as people seeking to excuse our own sometimes poor performances. Implicitly it is often assumed that the central use of the general performance equation is the accurate determination of abilities. We have suggested the somewhat problematic nature of the ability construct, and the presence of other than accuracy motives in the social situations in which ability questions arise. In doing so, we have attempted to indicate the connections that exist between the naive psychological analyses pioneered by Heider and the self-presentational theme in modern social psychology.

REFERENCES

Abelson, R. P. A script theory of understanding, attitude and behavior. In J. Carroll & T. Payne (Eds.), *Cognition and social behavior*. Hillsdale, N.J.: Erlbaum, 1976.

Bem, D. J. Self-perception: an alternative interpretation of dissonance phenomena. *Psychological Review* 1967, **74**, 183–200.

Berglas, S., & Jones, E. E. Drug choice as a self-handicapping strategy in response to noncontingent success. *Journal of Personality and Social Psychology*, 1978, **36**, 405–417.

Bradley, G. Self-serving bias in the attribution process; A reexamination of the fact or fiction question. *Journal of Personality and Social Psychology*, 1978, **36**, 56–71.

Butzin, C. A., & Anderson, N. H. Performance equals motivation times ability; an integration-theoretical analysis. *Journal of Personality and Social Psychology*, 1974, **30**, 598–604.

Cooper, H. M., & Burger, J. M. Categorizing open-ended academic attributions—replication of earlier findings. *Personality and Social Psychology Bulletin*, 1978, **4**, 350.

Dweck, C., Davidson, W., Nelson, G., & Enna, G. Sex differences in learned helplessness: (II) The contingencies of evaluative feedback in the classroom and (III) An experimental analysis. *Developmental Psychology,* 1978, **14,** 268–276.

Dweck, C., & Goetz, T. Attributions and learned helplessness. In J. H. Harvey, W. J. Ickes, & R. F. Kidd (Eds.), *New directions in attribution research.* Vol. 2. Hillsdale, N.J.: Erlbaum, 1978.

Elig, T., & Frieze, I. A multidimensional scheme for coding and interpreting perceived causality for success and failure events: The CSPS. *Catalog of Selected Documents in Psychology,* 1975, **5,** 313. (MS 1069.)

Feather, N. T. Attribution of responsibility and valence of success and failure in relation to initial confidence and task performance. *Journal of Personality and Social Psychology,* 1969, **13,** 129–144.

Feather, N. T., & Simon, J. G. Attribution of responsibility and valence of outcome in relation to initial confidence and success and failure of self and other. *Journal of Personality and Social Psychology,* 1971, **18,** 173–188.

Festinger, L. A theory of social comparison processes. *Human Relations,* 1954, **7,** 114–140.

French, E. G., & Thomas, F. H. The relation of achievement motivation to problem solving effectiveness. *Journal of Abnormal and Social Psychology,* 1958, **56,** 46–48.

Frieze, I. Studies of information processing and the attributional process in achievement related contexts. Unpublished doctoral dissertation, University of California at Los Angeles, 1973.

Frieze, I. Causal attributions and information seeking to explain success and failure. *Journal for Research in Personality,* 1976, **10,** 293–305.

Frieze, I., & Weiner, B. Cue utilization and attributional judgments for success and failure. *Journal of Personality,* 1971, **39,** 591–605.

Goethals, G. R., & Darley, J. M. Social comparison theory: An attributional approach. In J. Suls & R. Miller (Eds.), *Social comparison processes: Theoretical and empirical perspectives.* Washington, D.C.: Hemisphere/Halsted, 1977.

Goffman, E. *The presentation of self in everyday life.* Garden City, N.Y.: Doubleday, 1959.

Gould, R., Brounstein, P., & Sigall, M. Attributing ability to an opponent: public aggrandizement and private denigration. *Sociometry,* 1977, **40,** 254–261.

Heider, F. *The psychology of interpersonal relations.* New York: Wiley, 1958.

James, W. *The principles of style* (2 vols.). New York: Holt, 1950. (Originally published, 1890.)

Jones, E. E., & Berglas, S. Control of attributions about the self through self-handicapping strategies: the appeal of alcohol and the role of underachievement. *Personality and Social Psychology Bulletin,* 1978, **4,** 200–206.

Jones, E. E., & Davis, K. From acts to dispositions: The attribution process in person perception. In L. Berkowitz (Ed.), *Advances in experimental social psychology.* Vol. 2. New York: Academic Press, 1965.

Jones, E. E., Davis, K., & Gergen, K. Role playing variations and their informational value for person perception. *Journal of Abnormal and Social Psychology,* 1961, **63,** 1–9.

Jones, E. E., & Goethals, G. *Order effects in impression formation: Attribution context and the nature of the entity.* New York: General Learning Press, 1971.

Jones, E. E., & McGillis, D. Correspondent inferences and the attribution cube: A comparative reappraisal. In J. Harvey, W. J. Ickes, & R. F. Kidd (Eds.), *New directions in attribution research.* Vol. 1. Hillsdale, N.J.: Erlbaum, 1976.

Jones, E. E., & Nisbett, R. *The actor and the observer: Divergent perceptions of the causes of behavior.* New York: General Learning Press, 1971.

Karaz, V., & Perlman, D. Attribution at the wire: consistency and outcome finish strong. *Journal of Experimental Social Psychology,* 1975, **11,** 470–477.

Kelley, H. H. Attribution theory in social psychology. In D. Levine (Ed.), *Nebraska Symposium on Motivation.* Vol. 15. Lincoln: University of Nebraska Press, 1967.

Kelley, H. H. *Attribution in social interaction*. Morristown, N.J.: General Learning Press, 1971.

Kun, A., & Weiner, B. Necessary versus sufficient causal schemata for success and failure. *Journal of Research in Personality*, 1973, **7**, 197–207.

MacArthur, L. The how and what of why: Some determinants and consequences of causal attribution. *Journal of Personality and Social Psychology*, 1972, **22**, 171–193.

McClelland, D. C., Atkinson, J. W., Clark, R. A., & Lowell, E. L. *The achievement motive*. New York: Appleton, 1953.

McMahan, I. D. Relationships between causal attributions and expectancy of success. *Journal of Personality and Social Psychology*, 1973, **28**, 108–114.

Meichenbaum, D., Bowers, K., & Ross, R. A behavioral analysis of the teacher expectancy effect. *Journal of Personality and Social Psychology*, 1969, **13**, 306–316.

Miller, D., & Ross, L. Self-serving bias in the attribution of causality: Fact or fiction? *Psychological Bulletin*, 1975, **82**, 213–225.

Mills, C. W. Situated actions and vocabularies of motive. *American Sociological Review*, 1940, **5**, 904–913.

Nicholls, J. G. Causal attributions and other achievement-related cognitions: Effects of task outcomes, attainment, value and sex. *Journal of Personality and Social Psychology*, 1975, **31**, 379–389.

Orvis, B. R., Cunningham, J. D., & Kelley, H. H. A closer examination of causal inference: The roles of consensus, distinctiveness and consistency information. *Journal of Personality and Social Psychology*, 1975, **32**, 605–616.

Rosenbaum, R. A dimensional analysis of the perceived causes of success and failure. Unpublished doctoral dissertation, University of California at Los Angeles, 1972.

Rosenhan, D. On being sane in insane places. *Science*, 1973, **179**, 250–258.

Rosenthal, R. *Experimenter effects in behavioral research*. New York: Irvington, 1976.

Scott, M. B., & Lyman, S. Accounts. *American Sociological Review*, 1968, **33**, 46–62.

Simon J. G., & Feather, N. T. Causal attribution for success and failure at University examinations. *Journal of Educational Psychology*, 1973, **64**, 46–56.

Stephan, W. G., Bernstein, W. M., Stephan, C., & Davis, M. Attributions for achievement: Egoism vs. expectancy confirmation. *Social Psychology Quarterly*, 1979, **42**, 5–17.

Strodtbeck, F. L. Family interaction, values, and achievement. In D. C. McClelland, A. L. Baldwin, U. Bronfenbrenner, & F. L. Strodtbeck (Eds.), *Talent and society*. Princeton, Van Nostrand, 1958.

Trope, Y. Seeking information about one's own ability as a determinant of choice among tasks. *Journal of Personality and Social Psychology*, 1975, **32**, 1004–1013.

Trope, Y. Uncertainty-reducing properties of achievement tasks. *Journal of Personality and Social Psychology*, 1979, **37**, 1505–1518.

Trope, Y., & Brickman, P. Difficulty and diagnosticity as determinants of choice among tasks. *Journal of Personality and Social Psychology*, 1975, **31**, 918–925.

Valle, V., & Frieze, I. Stability of causal attributions as a mediator in changing expectations for success. *Journal of Personality and Social Psychology*, 1976, **33**, 579–587.

Weiner. B. *Achievement motivation and attribution theory*. New York: General Learning Press, 1974.

Weiner, B., Frieze, I., Kukla, A., Reed, L., Rest, S., & Rosenbaum, R. M. *Perceiving the causes of success and failure*. New York: General Learning Press, 1971.

Weiner, B., Heckhausen, H., Meyer, W., & Cook, R. Causal ascription of achievement behavior: A conceptual analysis of effort. *Journal of Personality and Social Psychology*, 1972, **21**, 239–248.

Word, C., Zanna, M. P., & Cooper, J. The nonverbal mediation of self-fulfilling prophecies in interracial interaction. *Journal of Experimental and Social Psychology*, 1974, **10**, 109–120.

THE EMPIRICAL EXPLORATION OF INTRINSIC MOTIVATIONAL PROCESSES[1]

Edward L. Deci and Richard M. Ryan

DEPARTMENT OF PSYCHOLOGY
UNIVERSITY OF ROCHESTER
ROCHESTER, NEW YORK

[1]Preparation of this chapter was facilitated by Research Grant MH 28600 from the National Institute of Mental Health to the first author.

39

ADVANCES IN EXPERIMENTAL SOCIAL
PSYCHOLOGY, VOL. 13

I.   Introduction

The study of motivation is intertwined with all areas of psychology and has been guided by many perspectives. Historically, there have been two major schools of thought in the psychological study of motivation: psychoanalytic theory (e.g., Freud, 1917/1949) and behavioral associationist theory (Hull, 1943). These two approaches are radically different in many respects, yet they share one fundamental assumption that is directly germane to our present concerns. That assumption holds that all behavior is basically carried out in an effort to reduce internal tension or stimulation and rests on a limited set of supposedly primary drives, such as those for food, water, and sex.

Increasingly this foundation of motivation theory has been seen as inadequate. In later psychoanalytic theory, Hartmann (1958) and White (1963) have asserted that there is an energy source inherent in the ego of the individual that is independent of the drives of the id. In experimental research on learning, reinforcement theorists began to discover that animals explored novel spaces and manipulated novel objects as if they were seeking additional stimulation rather than lessening inner excitation (Berlyne, 1966). Exploratory and manipulative behaviors defied extinction and even served as reinforcers for other behaviors (Butler, 1953).

Work in such diverse areas as cognitive development (Piaget, 1952), social motivation (McClelland, Atkinson, Clark, & Lowell, 1953), humanistic psychology (e.g., Maslow, 1954), and expectancy theory (Atkinson, 1964) also suggested the advisability of a motivational construct that was independent of the primary, tissue-based drives. In our work we assume such a motivation and refer to it as "intrinsic motivation."

INTRINSIC MOTIVATION

Intrinsic motivation has been investigated in a variety of ways at the physiological, psychological, and operational levels. Those who have focused on the psychological level have generally been guided by one of two general approaches: the incongruity theories and the competence and/or self-determination theories.

1.   Incongruity Theories

This approach suggests that organisms are intrinsically motivated by a need to encounter stimulus events that are moderately discrepant from some internal standard; in other words, they seek stimulation that is moderately discrepant from their accustomed stimulation (Berlyne, 1978; Dember & Earl, 1957; Hunt, 1965; McClelland *et al.*, 1953; Piaget, 1952; Walker, 1973).

Hunt, for example, stated that for effective functioning, organisms need an optimal amount of psychological incongruity between an internal standard and a stimulus event. An internal standard is simply some element of one's cognitive structure. For example, a child who has learned addition tables up through 10 plus 10 will have that as an internal standard; a person who has swum a maximum distance of 1 mile will have that as an internal standard. A stimulus event, such as the problem of 12 plus 11 or the goal of swimming a mile and an eighth, would provide a moderate discrepancy, so the child might be intrinsically motivated to solve the problem and the person might be intrinsically motivated to swim the mile and an eighth. Simply adding 10 plus 10 or swimming the mile provides no discrepancy and is therefore boring. On the other hand, an arithmetic problem of 127 plus 2481 or the goal of swimming 2 miles provides too much discrepancy from the existing standards and is therefore aversive. When the situation is either boring or aversive, people do not function as effectively as when there is moderate incongruity that stimulates their intrinsic interest.

Hunt's ideas have much in common with those of Piaget (1952), who has suggested that people seek moderately discrepant material to which they can accomodate, and with those of Berlyne (1978), who has suggested that people are inclined toward novel situations that provide conflicting cognitive elements requiring integration.

2. Competence and/or Self-determination Theories

White (1959) proposed the concept of competence to refer a person's capacity to deal effectively with his or her surroundings. People, he stated, are motivated to attain competence in their dealing with the environment, and this innate motivation energizes such things as exploratory play, aspects of cognitive development, and curiosity. White used the term effectance motivation to refer to this motivational propensity, which is ever present in the absence of homeostatic crises and which underlies much persistent, directed activity. Harter (1978) has also utilized the concept of effectance in her discussions of intrinsic motivation.

Bandura (1977) has presented a theory of behavior change that is based in the idea of efficacy. People, he suggested, will engage in behaviors only if they have expectations that they can do the behaviors efficaciously. His work is related to the idea of intrinsic motivation, yet Bandura has steadfastly refrained from positing any motivational underpinning to the importance of efficacy expectations. He has asserted that the idea of a generalized need for competence and self-determination has disutility because it is so vague. However, as we shall see in the following review of empirical research, the concept does have substantial heuristic value for integrating a wide range of research.

deCharms conceptualized intrinsic motivation in terms of the need for a sense of personal causation. People, he suggested, have a basic desire to experience themselves as causal agents, to view themselves as the originators of their own behaviors rather than pawns to external forces.

Recognizing the importance of striving for competence and personal causation, Deci (1975) defined intrinsic motivation in terms of the underlying need for a sense of competence and self-determination. The two, competence and self-determination, are inextricably related and generally covary in real-life situations. Yet, in a sense, self-determination (Deci, 1980) is the more fundamental component, for the attainment of competence must occur within the context of self-determination to be intrinsically rewarding. Competence acquisition that is forced by others rather than chosen by oneself is not intrinsically motivated. Fisher (1978), for example, found that when subjects' performance was constrained there was no correlation between the achievement of competence and intrinsic motivation, whereas when subjects had personal control there was a relationship between competence and intrinsic motivation.

3. Intrinsic Motivation Defined

Human beings are active organisms who are continually interacting with and adapting to their surroundings. They need to experience themselves as competent and self-determining in these interactions. Their sense of being competent and self-determining provides intrinsic gratification and is prerequisite for psychological health. The disruption of the experience of competence and self-determination has been shown to be deleterious to adaptive behavior and related to psychological disorders (Deci, 1980; Lefcourt, 1973; Seligman, 1975).

Intrinsically motivated behaviors are those behaviors that are motivated by the underlying need for competence and self-determination. As with all psychological constructs, operational definitions are necessary for research purposes. *Therefore, we operationally define intrinsically motivated behaviors as those that are performed in the absence of any apparent external contingency.* This is typically measured by observing behavioral persistence in a free-choice period following the removal of rewards or constraints. Several studies have also measured intrinsic motivation with paper and pencil measures of interest or enjoyment, thereby providing an additional operational definition of intrinsic motivation. We shall review research that has utilized either of these two operational definitions and their corresponding measures.

Let us characterize intrinsically motivated behaviors further. When they are intrinsically motivated, we suggest, people will be involved in an ongoing, cyclical process of seeking out (or creating) optimally challenging situations and then attempting to conquer those challenges. The idea of "optimal" here simply means that people have unique sets of abilities with regard to any given domain of activity and their attention will be directed toward those activities that require them to learn or to stretch their abilities a small amount.

In terms of the incongruity theories, one can understand such challenges in terms of an incongruity between an internal standard and a stimulus event. Optimal challenges require a modest amount of incongruity. We can see, therefore, that the incongruity theories and the competence and self-determination theories are quite compatible. The need for competence and self-determination leads people to encounter moderate incongruity and to create congruity from the incongruity.

Of course, people are not intrinsically motivated to engage in all kinds of behaviors that provide optimal challenges or moderate incongruity; they have preferences. Enduring a little more pain than one is accustomed to is a moderate incongruity and could provide an optimal challenge, yet people may prefer other types of challenges or incongruities as they strive to develop feelings of competence and self-determination. Those that are attractive can be distinguished from those that are not in terms of innate abilities and prior experiences. This review outlines processes through which activities and situations that provide moderate incongruity or optimal challenges may become either more or less intrinsically motivating as a result of various experiences.

II. Cognitive Evaluation Theory: Perceived Locus of Causality

Many recent studies have investigated the effects of extrinsic rewards, external constraints, and interpersonal communications on people's intrinsic motivation. In our laboratory, the general paradigm for the experiments has been to provide subjects with a mechanical, spatial relations puzzle called Soma—a puzzle that college students have generally found to be very interesting. We then introduce the experimental manipulation (e.g., reward some subjects and not reward others, or provide feedback to some subjects and not to others). Finally, we assess their intrinsic motivation following the puzzle solving by observing them in a free-choice situation. Subjects who spend more of their free-choice time working on the target activity are said to be more intrinsically motivated for that activity than subjects who spend less of their free-choice time working with the activity. The primary dependent measure of intrinsic motivation, therefore, is the number of seconds that subjects spend working on the target activity during the free-choice period. A supplemental measure used in some experiments was subjects' reported level of interest in or enjoyment of the activity.

In two early studies, Deci (1971, 1972b) explored the effects of monetary rewards on intrinsic motivation. The second investigation employed the paradigm described above, whereas the first employed a more elaborate three-session paradigm in which the first and third sessions provided the before and after measures of intrinsic motivation, respectively, whereas the second session contained the experimental manipulation of payments to half the subjects and no payments to the other half. In both experiments subjects worked on the Soma puzzles, with the experimental subjects being paid $1 for each of the four puzzles that they were able to solve in the allotted time and control subjects receiving no pay for the same activity. Intrinsic motivation was assessed using the free-choice measure wherein subjects were given an additional opportunity to work on the puzzle or engage in other activities with the experimenter absent. Results of both experiments indicated that the paid subjects evidenced a significant decrease in intrinsic motivation relative to the nonpaid subjects.

Results similar to Deci's were reported by Calder and Staw (1975b), who used "expressed interest" as their dependent measure. Thus, the phenomenon of undermining intrinsic motivation by extrinsic rewards emerged with a self-report, attitude-dependent measure as well as with Deci's free-choice, behavioral measure.

Utilizing the terminology employed by Heider (1958) and deCharms (1968), Deci suggested that the experience of being rewarded for the activity induced a shift in the perceived locus of causality for this behavior from internal to external, resulting in decreased intrinsic motivation. Whereas intrinsically motivated behavior is seen as internally caused, carrying out an activity in order to get a reward leads the actor to view his behavior an externally caused. In Deci's (1975) cognitive evaluation theory, this "change in perceived locus of causality process" was said to be one of two processes through which external considerations could affect a person's level of intrinsic motivation.

A. ATTRIBUTION AND MOTIVATIONAL SUBSYSTEMS

The concept of perceived locus of causality was introduced as part of Heider's commonsense psychology that has stimulated much current work in attribution theory. The general attribution approach, when applied intrapersonally, suggests that people make postbehavioral, cognitively determined inferences about their motivational or affective states after observing their actions. The cognitive inferences they draw are said to be causal antecedents of subsequent behavior. This approach, espoused by Bem (1972), Kruglanski (1975), Ross (1976), and others, has been widely used in interpreting the undermining of intrinsic motivation by extrinsic rewards. The notion suggests that the presence of extrinsic rewards leads to the attribution of an external cause of the behavior and therefore the absence of an internal one, viz., intrinsic motivation. The change in perceived locus of causality process as presented by Deci has often been interpreted as a function of attributional processes that work in the manner just outlined. However, we do not understand it in that way. We intend the statement of the process to be a heuristic description of the perceptions and cognitions that accompany changes in underlying motivational processes. We hold that the addition of rewards to a situation calls into play a different motivational subsystem (extrinsic rather than intrinsic) and that the resulting behavior (Soma puzzle solving in these experiments) becomes integrated into the extrinsic rather than the intrinsic motivational subsystem. The given behavior becomes instrumentally linked to the reward and tends not to be performed in its absence. Phenomenologically, the person does the behavior for an external reason, viz., the reward. Referring to the locus of causality as external here is heuristically valuable because it describes the developed dependency between performance and the presence of the external reward or constraint. The motivational cause, of course, remains internal; it is the operation of the extrinsic motivational subsystem.

This phenomenon of rewards undermining intrinsic motivation under certain conditions has been replicated frequently, as will become apparent in this review. Some of the studies were reported in earlier reviews by Deci (1975), Condry (1977), and Lepper and Greene (1978a) and have been discussed in relation to education (Levine and Fasnacht, 1974), work motivation (Notz, 1975), and psychotherapy (Arkes, 1978).

The phenomenon is generally referred to as the "overjustification effect," a term introduced by Lepper, Greene, and Nisbett (1973). That terminology developed out of the attributional, self-perception framework (Bem, 1972) and therefore is theoretically tied to that conception. Therefore, we shall tend not to use the term "overjustification" because it implies the operation of a theoretical process that we believe is incomplete as an explanation of the phenomenon. Lepper and Greene (1978b) have also realized the limitations of the overjustification effect in the study of intrinsically motivated behavior and have called for moving beyond the exclusive use of the concept in explicating intrinsic motivation.

B. PERFORMANCE MEDIATORS

Deci asserted that the change in intrinsic motivation was caused by changes in motivational processes. Others, such as Calder and Staw (1975a), suggested that the changes in intrinsic motivation in Deci's studies may have been an "artifact" of performance differences. For example, the payments may have caused subjects to work harder and then become satiated or fatigued, thereby leading them to display less intrinsic motivation. In response to this suggestion, Deci, Cascio, and Krusell (1975) reported that there were no performance differences between the payment and nonpayment groups, so this alternative interpretation is ruled out and the motivation interpretation remains plausible.

We do, of course, believe that performance can mediate between reward structures and one's level of intrinsic motivation, although we are asserting that reward structures can also directly affect intrinsic motivation through the change in perceived locus of causality process, independent of any performance-mediated effects. The term "performance-mediated effect" means simply that (1) reward structures can affect one's performance of an activity, and (2) those performance effects can in turn influence one's level of intrinsic motivation. For example, rewards could lead one to work faster and therefore become satiated or fatigued, or rewards could lead one to perform better at the activity and therefore feel good about one's performance. The satiation or fatigue and the satisfactions about one's performance could either lower (in the former case) or raise (in the latter case) one's level of intrinsic motivation.

McGraw (1978) surveyed many studies showing that rewards did affect performance. He concluded that rewards might be either detrimental to or facilitative of task performance, depending on two parameters. First, if the task is aversive, rewards will tend to facilitate task performance, presumably by adding some hedonically positive elements to the aversive situation. On the other side of the aversive–attractive coin, rewards may either enhance or diminish performance of an attractive task depending on a second parameter, viz., the algorithm vs. heuristic dimension. If an attractive task is well learned or has an algorithmic solution that is known or is easily discovered, rewards will tend to facilitate performance on the task. However, if the attractive task requires creativity, resourcefulness, and the use of ingenious heuristics, rewards will tend to impair performance (e.g., McGraw & McCullers, 1979). There is evidence, therefore, that rewards do affect performance.

Later in this contribution we shall review research demonstrating that the perception of one's performance as effective seems to enhance intrinsic motivation, whereas the belief that one's performance is ineffective seems to diminish intrinsic motivation. Therefore, performance differences can affect intrinsic motivation. These two types of evidence lead to the conclusion that rewards can affect intrinsic motivation through performance-mediated effects. However, we shall be primarily concerned with the effects of rewards on intrinsic motivation that are not mediated by such performance differences. These effects result from a change in motivational processes, the cognitive component of which is the change in perceived locus of causality.

C. OTHER REWARDS; OTHER ACTIVITIES

We reported three studies in which monetary rewards have decreased subjects' intrinsic motivation. We accounted for this phenomenon by invoking the process that Deci previously called a change in perceived locus of causality. Although we acknowledge that rewards may affect intrinsic motivation through determining the perceived effectiveness of the performance, we shall focus primarily on the direct, extrinsic influence on intrinsic motivation. If rewards affect intrinsic motivation through the change in perceived locus of causality process, then one would expect many rewards besides just monetary ones to decrease intrinsic motivation in this way. Several experiments have confirmed this expectation.

In one such experiment, Deci and Cascio (1972) used a modified "negative-reinforcement" procedure. Utilizing the Soma paradigm described earlier, they told experimental subjects that if they were unable to solve a puzzle in the allotted time a buzzer would sound indicating that their time for that puzzle was up. Subjects were briefly exposed to the buzzer so they would know that it was quite noxious. Control subjects, in contrast, carried out the same task under the same conditions without learning of the buzzer. In this experiment, therefore, the reward for solving puzzles was avoidance of noxious stimulation, a situation analogous to the typical threat-oriented conditions of everyday life.

In this experiment, as in the money studies, the rewarded subjects displayed less intrinsic motivation (a marginally significant result) than nonrewarded people. There are, of course, alternative interpretations for this result. For example, the "threats" may have induced anxiety in the experimental subjects. However, in spite of the plausible alternative interpretations, we regard the finding as consistent with the perceived locus of causality process; although it does not provide unequivocal support, it fits into a larger picture of being one type of controlling reward that seems to undermine intrinsic motivation.

As another example of a nonmonetary reward, Lepper *et al.* (1973) rewarded preschool children by giving them a "good player award" for using attractive art materials. The outcome was a decrease in the children's intrinsic motivation. The researchers employed a free-choice measure that was separated from the manipulation phase of the experiment by several days, thereby showing that the intrinsic motivational decrement persisted over time and was not merely a transitory phenomenon. Further, because the Lepper *et al.* study utilized young children as subjects, their experiment added to the generalizability of the phenomenon.

Similarly, Anderson, Manoogian, and Reznick (1976) reported that both monetary rewards and good player awards produced decrements in the intrinsic motivation of lower socioeconomic, largely Afro-American, preschool children. And Greene, Sternberg, and Lepper (1976) also found such decrements using a token economy procedure with fourth- and fifth-grade children.

Several studies have obtained results that are generally congruent with the undermining of intrinsic motivation phenomenon, although they do not test the proposition directly. Kruglanski, Freedman, and Zeevi (1971), for example, found that rewarding Israeli high school students with a tour of a university psychology laboratory for their work on a variety of tasks significantly decreased their creativity and task recall relative to a nonreward group. Further, Benware and Deci (1975) reported that rewarding subjects for arguing in favor of a position they initially supported actually led them to believe less strongly in the position. Then too, Garbarino (1975) showed that when sixth-grade girls were rewarded with movie tickets for tutoring first graders, the former became more critical and demanding and less effective than their nonrewarded counterparts. Garbarino suggested that rewards create an instrumental orientation that has deleterious social consequences. Such consequences, we assert, arise when people are shifted into an extrinsic rather than an intrinsic motivational orientation or subsystem.

Dienstbier and Leak (1976) discovered that persons who were paid to lose weight lost weight faster than nonpaid control subjects; however, when payments stopped, the former subjects regained some of the lost weight, whereas the control subjects continued to lose. Presumably, the paid subjects had come to believe there was an instrumental connection between weight loss and rewards so that cessation of the rewards caused a cessation of the instrumental behavior of losing weight. Also in keeping with our theme, T. S. Smith and Murphy (1978) found that symphony orchestra players expressed decreased satisfaction with their jobs as the judged quality of the orchestra, and so their pay, increased.

Deci, Benware, and Landy (1974) reported that subjects attributed less intrinsic motivation to others who received greater rewards for an activity than those who received lesser rewards. Therefore, it appears that rewards not only undermine people's intrinsic motivation for an activity but lead observers to assume that the rewardee is less intrinsically motivated.

D. EXPECTANCY, CONTINGENCY, AND SALIENCE

The finding that extrinsic rewards undermine intrinsic motivation for the rewarded activity seems quite robust. Experiments that employed several different rewards, several different activities, and variously aged subjects have produced the same results. There are, however, several limiting conditions to the process in which a change in perceived locus of causality leads to the undermining of intrinsic motivation. Those limiting conditions will continue to become evident throughout the remainder of this review, but we will consider three relevant dimensions in this section.

In the experiments discussed so far, rewarded subjects were told before they began working on the target activity that they would receive rewards for doing the activity. Therefore, the reward contingency was clear to the subjects before their initial engagement with the task; the rewards were expected. In such situations, where the reward contingencies were clear, perceived instrumentalities seemed to develop readily, resulting in the drop in intrinsic motivation. In the Lepper et al. (1973) study reported earlier, subjects who expected the good player award evidenced decreased intrinsic motivation relative to the no-reward controls. Subjects in another experimental group were given unexpected good player awards after they finished playing with the art materials. These subjects showed no decrements in intrinsic motivation relative to the control subjects. Thus, it appears that rewards need to be expected—the reward contingencies need to be clear—in order for intrinsic motivation to lessen. This, of course, makes good sense. If the effect of the reward is to create an instrumentality between the behavior and the reward, this is less likely to occur if the activity has not been conducted in order to get the reward. The motivational orientation during the performance was wholly intrinsic. If one were to receive "unexpected" rewards several times, however, this could easily begin to establish an instrumental relationship between the activity and the reward. The point is that the undermining occurs when the activity becomes subsumed by the person's extrinsic motivational subsystem, that is, when the activity becomes instrumental for a reward rather than rewarding in itself, and the perceived locus of causality shifts from internal to external. This process is unlikely to occur when an unexpected reward is received on one occasion.

In one published experiment an unexpected reward seems to have caused decreased enjoyment of an activity, although a methodological peculiarity makes the study difficult to compare with the Lepper, Greene, and Nisbett investigation. In that experiment, Kruglanski, Alon, and Lewis (1972) gave prizes to half of their elementary school subjects who had been on winning teams in group game competitions, whereas the other half received no prizes. The prizes were awarded following the announcement of the winner, although no mention of the prize had been made until that time. Therefore, the prize appears to be a straightforward, unexpected reward. However, when the prizes were presented, the experimenter falsely stated, "As we said before, members of the winning team will be awarded special prizes as tokens of their victory." It is difficult to say in this case just what produced the lowered expressed enjoyment of the games in the rewarded subjects, so the study's status is unclear.

Another feature of reward administration that has stimulated discussion as it relates to the undermining effect is whether the rewards are made contingent upon the nature or quality of performance or are simply given for participation in the activity regardless of the quality or quantity of performance. The undermining effect has been obtained after performance-contingent rewards (e.g., Deci, 1971, 1972b, in which subjects received $1 per puzzle solved) as well as following performance-noncontingent rewards (e.g., Lepper et al., 1973, in which subjects received a good player award regardless of the quality of their drawings). Therefore, rewards of either type can produce the undermining effect. However, several studies have shown that performance-contingent rewards have a more powerful undermining effect. An archetype of performance-contingent rewards is the piece-rate payment systems, in which wages are a direct function of output. It makes sense in terms of the change in perceived locus of causality process that contingent rewards would have a more deleterious effect on intrinsic motivation, for the contingency emphasizes the instrumental nature of the activity. Four experiments that utilized monetary rewards (Deci, 1972a; Pinder, 1976; Pritchard, Campbell, & Campbell, 1977; Weiner & Mander, 1978) and one that utilized prizes (Harackiewicz, 1979) demonstrated that performance-contingent rewards decrease intrinsic motivation. All but the Pritchard et al. study compared performance-contingent rewards to noncontingent rewards and found that contingent rewards tended to be more detrimental than noncontingent rewards. In fact, in the Deci (1972a) study, noncontingent rewards did not produce a decrement in intrinsic motivation.

In one study, Karniol and Ross (1977) found that performance-contingent rewards in conditions of high performance led to a higher level of intrinsic motivation than performance-noncontingent rewards. In this experiment with children, the instruction emphasized that the children should try to respond in a way that made a green light come on. The instructions emphasized the green light (as a source of positive performance feedback) much more than the rewards (marshmallows). Therefore, it was less a study of contingent rewards than a study of positive performance feedback conveyed through a green signal light. Later we will see that positive performance feedback increases intrinsic motivation, and we will return to a brief mention of this study at that time.

In sum, it appears that rewards which are contingent upon a specified level of performance are more deleterious to intrinsic motivation than rewards not having this relationship, although noncontingent rewards have also been shown in many instances to have the deleterious effect. In a later section we shall see that performance-contingent rewards can actually enhance intrinsic motivation when they are administered in a way that places emphasis on effective performance rather than on reward acquisition.

In order for rewards to undermine intrinsic motivation they must be a salient factor in the person's experience of the activity. Ross (1975) reported an experiment in which two groups of children were offered prizes for playing with a drum. For one group, the prize was under a box in plain view of the child; for the other group the prize was absent and there was no further mention of it during the performance. He found that the salient reward, the one in view of the subjects, produced a significant decrease in intrinsic motivation whereas the nonsalient prize did not. Apparently, rewards must be salient if there is to be an adverse effect on intrinsic motivation, although, as we will see later, salient rewards may either increase or decrease intrinsic motivation depending on other factors (namely the functional aspects of rewards; see Section IV).

E. NATURE OF THE TASK

Most of the studies of the effects of rewards on intrinsic motivation have employed a highly interesting task. With such tasks, rewards (particularly when salient, expected, and contingent) generally decrease intrinsic motivation. A few studies have examined the nature of the target activity as a factor influencing the undermining effect.

Arnold (1976), for example, acknowledged that most studies in this area have yielded the undermining effect, but he suggested that if the activity is extremely highly intrinsically motivating, the intrinsic motivation should be impervious to the negative effects of extrinsic rewards. In his study "subjects" were recruited for a game rather than an experiment and no mention was made of the rewards. Subjects worked on a very interesting computer game and were either paid or not paid $2.00 during their first session. The results indicated that rewards either left intrinsic motivation unchanged or enhanced it. In interpreting these results, we would note several points. First, the rewards were noncontingent, and as we saw previously, noncontingent rewards are less likely to decrease intrinsic motivation. Second, the subjects who received rewards were told of the rewards just before they began their actual experimental performance so they were recruited with no mention of money. Moreover, several events occurred before anything was said about money; a 10-min videotaped introduction to the game and a brief question and answer period. As a consequence of all this, they had been oriented to play the computer game before rewards entered their awareness, and we suggest that the rewards were relatively unexpected. Hence, the rewards in this experiment were really noncontingent, unexpected rewards, and both characteristics have been shown to lessen the deleterious effects of extrinsic rewards. A true test of Arnold's hypothesis would necessitate the use of contingent, expected rewards. We see no compelling reason to expect highly interesting tasks to escape the negative impact of extrinsic rewards, nor do we interpret Arnold's experiment as indicative that they do.

Calder and Staw (1975b) and Lee, Syrnyk, and Hallschmid (1977) did experiments in which subjects were rewarded for working on either relatively interesting or relatively dull activities. Calder and Staw used college students as subjects and employed both an interesting and a dull jigsaw puzzle activity. Half the subjects in each condition were monetarily rewarded and half were not. The results revealed that paid subjects in the interesting puzzle condition expressed less enjoyment in a postexperimental questionnaire than did the nonrewarded subjects. In the interesting puzzle condition, therefore, the undermining effect was replicated. However, in the dull puzzle task, paid subjects expressed greater enjoyment than the nonpayment subjects. This finding is often referred to as a reinforcement effect and was interpreted by Calder and Staw as indicating that extrinsic rewards increase subjects' intrinsic motivation for dull tasks.

We regard their interpretation as noncompelling and inappropriate. A task that is dull and uninteresting is certainly not intrinsically motivated initially; typically it would be performed for extrinsic reasons, such as rewards or compulsion. We do not see how adding extrinsic rewards to a dull task (which is most probably an instrumental activity to begin with) could possibly increase intrinsic motivation for the activity. Rewards should increase satisfaction with the activity, but only by virtue of the activity's instrumentality for the attainment of extrinsic satisfaction rather than because of its intrinsic interest. Said somewhat differently, people rewarded extrinsically for doing something that they would typically do only if rewarded should be more satisfied than other persons who are not rewarded for doing such an activity. However, that does not in any way speak to their level of intrinsic motivation. The result is somewhat parallel to the findings reported earlier that when rewards are added to an aversive task, performance is enhanced (McGraw, 1978). Rewards decrease the aversive elements of the situation, thereby improving performance, providing extrinsic satisfaction, and adding enjoyment. Part of the reason for confusion on this point is that the operational definitions of intrinsic motivation are not perfectly correlated with the psychological definition of intrinsic motivation. Whereas enjoyment and satisfaction with an activity are certainly related to intrinsic motivation and are therefore used as operational definitions of this motivation, they can also reflect other factors, such as the enjoyment of being extrinsically satisfied.

The study by Lee *et al.* used mentally deficient children as subjects. They worked on interesting vs. dull tasks and received rewards that had either high or low incentive value. These researchers found results similar to those of Calder and Staw. Our interpretation of this study is the same as we just outlined. Extrinsic rewards decrease intrinsic motivation, satisfaction, and enjoyment of intrinsically interesting activities, whereas extrinsic rewards increase extrinsic satisfaction and enjoyment of a dull activity, although they do not increase subjects' intrinsic motivation for the dull activity.

Kruglanski, Riter, Amitai, Margolin, Shabtai, and Zaksh (1975) have reported two experiments that bear theoretical similarity to the ones just described. Kruglanski *et al.* reasoned that if money were endogenous to an activity—in other words, an integral element of the activity (e.g., coin tossing)—then monetary rewards should increase intrinsic motivation. However, if the money is exogenous to the activity—in other words, not an integral element of it—then monetary rewards should decrease intrinsic motivation. Using "expressed interest" as their primary dependent measure, Kruglanski *et al.* found that subjects who were paid for money-exogenous tasks expressed less interest than their nonpayment counterparts, whereas subjects who were paid for money-endogenous tasks expressed greater interest than their nonpayment counterparts. Deci, Porac, and Shapira (1978) replicated one of Kruglanski's experiments and found that while payment for a money-endogenous task increased rated interest, it did not increase subjects' intrinsic motivation as measured by the standard free-choice measure. They reasoned that money-endogenous activities (like dull, boring ones) are ones that people tend to do for rewards; they actually are extrinsic activities. Such activities, whether dull or exciting, have been under the control of people's extrinsic motivational subsystems. Therefore, when people carry out "extrinsic activities" and receive extrinsic rewards for doing so, they will be more satisfied than if they perform the extrinsic activity without getting the extrinsic rewards. Again, however, that does not speak directly to the issue of their intrinsic motivation for the activity.

To summarize, research evidence as well as common sense indicate that the widely observed undermining of intrinsic motivation by extrinsic rewards does not occur unless there is some initial intrinsic motivation. The person being rewarded must be intrinsically motivated at the start, obviously, if his intrinsic motivation is to decline. Thus, leaving aside individual differences in people's attraction to particular activities, it is necessary to employ activities that are generally interesting and intrinsically involving in order to have a clear demonstration of the undermining effect. When activities are initially dull, boring, or money endogenous—in other words, when they are the types of activities people carry out largely for extrinsic rewards—the rewards will increase satisfaction with the activity, although there is no evidence to indicate that people's intrinsic motivation will be increased, nor is there any compelling theoretical basis for expecting it to be.

We suggest that it is important to start with a definition of intrinsic motivation that involves psychological substrates in order to make reasonable interpretations of experimental findings. These studies just reviewed seem to be excellent cases in point. Kruglanski *et al.* and Calder and Staw have tended to define intrinsic motivation as a postbehavioral, self-attribution while paying little or no attention to underlying motivational or affective processes. Such definitions, which are rather superficial in the dynamic or depth sense, facilitate the type of confusion that allows one to arrive at (what we consider) the false conclusion that extrinsic rewards will increase people's intrinsic motivation for a dull, boring task.

Lepper *et al.* (1973) usefully pointed out that rewards may get people engaged in activities they would not otherwise try but which they find interesting once they try them. Rewards therefore may play a part in people's discovering their intrinsic motivation for an activity, although that is quite different from saying that rewards increase people's intrinsic motivation for an activity.

F. COMPETITION AND INTRINSIC MOTIVATION

Competition is a component of many "play" activities; it would seem to be somehow intertwined with intrinsic motivation. Csikszentmihalyi (1975) has said that competition is one of the basic components of "autotelic" or intrinsically motivated activities, and McClelland *et al.* (1953) have suggested that achievement motivation involves competition against a standard of excellence. Deutsch (1962) spoke of competition in terms of two or more people or groups having directly opposing goals. This, then, would be competition as seen in the standard sporting activity in which one party wins and one party loses. It is important to distinguish between this latter use of the concept and that of McClelland *et al.* (1953) in which there need be only one person who is seeking to do well at some activity. Csikszentmihalyi (1975) made a similar distinction by differentiating the following two items: "measuring self against others" and "measuring self against own ideal." We shall use competition in the former sense, in which there are two or more parties involved and each is specifically attempting to beat the other. We consider the latter usage—seeking to do well and meet one's own standard—to be mastery rather than competition. Kelley and Thibaut (1969) used the term "perfect competition" to refer to the so-called zero-sum situations where there is a perfect negative relationship between the wins of one side and the losses of the other. Kelley and Thibaut reported that pure competition tends to foster a mutual mistrust (often even deceit), and much research (e.g., Berkowitz, 1962; Deutsch, 1969) has indicated that competition may impair performance and facilitate aggression.

Deci, Betley, Kahle, Abrams, and Porac (in press,a) reported an experiment which investigated the effects of competition on intrinsic motivation. They reasoned that competition was an extrinsic element since attempting to win, per se, was extrinsic to mastering the activity for its own sake. They therefore predicted that competition (i.e., trying to win) would decrease subjects' intrinsic motivation. To test their hypothesis they used a variant of the typical Soma puzzle paradigm and induced competition by instructing the actual subject and an experimental accomplice (posing as a second subject) to try to win by solving each puzzle faster than the other person.

It should be noted that many games have competition built into them as an integral element, whereas in this experiment the competition is, in a sense, exogenous to puzzle solving. In contrast, competition, although built into such games as basketball, is exogenous to shooting baskets well, to dribbling well, and to mastering other components of the game. Therefore, although competition (the *fact of winning or losing,* as opposed to mastery feedback) may be built in to some games, we assert that it is by nature an extrinsic element; its focus is on winning rather than engaging with the activity itself.

In the Deci *et al.* study, half the subjects were instructed to compete (i.e., to try to solve the puzzles faster than the other person) while half were simply instructed to work as quickly as they could so as to finish in the alloted time. As predicted, the results revealed that competition decreased the subjects' intrinsic motivation. This was particularly true for females; their score on the measure of intrinsic motivation was 115 sec (out of 480 sec of free-choice time) lower than their counterparts who did not compete, whereas the competing males had intrinsic motivation scores only 38 sec less than their noncompeting counterparts. This experiment was constructed so that each subject worked on three puzzles. In the competition condition the actual subjects were allowed to "beat" the confederate on all three. Thus, even though the subjects won, the competition undermined their intrinsic motivation, as measured by the standard free-choice measure.

Our interpretation of the results is that competition is by nature an extrinsic element which causes an external perceived locus of causality and engages a person's extrinsic motivational subsystem. As was seen in the Garbarino (1975) study of tutoring, the extrinsic orientation tends to be accompanied by certain affective behaviors, such as demandingness and criticism. Competition is a particularly keen form of extrinsic relating because of its face-to-face nature; therefore one often finds face-saving behaviors, performance disruption, and emotionality—as for instance the increased aggression reported by Berkowitz (1962) in competitive settings.

G. EFFECTS OF CONTROL STRUCTURES

In several of the preceding sections we have reported a variety of studies which provide strong support for the hypothesis that certain kinds of extrinsic rewards decrease people's intrinsic motivation for intersting activities. According to cognitive evaluation theory, this occurs when the reward contingency creates a perceived instrumental relationship between the activity and the reward, thereby placing the behavior within the realm of the person's extrinsic motivational subsystem and changing the person's corresponding perceived locus of causality from internal to external.

Persumably, if various desired extrinsic rewards induce such a change in one's perception of causality, other types of external constraints and structures should produce the same results. Several studies have supported this conjecture. Amabile, DeJong, and Lepper (1976) found that when external deadlines were imposed on college students who were working on interesting word games they expressed less interest subsequent to the experience than control subjects who were not given deadlines. Similarly, Lepper and Greene (1975) reported that children who worked on an interesting puzzle under conditions of adult surveillance via a television camera procedure displayed less intrinsic motivation for the puzzle activity in a follow-up session than did nonwatched children. Therefore, both deadlines and surveillance, two factors integrally involved with externally imposed control systems, have been shown to undermine intrinsic motivation.

H. FAILURES TO REPLICATE: THE BEHAVIORISTIC PERSPECTIVE

A few studies in the literature have reported failures to support the undermining of intrinsic motivation by extrinsic rewards (Farr, 1976; Finegold & Mahoney, 1975; Hamner & Foster, 1975; Reiss & Sushinsky, 1975). These studies were formulated with a behavior theory point of view. Traditionally, behavior theory has assumed that rewarded behavior would be strengthened, a phenomenon referred to as a "reinforcement effect." Focus has been on specific, observable responses with little or no attention paid to psychological events. For example, Finegold and Mahoney defined intrinsic motivation as operant level performance, and Hamner and Foster used as the dependent measure of intrinsic motivation the subjects' performance during the payment period.

We suggest therefore that the concerns of the behavior theorists are in a fundamental sense different from ours. We begin with an interest in internal psychological phenomena and their effects on subsequent behavior. Accordingly, for our purposes the relevant data in an operant paradigm appear during the extinction phase and involve a comparison of rewarded and nonrewarded subjects during the extinction period. There is no way to separate the intrinsic elements of performance from the extrinsic elements while the reward contingencies are still in effect. Given the theoretical and methodological differences between our analysis and the behavioral analysis, we suggest that these studies have not contradicted cognitive evaluation theory.

Finegold and Mahoney (1975) did a "token-economy" type of experiment with children. They observed children playing with a dot connection activity during a baseline phase and then rewarded the youngsters by giving them tokens (that could be exchanged for prizes) in accord with the number of dots connected (more tokens for more dots connected). Finally, they observed the children during two more baseline phases in which there were no rewards. They reported that there were sharp performance increases when rewards were introduced and that the postreward baseline performance was not lower than the prereward baseline performance. They therefore claimed failure to support the undermining effect.

There are aspects of this experiment that we believe vitiate the conclusions drawn by the authors. There were only five subjects, so their conclusions must be considered tenuous. More importantly, there was no nonreward group to control for extraneous factors, so there was no basis for drawing conclusions about the effects of rewards. For example, a nonrewarded group may have evidenced substantially higher responding during the posttreatment phase, thereby indicating relative decrements for the rewarded group.

As we mentioned above, the Hamner and Foster study has a similar shortcoming. They measured performance on and interest in the task during the period when reward contingencies were in effect. Their experiment used both a dull task and an interesting one—although it should be noted that both tasks were overlearned tasks (transcribing numbers with dull vs. interesting content) which required no creativity and were not in any way challenging. They claimed failure to support the undermining of intrinsic motivation; however, we assert that their interpretation of the results was inappropriate since they did not employ an intrinsically motivating task and did not look at behaviors and attitudes subsequent to the reward phase.

Farr, Vance, and McIntyre (1977) also reported a failure to support the undermining effect predicted by cognitive evaluation theory. Yet a careful inspection of their results shows considerable ambiguity. In the first of their two empirical studies they found a highly significant decrement in the intrinsic motivation of contingently rewarded subjects relative to nonrewarded subjects on the free-choice measure of intrinsic motivation but not on an attitudinal measure. In their second study there was no statistically significant effect for rewards. From these studies they concluded nonsupport for the undermining effect. Yet that conclusion is unwarranted. In fact, with the most important dependent measure they found strong support in the first of the two studies, and in the second study they found a trend in the direction of the undermining effect ($F = 1.55$; $p < .13$), thereby suggesting that rewards tended to affect intrinsic motivation. It is always difficult to interpret failures to reject the null hypothesis, so even if there had been no significant findings in their studies, the conclusion would need to be tempered.

Farr *et al.* did make a very interesting point in their paper. They reported that their free-choice data tended to be bimodally (rather than normally) distributed, and that the same was true for Deci's (1971) data. That point deserves investigation. It suggests one of two things. The less interesting possibility is that it is a function of the particular measure, that is, that some people tend to enjoy the target activity and some do not. The second and more interesting possibility is that the undermining effect, although on average significant across all subjects, really exists primarily for some subset of the population. If the latter hypothesis is correct, it would be very interesting to determine what characteristics distinguish the people whose intrinsic motivation will be undermined by extrinsic rewards from those whose intrinsic motivation will not be undermined.

Reiss and Sushinsky (1975), criticizing the "overjustification" experiments for utilizing only single-trial reinforcement procedures, reported two studies. In the first they used a single-trial reinforcement procedure with children and obtained a replication of the overjustification effect previously found by Lepper *et al.* (1973) and Greene and Lepper (1974). In the second experiment, however, they utilized a multiple-reinforcement procedure and reported increased intrinsic interest following token reinforcement. They therefore concluded that the overjustification effect was in actuality a short-term distraction effect and that rewards will generally enhance intrinsic motivation. However, the primary difficulty with their results, as noted by Lepper and Greene (1976), was that like Finegold and Mahoney they did not use a no-reward, control group. Although the subjects' interest in the target activity may have increased from pre- to posttreatment, it is impossible to know whether that is caused by reinforcement, passage of time, increased familiarity with the target activity, or any one of a host of other factors. With no control group, the data are impossible to interpret. Further, R. W. Smith and Pittman (1978) tested the "distraction" interpretation and found no evidence for it.

Some people who employ the behavioristic perspective to investigate the undermining of intrinsic motivation by extrinsic rewards still do not accept the phenomenon. Therefore, they tend to discredit the experimental procedures which have purported to demonstrate the effect. Others agree that such an effect may exist, but they then offer a reinforcement account of the effect. For example, Reiss and Sushinsky acknowledged that a decrement in interest may occur with a single-trial reinforcement procedure. Moreover, Scott (1976), although asserting that no good evidence exists for an undermining effect, provided a behavioral explanation for such a phenomenon.

The essence of a behavioral explanation (Mawhinney, 1979) is the assertion that situations have multiple reinforcing contingencies and that the introduction of rewards may distract attention from the rewarded activity (Reiss & Sushinsky, 1975), interfere with the optimal duration of the activity (Mawhinney, 1979), or change the contingencies so that the withdrawal of the new contingencies which control the behavior will result in a lowered response rate for the target behavior (Scott, 1976).

Deci (1976) replied to Scott's critique by noting that his assertion about a reinforcement explanation being preferable to a cognitive explanation is largely a statement of preferred metatheory. Scott began with the assumption that a reinforcement explanation is best and then used this formulation as an alternative explanation to Deci's. Given the behavioristic metatheory, Scott was primarily concerned with the way classes of reinforcing events affect the probability that organisms will emit certain classes of behavior. We want to explicate the psychological processes involved in the motivation of behavior and with the quantitative and qualitative differences in behaviors that are governed by what we have called intrinsic and extrinsic processes. Much of what concerns us is deliberately ignored by a behavioral analysis.

I.   EXTERNAL TO INTERNAL: THE IMPORTANCE OF SELF-DETERMINATION

In the preceding sections we reviewed considerable evidence indicating that controlling extrinsic rewards and constraints will often decrease people's intrinsic motivation for the rewarded activity, as they perceive an instrumental relationship between the activity and the reward or the constraint. The development of a perceived instrumental relationship between the behavior and reward involves a shift in the motivational subsystem that organizes and governs the behavior. Whereas the behavior had initially been in the domain of the intrinsic subsystem, it now moves into the domain of the extrinsic subsystem. The cognitive component of this shift is what we have referred to as the change in perceived locus of causality.

The decrease in intrinsic motivation has usually been attributed to a shift from internal to external causality. This is largely a reflection of the fact that the experimental research has explored the effects of rewards and constraints rather than the effects of the absence of rewards and constraints.

Actually, the perceived locus of causality may shift in either direction—from external to internal or from internal to external—depending on whether conditions fostering self-determination or non-self-determination are present. In the absence of external rewards and constraints, when people are free to do what they want, they should perceive the locus of causality to be internal. Their behavior in these situations could become governed by the intrinsic rather than the extrinsic motivational subsystem, the behavior would not be seen as instrumental to an external reward or constraint, and the locus of causality would be perceived as internal. They would feel self-determining.

In therapeutic and affective educational settings the aim of treatment is to foster self-determination and develop a perceived internal locus of causality (Ryan & Deci, 1980). Clients are encouraged to accept responsibility for their behavior so that treatment changes will persist in the absence of the therapeutic setting. This shift from external causality to internal causality is typically more difficult to accomplish than the shift from internal to external since in essence it involves not controlling behavior with readily manipulable external events rather than controlling it with such events. Nonetheless some research has been conducted which addresses the shift from external to internal causality.

Zuckerman, Porac, Lathin, Smith, and Deci (1978) sought to determine whether subjects who were given a modest amount of additional self-determination relative to other subjects not provided with the additional self-determination would show increased intrinsic motivation for the target activity. In this study, yoked pairs of college student subjects solved Soma puzzles. One member of each pair was given a choice as to which three of six puzzles to work on, and further, as to how to apportion the 30 min available for puzzle solving to the three chosen puzzles. The other member of each yoked pair was assigned the puzzles and time allotments chosen by the first person.

Results indicated that subjects who chose the activities and time allotments—in other words, who had additional self-determination—were more intrinsically motivated than subjects performing the same activity without choice. The "self-determining" subjects spent an average of 94 sec more of free-choice time (out of 480 sec available) working on the puzzles than did their yoked counterparts. They also indicated a greater willingness to return to the laboratory for additional puzzle solving than the subjects who had not been given the choice of puzzles. Both effects were statistically significant.

Because the "self-determining" subjects selected which puzzles they would work on, they might have chosen configurations that were easier for them, so that performance differences might have mediated the intrinsic motivation effects. To test this possibility the authors analyzed the average time to solve each puzzle and also the average number of puzzles not completed. There were no differences between the choice and no-choice groups on either measure (each of which yielded an F of less than 1.0). Further, an analysis of covariance was performed using both of the performance measures as covariates, and the significant main effect still remained on the dependent measures. Therefore, it seems clear that the opportunity for self-determination in regard to some activity enhances one's intrinsic motivation for the activity, presumably by facilitating an internal perceived locus of causality for performance of the activity.

Swann and Pittman (1977) reported experimental results that corroborated those of Zuckerman *et al*. They utilized children who played with an interesting drawing game. Half of their subjects were assigned the target activity, while the others were told that they could select which game they wanted to play with, although it was quickly added that since they were sitting in front of the drawing game they might as well start with it. Thus, the "choice" children were given the "illusion of choice" rather than actual choice about which activity to play with. The results indicated somewhat greater intrinsic motivation in the choice group than the no-choice group.

The "illusion of choice" manipulation has become a prominent one in experimental social psychology and deserves a few words of comment. The manipulation is intended to make people believe that they have choice when in fact they are induced by the experimenter to behave in a certain way. We suggest that this is a subtle form of control rather than an opportunity for self-determination. Therefore, we hypothesize that although the manipulation may work to enhance felt control over the short run it could decrease one's felt control and intrinsic motivation over a prolonged period. We know of no evidence on this matter, although relevant evidence would be important, for if the illusion of choice is really a subtle form of control, then the manipulation is not satisfactory for studying self-determination and self-control.

We have seen that choice of puzzles increased intrinsic motivation for puzzle solving and that the illusion of choice increased intrinsic motivation for a play activity. Fisher (1978) has shown that personal control over performance also increases subjects' intrinsic motivation. In her study, half the subjects was given puzzles in which difficulty levels constrained their performance to either low, medium, or high. The other subjects were given puzzles in which the moderate difficulty level gave them freedom to determine their own performance level. She found that even when matching for performance, the subjects with control of their performance felt freer and were more intrinsically motivated than constrained subjects.

A study by Margolis and Mynatt (1979) has shown that when subjects were given a choice about which rewards they would receive, the rewards did not undermine intrinsic motivation, even though the same rewards did undermine intrinsic motivation for a no-choice group. Those who selected the size of their own rewards were comparable to nonrewarded control subjects and were significantly more intrinsically motivated than subjects who were administered the same rewards that had been selected by their yoked counterparts. Thus, feelings of self-determination (and the concomitant perception of an internal locus of causality) seem to enhance intrinsic motivation. Further, feelings of self-determination that result from the self-administration of rewards may counteract the deleterious effects of the controlling aspect of the rewards and help to maintain an internal locus of causality. This latter conclusion remains somewhat tenuous, however, since a study by Dollinger and Thelen (1978) found that children who self-administered rewards when they thought they had done well showed decrements in intrinsic motivation. The reward involved their placing a "star" on their good player award which was on a bulletin board. We suggest that the reason these self-administered rewards decreased intrinsic motivation (rather than fostering an internal locus of causality and maintaining their intrinsic motivation) was that the instructions emphasized self-evaluation and may have elicited an evaluation apprehension that made the self-administration of rewards a somewhat aversive controlling experience.

Recent research on attribution theory and therapy also has relevance to our hypothesis that situational factors, such as the absence of extrinsic controls and the encouragement of choice, will strengthen the perception of an internal locus of causality and in turn increase intrinsic motivation. For example, Nentwig (1978) reported that modifications in smoking behavior were more likely to persist following treatment if clients perceived the cause of the modifications to be internal.

III. Cognitive Evaluation Theory: Perceived Competence

So far we have discussed the proposition that intrinsic motivation will be affected when elements of a situation—for example, the presence or absence of rewards and constraints and the opportunity or lack thereof for choice—cause a shift in perceived locus of causality from internal to external or from external to internal.

Deci (1975) has proposed that there is a second process through which one's intrinsic motivation may be affected. Intrinsic motivation is defined in terms of people's needs for competence and self-determination. The perceived locus of causality process is based in feelings and perceptions of self-determination. The second process is based in feelings and perceptions of competence. Intrinsic motivation will be affected if there is a change in one's perception of being competent. Perceiving oneself as competent at an activity will increase one's intrinsic motivation for the activity; perceiving oneself as incompetent will decrease one's intrinsic motivation for the activity. We said earlier that self-determination is the more fundamental of the two intrinsic needs. We now assert that one's perception of competence or incompetence must occur within the context of self-determination to affect intrinsic motivation. If one is forced to acquire competence at an activity, the activity will not be intrinsically motivating. Similarly, if one is forced to do badly it will not undermine intrinsic motivation since the poor performance will be understood as a result of the coercion. Fisher (1978) found support for this assertion. She reported that subjects whose performance had been constrained showed no correlation between felt competence and intrinsic motivation, whereas subjects whose performance had not been constrained did show a significant correlation.

The current statement of the second process through which intrinsic motivation can be affected differs from the 1975 statement of the process in two ways. First, the current statement utilizes "perceptions" of competence rather than "feelings." This was done so as to parallel the first process, which is stated in terms of "perceptions" of the locus of causality. Of course feelings accompany perceptions: people feel self-determining when they perceive the locus of causality to be internal and people feel competent when they perceive themselves as competent. The use of perceptions in both processes is done for consistency, since the theory is called a cognitive evaluation theory. The second difference between the 1975 and the present statement of the second process involves the separation of the self-determination and competence components of intrinsic motivation. The first process of cognitive evaluation theory is oriented around the need for self-determination; it involves perception of the locus of causality and feelings of self-determination. The second process is oriented around the need for competence; it involves perceptions of competence and feelings of competence. The 1975 statement of the second process employed "feelings of competence and self-determination"; we now assert that feelings of competence accompany the second process and that feelings of self-determination accompany the first process. Self-determination comes into the second process only insofar as one's perception of competence or incompetence must exist within the context of self-determination to affect one's intrinsic motivation.

When an informational input increases one's perceptions of (self-determined) competence it should enhance one's intrinsic motivation; when it decreases one's perceptions of (self-determined) competence it should diminish one's intrinsic motivation. For example, if one received positive feedback about a puzzle solution the person will have enhanced intrinsic motivation to move on to a new puzzle problem. If the person knows the solution to the old problem, the old problem will not be intrinsically interesting but the activity of solving those puzzle problems will. Each new puzzle needs to be a challenge and the person will be more intrinsically motivated to engage in that type of puzzle problem.

Ross (1976) made a point similar to Deci's. Utilizing an attribution framework, he suggested that if rewards provide competence cues they will cause an attribution of intrinsic motivation. Our point of divergence with Ross' attribution position is that we maintain that the changes that occur are changes in motivational process that have cognitive and affective components. The attributional changes are the cognitive component of the changes that theoretically, we assert, are organized by motivational changes.

There is considerable empirical evidence in support of the change in perceived competence hypothesis, just as there was in support of the change in perceived locus of causality process.

A. POSITIVE FEEDBACK AND PRAISE

More than a dozen experiments, variously utilizing children, students, and adults, have investigated the effects of positive feedback. Many authors have used the terms verbal rewards, praise, and positive feedback interchangeably. As we will see later, verbal rewards—like other rewards—can either enhance or diminish intrinsic motivation, and we assert that verbal rewards which increase intrinsic motivation are ones emphasizing competence feedback, whereas those decreasing intrinsic motivation are ones that are administered controllingly, in other words, administered to achieve a particular behavioral outcome. Thus, while verbal rewards may either increase or decrease intrinsic motivation, *positive competence feedback should always increase intrinsic motivation*. This will be explicated later in this section and in Section IV.

Anderson *et al.* (1976), in their study with lower socioeconomic 4- and 5-year-olds, found that verbal rewards increased children's intrinsic motivation. The rewards were such statements as ''That's real nice''; the activity was drawing; and the subjects were about two-thirds female.

Utilizing a slightly different paradigm, Martin (1977) found that after children had been praised for playing with a target activity they preferred that activity to other activities on which their behavior had not been praised. Further, their preference for the verbally rewarded activity seemed to generalize to other activities that were similar to the verbally rewarded one.

Swann and Pittman (1977) reported that verbal rewards increased the intrinsic motivation of children, although in their study the verbal rewards were paired with contingent tangible rewards so it is difficult to know whether the increased intrinsic motivation resulted from verbal rewards, the tangible rewards, or some interaction of the two.

Dollinger and Thelen (1978) and Lonky (1978) reported that verbally rewarded children did not differ from no-reward children in terms of their intrinsic motivation, although Lonky reported that subjects high in locus of control (internals) seem to have increased, while subjects low in locus of control (externals) seem to have decreased. He employed the Bialer (1961) scale for locus of control.

Boggiano and Ruble (1979) found that self-administered, positive competence feedback increased the intrinsic motivation of 9–11-year-olds, although it did not affect 4–6-year-olds. The information was taken by the children from a table of norms, so it is possible that the younger children did not adequately understand that they had performed well.

To summarize the studies with children, positive competence information—generally administered as verbal feedback—tended to increase intrinsic motivation, although this finding failed to appear in two studies. In one of them, however, the failure seems to have been caused by the averaging of an increase for internal locus of control subjects and a decrease for external locus of control subjects.

Experiments on the effects of positive feedback and praise that have utilized adults have yielded a more complex set of findings than those utilizing children.

Harackiewicz (1979) found that verbally rewarding high school students for solving hidden-word puzzles increased their intrinsic motivation on a free-choice measure and their enjoyment of the activity. About 70% of these subjects were males, and there were apparently no sex differences. Deci (1971) found that positive feedback to subjects, who were predominantly males, increased their intrinsic motivation relative to a no-reward, control group.

In the Arnold (1976) experiment with a computer game as the target activity, subjects who performed better reported higher feelings of competence than poorer performers, and those with higher felt competence in turn displayed greater intrinsic motivation as evidenced by a greater willingness to return for future sessions with the target activity. In this study there was apparently no analysis for sex effects. We see from these three studies that both positive verbal feedback and positive feedback that is "self-administered" from successful performance appear to enhance intrinsic motivation.

A study by W. E. Smith (1974) appears at first blush to have yielded results that are contradictory to those of Harackiewicz (1979), Arnold (1976), and Deci (1971). In his study, college student subjects were given "anticipated social rewards" for learning about art. The results showed that intrinsic motivation (with a free-choice measure) decreased for the anticipated social reward group. To induce the anticipation of social rewards, the experimenter emphasized in the instructions that the subject's work would be evaluated by the experimenter. These subjects received positive written evaluations following their performance and subsequently displayed less intrinsic motivation than nonrewarded, control subjects. Although this study was interpreted as indicating that social rewards (in the form of positive feedback) decreased intrinsic motivation, our interpretation is different. The most salient aspect of the experimental induction seems to be the emphasis on evaluation of the subjects. Evaluation lends an extrinsic character to feedback and is often experienced as highly controlling and aversive (e.g., Amabile, 1979, found that evaluation interfered with subjects' creativity). Thus, even when the final feedback is positive, the evaluation apprehension can undermine intrinsic motivation by making the activity instrumental to a positive evaluation. We understand the Smith results, like those of Dollinger and Thelen (1978) mentioned earlier, as resulting from the subject's reaction to being evaluated. There is no contradiction, therefore, between these results and the findings of enhancement of intrinsic motivation through positive feedback; the two are complementary.

There has been some indication in other studies that verbal rewards affect adult males and adult females differently, although this issue seems unsettled. Deci, Cascio, and Krusell (1975) reported that verbal rewards increased the intrinsic motivation of males but decreased the intrinsic motivation of females. This rather dramatic finding had been suggested in an earlier study (Deci, 1972b).

Carone (1975) replicated the Deci *et al.* study with females and also found that praise decreased their intrinsic motivation. In contrast, Weiner and Mander (1978) found that positive feedback to females increased their intrinsic motivation (the later finding was only marginally significant).

How then are we to make sense of these apparently contradictory findings? We said above that positive information about one's competence should increase intrinsic motivation through the change in perception of competence process. One would suspect, therefore, that any verbal praise or any positive feedback should initiate this process and increase intrinsic motivation. However, one must realize that verbal praise can mean many things. For example, people may offer praise as an ingratiation strategy or as a means to manipulate or cajole the praised person into doing something he or she does not want to do. In other words, praise, like money or threats, can be very controlling and therefore be negatively experienced by the person receiving the praise.

Deci (1975) suggested that all rewards, whether money, praise, candy, or trips to Europe (and in fact all situations in general), have two *functional properties*. They have a *controlling aspect*—that aspect which satisfies extrinsic needs and creates instrumentalities between behavior and rewards—and an *informational aspect*—that aspect which provides people with positive information about their self-competence or efficacy. When the controlling aspect of a situation is salient, it will initiate the change in perceived locus of causality. The salient presence of controlling, extrinsic rewards instigates a change from internal to external causality with a concomitant decrease in intrinsic motivation and a gratification of extrinsic needs. The salient absence of extrinsic rewards or constraints can initiate a change from external to internal causality with the concomitant strengthening of intrinsic motivation. If, in contrast, the informational aspect of a reward (or other situational factor) is more salient, it will initiate the change in perceived competence process, increasing intrinsic motivation when the information implies competence and decreasing intrinsic motivation when the information implies incompetence.

Now let us consider the sex differences reported in the Deci studies in light of the two functional aspects of rewards. Deci (1975) suggested that for females the controlling aspect of the verbal praise appears to have been more salient, resulting in decreased intrinsic motivation through the shift of perceived locus of causality, whereas for males the informational aspect seems to have been more salient, resulting in increased intrinsic motivation through the enhancement of perceived competence. He reasoned that with traditional socialization practices girls have learned to be more dependent and interpersonally focused, whereas boys have learned to be more independent and achievement focused. A study by Alegre and Murray (1974), which showed that females "condition" more readily with verbal reinforcement than do males, lends support to Deci's interpretation.

If Deci's interpretation is correct, how can other discrepancies be reconciled? First, consider the apparent contradiction between the results of Deci *et al.* and Carone (1975), on the one hand, and those of Weiner and Mander (1978), on the other. In the Deci experiments and the Carone experiment, subjects were praised at the end of each puzzle on which they worked. The praise was regular and salient in their experience. It was interpreted, therefore, as either controlling (by females) or informational (by males) and caused the observed effects. In the Weiner and Mander study, the procedure was quite different. At the end of all their problem-solving work, the verbally rewarded subjects were told that they did better than average. Thus, the feedback was not delivered as salient "praise" during their performance. Instead, it was simply positive information about their competence; hence, it enhanced their intrinsic motivation.

The important point is that females as well as males will become more intrinsically motivated when they receive positive competence information. However, the specific reward of praise tends to be more controlling for females and more informational for males. When verbal feedback is administered to females in a more informational way, as was the case in the Weiner and Mander study, it will of course increase their intrinsic motivation. We have noted, however, that if the positive feedback is given in a highly evaluative fashion, the controlling nature of the evaluation may override the information contained in the feedback and decrease the intrinsic motivation of both males and females (e.g., W. E. Smith, 1974).

It is necessary also to take note of the fact that there appeared to be no sex differences in the effects of praise on little children, only on adults. Presumably, either the socialization procedures have not had sufficient impact by the time a child is 3–6 years old to result in the type of sex differences observed in adults, or alternatively, the socialization procedures used in the late 1960s and the 1970s (which were applicable for the children in the reported research) were somewhat different from those of the 1950s (which were applicable to the adults in the reported research).

A study by Blanck, Jackson, and Reis (1979) would seem to argue for the latter. They reported that praise administered in the same fashion as in the Deci studies increased the intrinsic motivation of both males and females. They argued that consciousness of sex roles and changing beliefs about sex-typed behaviors and activities have lessened the tendency for praise to be interpreted differently by the two sexes. They found that women were more intrinsically motivated for feminine sex-typed tasks than masculine sex-typed tasks (the researchers used the same task for both but created a masculine vs. feminine set for the activity) and that males were more intrinsically motivated for masculine sex-typed tasks than feminine ones, but that the differential effects of praise that appeared in studies from the early part of the decade no longer appear, at least for the achievement conscious undergraduate women in their study.

B. NEGATIVE FEEDBACK

The studies reported above have confirmed that people's intrinsic motivation will increase when their perceptions and feelings of (self-determined) competence increase. Similarly, we hypothesized that people's intrinsic motivation will decrease when their perceptions and feelings of (self-determined) competence are diminished. Studies by Deci and Cascio (1972) and Deci, Cascio, and Krusell (1973) have supported this hypothesis. Employing the standard Soma paradigm, these investigators found that negative feedback, whether verbally administered by the experimenter or self-administered through failure at the target activity, decreased subjects' intrinsic motivation as measured by free-choice involvement with the target activity.

It is important to realize that not all so-called negative feedback will decrease intrinsic motivation, only that which signifies that one is incompetent. For example, trial-and-error learning is perhaps an archetype of intrinsically motivated behavior. People try things and sometimes find that they were wrong; however, that information may be useful in helping them figure out the solution. It does not imply incompetence; it gives clues toward competence. The nature of the "negative" feedback is important: If it implies incompetence it will decrease intrinsic motivation; if not, it will not.

IV. The Functional Aspects of Rewards

In Section III, A, we discussed Deci's proposition that rewards have two functional properties: a controlling aspect, which satisfies extrinsic needs and creates instrumentalities between behavior and rewards, and an informational aspect, which provides competence feedback. The relative salience of the two aspects is hypothesized to determine whether the rewards will increase or decrease intrinsic motivation. If the controlling aspect is more salient, it will provide extrinsic satisfaction, as we noted earlier for the Calder and Staw and Kruglanski et al. studies. Further, it will decrease intrinsic motivation by inducing a change in perceived locus of causality from internal to external. If the informational aspect is more salient (and if the information is positive), intrinsic motivation will increase through a change in perceptions of competence. (Of course, if the information is negative, intrinsic motivation will decrease.)

As a preliminary test of the hypothesis, Deci and Porac (1978) reported a pilot study in which two groups of subjects were paid $.50 for each of four puzzles they solved. Subjects in one group were simply given the payments in the standard fashion of earlier studies. Subjects in the other group were told that they would receive $.50 for each puzzle they solved faster than 80% of previous subjects, $.25 for each puzzle they solved faster than 50% of previous subjects, and no pay when they were in the bottom half. In fact, they, like the other group, always received $.50 when they solved a puzzle and no money when they failed to solve one. The results showed a significant difference in the intrinsic motivation of the two groups. This study was only preliminary, yet it suggested that even monetary rewards will affect intrinsic motivation differently depending on whether they are primarily controllers or primarily conveyors of positive competence information.

Before we report other studies that have supported the present hypothesis, let us raise the question of what determines which aspect of a reward will be more salient? Our answer is that there are factors in (1) the rewardee, (2) the situation, and (3) the rewarder that will determine which aspect of the reward is more salient. We shall consider these categories in turn, reporting studies that support the general hypothesis as well as more specific ones related to the three categories of factors.

A.   FACTORS IN THE REWARDEE

Individuals differ on every psychological dimension that has ever been investigated. A variety of these factors is likely to affect the way they interpret rewards and therefore the effects of those rewards on their intrinsic motivation. There has been little direct attention paid to person factors, in the recipient of rewards, that determine how those rewards will be perceived; however, in preceding sections we have reported research indicating two such factors that have significantly mediated the effects of rewards. The first is sex of the subject in relation to praise. On average it appears that males vs. females, presumably because of socialization practices, have come to respond differentially to the controlling vs. informational aspect of praise. Further, the study by Lonky suggests that the locus of control variable may mediate subjects' responses to praise with praise increasing the intrinsic motivation of internal children and decreasing it for external children. Baron and Ganz (1972) reported a related result. Internal versus external locus of control children responded differentially to intrinsic vs. extrinsic feedback. Internal children worked better with intrinsic feedback; external children, with extrinsic feedback. We know of no study that has isolated factors in the rewardee that mediate the salience of the two aspects of rewards other than praise.

B. FACTORS IN THE SITUATION (EXPECTANCY, CONTINGENCY, AND
SALIENCE REVISITED)

There have been a few studies that have specifically manipulated situation variables to investigate their effects on the relative salience of the aspects of rewards and in turn on intrinsic motivation. The Deci and Porac pilot study mentioned at the beginning of Section IV was one such example. A more substantive investigation of this matter has been reported by Enzle and Ross (1978). They found that when highly valued monetary rewards were contingent upon "skilled" performance the rewards increased intrinsic motivation, whereas the same rewards given simply for doing the task decreased intrinsic motivation. When the rewards conveyed positive competence information, they enhanced subjects' interest in the puzzle activity. Rosenfield, Folger, and Adelman (in press) similarly have reported that when rewards reflect competence they will increase intrinsic motivation, whereas they will decrease intrinsic motivation when they do not. Finally, Pittman, Davey, Alafat, Wetherill, and Wirsul (in press) found that when verbal rewards were administered "informationally" they enhanced intrinsic motivation, although when they were administered "controllingly" they tended to decrease or leave unchanged subjects' intrinsic motivation.

The Enzle and Ross study can be viewed as an investigation of the contingency question outlined in Section II, D. Most studies that investigated the effects of contingent rewards found that they undermined intrinsic motivation, whereas this study found an enhancement. We are suggesting now that it is not contingency per se that determines whether rewards will undermine or enhance intrinsic motivation, for contingencies can be constructed very differently. They too can be set up to control behavior or to provide competence feedback. People often feel controlled when their rewards depend on a certain level of output or type of performance. For example, the piece-rate payment practice is a very controlling form of contingent payment. In such cases, as we said earlier, intrinsic motivation will decrease. However, in the Enzle and Ross study it was highlighted that rewards imply a certain skill level at the activity. They therefore structured the situation so that the informational aspect of the contingent reward was more salient; hence, intrinsic motivation increased. The same was true of the Karniol and Ross (1977) study previously mentioned. They used contingent rewards, and yet they paired them with a very informational blinking green light which signaled competence; and indeed the rewards (green light plus marshmallows) increased the children's intrinsic motivation.

Deci and Porac (1978) suggested that in organizations monetary bonuses are likely to be perceived as informational, unlike the piece-rate payments, which tend to be perceived as controlling. Both are contingent rewards, but they are experienced quite differently. A study by Lopez (1979) supports their speculation. She found that good performance bonus prizes increased the intrinsic motivation of a telephone company's employees.

The question of expectancy can also be understood within the context of the relative salience of the two aspects of rewards. When rewards are expected they are likely to be experienced as more controlling (all other things equal) because the rewardee begins doing the activity in order to get the reward. With unexpected rewards, however, there is no appreciable control factor; they come along after the performance and are likely to be interpreted as an indication of good performance.

Finally, it should be clear that salience of a reward is not the parameter that will determine whether rewards will decrease intrinsic motivation. Rewards will need to be salient to have an effect, but salient rewards can either bolster or drain one's intrinsic motivation. The important parameter is the salience of the two aspects of the reward, not the salience of the reward per se.

C. FACTORS IN THE REWARDER

Finally, we suggest that characteristics of the rewarder are likely to influence how rewards are perceived. For example, a highly authoritarian person is likely to use rewards for purposes quite different from those of a less authoritarian person. The former person will tend to have a more controlling orientation toward the use of rewards and is likely to convey this orientation in some way, whether blatant or subtle. We assert that the use of rewards by different types of rewarders will have a different effect on intrinsic motivation, even when the same behaviors are being rewarded. We know of only one study that has investigated this general question: the study, by Deci, Nezlek, and Sheinman (in press, b) which supported the current reasoning, is presented in Section V.

V. Intrinsic Motivation and Perceived Competence in the Schools

In this section we shall describe a field study conducted in the fourth, fifth, and sixth grades of four elementary schools. The data and conclusions we present deal with two issues: whether teacher orientations affect the intrinsic motivation and perceived competence of their pupils, presumably as a result of their using rewards and other structures in a primarily controlling vs. informational fashion; and how patterns of intrinsic motivation and perceived competence differ between the sexes and among the grade levels studied.

A. THE IMPACT OF TEACHER CHARACTERISTICS

The study (Deci *et al.*, in press, b) was conducted in 35 classrooms and looked at the relation of teachers' orientation toward the use of rewards as they related to children's intrinsic motivation and perceived competence during one school year.

The basic design of the study was the administration of an intrinsic motivation measure and a perceived competence (i.e., self-esteem) measure to 610 children in late October and then again in May of one school year. In addition, teachers' attitudes toward control vs. autonomy were assessed and related to the children measures using correlational procedures. It was hypothesized that teachers who believe in dealing with children in a way that encourages them to be autonomous (i.e., who use rewards informationally) would tend to facilitate the intrinsic motivation and perceived competence of their pupils, whereas teachers who are more controlling will tend to discourage the intrinsic motivation and perceived competence of their pupils.

The two children measures were developed by Harter (1979, in press). The first measure assessed intrinsic motivation in the classroom. It has five subscales that Harter designed to reflect various dimensions of intrinsic motivation: (a) preference for vs. avoidance of challenge; (b) curiosity vs. preference for familiar material; (c) desire for independent mastery vs. dependence on teacher; (d) desire to work for one's own satisfaction vs. working for grades and teacher approval; and (e) internal vs. external criteria for success. The first three subscales have been shown to be primarily motivational, whereas the last two are primarily evaluative (Harter, 1979).

The second measure was a self-esteem measure defined in terms of children's perceptions of their own competence and self-determination (Harter, in press). This measure has four subscales, a general subscale plus a subscale reflecting perceived competence in three content domains—cognitive, social, and physical.

Further, each child also completed a classroom climate questionnaire developed by deCharms (1976) in which children described their classroom and teacher on intrinsic vs. extrinsic dimensions.

Finally, the researchers developed a measure to assess teachers' attitudes toward control vs. autonomy, reasoning that teachers who favor control will use rewards as sanctions, whereas those who favor autonomy will use rewards informationally. The control vs. autonomy categorization, although binary, really represents a continuum. Therefore, four types of orientations for teachers dealing with children were characterized. They ranged from being very controlling to being informational (supportive and encouraging of autonomous behavior).

The four "styles" used in the questionnaire were: a "hard-line" style in which teachers make decisions about what is right, require pupils to do this "right" thing, and use highly controlling sanctions to produce the behavior; a "do-what-you-ought" style, which emphasizes shoulds and oughts and utilizes guilt to get the children to do what the teacher thinks they should do but which does not have the teacher "making" them do it in the more overt sense; a "compare-yourself-to-others" style in which teachers do not tell kids what they should do but rather encourage them to compare themselves with others so as to see where they stand relative to others on the behavior of concern; and finally, an "autonomous" style, in which teachers encourage children to consider the relevant elements of the situation and to take responsibility for working out a solution to the problem.

Teachers considered eight typical problem vignettes and responded in a way that reflected their preferences for ways of handling the problems. Their responses were combined algebraically to give an index that placed them along the control–autonomy continuum.

In the analysis the children were aggregated within each classroom on their intrinsic motivation, perceived competence, and classroom climate responses. Since the intrinsic motivation and perceived competence measures were administered twice, change scores for spring minus fall and also averages for the spring and fall values were created and correlated with the teacher measure. For the teachers, their total "attitude toward control–autonomy" scores were used. Finally, there was the "origin climate questionnaire," which children completed to describe their classrooms and teachers. This was administered once, in the winter, so these scores, aggregated within classrooms, were correlated both with the teacher measures and with the changes and averages on intrinsic motivation and perceived competence.

First, let us consider the correlations between the teacher measures and the children's change and average scores on intrinsic motivation and perceived competence. According to cognitive evaluation theory, there should be consistent correlations between the "attitude toward control–autonomy" measure and changes in intrinsic motivation. Presumably, those teachers who use rewards more informationally will have children who become more intrinsically motivated and feel more competent, whereas those who use them more controllingly will have children who tend to lose intrinsic motivation and felt competence. Alternatively, if this measure does not correlate with changes (assuming the changes are not large enough to yield a consistent effect), one would expect correlations between teacher measures and average scores on children's intrinsic motivation and perceived competence. The theoretical implications of one versus the other type of correlation will be discussed following presentation of the data.

The teachers' "attitude toward control–autonomy" measure correlated with fall to spring average scores on all three of the motivational subscales of the intrinsic–extrinsic scale, although it did not correlate with the evaluative subscales. Further, it correlated with the general perceived competence subscale and the cognitive subscale, it correlated marginally with the social subscale, and it did not correlate with the physical subscale. There was a very strong relationship, therefore, of teachers' characteristics to children's intrinsic motivation and to classroom-relevant dimensions of perceived competence. The teacher measure, however, did not correlate with Fall to Spring change scores.

There was also a relationship between the teachers' "attitude toward control–autonomy" measure and the children's responses on the origin climate questionnaire (the total scores on each measure correlated significantly, with $r = .354$). The teacher measure correlated especially highly ($r = .511$) with the children measure subscale "facilitating acceptance of personal responsibility." Apparently one thing which is highly stressed by "autonomy"-oriented teachers is the importance of children's accepting responsibility for their own behavior.

In considering the relationship between the children's perceptions of their classroom and the intrinsic motivation and perceived competence of the children there was a stronger relationship between the classroom climate and the averages of the children's fall and spring scores than between the classroom climate and the changes from the children's fall to spring scores. There was a fairly consistent relationship between the children's perceptions of the origin (or intrinsic) nature of the classroom/teacher (deCharms, 1976) and their average intrinsic motivation, and there was a very strong and consistent relationship between their perceptions of the origin nature of the classroom/teacher and their feelings of competence in all domains. When children perceive their classroom/teacher as more intrinsically oriented, they have higher self-esteem, that is, they perceive themselves as being more competent, and they are more intrinsically motivated.

These results of the Deci *et al.* study complement the work of deCharms (1976). He and his colleagues found, in a large field experiment, that when they trained teachers to be more intrinsically oriented, their children became more intrinsically motivated and performed better on standardized achievement tests.

B. MOTIVATIONAL SUBSYSTEMS (ONCE AGAIN)

One of the things that stood out most clearly in the data was the fact that the "attitudes toward control–autonomy" measure related consistently and quite strongly to the averages of the children's fall and spring scores on intrinsic motivation and perceived competence. However, there was little relationship between teacher characteristics and change scores of the children over the course of the 7-month period. This was a striking effect which has interesting theoretical implications in line with some points made earlier in this review.

Deci *et al.* found strong and virtually identical relationships between the teachers' orientations and the children's measures in the fall, the spring, and the average of fall and spring. In short, the relationship between teachers' orientation and children's intrinsic motivation and self-esteem had become established in the first 6–8 weeks of the school year and remained constant over the next 7 months.

There is no indication that the relationship was caused by selection procedures or other extraneous factors; it appears that all grades were the same (save for random variation) at the beginning of the year. It seems quite clear that the results are not spurious. They are generally consistent with our theoretical orientation, and the possibility of getting this pattern of results by chance is essentially zero.

A "trait approach" to the understanding of intrinsic motivation does not seem to fit the data, for such a conceptualization would be more consistent with the prediction of an increase in relationship over the course of the year. The teachers' orientations would gradually impact the children's "trait," so one would expect a relationship between the teacher measure and the children's change scores. Instead, a conceptualization that does fit the data views the children as having an intrinsic orientation that is a subsystem of the human organism. A *motivational subsystem* (intrinsic or extrinsic) is defined as a set of beliefs about self and others, programs for interacting with the environment, and affective experiences all of which are organized by motivational processes. A subsystem is ever present for the individual, although it would be more or less operative from person to person and for each person from time to time. Intrinsic motivation is the heart of the intrinsic motivational subsystem and would be the primary motivational force operating when the intrinsic subsystem is centrally salient for the person. With the motivation comes corresponding beliefs and attitudes. Children who were more intrinsic also had more positive self-concepts; they perceived themselves to be more competent. Each person also is conceptualized as having an extrinsic motivational subsystem, which is more oriented toward rewards, is more concerned with control, is less supportive and less concerned with autonomy, involves a lower self-esteem, and so on.

What this conceptualization suggests in terms of the current data is that within the first couple of months of school the children have "adapted" to the teacher. Those who are with teachers who are oriented toward intrinsic motivation, autonomy, and the use of rewards as information rather than control will adapt to the situation by operating more out of their intrinsic subsystem. Once this adaptation is made, which for elementary school children seems to occur fairly quickly, it tends to be stable as long as the situation remains constant.

It is probable that as one versus the other human motivational subsystem (intrinsic versus extrinsic) is used more, it will become a more dominant aspect of the personality and will have a greater influence on the person's general interactions with the physical and social environment.

In terms of cognitive evaluation theory, this theoretical point of view suggests that, at the motivational level, the "undermining of intrinsic motivation" involves an engagement of the extrinsic subsystem as the dominant motivational orientation in relation to certain behaviors and the concomitant disengagement of the intrinsic subsystem with those behaviors. The cognitive aspect of this shift in subsystems is the "change in perceived locus of causality."

C. DESCRIPTIVE INFORMATION ON SCHOOL CHILDREN

On all five intrinsic motivation subscales as well as the total intrinsic score, spring scores were more intrinsic than fall scores. On average, children came to see themselves as more intrinsic over the 7-month period. Boys were more intrinsically motivated than girls on two subscales and the total scale, whereas there was no scale on which girls were more intrinsic than boys. On three of the intrinsic motivation subscales plus the total score, there were grade differences. Sixth graders were more intrinsic than fifth graders, who were in turn more intrinsic than fourth graders. This was more so for males than females, although it was true for both sexes. The greater intrinsic orientation was indicated by the acquisition of greater independence of judgment and evaluation, although this was accompanied by some loss of curiosity.

On the perceived competence scale, there was not a clear increase over the course of the 7-month period. Only the general subscale tended to be higher. There were, however, quite clear sex effects. On the social, physical, and general subscales, boys perceived themselves as more competent than girls. Only on the cognitive subscale did boys and girls perceive themselves as equally competent. On two of the four subscales, there were differences between grades. On the cognitive and general subscales, fifth graders perceived themselves as more competent than either fourth or sixth graders.

In sum, boys tend to have higher self-esteem (or perceived competence) than girls during these grades, and fifth graders tend to have a higher self-esteem than fourth or sixth. Perhaps there is a peak at the fifth grade where children feel good about themselves after several years in school and before the time in sixth grade when they begin to fear going into new school settings at the junior high level.

Analyses were also done on the sex of the teacher to determine whether male vs. female teachers tended to affect children's intrinsic motivation and perceived competence differently. In general the answer was no. On the six intrinsic motivation scales and the four perceived competence scales there was only one difference that was conventionally significant. On the general subscale of the perceived competence measure, female teachers had children with greater felt competence than male teachers. Thus, there is little evidence of meaningful difference between male and female teachers in terms of their impact on the intrinsic motivation and perceived competence of children.

VI.   A Final Statement

The research literature that has explored the nature of intrinsic motivation and the effects of rewards and controls on intrinsic motivation appears to have been highly supportive of the competence and self-determination formulation of intrinsic motivation and also of the propositions of cognitive evaluation theory (Deci, 1975). The results of individual studies have provided the basis for greater understanding of the phenomena and greater specificity of the theory. One conclusion to be reached from this is that, in general, an understanding of motivational processes is critical for explicating and predicting human behavior as well as a variety of interrelated beliefs, attitudes, and affects, the complex of which we have referred to as motivational subsystems. It seems probable that continued investigation will further illuminate these phenomena and processes.

REFERENCES

Alegre, C., & Murray, E. J. Locus of control, behavioral intention, and verbal conditioning. *Journal of Personality*, 1974, **42**, 668–681.
Amabile, T. M. Effects of external evaluation on artistic creativity. *Journal of Personality and Social Psychology*, 1979, **37**, 221–233.
Amabile, T. M., DeJong, W., & Lepper, M. R. Effects of externally imposed deadlines on subsequent intrinsic motivation. *Journal of Personality and Social Psychology*, 1976, **34**, 92–98.
Anderson, R., Manoogian, S. T., & Reznick, J. S. The undermining and enhancing of intrinsic motivation in preschool children. *Journal of Personality and Social Psychology*, 1976, **34**, 915–922.
Arkes, H. R. Competence and the maintenance of behavior. *Motivation and Emotion*, 1978, **2**, 201–211.
Arnold, H. J. Effects of performance feedback and extrinsic reward upon high intrinsic motivation. *Organizational Behavior and Human Performance*, 1976, **17**, 275–288.
Atkinson, J. W. *An introduction to motivation*. Princeton, N.J.: Van Nostrand, 1964.
Bandura, A. *Social learning theory*. Englewood Cliffs, N.J.: Prentice-Hall, 1977.
Baron, R. M., & Ganz, R. L. Effects of locus of control and type of feedback on the task performance of lower-class, black children. *Journal of Personality and Social Psychology*, 1972, **21**, 124–130.
Bem, D. J. Self-perception theory. In L. Berkowitz (Ed.), *Advances in experimental social psychology*. Vol. 6. New York: Academic Press, 1972. Pp. 1–62.
Benware, C., & Deci, E. L. Attitude change as a function of the inducement for espousing a pro-attitudinal communication. *Journal of Experimental Social Psychology*, 1975, **11**, 271–278.
Berkowitz, L. *Aggression: A social psychological analysis*. New York: McGraw-Hill, 1962.
Berlyne, D. E. Exploration and curiosity. *Science*, 1966, **153**, 25–33.
Berlyne, D. E. Curiosity and learning. *Motivation and Emotion*, 1978, **2**, 97–175.
Bialer, I. Conceptualization of success and failure in mentally retarded and normal children. *Journal of Personality*, 1961, **29**, 303–320.
Blanck, P., Jackson, L., & Reis, H. T. Effects of verbal praise on intrinsic motivation for sex-typed tasks. Paper presented at the meeting of the American Psychological Association, New York, September, 1979.
Boggiano, A. K., & Ruble, D. N. Competence and the overjustification effect: A developmental study. *Journal of Personality and Social Psychology*, 1979, **37**, 1462–1468.
Butler, R. A. Discrimination learning by rhesus monkeys to visual exploration motivation. *Journal of Comparative and Physiological Psychology*, 1953, **46**, 95–98.

Calder, B. J., & Staw, B. M. The interaction of intrinsic and extrinsic motivation: Some methodological notes. *Journal of Personality and Social Psychology*, 1975, **31**, 76–80. (a)

Calder, B. J., & Staw, B. M. Self-perception of intrinsic and extrinsic motivation. *Journal of Personality and Social Psychology*, 1975, **31**, 599–605. (b)

Carone, D. P. The effects of positive verbal feedback on female intrinsic motivation. Unpublished master's thesis, University of Bridgeport, 1975.

Condry, J. C. Enemies of exploration: Self-initiated versus other-initiated learning. *Journal of Personality and Social Psychology*, 1977, **35**, 459–477.

Csikszentmihalyi, M. *Beyond boredom and anxiety*. San Francisco: Jossey-Bass, 1975.

deCharms, R. *Personal causation: The internal affective determinants of behavior*. New York: Academic Press, 1968.

deCharms, R. *Enhancing motivation: Change in the classroom*. New York: Irvington, 1976.

Deci, E. L. Effects of externally mediated rewards on intrinsic motivation. *Journal of Personality and Social Psychology*, 1971, **18**, 105–115.

Deci, E. L. Effects of contingent and non-contingent rewards and controls on intrinsic motivation. *Organizational Behavior and Human Performance*, 1972, **8**, 217–229. (a)

Deci, E. L. Intrinsic motivation, extrinsic reinforcement and inequity. *Journal of Personality and Social Psychology*, 1972, **22**, 113–120. (b)

Deci, E. L. *Intrinsic motivation*. New York: Plenum, 1975.

Deci, E. L. Notes on the theory and meta-theory of intrinsic motivation. *Organizational Behavior and Human Performance*, 1976, **15**, 130–145.

Deci, E. L. *The psychology of self-determination*. Lexington, Mass.: D.C. Heath, Lexington Books, 1980.

Deci, E. L., Benware, C., & Landy, D. A. The attribution of motivation as a function of output and rewards. *Journal of Personality*, 1974, **42**, 652–667.

Deci, E. L., Betley, G., Kahle, J., Abrams, L., & Porac, J. When trying to win: Competition and intrinsic motivation. *Personality and Social Psychology Bulletin*, in press. (a)

Deci, E. L., & Cascio, W. F. Changes in intrinsic motivation as a function of negative feedback and threats. Paper presented at the meeting of the Eastern Psychological Association, Boston, April, 1972.

Deci, E. L., Cascio, W. F., & Krusell, J. Sex differences, positive feedback and intrinsic motivation. Paper presented at the meeting of the Eastern Psychological Association, Washington, D.C., May, 1973.

Deci, E. L., Cascio, W. F., & Krusell, J. Cognitive evaluation theory and some comments on the Calder, Staw critique. *Journal of Personality and Social Psychology*, 1975, **31**, 81–85.

Deci, E. L., Nezlek, J., & Sheinman, L. Characteristics of the rewarder and intrinsic motivation of the rewardee. *Journal of Personality and Social Psychology*, in press. (b)

Deci, E. L., & Porac, J. F. Cognitive evaluation theory and the study of human motivation. In M. R. Lepper & D. Greene (Eds.), *The hidden costs of reward*. Hillsdale, N.J.: Erlbaum, 1978. Pp. 149–176.

Deci, E. L., Porac, J., & Shapira, Z. Effects of rewards on interest and intrinsic motivation for an extrinsic activity. Unpublished manuscript, University of Rochester, 1978.

Dember, W. N., & Earl, R. W. Analysis of exploratory, manipulatory, and curiosity behaviors. *Psychological Review*, 1957, **64**, 91–96.

Deutsch, M. Cooperation and trust: Some theoretical notes. In M. R. Jones (Ed.), *Nebraska Symposium on Motivation*. Vol. 10. Lincoln: University of Nebraska Press, 1962. Pp. 275–319.

Deutsch, M. Socially relevant science: Reflections on some studies of interpersonal conflict. *American Psychologist*, 1969, **24**, 1076–1092.

Dienstbier, R. A., & Leak, G. K. Effects of monetary reward on maintenance of weight loss: An extension of the overjustification effect. Paper presented at the meeting of the American Psychological Association, Washington, D.C., September, 1976.

Dollinger, S. J., & Thelen, M. H. Overjustification and children's intrinsic motivation: Comparative effects of four rewards. *Journal of Personality and Social Psychology*, 1978, **36**, 1259–1269.

Enzle, M. A., & Ross, J. M. Increasing and decreasing intrinsic interest with contingent rewards: A test of cognitive evaluation theory. *Journal of Experimental Social Psychology*, 1978, **14**, 588–597.

Farr, J. L. Task characteristics, reward contingency, and intrinsic motivation. *Organizational Behavior and Human Performance*, 1976, **16**, 294–307.

Farr, J. L., Vance, R. J., & McIntyre, R. M. Further examination of the relationship between reward contingency and intrinsic motivation. *Organizational Behavior and Human Performance*, 1977, **20**, 31–53.

Finegold, B. D., & Mahoney, M. J. Reinforcement effects on intrinsic interest: Undermining the overjustification hypothesis. *Behavior Therapy*, 1975, **6**, 367–377.

Fisher, C. D. The effects of personal control, competence, and extrinsic reward systems on intrinsic motivation. *Organizational Behavior and Human Performance*, 1978, **21**, 273–288.

Freud, S. *A general introduction to psycho-analysis*. New York: Perma-Giants, 1949. (Originally published, 1917.)

Garbarino, J. The impact of anticipated reward upon cross-aged tutoring. *Journal of Personality and Social Psychology*, 1975, **32**, 421–428.

Greene, D., & Lepper, M. R. Effects of extrinsic rewards on children's subsequent intrinsic interst. *Child Development*, 1974, **45**, 1141–1145.

Greene, D., Sternberg, B., & Lepper, M. R. Overjustification in a token economy. *Journal of Personality and Social Psychology*, 1976, **34**, 1219–1234.

Hamner, W. C., & Foster, L. W. Are intrinsic and extrinsic rewards additive: A test of Deci's cognitive evaluation theory of task motivation. *Organizational Behavior and Human Performance*, 1975, **14**, 398–415.

Harackiewicz, J. M. The effects of reward contingency and performance feedback on intrinsic motivation. *Journal of Personality and Social Psychology*, 1979, **37**, 1352–1363.

Harter, S. Effectance motivation reconsidered: Toward a developmental model. *Human Development*, 1978, **21**, 34–64.

Harter, S. A new self-report scale of intrinsic versus extrinsic motivation in the classroom: Motivational and informational components. Society for Research in Child Development, 1979.

Harter, S. Perceived competence scale for children. *Child Development*, in press.

Hartmann, H. *Ego psychology and the problem of adaptation*. New York: International Universities Press, 1958.

Heider, F. *The psychology of interpersonal relations*. New York: Wiley, 1958.

Hull, C. L. *Principles of behavior*. New York: Appleton, 1943.

Hunt, J. McV. Intrinsic motivation and its role in psychological development. In D. Levine (Ed.), *Nebraska Symposium on Motivation*. Vol. 13. Lincoln: University of Nebraska Press, 1965. Pp. 189–282.

Karniol, R., & Ross, M. The effect of performance-relevant and performance-irrelevant rewards on children's intrinsic motivation. *Child Development*, 1977, **48**, 482–487.

Kelley, H. H., & Thibaut, J. W. Group problem solving. In G. Lindzey & E. Aronson (Eds.), *The handbook of social psychology*. (2nd ed.) Vol. 4. Reading, Mass.: Addison-Wesley, 1969. Pp. 1–101.

Kruglanski, A. W. The endogenous-exogenous partition in attribution theory. *Psychological Review*, 1975, **82**, 387–406.

Kruglanski, A. W., Alon, S., & Lewis, T. Retrospective misattribution and task enjoyment. *Journal of Experimental Social Psychology*, 1972, **8**, 493–501.

Kruglanski, A. W., Freedman, I., & Zeevi, G. The effects of extrinsic incentives on some qualitative aspects of task performance. *Journal of Personality*, 1971, **39**, 606–617.

Kruglanski, A. W., Riter, A., Amitai, A., Margolin, B., Shabtai, L., & Zaksh, D. Can money enhance intrinsic motivation?: A test of the content-consequence hypothesis. *Journal of Personality and Social Psychology,* 1975, **31,** 744–750.

Lee, D. Y., Syrnyk, R., & Hallschmid, C. Self-perception of intrinsic and extrinsic motivation: Effects on institutionalized mentally retarded adolescents. *American Journal of Mental Deficiency,* 1977, **81,** 331–337.

Lefcourt, H. M. The function of the illusion of control. *American Psychologist,* 1973, **28,** 417–425.

Lepper, M. R., & Greene, D. Turning play into work: Effects of adult surveillance and extrinsic rewards on children's intrinsic motivation. *Journal of Personality and Social Psychology,* 1975, **31,** 479–486.

Lepper, M. R., & Greene, D. On understanding "overjustification": A reply to Reiss and Sushinsky. *Journal of Personality and Social Psychology,* 1976, **33,** 25–35.

Lepper, M. R., & Greene, D. (Eds.) *The hidden costs of reward.* Hillsdale, N.J.: Erlbaum, 1978. (a)

Lepper, M. R., & Greene, D. Overjustification research and beyond. In M. R. Lepper & D. Greene (Eds.), *The hidden costs of reward.* Hillsdale, N.J.: Erlbaum, 1978. (b)

Lepper, M. R., Greene, D., & Nisbett, R. E. Undermining children's intrinsic interest with extrinsic rewards: A test of the "overjustification" hypothesis. *Journal of Personality and Social Psychology,* 1973, **28,** 129–137.

Levine, F. M., & Fasnacht, G. Token rewards may lead to token learning. *American Psychologist,* 1974, **29,** 816–820.

Lonky, E. I. The effects of extrinsic rewards and praise on intrinsic motivation: A cognitive-developmental perspective. Unpublished doctoral dissertation, University of Wisconsin-Madison, 1978.

Lopez, E. M. A field study of the effect of contingent reward on intrinsic motivation. Unpublished manuscript, St. John's University, 1979.

Margolis, R. B., & Mynatt, C. R. The effects of self and externally administered reward on high base rate behavior. Unpublished manuscript, Bowling Green State University, 1979.

Martin, J. A. Effects of positive and negative adult-child interactions on children's task performance and task preferences. *Journal of Experimental Child Psychology,* 1977, **23,** 493–502.

Maslow, A. H. *Motivation and personality.* New York: Harper, 1954.

Mawhinney, T. C. Intrinsic X extrinsic motivation: Perspectives from behaviorism. *Organizational Behavior and Human Performance,* 1979, **24,** 411–440.

McClelland, D. C., Atkinson, J. W., Clark, R. W., & Lowell, E. L. *The achievement motive.* New York: Appleton, 1953.

McGraw, K. D. The detrimental effect of reward on performance: A literature review and a prediction model. In M. R. Lepper & D. Greene (Eds.), *The hidden costs of reward.* Hillsdale, N.J.: Erlbaum, 1978. Pp. 33–60.

McGraw, K. D., & McCullers, J. C. Evidence of a detrimental effect of extrinsic incentives on breaking a mental set. *Journal of Experimental Social Psychology,* 1979, **15,** 285–294.

Nentwig, C. G. Attribution of cause and long term effects of the modification of smoking behavior. *Behavior Analysis and Modification,* 1978, **2,** 285–295.

Notz, W. W. Work motivation and the negative effects of extrinsic rewards: A review with implications for theory and practice. *American Psychologist,* 1975, **30,** 884–891.

Piaget, J. *The origin of intelligence in children.* New York: International Universities Press, 1952.

Pinder, C. C. Additivity versus nonadditivity of intrinsic and extrinsic incentives: Implications for work motivation, performance, and attitudes. *Journal of Applied Psychology,* 1976, **61,** 693–700.

Pittman, T. S., Davey, M. E., Alafat, K. A., Wetherill, K. V., & Wirsul, N. A. Informational vs. controlling rewards, levels of surveillance and intrinsic motivation. *Personality and Social Psychology Bulletin,* in press.

Pritchard, R. D., Campbell, K. M., & Campbell, D. J. Effects of extrinsic financial rewards on intrinsic motivation. *Journal of Applied Psychology*, 1977, **62**, 9–15.

Reiss, S., & Sushinsky, L. W. Overjustification, competing responses, and the acquisition of intrinsic interest. *Journal of Personality and Social Psychology*, 1975, **31**, 1116–1125.

Rosenfield, D., Folger, R., & Adelman, H. F. When rewards reflect competence: A qualification of the overjustification effect. *Journal of Personality and Social Psychology*, in press.

Ross, M. Salience of reward and intrinsic motivation. *Journal of Personality and Social Psychology*, 1975, **32**, 245–254.

Ross, M. The self-perception of intrinsic motivation. In J. H. Harvey, W. J. Ickes, & R. F. Kidd (Eds.), *New directions in attribution research*. Vol. 1. Hillsdale, N.J.: Erlbaum, 1976.

Ryan, R. M., & Deci, E. L. The importance of intrinsic motivation for maintenance and transfer of treatment gains in psychotherapy. Unpublished manuscript, University of Rochester, 1980.

Scott, W. E., Jr. The effects of extrinsic rewards on "intrinsic motivation": A critique. *Organizational Behavior and Human Performance*, 1976, **15**, 117–129.

Seligman, M. E. P. *Helplessness: On depression, development and death*. San Francisco: Freeman, 1975.

Smith, R. W., & Pittman, T. S. Reward, distraction and the overjustification effect. *Journal of Personality and Social Psychology*, 1978, **36**, 565–572.

Smith, T. S., & Murphy, R. J. Conflicting criteria of success in the careers of symphony musicians. Unpublished manuscript, University of Rochester, Department of Sociology, 1978.

Smith, W. E. The effects of social and monetary rewards on intrinsic motivation. Unpublished doctoral dissertation, Cornell University, 1974.

Swann, W. B., & Pittman, T. S. Initiating play activity of children: The moderating influence of verbal cues on intrinsic motivation. *Child Development*, 1977, **48**, 1128–1132.

Walker, E. L. Psychological complexity and preference: A hedgehog theory of behavior. In D. E. Berlyne, & K. B. Madsen (Eds.), *Pleasure, reward, and preference*. New York: Academic Press, 1973. Pp. 65–97.

Weiner, M. J., & Mander, A. M. The effects of reward and perception of competency upon intrinsic motivation. *Motivation and Emotion*, 1978, **2**, 67–73.

White, R. W. Motivation reconsidered: The concept of competence. *Psychological Review*, 1959, **66**, 297–333.

White, R. W. *Ego and reality in psychoanalytic theory. (Psychological Issues*, Monogr. 11.) New York: International Universities Press, 1963.

Zuckerman, M., Porac, J., Lathin, D., Smith, R., & Deci, E. L. On the importance of self-determination for intrinsically motivated behavior. *Personality and Social Psychology Bulletin*, 1978, **4**, 443–446.

ATTRIBUTION OF RESPONSIBILITY: FROM MAN THE SCIENTIST TO MAN AS LAWYER

Frank D. Fincham* and
Joseph M. Jaspars

DEPARTMENT OF EXPERIMENTAL PSYCHOLOGY
UNIVERSITY OF OXFORD
OXFORD, ENGLAND

*Present address: Department of Psychology, State University of New York at Stony Brook, Stony Brook, New York 11794.

ADVANCES IN EXPERIMENTAL SOCIAL
PSYCHOLOGY, VOL. 13

I. Introduction

The expression "attribution of responsibility" as commonly used in psychological literature has two major connotations. First, it suggests a clearly demarcated area of research concerned with the study of how responsibility is assigned. Second, the use of the term "attribution" in the expression apparently implies that the assignment of responsibility can be described as a process which is directly comparable to the perception of causality as studied in attribution research. Both these inferences are challenged in this review, for the recent popularity of attribution theory has not been matched by an equally discriminating terminology.

A. ATTRIBUTION THEORY AND ATTRIBUTION OF RESPONSIBILITY

In its broadest conception attribution theory refers to the general process by which the layman explains events, although traditionally it has been associated with the study of perceived causality. However, attribution theory is probably best identified with the work of Jones and Davis (1965), Kelley (1967, 1971a, 1972, 1973), and especially Heider (1944, 1958), for despite the recent explosion of attribution research [Kelley and Michela (1980) report over 900 references in the last decade], conceptual advances over and above these earlier and by now classical statements have been rather limited (Jones, 1978; Jones & McGillis, 1976; Kelley & Michela, 1980). Consequently, it is these core "theories" that are considered here in assessing the relationship between attribution theory and attribution of responsibility.

In an early publication, Heider (1944) frequently referred to responsibility in discussing unit formation between effect and origin, which he saw primarily in terms of causal integration. For instance, he freely quoted Fauconnet's theory of responsibility to justify his view of persons as the prototype of causal origins: "Is a first and personal cause anything else but a cause conceived in such a way that it can be held responsible, that it can furnish something fixed and constant to which sanction can be applied?" (p. 361). Similarly, responsibility by contiguity and responsibility by similarity (Heider, 1944, p. 362) are used to illustrate the extension of these Gestalt principles from figural to causal unit formation. However, Heider does not define responsibility[1] or state the extent to which it is synonymous with or related to phenomenal causality. It is only in a later work that Heider (1958, p. 114) briefly addresses this issue, suggesting that attribution of responsibility includes problems related to the attribution of action. However, in describing several levels at which a person may be held responsible, it is clearly implied that the question of responsibility goes beyond the naive analysis of action he presents.

---

[1]Heider (1944, p. 362) parenthetically describes responsibility as "the attribution of a crime to a person," although it is not clear whether this represents his own or Fauconnet's view.

Although Heider's remarks on responsibility are only brief summary state-ments made in passing, they have come to dominate the literature, partly because there has been no other work on responsibility attribution per se. Neither Jones and Davis (1965) nor Kelley (1967) specifically addresses this issue, although Kelley does use the term in discussing moral evaluations (e.g., Kelley, 1971, pp. 17, 23, 1973, p. 121). In this respect it is worth noting Kelley's (1971, p. 17) belief that attribution theory cannot provide more than a partial understanding of such phenomena as evaluation.

Even if one rejects the equation of responsibility with moral judgments (cf. Heider, who does not include the question of responsibility in his treatment of "oughts"), Kelley's conclusion seems nonetheless to remain true for attribution of responsibility. Holding someone responsible does not explain anything di-rectly but may be related to the explanation one gives. Neither does it merely involve the perception of causality, although here too there may be a relationship with attributed responsibility. However, it seems unlikely that the mere specifica-tion of such relationships can be sufficient for understanding the process of responsibility attribution. Indeed, it is questionable whether such a task can be undertaken without a conceptual analysis of the notion of "responsibility."

Perhaps the most effective means of illustrating the limited role of attribu-tion theory vis-à-vis determination of responsibility is to consider some com-monplace examples where the question of responsibility arises. In doing so several conceptual distinctions will be made which serve to introduce the reanalysis of responsibility offered in Section II.

a. *John, while driving to work in his car, rides into a lamp post and dies.* It is not easy to see how Jones and Davis' (1965) theory of correspondent in-ferences can be applied to the case of an accident such as this. According to Jones and Davis (1965, p. 221), knowledge on the part of an actor that an action has certain effects and the ability to bring about the effects observed are precondi-tions for the assignment of intentions. In this case John presumably has both, but we still call it an accident because the effect is unlikely to have been intentional. According to Jones and Davis' (1965) criteria, the act should be seen as inten-tional (i.e., John committed suicide), in which case our attribution of responsibil-ity would probably be very different. The attribution of intentions based on knowledge and ability of the actor or the (noncommon) nature of the effect does not seem to apply in this example.

Kelley's (1967) analysis is similarly problematic. It is not clear how, or even if, the covariation principle is applicable in such cases.[2] However, even if it

[2]Presumably such an analysis would in most cases of this sort yield a data pattern indicating attribution to the circumstances (see Kelley, 1973, p. 111, Fig. 5), as it is unlikely that John regularly rides into poles (low consistency), that other people do so (low consensus), or that John knocks into other objects (high distinctiveness).

does allow an unambiguous attribution to "something" in the person, situation, etc., this allowance is insufficient for establishing responsibility. Again, intent, which is crucial to the question of responsibility in both commonsense terms and Heider's theory, is neither ruled out nor established by covariation. Moreover, if our hypothetical event is seen as an accident arising from John's action, John may not be held responsible unless he has acted negligently or recklessly. It is such additional considerations in the following examples that do not allow attribution of responsibility to be considered only in terms of causal attribution theory.

b. *David puts pressure on Peter, who consequently lies to the disadvantage of a third party.* That David's pressure constituted (or was part of) Peter's reason for lying does not rest on the fact that if the same circumstances recurred Peter would lie again. As the perceiver "seeks to find a sufficient reason" (Jones & Davis, 1965, p. 284) for the action, an honest report of Peter's decision making establishes the causal status of David's action. The case, therefore, is treated here as a single observation that comprises the basis of Kelley's (1972) scheme analysis and correspondent inference theory.[3]

To the extent that David's pressure constitutes a plausible reason for the lie, the discounting principle and analogous noncommon effects analysis hypothesize that its effect is less likely to be attributed to Peter. However, the mere presence of such an alternative cause is insufficient to alter perceived responsibility. What is crucial is not the fact that Peter was influenced by David but whether he should have resisted such influence. Clearly, the exact nature of the plausible cause, a factor ignored in attribution theory, becomes important in deciding whether it constitutes an excusing condition which relieves Peter of responsibility.

c. *Joan leaves her bicycle unlocked and returns to find it has been removed.* Joan's omission merely provides the occasion for the theft, and hence the effect is dependent on something other than her omitted act. Both the degree of dependence and the nature of the "something else" may alter perceptions of her responsibility. Such cases do not appear to have been considered in attribution theory and indeed give rise to considerable dispute in philosophical discussions of causality (e.g., Mackie, 1974).

There is little objection to admitting that the theft was a (causal) consequence of Joan's act, yet the suggestion that her omission caused the bicycle to be stolen seems counterintuitive. Nor does a covariation test in respect to the number of thefts, Joan's behavior regarding other cycles, etc., resolve this issue. In any event whether such causal questions are relevant in attributing responsibility is open to question, as illustrated in the final example.

---

[3]The configuration of possible causes is meaningful because it can be assimilated to "an assumed pattern of data in a complete analysis of variance" (Kelley, 1972, p. 2). To the extent that these schema derive their validity from the covariance principle they can be criticized on similar grounds.

d. *Mary, Mrs. Jona's newly adopted daughter, throws a stone through the store window on her way home from school.* Even though Mrs. Jona has not done anything, her responsibility for the damage arises because of her relationship to Mary. Being held responsible in this case does not carry any implication that the person involved actually produced the harm. Instead, it is liability according to a set of rules that is at issue (cf. Section II). The lack of any connection between this case and those studied in attribution research possibly stems from the fact that producing harm often constitutes the ground for holding someone responsible or liable in the above sense. Nor is attribution theory's exclusive consideration of cases where an outcome is directly caused or produced by a commissive act particularly surprising, given that it explicitly attempts to model perceived causality.

Thus it appears that attribution of responsibility may involve very different questions from those addressed in attribution theory. Despite the use of the term "responsibility" in discussions of attribution theory, the fact that there has been no attempt to relate attribution of responsibility to more general attribution theories suggests that the preceding conclusions are implicitly recognized by social psychologists. Despite a wealth of empirical findings, psychological research has done little to clarify the process of responsibility attribution, partly because fundamental conceptual issues regarding the notion of responsibility remain implicit in the literature, or, where articulated, are dealt with only superficially. This conclusion is perhaps most apparent in research on responsibility for an accident, which, together with work on the developmental nature of Heider's (1958) levels model, constitutes the focus of social psychological investigations on responsibility attribution (Hamilton, 1978).

B. ACCIDENT RESEARCH AND DEFENSIVE ATTRIBUTION

The major impetus to the research on perceptions of responsibility for accidents is a provocative study by Walster (1966). Her experiment demonstrated that outcome severity determined the amount of responsibility assigned to a hypothetical story character. Walster had predicted that most people would find it threatening to believe in chance happenings that might drastically affect their lives and over which they had no control. Consequently, subjects were held to have attributed more responsibility in the serious accident to protect themselves from the idea that they too could experience such unfortunate events. Explanations in terms of motivational biases have remained the dominant theme in subsequent research. Hence, failures to replicate the original finding (e.g., Chaikin & Darley, 1973; Shaver, 1970; J. I. Shaw & Skolnick, 1971; Walster, 1967) soon led to refinements of the hypothesis rather than the construction and testing of normative models.

to clear up interactions

Because subsequent experimental work derives almost exclusively from some version of the defensive attribution hypothesis, the variables investigated in relation to responsibility attribution are somewhat limited. Outcome severity remains the most frequently used, although its posited interaction with other factors has led to the manipulation of relevance (e.g., Chaikin & Darley, 1973; Lowe & Medway, 1976; Pliner & Cappell, 1977; J. I. Shaw & McMartin, 1977), outcome valence (e.g., Medway & Lowe, 1975; McKillip & Posavac, 1975; Reisman & Schopler, 1973; J. I. Shaw & Skolnick, 1971), causal ambiguity (e.g., Phares & Wilson, 1972; Schroeder & Linder, 1976), and personality characteristics, such as locus of control, empathy, and punitiveness (Lowe & Medway, 1976; Phares & Wilson, 1972; Sosis, 1974; Sulzer & Burglass, 1968).

half . missing

Consequently, any theory of responsibility attribution based on current accident research is likely to yield a truncated and possibly distorted picture, for it is by no means established that the variables important in such research operate in the same way, or are even implicated in nondefensive attributions. In fact, there is even evidence to the contrary; when outcome severity is placed in the "open market" with such factors as vehicle speed, road conditions, brake functioning, traffic, and the driver's record in a road accident, this variable has no effect (Arkellin, Oakley, & Mynatt, 1979). Even when information regarding these factors was removed to the extent that subjects felt they could no longer decide responsibility, outcome severity remained as a possible but unused cue. No doubt such results will be dismissed, presumably because the necessary set, ambiguity, situational possibility, personal similarity, causal role or ego involvement will be found missing.

The continued popularity of defensive attribution research is perhaps surprising in view of the increasing number of constraints imposed on the hypothesis, which suggests that such defensive attributions are indeed rare. Far more worrying, however, is the uneven growth of data collection and conceptual development, since defensive attribution research has proceeded in an ad hoc manner without any attempted theoretical integration of various hypotheses and findings. Moreover, the very basis of the hypothesis appears to be conceptually inadequate, an issue totally neglected in the literature and which is now addressed.

The titles of major articles in the area (e.g., Shaver, 1970; Walster, 1966) show that the work is typically discussed in terms of a question that explicitly asks how responsible the stimulus character is for the outcome. Central to the hypothesis, however, is the assumption that "where the perceiver is concerned about having caused pain to others," he is motivated to avoid "blame"; hence "unavoidable chance is the preferred attribution" (Shaver, 1970, p. 113). This assumption reveals an implicit model of the relationship between cause, blame, and responsibility, which is largely ignored in research where dependent measures include, in addition, punishment and legal sanction. It is questionable whether all of these dependent measures are truly comparable, since a great deal of evidence now shows that people respond to questions of causality, responsibility, blame, and punishment in different ways (e.g., Fincham, 1980d; Fincham & Jaspars, 1979; Fincham & Shultz, 1980; Hamilton, 1976; Harvey & Rule, 1978; Shultz, Schleifer, & Altman, 1979; M. E. Shaw & Reitan, 1969).

This difficulty is generic not only to defensive attribution research; even the most recent theoretical statement on responsibility (Hamilton, 1978) sees Heider's notion of levels of responsibility as "referring primarily to general liability for blame or punishment" (p. 317) but refers to this notion as involving levels of causality. If this widely shared but untested model of the various judgments were the only problem with the defensive attribution hypothesis, the considerable research effort it generated might still be justified. Unfortunately, there are also fundamental internal contradictions that destroy the utility of the hypothesis as developed thus far.

Shaver (1970) refined Walster's (1966) original hypothesis by postulating that defensive attributions would only occur if the situation portrayed were relevant to the subject, although the direction of the distortion presumably would be determined by perceived similarity to the stimulus person. Shaver posited that greater responsibility is attributed the more severe the outcome of the accident in the case of high dissimilarity, whereas identification with the perpetrator is held to diminish responsibility. However, Shaver (1970) also went on to suggest that where the perceiver was "a possible victim the attribution is different" (p. 113). Whereas attributions to chance were formerly preferred because they relieved the subject of possible blame, they now become threatening and hence responsibility attributed to the perpetrator is high.

In much of the research investigating the defensive attribution hypothesis the stimulus character is both perpetrator and victim of an accident. The problem this raises does not seem to have been recognized. According to Shaver's reasoning the perceiver as possible perpetrator/victim should both decrease and increase attributed responsibility, respectively. However, Shaver's (1970) concluding suggestion that "avoidance of blame for an accidental occurrence is more important than avoidance of the outcome itself" (p. 112) seems to resolve the dilemma. This would mean that in the case of perpetrator/victims, subjects presumably relinquish their perceived control over the event by denying responsibility and hence allow that the misfortune could befall them again. This threatening thought, which usually motivates subjects to assume responsibility, is now tolerated because of their motivation to avoid blame. No justification is given for this crucial assumption and one can imagine many instances where the reverse might apply. The question now becomes: At what point does the threat of the damage recurring begin to exceed the need to avoid blame? This question would be extremely difficult to resolve, and indeed defensive attribution research does not have a good track record when it comes to a priori specifications of crucial parameters. For instance, it is very seldom that any rationale is given to predict with whom the perceiver will identify, or what is sufficient to constitute such factors as situational or personal similarity. However, this is not really a problem in most of the current research, which, as pointed out earlier, consists of perpetrator/victim cases.[4]

These difficulties notwithstanding, support has been claimed for Shaver's (1970) views. Thus, McKillip and Posavac (1975, Experiment 1) interpret the decreased responsibility assigned by marijuana users in automobile accidents involving the drug in terms of perceived similarity. (Interestingly, perceived severity did not correlate with attributed responsibility or with the fines assigned by the subjects.) An identical result obtained in regard to nonteetotalers and alcohol-related accidents (Pliner & Cappell, 1977) raises the question of what mediates the decreased judgments made by similar observers. Quite possibly, users of drugs or alcohol are more familiar with their effects on driving and hence perceive the drug's role differently. Alternatively, personal similarity may transform the observer into a quasi "actor," thereby altering the meaning given to questions of responsibility from causal to reason explanations (e.g., Buss, 1978). Likewise, perhaps similarlity elicits empathy from perceivers, a variable which has been found to decrease attributed responsibility (Sulzer & Burglass, 1968). The failure to acknowledge and test these obvious alternative explanations again emphasizes the stunted conceptual growth in this area.

The conceptual confusion is perhaps most dramatically illustrated in a recent version of the hypothesis where perceived causality is explicitly cited as a (yet another) limiting condition for defensive attributions. Schroeder and Linder (1976) argue that when situational factors are seen to cause an accident "defensive tendencies are not aroused, and responsibility assignments that correspond to an entity's causal role are made" (p. 354). Hence, outcome severity has no effect. However, the whole notion of defensive attribution arises from the supposed need to avoid seeing severe accidents as resulting from chance precisely

---

[4]As Vidmar and Crinklaw (1974, p. 121) have reviewed the literature and found no "consistent support in attempts at replication" of the defensive attribution hypothesis, only research published since then is considered here. Furthermore, Lerner and Miller's (1978) recent survey of "just world" research and attribution processes makes it unnecessary to detail the related research in this area. Finally, defensive attribution research in relation to positive outcomes [J. I. Shaw and Skolnick's (1971) "happy accident effect"] is not specifically mentioned, as many of the criticisms made are not contingent on outcome valence.

because this is too threatening. Moreover, the data they offer to support their contention are less than convincing. Using a factory accident in which an explosion leads to a splinter's blinding (severe outcome) or scratching (mild outcome) a visiting child (a situation low in relevance and with little personal similarity), they found a decrease in responsibility for the severe outcome only where there had been two (as opposed to many) previous accidents. According to the authors' interpretation of Kelley's ANOVA cube, the stimulus person is more likely to be seen as the cause of the accident in this condition. The experimenters cling to an explanation that incorporates causal role despite the fact that they obtained no differences in perceived causality across their manipulation of this variable.

Such misinterpretations, however, are not atypical of this research. Investigators often stick to the defensive attribution hypothesis when their own results with other variables offer a clearer and more parsimonious explanation of the findings (possibly the clearest evidence of motivated distortions in the psychological literature). However, as Miller and Ross (1975) point out, the idea of attribution biases remains intuitively compelling even in the face of contradictory evidence. The notion of such biases has given rise to a great deal of controversy in regard to self-attributions of interpersonal influence and success/failure perceptions (cf. Bradley, 1978; Miller, 1978; Miller & Ross, 1975; Weary, 1979; Zuckerman, 1979) but remains strong in accident research. Indeed, there is virtually no unambiguous support for the hypothesis despite its continued dominance in the accident literature. This may result in part from the absence of work that attempts to evaluate defensive attribution qua defensive attribution. Typically, the confusing results are noted and a single non-motivation-derived parameter is offered as a solution (cf. Brewer, 1977; Fishbein & Ajzen, 1973), which tends to have little impact on subsequent research. This is perhaps not surprising, given the ad hoc manner in which this research has proceeded.

For instance, Fishbein and Ajzen (1973, 1975) use Heider's levels model to argue that attributed responsibility is a function of both the observer's development or response level and the contextual (Heiderian) level of the stimulus information. They maintain that defensive attribution data are destined to remain ambiguous and confusing until these two parameters are clearly specified as experimental variables, a viewpoint also taken by Vidmar and Crinklaw (1974). However, as Shaver (1974) points out in an unpublished reply, motivational biases can operate only when stimuli display contextual ambiguity and hence are not classifiable in Heiderian terms. In contrast, we believe that this critical analysis of defensive attribution within its own framework is sufficient to show its limited scope. We point to the need for a more comprehensive theory regarding the process of responsibility attribution. However, we do not suggest that Fishbein and Ajzen's (1973, 1975) analysis is irrelevant, but that it is more appropriately considered in relation to the other major area of responsibility attribution investigation, developmental research.

C. DEVELOPMENTAL STUDIES

The emergence of a social psychological research tradition in developmental investigations of responsibility judgment is largely a historical accident. General factors that may account for its increasing popularity include dissatisfaction with the dominant Piagetian paradigm commonly used in such research (cf. Keasey, 1977; Lickona, 1976; Tomlinson, 1979), the establishment of social cognition as a distinct field within developmental psychology (see Shantz, 1975), and a recent emphasis on the reciprocal relation between social and developmental psychology (cf. Flavell, 1974; Geber, 1977). More important than any of these, however, is Heider's development of a responsibility model and the way in which he presents it (Heider, 1958, pp. 113–114).

Although Heider never directly defines responsibility, he describes several criteria used by the naive observer in its description. These are ordered according to the relative contribution of environmental and personal forces to the action outcome and comprise five distinct levels (see Table I). These represent a progression from "primitive," undifferentiated cognitive functioning to highly differentiated, "sophisticated" attributions. From his presentation of the model, it is not altogether clear to what extent Heider intends his levels to represent developmental stages in the cognitive developmental sense (i.e., structured wholes following an invariant sequence in which each is a preparatory condition for the next and is assimilated to it, see Kohlberg, 1969). By pointing out the similarity between his criteria of causality and intentionality and Piaget's (1932) phases of heteronomous and autonomous morality, however, he implies that his levels are age related. Heider has subsequently claimed that "I did not want to imply that they followed each other in time in child development . . . [but] thought of this only as a simple way of presenting these different kinds of attribution . . . as different forms of mental structure with different cognitive 'depth' " (written communication, December 13, 1978). Yet this perhaps unfortunate association has generally given rise to a developmental interpretation of his model.

Tests of the scheme, however, tend not to use a strict stage interpretation of the levels but merely examine quantitative variations in response patterns across age. Perhaps the most widely cited study is that by M. E. Shaw and Sulzer (1964). This investigation is prototypic of research in this area and hence serves to illustrate some of the difficulties with these studies. (For further discussion of this research, see Section IV, C.)

TABLE I

HEIDER'S LEVELS OF RESPONSIBILITY ATTRIBUTION

Level	Definition
1. Association	According to the global concept manifest at this level, "the person is held responsible for each effect that is in any way connected with him or that seems in any way to belong to him" (Heider, 1958, p. 113).
2. Causality	Anything "caused by (a person) P is ascribed to him. Causation is understood in the sense that P was a necessary condition for the happening, even though he could not have foreseen the outcome however cautiously he had proceeded . . . the person is judged not according to his intention, but according to the actual results of what he does . . . what Piaget (1932) refers to as objective responsibility" (Heider, 1958, p. 113).
3. Foreseeability	Here, "P is considered responsible, directly or indirectly, for any aftereffect he may have foreseen even though it was not a part of his own goal and therefore still not a part of the framework of personal causality" (Heider, 1958, p. 113).
4. Intention	At this level "only what P intended is perceived as having its source in him. This corresponds to what Piaget has called subjective responsibility"(Heider, 1958, p. 113).
5. Justification	Finally, "even the P's own motives are not entirely ascribed to him but are seen as having their source in the environment . . . responsibility for the act is at least shared by the environment" (Heider, 1958, p. 114).

Stories concerning a boy named Perry were administered to two different age groups (6- to 9-year-olds and college students) who rated his responsibility for story outcomes which differed in both valence and intensity. Each contained only the minimum information to be classified at one of Heider's levels. Although some support was found for age-related changes regarding some of the levels (a levels × populations interaction), the results are open to alternative interpretations. For example, Harris (1977) shows how the use of only two groups differing so widely in age may have yielded results that merely reflect differential understanding of the task requirements, a possibility which is not unrealistic in view of the large group testing procedure and the utilization of the rather complex term "responsibility" in eliciting responses from young children.[5]

Several crucial problems relating to the operationalization of Heider's levels (see Fincham & Jaspars, 1979) create further interpretational difficulties and

---

[5]Indeed an even greater variety of dependent measures is used in developmental research (e.g., blame, naughty, bad, like, punish, cause, etc.), which obscures the important question as to what developmental factors are important in differentiating these related concepts.

impose severe limitations on subsequent research by Shaw and his associates (e.g., Shaw, Briscoe, & Garcia-Esteve, 1968; Shaw & Schneider, 1969a). This is implicitly recognized by these researchers who have turned to alternative stimuli. For instance, "abstract structures" have been employed such as the following: "Steve caused something to happen that was a little bit bad. He intended to cause it. Is Steve responsible for the bad thing he caused?" The abstract nature and linguistic complexity of such stories is obviously prejudicial to the young child's performance. Moreover, the explicit presentation of Heider's attribution criteria may draw older children's attention to them, leading to more differentiated attributions than might otherwise be made and thereby creating inflated developmental differences. Awareness of child development is crucial if social psychologists are to decenter from an egocentric, adult perspective and investigate children's competence instead of arbitrary performance variables, a distinction which recently has revolutionized the appreciation of Piaget's work (cf. Bryant, 1974; Fincham, 1980b).

Besides attempts to evaluate the developmental nature of Heider's model (see Section IV, C) and its general implications for moral development research (see Keasey, 1977), his criteria have also been suggested as general rule sets representing distinct bases for judging responsibility (e.g., Fishbein & Ajzen, 1973; Hamilton, 1978; Vidmar & Crinklaw, 1974). Vidmar and Crinklaw (1974) propose that research subjects be allowed to choose the type of responsibility they wish to assign and, furthermore, to designate a certain magnitude of responsibility within the type selected. Except for the aforementioned developmental research, and an attempt to use the rules/criteria to test the limitations of the young child's notions regarding responsibility (Fincham, 1980a), there has been no investigation of the conditions determining the use of such rule sets. However, it has been suggested by Ross and Di Tecco (1975, p. 103) that "primitive" and self-effacing attributions occur when the results of the attribution have little future significance for the perceiver in his attempts to control or predict his environment.

A final set of studies, although neither strictly developmental in origin nor adequately reported, bears mentioning because they point to a fruitful connection in Heider's work. In addition to his levels schema, Heider presents a model for the naive analysis of action which also includes internal and external forces as basic building blocks. The internal side of the equation is further subdivided into trying (involving effort and intentions) and ability. Whereas Heider clearly exploits the notion of intention in regard to responsibility attribution, no mention is made of effort. Dillehay and his colleagues (Dillehay, Woods, & Raymond, 1973; Raymond & Dillehay, 1973; Schultz & Dillehay, 1970), however, repeatedly have found that perceived effort influences responsibility judgments of both children and adults. They also manipulated incidental outcome or consequences that were not contingent on the protagonists' actions in an attempt to demonstrate unit formation between outcome and actor. Although this produced inconsistent results and was perhaps merely an instance of global association (Level 1), their work is of important heuristic value. Although the authors do not mention Heider's analysis of responsibility in relation to their own work, the exploration of such possible links requires serious consideration. In addition, their results pose several obvious interpretational difficulties (e.g., the confounding of ability and trying, whether the effort manipulation is not more parsimoniously accounted for in terms of perceived intention, etc.) that raise questions for further research.

This connection is also suggested by the work of Weiner and his associates (e.g., Weiner, Kun, & Benesh-Weiner, 1978; Weiner & Peter, 1973), who have investigated the determinants of achievement evaluations in relation to moral judgment development. By manipulating intent,[6] ability and (in later work) task difficulty, they have at least extended elements of Heider's naive analysis of action model to the responsibility attribution domain. The fact that all three variables influenced judgments emphasizes the need for some rapprochement between Heiderian elements used in making general attributions regarding action and those proposed to influence responsibility attribution in particular.

D. CONCLUSIONS

It is apparent that the term "attribution of responsibility" does not denote a simple judgmental process. In addition to the inherently ambiguous nature of the concept, a great deal of confusion arises because social psychologists have tended to ignore fundamental questions regarding responsibility assignment. Consequently, psychological statements regarding the assignment of responsibility often rely on implicit, shared assumptions and contextual cues for their intelligibility. However, the unacknowledged vacillation between different uses of the term "responsibility" and its lack of differentiation from related concepts (e.g., punishment) generates a lack of conceptual clarity for the reader. Not only does this call for a more adequate conceptual analysis of the notion in the psychological literature, but it also points to a potentially useful research program. Explicitly identifying and testing social psychologists' preconceptions in this area may yield some important insights to the extent that psychologists themselves constitute attributors drawing heavily on common sense in the absence of an extensive literature on responsibility judgments per se.

Given the nature of research to date, this confusion is perhaps not at all surprising. Insofar as there have been investigations of attribution of responsibility, as opposed to general attribution research parading under this title, it has not

---

[6]Intent is equated with effort but, from examination of their stimuli, may be more appropriately encapsulated by the superordinate concept of trying (motivation).

specifically addressed this responsibility judgment process per se; instead, it has concentrated on the related issues of motivational biases and child development. Two rather unfortunate ironies follow. First, by elevating defensive attribution to such a dominant role in the research literature, social psychologists themselves may be guilty of an attribution error. It is indeed unfortunate that the research started by focusing on a (motivational) bias in a psychological process that is itself little understood. Under these circumstances it therefore is not surprising that as yet no coherent conception of defensive attribution has emerged. Second, the model which was proposed as a conceptual framework for investigating responsibility attribution in a more general sense has mainly been used in developmental research and not as a conceptual tool.

We argue that considerable conceptual clarification is needed in order to put the results already obtained in their proper perspective and produce more meaningful research. This does not mean that existing responsibility attribution research has to be rejected. On the contrary, some considerable progress has been made. Nor should the argument that classical attribution theory has not, and indeed cannot, provide an adequate framework for investigating attribution of responsibility be interpreted as implying that the classical analysis should therefore be ignored. Attributions of responsibility are quite possibly related to the kinds of explanation one gives for events. Determining the nature of this relationship might provide a substantial link between more general theories of attribution and attributions of responsibility. Consequently, the ensuing sections draw liberally from social psychological research, where appropriate, although the analysis offered in response to the aforementioned criticisms derives mainly from commonsense and legal notions of responsibility.

II. A Conceptual Analysis of Responsibility

In this section we will consider the attribution of responsibility from three different points of view which have not been taken explicitly into account in social psychology.

Since we are concerned primarily with the commonsense notion of responsibility, an analysis of responsibility attribution should perhaps start by considering the meaning of responsibility in everyday life. To the extent that this meaning is reflected in a dictionary definition of the word "responsibility," a simple linguistic analysis may suffice as a first step. Responsibility considered from this point of view therefore is discussed in the first part of this section.

A much more important consideration, however, is to analyze commonsense notions of responsibility in a context of great social relevance, namely, the law. We saw in Section I that several authors (Hamilton, 1978; Heider, 1944) mention various legal ideas at an anecdotal level but do not attempt a systematic analysis of commonsense ideas about responsibility implicit in the law or legal proceedings. However, such an analysis has been undertaken in legal philosophy by Hart (1968) and Hart and Honoré (1959). In the second part of this section, therefore, we shall discuss the commonsense notion of responsibility and the related notion of causality as analyzed by these writers.

Since the Hart and Honoré analysis is intended to clarify legal proceedings and not psychological processes per se, direct consideration of various legal notions from a social psychological perspective may also assist in understanding commonsense thinking about responsibility. Where Hart and Honoré are concerned with the ideas of lawyers about commonsense, social psychologists may consider legal thinking about responsibility as a paradigm for the analysis of responsibility attribution in common sense. "Man the lawyer" might be a more adequate model for the study of responsibility attribution in everyday life than "man the scientist." Consequently, some relevant legal concepts which suggest a further perspective on the study of responsibility attribution in everyday life are discussed in the third part of this section. Finally, an attempt is made to compare the notions of responsibility that are presented here with the way in which attribution of responsibility has been studied in social psychology.

A. COMMONSENSE NOTIONS OF RESPONSIBILITY

According to the Oxford English Dictionary, the terms "responsible" and "responsibility" have a variety of meanings. Excluding obsolete and rare ones, the central meanings of the word "responsible" appear to be (1) "answerable, accountable to another for something; liable to be called to account" and (2) "morally accountable for one's actions."

These two definitions immediately suggest that any theory dealing with the attribution of responsibility in the first sense may have to consider what one is to account for and to whom. The second definition indicates that one can be held accountable for one's actions, but it is clear from the various examples given that one may also be held accountable for the results or outcomes of one's actions, or even for events which are not the direct outcome of these actions. The qualification "morally" in the second definition suggests, moreover, that one also can be held responsible in different ways. Such adjectives as "legal" and "criminal" immediately come to mind.

These definitions, however, and their implications do not exhaust the variety of commonsense meanings associated with the word. "Responsible" can also be used in the sense of "being capable of rational conduct," a notion that plays an important role in criminal law, as we shall see shortly. The concept of capability, however, also is combined with the fulfilment of an obligation/trust, or even a charge/duty, which suggests that a responsibility often characterizes a particular social position or social role. This notion may even generalize so that a person may be considered responsible on the basis of good credit, repute, or even respectable appearance.

It therefore appears that the central notion of responsibility in common sense is the idea that a person can be held accountable for something; he is answerable to someone or some social institution for his actions or the outcomes of those actions, although he may also be asked to answer for acts not performed but that may have been expected on account of his position. Finally, he may be regarded as someone who is not accountable for some act because he lacks the capability of fulfilling certain obligations.

B.   COMMONSENSE NOTIONS OF RESPONSIBILITY IN LEGAL PHILOSOPHY

The notion of accountability discussed in the previous section is in fact a very old one found in early Greek writings (Adkins, 1960), and has been used in legal philosophy to express the quintessence of the concept of responsibility. The legal theorist Hart (1968) has made a very detailed analysis, not only of responsibility but also of the concepts of causality and punishment in the law. Before we discuss Hart's work it is perhaps important to note that the concept of causality is not explicitly included in the commonsense notion of responsibility. Hart also excludes causality from the concept of responsibility, at least when he describes what, according to him, constitutes its central idea. That idea is answerability, but in a slightly different sense from its usage in the above analysis of common sense. Someone is made responsible, or can be held responsible, by a demand that he rebut accusations or charges that, if established, carry liability to punishment, blame, or other adverse treatment. In short, responsibility exists when a person is answerable for loss or damage, or for his actions. This notion, according to Hart, is extended to the infliction of harm by action or omission, the person causing the harm, and the possession of normal capacities to conform to the requirements of law and morals. In an even more extended sense, causal connections outside the context of blame and punishment are included. Moreover, good outcomes, as well as bad ones, may be taken into account and, finally, the duties defining a person's position may be included. Hart is less certain about the last form of responsibility, which he calls *role responsibility,* as he is not sure whether it can really be seen as an extension of the central notion of rebutting charges or accusations. According to Hart, role responsibility implies the performance of a relatively complex and extensive set of duties which require care and attention over a protracted period of time. These are usually attached to a distinctive place or office in a social organization either to provide for the welfare of others or to advance in some specific way the aims and purposes of the organization. If one wants to distinguish role responsibility from other forms of responsibility, it is perhaps useful to remember that we usually refer to role responsibility in the form of "a responsibility" or in the plural.

In exploring the various types of responsibility Hart outlines, the concept of *legal liability responsibility* appears as the central notion of responsibility in legal philosophy. This implies that one is liable to punishment and/or enforced compensation if certain mental or psychological criteria are met. The notion itself is clear enough, but the important aspect of this conception of responsibility is that certain criteria are mentioned which have to be met before one can be held responsible by the law. These criteria are, for example, a guilty mind (*mens rea*), normal capacities in the sense previously mentioned, and either a connection (causal or otherwise) with the harm or relationship with the agent. It is interesting to note that Hart does not use causation as the sole criterion for the assignment of responsibility. A (direct) causal connection between the actor and the outcome is apparently neither necessary nor sufficient for the attribution of responsibility.

Hart's discussion of *moral responsibility* is not essentially different from his discussion of legal liability responsibility, although he clearly recognizes the differences between these two forms of responsibility. It seems that such differences are to be sought primarily in a less explicit formulation of the relevant conditions and the purpose for which a person is to be held responsible in moral as opposed to legal judgments (Lloyd-Bostock, 1979b).

Finally, Hart points out that responsibility can be used in the sense of *causal responsibility*. Here responsibility is actually synonymous with causality and can be applied to human beings (their actions or omissions), to things, conditions, and events when explaining consequences, results, and outcomes. In this sense the term "responsibility" is virtually always used in the past tense.

It appears, therefore, that we face at least a twofold problem in discussing the attribution of responsibility. In the first instance the concept may not be used in the sense of accountability but refers to conditions which have to be met before a person can be held responsible. However, responsibility may indeed refer to accountability, although this meaning requires that one specifies to whom and for what one is held responsible. The type of responsibility meant in a particular explanation should therefore be made clear. We should not explain the attribution of causal responsibility in the same way as the attribution of responsibility in the sense of moral, legal, or role responsibility. In the first case we are simply talking about causality, whereas the second case involves rebutting charges or accusations. The fact that attributed causality may be a condition for attributing responsibility does not make the two concepts identical. Causality has in this respect the same conceptual or theoretical status as normal capacities, without which a person cannot be held responsible. Capacity responsibility therefore also has a theoretical status distinct from legal, moral, and role responsibility because it can be combined with either of these notions as one of the criteria which has to be met for "accountability."

In the case of legal, moral, and role responsibility it appears that we are talking not about different meanings of the general concept of responsibility but about different forms of answerability or accountability regarding to whom one is responsible. It may be that these different forms of "liability" responsibility require completely different explanations but a more general theory of responsibility attribution is of course not inconceivable if the differences between various forms of responsibility can be expressed in terms of only a few parameters. One possibility is, for example, that role, legal, and moral responsibility differ mainly in terms of the perceived seriousness of the consequences or outcomes of the acts under consideration.

Whatever the case may be, the central issue in responsibility attribution, according to Hart's analysis, is whether a person can be held accountable for certain acts or the outcomes of those acts. In order to hold someone responsible, however, the person who is made to answer must stand in a particular relationship to the act or outcome under consideration. It is the nature of the relationship that is crucial in determining responsibility. Although it need not necessarily be a causal one, a direct causal link between the person and the act or outcome is the clearest instance of a sufficiently close connection for attributing responsibility and may therefore exert considerable influence over our thoughts about responsibility in other cases. It is for this reason that the Hart and Honoré (1959) analysis regarding commonsense notions of causality is now considered.

Hart and Honoré on Causation

In contrast to attribution theory in social psychology, which is based upon philosophical and scientific notions of causality, Hart and Honoré (1959) see causation and responsibility in the law as rooted in common sense. They point out that philosophical notions of causation have always seemed irrelevant to the lawyer and historian because they are primarily concerned with causal statements about particulars, whereas science and philosophy deal with connections between types of events which can be formulated as laws or generalizations. As in ordinary life, the causal statements of lawyers are singular statements identifying in complex situations certain particular events as causes or consequences. In the philosophical tradition of Hume and Mill, every singular statement is seen as an instance of one or more general propositions asserting invariable sequence. In practice, however, a major difficulty arises when generalizations are used to identify the cause of a particular event on a particular occasion. How does one distinguish between something that can be said to cause something else and something that is only "its occasion," "a mere condition," or "part of the circumstances"? Hart and Honoré illustrate this problem by arguing that the lawyer and the ordinary man would refuse to say that the cause of a fire was the presence of oxygen. They would reserve the title of cause for something of the order of a shortcircuit, the dropping of a lighted cigarette, or lightning. On some occasions, however, it would be perfectly normal to consider the presence of oxygen as the cause of a fire (e.g., when the fire occurs within part of a manufac- turing process where oxygen has to be excluded).

The most important issue in their discussion seems to be that the general laws we may need to demonstrate causal connection do not tell us which of all possible conditions necessary for the occurrence of an event can be cited as the cause in a particular case. Instead of regarding the process of causal attribution as an inference process based upon an intuitive analysis of observed covariation of events, as Kelley's approach would suggest, Hart and Honoré seem to view causal attribution as a process of focusing on one condition among many that may be present.

The second major point made by Hart and Honoré is that there seem to be, both within the law and in common sense, rational limits to "the pursuing of causal connections, backwards or forwards in time" (Hart & Honoré, 1959, p. 12). To cite just one of their examples:

> If a man has been shot it would usually be stupid or inappropriate, though not false, to give as the cause of his death the fact that his blood cells were deprived of oxygen, and equally inappropriate to give the manufacturer's action in selling the gun to his father from whom he had inherited it. (p. 11)

According to Hart and Honoré, the central commonsense notion of causa- tion is that a contingency, usually a human intervention, initiates a series of physical changes which exemplify general connections between types of events. Its features, they argue, are seen in the simplest case of all where a human being manipulates things in order to bring about intended change. In some complex cases, however, it is necessary to draw distinctions between voluntary interven- tions and abnormal events as "causes" and other events as mere conditions.

In this central notion of causation only those conditions necessary for the occurrence of an event (and which are not part of the usual state or mode of operation of the thing under inquiry) are interpreted as causes. Such conditions are abnormal in the sense that they represent a departure from the ordinary or reasonably expected course of events. They "make the difference" between, for instance, an accident and things going on as usual and are thought of as interven- ing or intruding into the existing state of affairs. However, which conditions are treated as abnormal is to some extent dependent upon the context of the inquiry. Collingwood (see Hart & Honoré, 1959, p. 31) has suggested that the perceived context is very often constituted by the practical interests of the persons involved, a suggestion which also is considered by Kelley (1971a, p. 22).

The second contrast between causes and mere conditions is defined by the status accorded to human actions in Hart and Honoré's analysis. A voluntary human action intended to bring about what in fact happens, and in the manner in which it happens, is given a special place in causal inquiries because such acts are very often regarded as a limit or a barrier in tracing causality. We do not trace the cause of a later event through a voluntary human act, but we do trace the cause of an event back through intermediate causes of other kinds to voluntary action.

The notion of causality, however, is not limited to voluntary human action and abnormal conditions. A special case of "causality" exists when one human being by words or deeds influences another's action. Hart and Honoré argue that in such cases, which involve relationships between two human actions, we are no longer concerned with causes of events in the above sense but with reasons for actions. This is not to say that causal relationships cannot exist between two human actions, and it certainly does not exclude transitional cases. Relationships of this type, however, are distinguished from causal relationships in a strict sense by the following features: (1) The second actor knows of and understands the significance of what the first actor has said or done; (2) the first actor's words or deeds are part of the second actor's reasons for acting; (3) the second actor forms the intention to perform the act in question only after the first actor's intervention; and (4) except in the case when the first actor has merely advised the second actor, he intends the second actor to do the act in question.

Finally, Hart and Honoré distinguish a class of relationships between actions that is analogous to interpersonal transactions involving reasons, namely, situations in which one person provides another with an opportunity for doing something. It is argued that two essential features characterize this type of relationship: first, that providing or failing to provide another with an opportunity to act must be a deviation from a standard practice or procedure; second, the argumentation on which statements of this kind rely are mainly hypothetical, showing what could have happened had the opportunity (not) been provided.

In summary, Hart and Honoré (1959) argue that in common sense a cause is perceived as an "abnormal" condition, a condition which "makes the difference" because it is not present as part of the usual state or mode of operation of a thing but interferes with or intervenes in the normal course of events. A voluntary human action appears to be the prototype of such an abnormal condition. It occupies a special place in causal inquiries because it is seen as a primary or ultimate cause through which we do not trace the cause of a later event and to which we do trace the cause through intermediate causes of other kinds. Finally, this central notion of causality is distinguished from cases wherein one person "causes" another to act by providing him or her with a reason or an opportunity for acting.

Any of these forms of causation can be a ground for holding someone responsible, but whether responsibility will be attributed at all depends on their precise nature in a particular case. Unfortunately, there do not appear to be any simple means of relating these precise forms of connection to the determination of responsibility. It is not possible to present here Hart and Honoré's suggestions regarding the intricate ways in which responsibility may be attributed by way of summary principles. The interested reader is therefore referred to the original text. In the present context it suffices to note that the aforementioned distinctions are not only useful for investigating the relationship between act and outcome as it relates to responsibility attribution but also point to several refinements in psychological studies of perceived causality. A final rather more concrete approach to understanding the use of various criteria in assigning responsibility is to consider how responsibility is determined in the law. After all, the law itself presents us with centuries of accumulated experience in trying to systematize such criteria.

C. SOME RELEVANT LEGAL CONCEPTS

This contribution is not the place to present an exhaustive treatment of the legal criteria for attributing responsibility because we are concerned not with legal proceedings but with the attribution of (legal) responsibility by ordinary people in everyday life. The idea is, however, that certain legal rules have a parallel in lay attributions of responsibility (see Hart & Honoré, 1959, pp. 58-64), an idea which is comparable with the traditional notion that common law expounds or reflects common sense.

A cursory glance at handbooks of criminal and civil law, especially the law of torts in the latter case (Rogers, 1979; Smith & Hogan, 1978), shows immediately the enormous complexity of the conditions which have to be met for legal responsibility in various cases. Some of those used in criminal law are briefly considered, to illustrate their potential value for understanding the ordinary person's notions of responsibility.

Criminal Responsibility

In English criminal law, responsibility exists when a person's act or omission results in a state of affairs which the law seeks to prevent. The cardinal doctrine of criminal law requires that the act is intentional (*actus non facit reum nisi mens sit rea*). The physical element (*actus reus*) and the mental element (*mens rea*) are both essential. However, the concept of *actus reus* does not just refer to an act in the usual sense of the word, as it also involves the results and the surrounding circumstances that are included in the definition of the offence. Moreoever, the prosecution must usually prove beyond reasonable doubt that the state of affairs the law desires to prevent has been created as a result of the person's conduct and that the conduct has been accompanied by a certain condition of mind.

These legal considerations may not seem directly relevant to a theory of responsibility attribution in psychology, as lay observers need not carefully consider whether they can prove beyond reasonable doubt that it was a person's conduct which resulted in a particular outcome. It is quite likely, however, that ordinary people use criteria similar to those specified in the law in a less strict sense to attribute responsibility. In most psychological experiments the problems of proof and evidence are usually circumvented by presenting the subject directly with the relevant information, but it may be worth considering in future research how attribution of responsibility is affected by different types of evidence (e.g., direct evidence, circumstantial evidence, oral evidence, documentary evidence, real evidence, and hearsay evidence). More important for attributing criminal responsibility, however, is the extent to which it can be said that specific consequences have been "caused" by the accused. In general, a person will not be held to have caused a particular event unless it is possible to establish a sufficiently direct link between that person's conduct and that event. The variety of criminal cases in this respect is bewildering, and it is quite obvious that it is a very difficult task to state in a general way whether a link is sufficiently direct. The whole issue of the chain of causation is of such importance, however, that any psychological theory of responsibility attribution should allow for some measure of the link between person and consequences.

The problem becomes especially difficult when we are dealing with omissions. In general, the harmful effects of an omission will result in criminal responsibility only when the law has imposed a duty to act in those circumstances. That omission may create criminal responsibility suggests that responsibility attribution in everyday life may very well be determined to some extent by implicit or explicit notions people have about the duties of the actor in a particular situation.

Legal rules for determining criminal responsibility become even more relevant for a psychological theory of responsibility attribution when we consider *mens rea* as an essential prerequisite for its ascription. Almost all legal systems recognize the importance of a guilty mind, or *mens rea,* but statutes have not always spelled out exactly what is meant by this concept. The American Law Institute's model penal code (Hart and Honoré, 1959, p. 353) has attempted to clarify the concept by reducing the variety of mental states to four: Guilt is attributed to a person who acts "purposely," "knowingly," "recklessly," or "negligently." These terms correspond roughly to those used in European legal theory and to commonsense notions, as expressed in Heider's scheme of responsibility attribution. The major issue with respect to *mens rea,* however, is not so much the definition of the concept but the demonstration of its absence on the part of the accused. General defenses against a charge of criminal responsibility, claiming mistake, compulsion, intoxication, automatism, and insanity, apparently rely on the indirect inference that their presence rules out the existence of a particular state of mind. It seems that *mens rea* is always present unless negated by the defense. The clearest case of this is probably the M'Naghten Rules, which state that every person is presumed to be sane and to possess sufficient reason to be responsible for his crimes until proved otherwise. The interesting hypothesis that follows from this general notion is that attribution of responsibility in everyday life also relies on the presumption of intentionality unless there are situational or incapacitating factors which rule out its presence.

If the above hypothesis were to hold, it would mean that commonsense proofs of *actus reus* and *mens rea* are essentially different. In the first case there would have to be positive evidence that a person had produced, directly or indirectly, a certain outcome. In the second, however, it is supposed that we rely essentially on negative and contrary evidence, using a discounting procedure to determine intentionality. In other words, the extent to which an act is perceived as intentional is the inverse of the extent to which it is seen as determined by situational or incapacitating factors. It would be interesting to determine whether direct evidence of intentionality, based either on self-report or on observation of ongoing behavior, operates in accordance with such a discounting process.

In order to complete our picture of criminal responsibility it is necessary to discuss strict liability and vicarious responsibility. In both cases the demonstration of *mens rea* is not required. It is interesting to note that where statutes do not deal with *mens rea* a presumption of *mens rea* may be made. It would seem that the notion of strict liability is unjust by convicting those whose behavior has been correct. The case for strict liability, however, is based on the argument that certain important regulations necessary for the welfare of the community have to be obeyed, that *mens rea* is very often difficult to prove, and that a high degree of "social danger" may be created by certain acts. Instead of being a special criterion for attribution of responsibility, it appears that strict liability is instituted because of the social importance of the consequences it seeks to avoid. The fact that *mens rea* may be difficult to prove does not introduce a new criterion because it is entirely in line with the present argument that intentionality cannot be determined positively after the fact. However, the extent to which attribution of responsibility in everyday life depends upon the social importance of consequences is an interesting question to be determined by empirical research.

Vicarious responsibility similarly can be conceived as an exception to the general rule of *actus reus* and *mens rea* because the law states that a person is in general not vicariously liable for a crime committed by his servant. Exceptions to this rule are apparently made in order to prevent certain offences in the future or when, under statute, a general and/or complete delegation of authority has taken place. This particular form of responsibility can be seen as analogous to that associated with certain social roles and is discussed more fully in relation to recent social psychological work in this area (Section III,B).

The preceding analysis has only touched upon a few important concepts in criminal law. Space restrictions do not permit a consideration of similar concepts in other areas of the law (e.g., the law of torts and contract law) which may be equally relevant to the psychologist interested in attribution of responsibility. The

ideas presented so far, however, are sufficient to point out how social psychological research may benefit from considering legal criteria for determining responsibility. This theme is pursued further in the next subsection, which relates the
analyses presented to attribution theory and research.

D. THE RELATION TO ATTRIBUTION THEORY AND RESEARCH

That responsibility should not be equated with causality becomes apparent
from the preceding analysis. The confusion in psychological writings arises
partly because causality constitutes one meaning of the word "responsibility."
Apparently, it has not been noticed that the term "responsible" in a causal sense
is normally used in combination with the past tense of verbs. The central meaning of responsibility, however, is different from that of causality. Holding someone responsible by demanding that he rebut an accusation does not explain his
actions but simply indicates liability for punishment (praise), or compensation.
The confusing results obtained in accident research may be partly caused by
certain studies having used responsibility in a causal sense, whereas others have
used it to mean moral blame or evaluation. In Walster's (1966) original study
both causal and moral responsibility questions were asked (the causal responsibility questions are even phrased in the past tense!) but not considered separately.

The central meaning of responsibility (i.e., accountability) is nevertheless
closely related to the question of causation because perceived causality appears to
be a crucial factor in determining a person's responsibility both in the law and
common sense. It is important to realize, however, that the notion of causality
used in attribution theories is different from that used in the law and ordinary
thought. In Kelley's theory a cause is equated with the covariants of the observed
event, which places his causal attribution model in the empiricist tradition of
Hume and Mill. In contrast, Hart and Honoré argue that a cause is usually seen as
(a metaphor or analog of) a voluntary human action, which in a relative sense
constitutes an abnormal event and brings about a change in the environment. The
crucial element in this commonsense notion of causality is the emphasis placed
on the production of the outcome by the cause, a notion which is lacking in the
covariation model.[7] It seems that the implicit notion of causality used by Jones
and Davis (1965) is partly comparable to that advanced by Hart and Honoré.
However, they do not distinguish clearly between causality and intentionality
because correspondent inference theory is confined to intentional behavior.

Only Heider clearly differentiates personal from impersonal causality, a
distinction paralleling the legal distinction between *actus reus* and *mens rea*. It is
therefore not surprising that Hamilton (1978) has been able to point out the

---

[7]Bunge's analysis of the scientific concept of causality (Bunge, 1959) shows that in this respect
Hart and Honoré's commonsense notion of causality may be closer to current scientific notions than
the covariance model.

similarity between Heider's levels and various legal criteria for assigning responsibility (see Section III).

This distinction allows the most important point regarding the relation between attribution of causality and responsibility judgments to be clarified. It is
not simply that people may use a notion of causality which is different from the
one advanced in attribution theories. Instead, the causal questions involved in
determining responsibility refer in part to actor–act–outcome relationships which
are different from the ones studied in attribution research.

Both Kelley's covariation–configuration model and the Jones and Davis
correspondent inference theory deal primarily with the "causal" relation between acts or behavior and "something in the person" (i.e., intentions, dispositions). This emphasizes the explanation of behavior in terms of an underlying
"effective personal force" (Heider, 1958). Questions of responsibility, however, concentrate primarily on the explanation of events which are perceived, at
least in part, as the outcome of an act. In attribution theories, for example, the
central relation is between intention/disposition and behavior, whereas in attribution of responsibility it is that between act and outcome.

Careful inspection of the actual material considered in attribution research
and legal decision making illustrates this difference in emphasis. In many experiments, and in the original theoretical papers, attention has been given mainly
either to expressive behavior, which does not produce an external outcome in the
ordinary sense of the word (enjoyment of a movie; see Kelley, 1967), or to
instrumental behavior, in which the relation between act and outcome in not in
dispute (Miss Adams choses Bagby; see Jones & Davis, 1965). However, in
most legal cases the relationship between act and outcome is not immanent or
undisputed but one of the two basic criteria which have to be taken into account
in order to establish responsibility. Consider the following case: A person X
intends to murder a child Y and gives laudanum to Y's nurse, stating that it is a
medicine to be administered to Y. The nurse decides that Y does not need it and
leaves the bottle on a shelf from which her daughter, aged 5 years, later takes it
and administers it to Y. Y dies. Is X's conduct then the cause of Y's death?[8]

Problems of this kind have not been considered in psychological studies of
perceived causality and/or responsibility. It is not suggested that one should
therefore study such incredibly complex cases as the one just mentioned; we
merely wish to indicate that in addition to the question of the causal relationship
between "something in the person" and his behavior, that between act and
outcome should also be explicitly taken into account in responsibility attribution
research.

It is the aforementioned relationship that cannot be taken for granted in
many real-life situations and that opens a whole new field of attributional ques-

[8]The answer is yes. (See RvMichael, 1840, cited in Curzon, 1977, p. 19.)

tions having to do with intervening causes, the perception of intentionality, the importance of reasons and opportunities, and so on. In recent theoretical papers, some vaguely similar suggestions have been made by authors presenting either quantitative models or alternative explanations of attribution processes. In Section III we discuss these developments.

III.   Recent Theoretical Developments in Attribution Research

A.   QUANTITATIVE MODELS

1.   A Bayesian Analysis of Attribution Processes

Ajzen and Fishbein (1975) suggest that it may be possible to employ Bayes' theorem as a model of causal attribution. This article is one of several recent attempts to develop quantitative models for attribution processes (e.g., Anderson, 1978; Brewer, 1977; Fincham, 1980d). Although Ajzen and Fishbein do not specifically address themselves to the problem of responsibility attribution, the general model they propose has certain implications for the attribution of responsibility.

In general, Ajzen and Fishbein suggest that causal attribution can be equated with the likelihood ratio in Bayes' theorem. Interpreting an actor's observed behavior (B) as the datum in Bayes' theorem and a proposed explanation as the hypothesis (H), the extent to which the behavior can be viewed as being produced by a given factor is represented by the likelihood ratio (LR)

$$LR = p(B/H)/p(B/\bar{H})$$

According to Bayes' theorem, the likelihood ratio indicates the diagnostic value of the new item of information (B) and is equivalent to the revision of the hypothesis (H) under consideration:

$$p(H/B)/p(\bar{H}/B) = [p(B/H)/p(B/\bar{H})] \times [p(H)/p(\bar{H})]$$

This can be written in the usual form as

$$\Omega_B = LR\,\Omega_0$$

where Ω_B indicates the posterior odds that H is more or less likely than $\bar{H}$ given B and Ω_0 is the comparable prior odds.

It is important to remember that Bayes' theorem can be applied sequentially in a simple way when conditional independence can be assumed between various items of information (Slovic & Lichtenstein, 1971). In that case the final posterior odds after n items of information become

$$\Omega_{Bn} = \prod_{i=1}^{n} LR_i\,\Omega_0$$

Ajzen and Fishbein have applied these ideas to a number of questions in attribution theory, such as the consistency of behavior across occasions, objects, and actions; attributions based on success and failure; the effect of multiple causes; the attribution of dispositions; attribution to self and other; and attributional biases. One example perhaps suffices in illustrating these applications. According to Jones and Davis (1965), behavior is more likely to be attributed to an actor's disposition, rather than to some external factor, when the actor is perceived as having behaved under high freedom of choice. Ajzen and Fishbein argue that

> a behaviour performed under low freedom of choice has little diagnostic value; that is, the behaviour (B) is as likely to be performed with or without disposition (D) in question. Under high freedom of choice, however, the behaviour is more likely to be performed when the actor has the appropriate disposition than when he does not. To put this more formally, the likelihood ratio $p(B/D)/p(B/\bar{D})$ should be close to unity in the case of low decision freedom, while it should exceed unity under high freedom of choice. (Ajzen & Fishbein, 1975, p. 269)

Fischhoff and Lichtenstein (1978) have expressed doubts about the applicability of Bayes' theorem as either a normative or descriptive model of causal attributions. We share most of their reservations but also agree with Ajzen and Fishbein (1978) that the points raised by Fischhoff and Lichtenstein do not preclude the use of Bayes' theorem as a possible unifying framework for research on causal attribution.

Because the Fischhoff and Lichtenstein criticism does not in any event apply to responsibility attribution, it may be worth considering the application of Bayes' theorem in this area of research. Although Fishbein and Ajzen (1973) have specifically criticized research on attribution of responsibility, they have unfortunately little to say about the extent to which the assignment of responsibility obeys Bayes' theorem (p. 275). In their analysis they refer only to defensive attribution and conclude that there is little empirical support for an ego-defensive bias in attributing responsibility for accidents. The results of accident research are indeed confusing, as was pointed out in Section I, but instead of dismissing the notion of defensive attribution altogether, one might consider whether Bayes' theorem possibly could be used in understanding this literature.

One reason that Ajzen and Fishbein do not seem to deal adequately with attribution of responsibility from a Bayesian viewpoint may be their own conceptual confusion in analyzing this particular aspect of attribution theory. They do not draw a distinction between attribution of responsibility and causal attribution in this publication.[9] Moreover, they do not seem to realize that in attributing

[9]Although Ajzen and Fishbein frequently refer to "causal attribution" in their paper, they include research on attribution of responsibility for accidents in their discussion of attributional errors and biases. In fact, they even refer the reader to their earlier work on this subject (Fishbein & Ajzen, 1973) in which they suggest responsibility attribution is best viewed as a moral judgment.

responsibility for an accident we are no longer concerned with behavior as the explanandum, but with the outcome of the behavior or in general with an event (e.g., an accident). It is not the relation between behavior and some unknown internal or external cause but the connection between behavior and its outcome that is of direct concern.

It would seem to follow from the Ajzen and Fishbein application of Bayes' theorem that responsibility attribution can perhaps be equated with the likelihood ratio of the probability of an outcome, given the behavior and the probability of the outcome in the absence of the act. Attributed responsibility therefore might be represented as

$$LR = p(O/A)/p(O/\bar{A})$$

where the outcome (O) is interpreted as the datum and the act (A) as the hypothesis in Bayes' theorem. This interpretation, however, raises certain problems, because we are no longer dealing with estimating the probability of an unknown cause in the case of a single, particular act. We usually take it for granted that the act has occurred, although this depends of course on the available evidence other than its outcome. It does not seem sensible to ask what the probability of the act is, given this outcome, when it is known that the act has occurred. What we appear to be uncertain of is whether this particular act can be seen as the cause of this particular event. If we wish to apply a probabilistic model to the attribution of responsibility, it seems that we must either make the cause unknown in a particular case or deal with types of events and types of acts. In the first case, it seems reasonable to ask for subjective probability estimates of an act of a particular kind, such as a deliberate or intentional act. If we consider the act and the outcome of the act as a unit (Heider, 1944), we are dealing again with probability estimates of unknown causes such as intentions. Thus, in considering types of outcomes and acts, a probabilistic model of responsibility attribution does not appear problematic except for the fact that we do not know whether people do indeed use such estimates when making responsibility attributions in a particular case. The fact that an outcome of a certain type occurs very often given a preceding act of a certain type may not be important at all. What matters, according to Hart and Honoré (1959, p. 33), is whether this particular act can be seen as the cause of this particular event. Although Fischhoff (1976) and Fischhoff and Lichtenstein (1978) express some reservation regarding the application of probabilistic models in attribution theory, there is some evidence directly concerned with their use in attribution of responsibility (Brewer, 1977). It is this work that is now considered.

2.   An Information-Processing Approach to Attribution of Responsibility

Brewer (1977) has reviewed the literature on defensive attribution and has argued that many of the results which have been attributed to self-serving biases can be reevaluated in terms of an information-processing analysis. Based upon an extension of the Schopler and Layton (1972) model of attribution of power, Brewer suggests that attribution of responsibility is an additive function of prior expectancy (PE) of the outcome and the congruence (C) between outcome and action. More specifically, attribution of responsibility is hypothesized to be (1) inversely related to the subjective probability that the outcome would have occurred given prior conditions or the natural course of events in the absence of the perpetrator's intervention, and (2) directly related to the subjective probability that the outcome could have been expected to occur given the action perpetrated by the actor.

The composite judgment of attributed responsibility (AR) is defined by Brewer as

$$AR = C - PE$$

Brewer (1977) does not regard the precise form of the combination rule to be critical, as "a multiplicative model of the form $AR = C/PE$ may prove to be more appropriate than our additive model" (p. 59). She recognizes that in this case her information-processing analysis is analogous to the Bayesian model developed by Ajzen and Fishbein but points out that the analogy is not perfect because her model deals with the relative contribution of a known cause to a known outcome, and not with estimating the probability of an unknown cause.

In addition, Brewer argues that the "developmental" levels of responsibility suggested by Heider (1958) can be viewed as variations in the congruence component; that is, the subjective probability of the outcome given the act should increase from commission, through foreseeability to intentionality (M. E. Shaw & Sulzer, 1964). Similar interpretations are given for outcome severity and role similarity. For instance, it is argued that severe outcomes, almost by definition, have a low probability of occurring. Hence, the marginal impact of specific actions is potentially quite large, which would account for increased attributions of responsibility in such cases. In contrast, it may be that a severe consequence is seen as less congruent with the act, which should have a negative effect on the attribution of responsibility.

Brewer's (1977) work is important not only with regard to her conceptual analysis but also because she claims to have tested the predictive validity of the model with data obtained by Brickman, Ryan, and Wortman (1975). In this study responsibility ratings were obtained for 24 insurance reports of automobile accidents, which varied according to the nature of the immediate cause (internal or external to the actor) and the presence and nature of prior causes (again either internal or external). Subjective probabilities that the accident would have occurred given that each cause was either true (C) or false (PE) were also obtained. Brewer found that in four cases where there was at least one internal cause present, the model predicted responsibility ratings fairly well $(r = .78)$. Similarly, where only an external cause was present prior expectations appeared to correlate negatively ($r = -.70$) with attribution of responsibility, as predicted. Strictly speaking these results do not prove that subjects actually base their ratings of responsibility on the subjective probabilities, since both these judgments and the responsibility ratings comprised dependent variables in the experiment. In fact, the probability judgments were made after the responsibility ratings. Even so, a reanalysis of these data shows that the model is less successful in cases where *both* internal and external causes are present. Although the value of $C - PE$ is virtually the same for situations with only one internal cause and cases in which there is both a prior internal and an immediate external cause, responsibility attribution is considerably higher in the first case. Moreover, in the case with a prior external and an immediate internal cause, responsibility attribution is only marginally higher than when only one external cause is present. Unfortunately, in the reports by Brickman *et al.* (1975) and Brewer (1977) it is not clear what the relationship is between internal and external causes in these instances. The description of some examples gives the impression that in the case of a prior internal cause and an immediate external cause, the external cause is itself the result of the preceding act by the perpetrator (e.g., the car in front swerved [immediate external cause], because the insured blinded the driver with his bright lights [prior internal cause]). In the case of a prior external cause (e.g., the presence of thick fog) and an immediate internal cause (the insured was driving only 10 feet behind the other car), the external prior condition may have brought about the internal cause.[10] One can represent the six conditions studied by Brewer by simple directed graphs as in Table II.

As can be seen in Table II, the most important factor which seems to determine attribution of responsibility is whether the origin of the outcome (the ultimate cause, UC) is an act of the person concerned or an external situational influence. In addition, the presence or absence or an intermediate cause (IC) and the nature of that cause (internal, external), when present, appear to explain any additional variance in mean ratings of responsibility attribution. A linear model which combines the information about the six conditions in this way (see Table II) predicts the mean ratings of responsibility almost perfectly ($R = .98$). The multiple regression equation indicates that the nature of the ultimate cause is by far the most important determinant of attribution of responsibility in this particular study ($R = .94 \ UC + .30 \ IC$).[11]

This result is of course no great achievement since the weights are determined post hoc. However, one can see from Table II that it is not difficult to

---

[10]These are of course not the only two ways in which internal and external causes may be related, as is evident from our discussion of Hart and Honoré's work.

[11]A differentially weighted additive model (Anderson, 1978) predicts the responsibility ratings with even greater accuracy ($R = .99$).

TABLE II

Attribution of Responsibility as a Function of Ultimate and Intermediate Causes[a]

Condition	1	2	3	4	5	6
Type of Cause[b]	I_u/I_i	I_u	I_u/E_i	E_u/I_i	E_u	E_u/E_i
Structural representation	$I_u \downarrow I_i \downarrow O$	$I_u \downarrow O$	$I_u \to E_i \downarrow O$	$I_i \leftarrow E_u \downarrow O$	$E_u \downarrow O$	$E_u \downarrow E_i \downarrow O$
Responsibility rating	5.54	5.42	4.46	2.71	2.33	1.29

[a] After Brewer (1977).

[b] I_u, E_u is ultimate internal/external cause; I_i, E_i is intermediate internal/external cause; and O is outcome. The design matrix for the ultimate/intermediate cause model would be:

	1	2	3	4	5	6
Ultimate cause, I or E	1	1	1	-1	-1	-1
Intermediate cause, I or E	1	0	-1	1	0	-1

where 1 indicates the presence of an internal cause and -1 the presence of an external cause. Absence of an internal cause is indicated by 0.

assign weights a priori depending upon the nature of the cause (internal–external) and the position of the cause in the chain of events (ultimate–intermediate). If we suppose that the weight of an intermediate cause depends upon its distance from the outcome in relation to the length of the chain from ultimate cause to outcome, we obtain an almost equally good prediction of attributed responsibility.

All this does not imply that Brewer's probability model of responsibility attribution has no heuristic value. The point is that her results do not show convincingly that attribution of responsibility is based upon subjective probability estimates. A model which takes into account the interrelationship of internal and external causes without invoking the notion of subjective probabilities gives at least equally good predictions. As pointed out in the previous section, the Hart and Honoré analysis of causation in common sense and the law suggests that the relationship between internal and external causes is of vital importance for understanding the attribution of responsibility, a suggestion which receives further support in Section IV.

3. Information Integration and the Attribution of Responsibility

A final nonprobabilistic but quantitative model of attribution processes to be considered is Anderson's information integration model (Anderson, 1974, 1978). Anderson's theory of information integration has been applied to a great variety of problems, but only a few of these are important for the analysis of responsibility attributions.

In applying information integration theory to attributions, Anderson makes a distinction between forward and inverse inferences. In the first case information is given about causal forces and the problem is to infer something about the consequences. For an inverse inference, in contrast, information is given about the consequence and the problem is to infer something about one of the causal forces. According to Anderson, these inverse causal inferences are important in making causal attributions. The further application of information integration theory to attribution of responsibility leads to a rather ad hoc additive model for the assignment of blame. Anderson's treatment of responsibility attribution typifies the confusion that has arisen in the literature, since he uses the term responsibility in at least three different ways in one paragraph (Anderson, 1978, p. 109). As an "obvious" informational model of responsibility judgment he presents the following:

$$\text{Blame} = \text{intent} + \text{consequence} - \text{extenuation} - \text{personal goodness}$$

This gives an eclectic summary of the literature but can hardly be called a substantial theory. Published data are interpreted in the light of this blame model. For example, similarity between perceiver and actor in defensive attribution studies is interpreted as personal goodness and hence less blame is assigned. Severity of outcome is related to the consequence term in the model and blame is therefore increased unless the consequences are beyond the control of the actor ("act of God"), in which case a zero weight is given to the consequence term. Anderson suggests that similar informational analyses may account for Lerner's (1971) "just world" hypothesis and a study by Nelson (1975) is cited as evidence that attribution of responsibility for a harmful act is an additive function of the actor's intent and the consequences of the action.

Obviously, Anderson's information integration approach does not take us very far. All this approach appears to tell us is that we can describe ratings of blame, responsibility, and causality as additive functions of whatever information we want to give a person. There is no attempt to specify in advance which information is relevant in the case of responsibility attribution, nor is the concept of responsibility clearly defined. In this respect some of the recent attempts to formulate alternative theories of responsibility attribution have provided us with several interesting and conceptually much more sophisticated analyses. However, for the determination of scale values and weights of conceptually sound variables in a theory of responsibility attribution, Anderson's work, conjoint measurement, or a path-analytical approach may be quite useful.

B. ALTERNATIVE "THEORIES" FOR ASSIGNING RESPONSIBILITY

1. Roles and Responsibility

In contrast to quantitative models of responsibility attribution which deal mainly with Heider's levels and defensive attribution, Hamilton (1978) has sought to broaden the framework for understanding responsibility judgments and to provide a more adequately social psychological approach. According to Hamilton, responsibility refers to liability for sanctions based on a rule. Attribution of responsibility is therefore, in Hamilton's view, a function of that rule, the actor's deeds and the expectations of others regarding what the actor should do. The expectations are defined by the actor's social role, and Hamilton therefore argues for the inclusion of roles in an understanding of responsibility judgments.

Hamilton, as mentioned in Section II, also notes the similarity between Heider's levels of responsibility and various legal categories. There is, however, an important difference between the legal rules for attributing responsibility and commonsense notions in this respect. Heider hypothesizes that responsibility attribution will increase from levels 1 to 4 and decrease at level 5. According to legal rules, however, one can be held fully responsible, as Hamilton correctly points out, at each Heiderian level. The difference is that not everyone can be held responsible according to each rule. For instance, only people occupying certain social positions can be held responsible at the level of association, whereas every adult can be held responsible at the level of intentionality. In this view Hart's notion of role responsibility becomes more important. Hamilton also argues that roles cannot simply be treated as external forces determining action, because in-role behavior is normative, which means that roles are generally more binding than customs but less compelling than acting under duress. Such role-related normative forces or oughts are, according to Hamilton, more difficult to classify as either internal or external because they are in fact both, that is, internal manifestations of an external social order.

In general, Hamilton suggests that authorities are held to more stringent standards of accountability, because of a liability for relatively diffuse obligations to act, to exercise foresight and to oversee others. She goes on to analyze in some detail the normative conflict which may arise over wrongdoing committed by subordinates under orders. In such a case attributors can focus on either the actor's causation of the blameworthy consequences or the actor's motive for obedience. In the first case, attribution of responsibility will probably be higher than in the second. Moreover, it is suggested that the perceiver's own position in

the social structure will influence the judgments made. Lower status is characterized by emphasizing the subordinate's duty or a motive grammar orientation,
whereas in higher status a consequence grammar stressing the actor's causation is
more likely to occur.

Hamilton's conceptual analysis appears to be a valuable extension and elaboration of Hart's notion of role responsibility. It remains to be seen, however, to
what extent role responsibility requires a treatment different from the attribution
of responsibility under conditions as described at levels 1, 2, and 3 of Heider's
theory. Hamilton is probably right in pointing out that the effect of roles in the
attribution of responsibility is different from the effect of other situational forces.
However, it seems that there are at least two quite different processes involved
following from an individual's position in a social structure. These are implicitly
reflected in Heider's views of responsibility attribution and various legal notions
of responsibility. Simply stated, the question concerns whether we are considering to whom or for whom one is responsible. The authority, institution or person
to whom one is responsible can act as an external force, and thereby absolve us to
some extent of the responsibility, depending upon the nature of the relationship.
This is one use of role responsibility made by Hamilton. The actor, or act,
occupies an intermediate position between the authority and the actor or outcome
of the action. In the second case, however, the position of the actor is quite
different. Here we are concerned with reasons, with role responsibility as defined
by Hart in terms of duties to provide for the welfare of others. It is "the others"
who now occupy the intermediate position between the actor and the act or outcome. It is here that we find cases of vicarious responsibility, strict liability, and
negligence. The "actor" has in a sense now become the situational force that
indirectly causes an event, provides the opportunity, or constitutes the reason for
someone else causing the event. Although in general he will be held responsible
for such events, it seems reasonable to assume that he will be seen as less
responsible in such cases than in those where he is the direct cause of the event.
Such situations as these in fact constitute the core of Hart and Honoré's elaborate
discussion of causation and responsibility in the law. Almost every single case
mentioned by them can be interpreted as a social psychological hypothesis about
everyday responsibility attribution.

2. Causes and Reasons

Recent discussions in causal attribution theory (Buss, 1978; Calder, 1977;
Fischhoff, 1976; Kruglanski, 1975; Zuckerman, 1977a, 1977b) have begun to
question the way in which attribution theory represents the explanations people
offer for their own and others' behavior. To a large extent the work by Hart and
Honoré foreshadows these discussions. One may still argue, however, that some
very old philosophical notions in the philosophy of science, recently reemerged
in a new guise as applied to social psychology (e.g., Harré & Secord, 1973), are

beginning to have an impact on attribution theory. In a way, this is not very surprising. It would seem unlikely that commonsense explanations of behavior should completely follow a causal analysis in the tradition of Hume and Mill, as suggested by Kelley's covariation model. Indeed, the analysis of variance interpretation of Heider's original naive analysis of action has to some extent perverted the original notions of commonsense explanations as put forward by Heider. Instead of suggesting that the ordinary citizen could be seen as an amateur scientist in the Humean tradition, Heider emphasized that commonsense explanations were interesting in their own right and might further our understanding of social behavior in everyday life. Heider therefore devoted a great deal of attention to the difference between personal and impersonal causality (intentionality), a distinction that does not fit into a Humean analysis of causal inferences.

Heider's original questions about phenomenal causality, moreover, have little to do with causal analysis in the scientific sense, but much more with unit formation in the tradition of Gestalt psychology (Heider, 1944). Cause and effect, actor and act, act and outcome are seen as special instances of Gestalt-like units. For example, Buss's (1978) discussion of causes and reasons appears to reinstate in the psychology of commonsense explanations some of the original notions put forward by Heider. It is to some extent unfortunate that Buss has chosen the term "reason" to make a distinction between what Heider has called impersonal and personal causality or cause and intention. The word "reason" has obviously a much wider meaning in everyday use than is suggested by Buss (see the Oxford English Dictionary) and is used in general to justify one's actions. One can justify, and to some extent explain, one's actions by referring to "that for which change is brought about" (e.g., goals, purposes, *causa finalis*) but that is not the usual way in which the term is used, as is evident from the Hart and Honoré (1959) discussion. In their use, the term "reason" refers primarily to interpersonal transactions in which one person induces or persuades another to act in a particular way. A "reason" explanation in the Hart and Honoré approach would therefore refer to the interpersonal relation and not necessarily to the intention of the actor or the purpose of the act.

If, as suggested, Buss is primarily referring to the distinction between intentional and unintentional behavior, it is odd that he claims that Heider did not make a distinction between causes and reasons (Buss, 1978, p. 1313), and we must assume that he has simply overlooked Heider's analysis of personal and impersonal causality. Whatever the case may be, the emphasis which Buss has placed upon this distinction may serve a useful purpose, not just because it helps us to understand the actor–observer difference in attribution theory but also because it probably has important implications for the attribution of responsibility. Both legal notions of responsibility and Heider's theory suggest that perceived intentionality is an important determinant in responsibility attribution. It seems that we have not paid sufficient attention to the difference between causes and intentions in drawing the distinction between internal and external attributions. External attributions that refer to interpersonal transactions in which reasons or opportunities are involved do not affect the perceived intentionality of an act in the same way external causal attributions do. The same is true for internal attributions, which may refer to either a person's intentions and goals, or his ability, lack of understanding, or even age. In line with this distinction, it seems reasonable to predict that attribution of responsibility is not so much a function of internal or external attribution as it is of the extent to which the actor's personal causality is affected by external or internal factors. In addition to this distinction within internal and external explanations, it may be useful to pay attention to a somewhat nebulous partition that has been proposed by Kruglanski, the distinction between endogenous and exogenous attributions (Calder, 1977; Kruglanski, 1975; Zuckerman, 1977a, 1977b). The best interpretation of this distinction appears to be offered by Zuckerman (1977a, p. 610) who points out that Kruglanski's model actually constitutes a theory of cognitive motivation, distinguishing between intentional acts that are intrinsically motivated (an end in themselves) and those that are merely instrumental (means to attain some further end). It seems reasonable to assume that an intentional endogenous act is the most personal act an individual can perform and therefore can increase attributed responsibility, whereas an exogenous act can in principle find justification in the value of the external end toward which it is directed.

In summary, it appears that ideas which are partly compatible with those already advanced in legal philosophy and some aspects of legal thinking have begun to emerge in psychological writings. It is too early to tell whether a probabilistic model of perceived relations between act, situation, and outcome will provide us with a comprehensive framework for the analysis of responsibility attribution. Studies conducted thus far (Brewer, 1977; Brickman *et al.*, 1975; Fincham, 1980d) suggest that the relation between internal and external causes (person or act and situation) is of great importance. In addition, it seems important to consider this relationship with regard to the positions people occupy in a social structure, as Hamilton has argued.

Finally, Buss's distinction between causes and reasons emphasizes the different conceptions of causality to be considered in studying responsibility attribution. When attributing responsibility it seems necessary to distinguish between impersonal, personal, and interpersonal causality. In the next section we shall report research relating to some of the issues discussed thus far.

IV. Some Unanswered Questions and Partial Solutions

Despite the voluminous and increasing literature purporting to deal with attribution of responsibility, empirical research on this topic appears deficient in several respects. First, and possibly most important, some basic questions posed by Heider's model have been neglected, while others are only inadequately researched. Second, the recent quantitative and conceptual developments outlined in the preceding section have not been empirically evaluated. Third, with the exception of Hamilton's work relatively little attention has been given to the distinctions or criteria commonly used to assess responsibility in social institutions, such as the law. It has been argued that, insofar as these criteria are often held to reflect common sense, they need to be evaluated in constructing a psychological theory of responsibility attribution.

Partial solutions to questions arising in each of these areas are presented on the basis of our current research. Lest the suggestion be otherwise, it must be stated explicitly that these studies address issues that are highly selective rather than representative or exhaustive. Nevertheless, they do serve to illustrate many of the points made thus far and emphasize the contribution of legal philosophy to psychological research on attribution of responsibility. Finally, it should be noted that the studies are exploratory investigations in a continuing research program.

A. HEIDER'S LEVELS

In view of its dominant place in the responsibility attribution literature, unanswered questions regarding Heider's model will be dealt with in some detail before other issues are addressed.

1. The Cumulative Nature of Heider's Model

Perhaps the most basic, yet neglected, issue arising from Heider's work is whether his criteria represent response levels according to which environment attributions become more likely with increasing level. More specifically, the implicit assumption that attribution of responsibility is cumulative, as higher levels imply lower levels of attribution (e.g., perceived intention implies perceived foreseeability, causality, etc.), has not been directly evaluated. Instead, differences in judgments, perhaps because they are usually age related, are tacitly accepted as reflecting differences in response level.

The preceding omission is all the more surprising as the data necessary for testing such an assumption are available in several studies using Heider's levels (e.g., M. E. Shaw & Reitan, 1969; M. E. Shaw & Sulzer, 1964). This oversight may be partly because Heider's criteria have been more explicitly used to define stimulus levels, or behavior contexts. Therefore, the protagonist himself may be related to the outcome in various ways (e.g., mere association, intention, etc.). By reversing Heider's last two criteria (intentionality and justification), his levels can be used to portray an action–outcome which becomes increasingly attributable to internal (personal) factors with each level. As Fishbein and Ajzen (1973,

1975) point out, when the criteria are seen as defining both response and stimulus levels, the two dimensions in combination generate a classification scheme representing the pattern of a perfect Guttman scale.

To test the scalability of Heider's levels (even if only at a probabilistic level) and the allied question as to whether any response levels found represent developmental stages, stories representing Heider's levels were administered to 240 persons from five age groups (see Fincham & Jaspars, 1979). Subjects were asked to respond in terms of perceived cause and blame on seven-point pictorial scales. As expected, a highly significant effect was found when each dependent measure was entered as a separate factor in the analysis, showing that the response patterns for perceived cause and blame did indeed differ. Using a fairly stringent criterion (a single cutoff point determined by the presence/absence of perceived cause/blame) this difference also emerged in testing the cumulative nature of the levels. A Guttman scale was found for perceived blame, but not for perceived cause. As might be expected, 81% of subjects attributed causality by level 2. In contrast, 87% of the sample constituted pure scale types for perceived blame. Most respondents based their absolute ascription of blame on intentional (even where the act might be justified) and foreseeable actor-produced accidents. This directly parallels the *mens rea* and objective "reasonable man" tests used in criminal and civil law, respectively. The criterion of justification (Heider's last level), however, did serve to mitigate or reduce judgments of blame in comparison with a similar act committed without justification, even though it did not (except in 19 cases) constitute an excusing condition.

Turning to the related question of developmental stages, analysis of the age by scale type distribution revealed no clear age-related pattern, except that a greater proportion of adults than of any other age group used the aforementioned criteria of foreseeability and justification, while some younger children, unlike adults, made no distinctions between the levels. It therefore appears that Heider's model does represent a single cumulative dimension at least with regard to perceived blame, although the use of this structure was not found to be clearly age related. However, if Heider's levels do not represent developmental stages, it seems reasonable to ask whether they are at all relevant to development.

2.   The Developmental Status of Heider's Model

Most investigations of Heider's levels have analyzed age differences in terms of quantitative group scores, rather than individual response patterns. Considered in these terms there has generally been some support for a developmental interpretation of Heider's levels (e.g., Lipton & Garza, 1977; M. E. Shaw & Sulzer, 1964). However, as pointed out previously (Section I, C) several relevant developmental data pose interpretational difficulties owing to methodological inadequacies and the presence of irrelevant age-related performance variables. In addition, the exact nature of any developmental differences often has to be inferred in the absence of explicit tests between age groups or between levels within age groups (e.g., M. E. Shaw & Sulzer, 1964). Consequently, only more recent studies that have attempted to meet these problems are reported here in any detail.

The importance of operationalizing Heider's criteria appropriately is illustrated in two developmental studies using subjects of similar age. Harris (1977) responded to the earlier mentioned methodological criticisms by varying Heider's levels in the context of a single behavioral situation. Hence, his videotape recordings showed a young girl walking into a room and either accidentally damaging a chair by sitting on it (levels 1–3), or intentionally kicking (breaking) it (levels 4–5). Consistent with previous research results, an age $\times$ levels interaction was found. Closer examination, however, revealed that none of the five age groups used distinguished between Heider's first three levels, despite a successful manipulation check of these criteria, and that only older subjects differed in their responses to any adjacent level pair.

In contrast, all age groups distinguished at least one adjacent level pair in the previously mentioned study by Fincham and Jaspars (1979), which presented several rather more natural and familiar behavioral contexts. Moreover, each group distinguished between all the levels in the manner predicted by Heider, the age $\times$ levels interaction resulting from a relatively greater differentiation with increasing age. Unlike Harris' (1977) data, these results held not only for perceived blame, but also for perceived causality where even 6-year-olds made the adult distinction between the first two levels. These findings did not appear to be purely fortuitous, for a similar use of Heider's criteria was again found when the study was partially replicated on an independent sample of 6-year-olds (Fincham, 1980a). Keasey (1977) also cites unpublished data which similarly suggest there is little increase in the use of Heider's criteria in 6-, 8-, and 10-year-olds, precisely because they are already used by the youngest age group.

Further corroborating evidence, but of a rather different sort, comes from an interesting study by Sedlak (1979). In a multidimensional scaling analysis she showed that 8-year-olds, 11-year-olds, and adults utilize Heider's critiera in their cognitive representation of stimulus stories. However, the salience (relative weight) of this dimension in predicting moral judgments did increase with age. Although this result requires replication in view of the extremely small sample used, and the fact that the structure found depends heavily on the precise questions asked in presenting the stimuli, it also supports the view that age differences are merely quantitative.

Research to date therefore suggests that a developmental interpretation of Heider's model is not as appropriate as was initially thought. Developmental differences seem to arise, not so much because different age groups use different criteria, but because they use the criteria to differing degrees. However, this should be seen as a tentative rather than a final conclusion in view of the restricted lower age limit used thus far. No attempt has been made to investigate children younger than 6 years, possibly because of the severe methodological difficulties this would pose. If the levels are indeed learned with age, however, an alternative may be to investigate their use in groups with limited or deprived learning experiences. One such study (Fincham, 1980c) showed that culturally deprived 6- and 8-year-olds only used the basic principles of association and causality (levels 1 and 2) in assigning blame, suggesting that the levels may indeed be learned in the order implied by Heider. Such results emphasize the need for research with preschool subjects. In the absence of such investigations, the precise developmental status of Heider's model will remain unclear.

3. The Generality of the Model

In addition to age, several other variables have been investigated in studies using Heider's levels. In most instances these have been included because of their expected interaction with age and hence implications for a developmental interpretation of Heider's levels. Consequently outcome intensity, story protagonist, respondent's ethnic group, outcome valence, and judgments of self versus other have been manipulated (e.g., Fincham, 1980a, 1980c, 1980d; Fincham & Jaspars, 1979; Lipton & Gaza, 1977; Sedlak, 1979; M. E. Shaw & Iwawaki, 1972; M. E. Shaw & Schneider, 1969a, 1969b; M. E. Shaw & Sulzer, 1964). These have to some extent served as a partial test of the model's generality, although, as is readily apparent, the above set of variables is rather limited. Despite some complex interactions, none has seriously challenged the validity of Heider's model. To the extent that these variables may indicate specific limitations, they are reviewed before additional factors which question the model's generality are considered.

a. Outcome Valence. In his earlier work, Heider (1944) clearly considers responsibility attribution in terms of crime and similar negative outcome events. Even though his levels are described primarily in these terms, he does provide a brief positive outcome example in relation to his first criterion of global association. It therefore appears that the model is intended as a general one, although it is by no means clear that Heider considered outcome valence in its construction. However, when considering positive behaviors the incompleteness of the model becomes apparent. The mere existence of special accolades, medals, etc., and the word "supererogation" suggests an intentional act may not define the upper limit of responsibility attribution, at least insofar as it may involve inherently an evaluative component. Indeed, going beyond one's duty or acting against an inhibitory environmental force is implied by the model. While a facilitative cause is held to diminish responsibility, presumably via discounting (the level of justification), no mention is made of a converse negative or inhibitory environmental force. Theoretically, the presence of an inhibitory cause should, in accordance with the complementary augmentation principle (Kelley, 1971a), increase responsibility. Conceptualized in Jones and Davis' (1965) terms it may be argued that the intentional production of a negative outcome is "out of role" behavior and hence completely diagnostic, eliciting maximum responsibility. For positive actions, however, it is "in role," so to speak, and only becomes attributionally unambiguous when it goes beyond one's role or duty. Both Sedlak's (1979) and M. E. Shaw and Sulzer's (1964) inability to show that adults distinguish between justification and intentionality (levels 4 and 5) with regard to positive outcomes supports this view.

Investigation of this effect (Fincham, 1978; Fincham & Jaspars, 1979) has yielded largely negative results. However, when a forced-choice technique, rather than responsibility ratings, was used, subjects chose a supererogatory act as more praiseworthy than an unsolicited intentional one. No effect was found for attributed responsibility or negative outcome cases. The difficulty encountered in establishing an augmentation effect is consistent with the finding by Kruglanski, Schwartz, Maides, and Hamel (1978) that discounting and augmentation may influence different aspects of the attribution process, as the former yields inferences concerning the validity of any among several causes, whereas the latter deals with the magnitude of what could be accepted as a plausible cause. In any event the consideration of outcome valence does suggest this extension of Heider's levels.

It also points, paradoxically, to a possible contraction of the existing model, as there is evidence to suggest that the criteria are not used as much in judging positive events (e.g., M. E. Shaw & Sulzer, 1964). There have been no specific attempts to investigate this issue; hence, controls regarding outcome valence are less than satisfactory. However, the prominent role accorded to punishment in Piaget's (1932) theory of moral judgment development suggests that there may be good grounds for suspecting that concepts used in judging positive behaviors are less differentiated than their negative counterparts. Indeed there is developmental evidence to support this view (cf. Fincham, 1979; Karniol, 1978), although it remains to be adequately tested in relation to both adults and Heider's levels.

Apart from the aforementioned possibilities, the data obtained to date support the generality of Heider's model. These results are perhaps hardly surprising as most of the research does not investigate the model itself but rather uses it as a tool in exploring other issues, such as development (e.g., M. E. Shaw & Sulzer, 1964), self/other attributions (e.g., Fincham & Jaspars, 1979), the relationship between responsibility attribution and punishment (e.g., M. E. Shaw & Reitan, 1969), cultural differences (e.g., Lipton & Garza, 1977), and the role of empathy in attributing responsibility (e.g., Sulzer & Burglass, 1968). Unfortunately, with the exception of developmental research, most of the studies represent isolated pockets of information. Instead of being united by a common concern in evaluating Heider's levels, they tend merely to accept the model and instead try to establish a relationship between responsibility attribution and the variable of interest. It is therefore necessary, in exploring the generality of the model as a conceptual tool, to consider some legal distinctions made in analyzing the notion of responsibility. It should be noted in turning to legal writings, that the law deals exclusively with negative sanctions and does not prescribe positive behaviors. Although the distinctions made may be important in judging negative behavior, therefore, it does not necessarily follow that they are useful, or indeed relevant, for positive evaluations.

b. Omissions. Perhaps the most obvious problem with Heider's model is that it is constructed (and has been tested exclusively) in relation to commissive acts only. Yet the law, as previously indicated, often deals with harm resulting from omissions. It is in considering such cases that the limitations of Heider's analysis are most apparent. However, such an assertion presupposes that the omission/commission distinction is in fact relevant to responsibility attribution. Two experiments have investigated this issue.

In the first experiment, stories were constructed in which a protagonist either failed to observe a safety precaution (e.g., install lifebuoys on his boat) or actually removed safety equipment to defray expenses. The omission/act resulted in an accident (e.g., the death of a passenger, who drowned), which was either high or low in foreseeability (Heider's levels 2 and 3). Under these conditions no effect was found in relation to the nature of the action, although foreseeability was, once again, found to be important in determining responsibility. In contrast, the second experiment showed that a protagonist who placed an object in another's path was seen as far more responsible and blameworthy for the damage caused by the person tripping over the object than when he failed to remove, or even warn the other of, an existing object lying in his path.

These results suggest that the nature of the duty in relation to which the omission takes place may be important. In the first experiment there is a strong obligation not to commit either the omission or the commission, whereas in the second any duty to remove the object is much weaker than the corresponding prohibition not to put it there in the first place. With the possible exception of the first level (association), which can be interpreted in terms of role or vicarious responsibilities (see Hamilton, 1978), Heider's model does not incorporate the notion of obligations or duties. Yet, as Hart and Honoré (1959) note, there can be no omission without a corresponding duty, and it is consideration of such cases that sensitizes one to the crucial element of duties to act, or not act, in determining responsibility.

Another important legal concept also arises most obviously in relation to acts of omission. For many omissions the act–outcome link is less direct than for commissions because the harm is dependent on something else in addition to the initial failure to act. Therefore, responsibility may at least be partly shared, or even negated, by intervening events or acts. Determining when the act–outcome link is in fact negated by the presence of what have been called "intervening" or "superseding" causes has constituted one of the more intractible problems in law. Moreover, there is some evidence that lay observers do consider such factors in assigning responsibility, yet the notion is alien to Heider's model, and indeed to the psychological literature (see Sections II and IV, D).

In sum, Heider's model appears to be general insofar as his criteria are used by respondents from differing cultures, for varying stimulus protagonists, outcome intensities, and so on. It is less clear whether the model is complete at the higher levels, applies equally to positive and negative behaviors, and is appropriate in relation to omissive acts, which by definition involve evaluation of corresponding duties. However, such accountability, or answerability, constitutes the primary sense of the word "responsibility." It is difficult to imagine how the notion of intervening cause, which seeks to delimit this answerability, can be incorporated in Heider's model. Consequently, it seems lacking as a general model of responsibility attribution. We do not suggest that it does not provide valuable insights, or that it should be neglected as a conceptual tool in social psychological research. Insofar as they go, Heider's criteria have consistently been found to affect responsibility attributions, although it is not at all clear what process underlies their operation.

B. SUBJECTIVE PROBABILITIES AND ATTRIBUTION OF RESPONSIBILITY

As shown in Section III, process models of Heider's responsibility attribution levels have been limited to one quantitative subjective probability approach. This may, in part, result from the prevalent view that Heider's levels represent qualitatively different rule sets each with its own qualitatively distinct criteria (cf. Fishbein & Ajzen, 1973, 1975; Vidmar & Crinklaw, 1974). As mentioned earlier, however, Brewer (1977) challenges this viewpoint in suggesting a quantitative information-processing model (cf. Section III,A,2) specifically for attribution of responsibility, and clearly outlines its implications for Heider's criteria. However, it was argued that the data Brewer presents do not necessarily support her model. More specifically, it was shown that a model incorporating the interrelationship between internal and external causes, accounted equally well for the variance in responsibility judgments.

By stressing the role of the act (internal) and situation (external) in producing the outcome, Brewer neglects the relationship between act and situation, thereby omitting an essential element in determining responsibility. This is apparent not only because of the reanalysis we have offered, but also from consideration of legal processes. For instance, in civil law the question is not simply whether the person produced the damage (except in cases of strict liability) but whether he acted negligently or recklessly in doing so—the reasonable man standard. Similarly, showing that the person was influenced by the contextual conditions surrounding his act (e.g., duress, provocation) can often serve as an excusing, or at least mitigating, condition in determining criminal responsibility. It would be surprising if the subjective probability of a reasonable man performing the act given the situation were not an important element in any subjective probability model of responsibility attribution. Such an estimate yields an index of the extent to which the act is validated by cultural norms and may serve to locate the perceived source of the act as either internal or external.

Notwithstanding the reservations expressed in relation to a probabilistic approach to attribution of responsibility (cf. Section III,A,1), several exploratory experiments were conducted in this area. In the first two, perceived cause, responsibility, and blame were regressed on Brewer's estimates and the probability (validation) suggested above. The first experiment presented stimuli representing an accident either high or low in foreseeability (levels 2 and 3), whereas the second used negative and positive outcome stories in which an intentional act was presented together with a facilitative, or inhibitory, cause and also where no cause was mentioned. For positive outcomes the subjective probabilities were not very successful in predicting attributions. In contrast, the regression equations computed for negative outcome events accounted for a significant proportion of the variance in the attribution ratings (Experiment 1, perceived cause, $R^2 = .16$; responsibility, $R^2 = .36$; blame, $R^2 = .50$; corresponding figures for intentional acts are .10, .51, and .43). Although Brewer equates responsibility with causality, this measure was predicted least well. It is therefore noteworthy that Brewer's (1977) evidence for her model is based on responses to a general question regarding responsibility and not causality. Moreover, the beta weights for prior expectancy (PE) in the first experiment and for congruence (C) in the second were not significant. Consequently it is not surprising that the joint probability indices (additive and multiplicative) were not particularly successful as predictors. When Brewer's components were appropriately weighed only one was necessary for predicting responsibility. In contrast, the hypothesized validation estimate was significantly related to perceived responsibility and blame, but not cause, in both experiments. However it accounted for very little variance in the positive outcome condition. Indeed, the subjective probabilities were not very useful in predicting responses to positive behaviors, suggesting that the process underlying responsibility attribution may differ according to outcome valence.

Two of the conditions in the second experiment represent Heider's last two levels (justification and intention), whereas causality versus foreseeability is varied in the first. It therefore seems that if any one dimension can model Heider's levels, it is validation rather than congruence. In any event, validation emerged as the single most important predictor, and hence an attempt was made to manipulate this variable by supplying directly information regarding the probability of the act described. It was earlier suggested that even if responsibility judgments could be modeled in subjective probability terms, it remained to be demonstrated whether observers actually utilized such information in making their judgments.

Despite problems in successfully manipulating this variable (respondents seemed to have fairly clear ideas about the probability of particular behaviors), some evidence was obtained to show that the more people who would have acted as the protagonist did, the less he is blamed for the outcome. This supports Kelley's (1971b) observation that moral evaluation derives partly from the reality attribution system so that what is, in fact, is also seen as what ought to be. More direct manipulation of these probabilities is currently being used to obtain further evidence on their causal status.

Although the preceding data are far from definitive, they point to an important gap in the research literature. Whether responsibility attributions ultimately turn out to be made on the basis of probabilistic estimates or not, a more precise structural model than Heider's has obvious advantages. It is quite likely that the inconsistent results obtained in responsibility attribution research reflect, at least in part, differences in the content of stimulus materials, which purportedly reflect the same underlying variables (e.g., Heider's levels). Indeed M. E. Shaw and Sulzer (1964) stressed the influence of story content on the basis of their "qualitative observations." Perhaps a more immediate task, presupposed in any event by a formal model of responsibility judgments and also serving to clarify the existing literature, is to determine the relationship between perceived cause, responsibility, blame, and punishment. Again, legal and commonsense concepts assist a great deal in analyzing this issue.

C. THE ENTAILMENT MODEL OF CAUSE, RESPONSIBILITY, BLAME, AND PUNISHMENT

In reviewing the social psychological research on responsibility attribution (Section I) it became clear that the related notions of cause, blame, punishment, compensation, sanction, etc., were frequently used interchangeably as dependent measures. Yet, as can be seen from the defensive attribution hypothesis, these concepts are also used in specific ways, manifesting intuitive but untested ideas about the relationships between them. Hence, the commonsense notion that judgments of causation partly determine those of responsibility, which in turn affect judgments of blame and punishment, implicitly informs much of this research. More specifically, causation, responsibility, blame, and punishment are normally conceived in such a manner that those mentioned earlier in the above sequence constitute either necessary or necessary and sufficient conditions for later ones.

The few studies explicitly investigating these relationships have been limited largely to exploring the link between responsibility and punishment. For instance, M. E. Shaw and Reitan (1969) note the confusion between punishment and responsibility in both Piaget's and Heider's work and argue that being held responsible constitutes the basis for sanctioning, which may, but need not necessarily, follow. Data from two experiments supported this view in that the mean difference between attributed responsibility and sanctions was in the hypothesized direction across all Heiderian levels for both outcomes of differing intensity and valence. Hamilton (1976) also develops this viewpoint in the legal context on the basis of two jury simulation studies which showed that judgments of responsibility and legal guilt were more closely related to each other than either was to punishment. She argues that assigning sanction for an offence only occurs after it has been appropriately labeled and responsibility determined. In a similar vein it has been found that a higher rating is invariably given for perceived cause than blame, suggesting that causation may constitute a necessary condition for blame (Fincham & Jaspars, 1979).

These relationships have been more extensively investigated under the influence of legal writings. For example, Hart and Honoré (1959) note that the previously mentioned relationships between cause, blame, and compensation in ordinary life judgments constitute the moral analogs of more precise legal conceptions (p. 59). More specifically, in all legal systems, responsibility, and hence liability to punishment, often depends on whether the act (omission) actually caused the harm. Consequently, Shultz *et al.* (1979), in specifying the earlier mentioned set of relationships between cause, blame, and punishment, have tested this "entailment model" suggested by both common sense and the jurisprudence literature. Computing the path coefficients between these three variables, they found that in four different experiments the path between cause and punishment was invariably weak (mean = .09) in relation to that between cause and blame (mean = .51) and blame and punishment (mean = .31). Although they interpret this as evidence for the above linear set of relations (which may be diagrammed $C \rightarrow B \rightarrow P$), these analyses are unsatisfactory for two reasons. First, the correlations between the measures used to compute the path coefficients may be affected by the experimental manipulations. Second, the strength of the path between cause and punishment is not directly tested to determine whether it is superfluous.

In a recent study, Fincham and Shultz (1980) attempted to meet both these difficulties by specifically testing the linear $(C \rightarrow B \rightarrow P)$ model against one which in addition specified a direct relation between judgments of causation and restitution. A similar set of analyses has also been conducted with regard to perceived cause, responsibility, and blame on the data obtained in investigating the subjective probability model discussed in Section IV, B. Although in both cases the indirect path connecting cause to compensation, and cause to blame, respectively, is not found to be necessary, these results are not completely diagnostic. Any set of path coefficients that supports the linear model also, by definition, supports two alternative models of possible theoretical interest. One of these (which can be diagrammed $P \rightarrow B \rightarrow C$) assumes that a judgment of punishment precedes assignment of either blame or causation. This is consistent with Fauconnet's views as quoted by Heider (Section I) and requires serious consideration. Indeed, Lloyd-Bostock (1979a) presented some evidence to suggest that this might indeed occur in industrial accidents involving compensation.

The other consistent model, diagrammed as

assumes that an initial judgment of blame comes to determine those of causation and punishment. This latter model clashes with the intuitive notion that blame can only be attributed to someone who has caused harm. Nonetheless, it may be premature to rule out this model without further investigation. It is possible, for example, that an implicit judgment of blame precedes or accompanies any judgment regarding the causation of harm. In view of the analysis of responsibility offered earlier, this might be especially likely with respect to the relationship between cause, responsibility, and blame. It was suggested (cf. Section II) that the notion of answerability or accountability in commonsense concepts of responsibility does not entail causation. However, because judgments of responsibility also often assert that the person held responsible did or caused the harm, being held responsible in the answerability sense may be used to determine whether the person can be said to have caused the harm. To the extent that this is not the case, and responsibility is determined according to liability specified by rules, the perception of causality in any event carries no implications for such judgments.

Clearly the relationships between the related notions of cause, responsibility, blame, and punishment may be far more complex than considered to date. Although some support has been obtained for the simple linear model implicit in much of the research, the legal use of such terms suggests alternative relations, which require testing. In this respect an interesting question is to determine whether in a clear-cut case of role or vicarious responsibility, where the protagonist does not in fact produce the outcome, he is seen by lay attributors as a cause of it. We now consider the converse question of when the causal role of someone who helps produce the outcome is negated.

D. INTERVENING CAUSES

The occurrence of an event, between a behavior and an outcome, which helps to produce the outcome, may pose severe problems in determining responsibility for the harm produced. In law, it is widely recognized that such intervening causes are crucial factors in limiting responsibility. Yet, as previously mentioned, they are largely neglected in psychological research. Insofar as two studies can be interpreted in terms of intervening cause, there is no evidence for its operation in ordinary persons' judgments (e.g., Brickman *et al.*, 1975; Shultz *et al.*, 1979). As neither study examines or provides any of the preconditions suggested by legal theorists for the effective use of intervening causation as a factor negating or mitigating responsibility, however, these findings are hardly surprising. For instance, Hart and Honoré (1959) suggest that if the initial act is causally sufficient to produce the harm, a feature which characterizes the stimuli used by Brickman *et al.*, the concept of intervening causation is unlikely to be used. Nor, they suggest, does it arise where there is a clear duty not to perform the initial act or omission, as in the case of the Shultz *et al.* (1979) study, where the person judged clearly failed to exercise an obvious role-related duty. Hart and Honoré (1959) also mention that the wrongness of the initial act is probably inversely related to the extent of mitigation via intervening causation. If these conditions are met it is quite possible that the presence of an intervening cause will affect responsibility attributions.

Consequently, an experiment was undertaken to clarify the conditions under which an ordinary observer will use the concept of intervening causation to mitigate judgments of causation, blame, and restitution. Two hypotheses suggested by the extensive legal literature on this topic were tested. One hypothesis was that an intervening cause will be used as a mitigating factor only insofar as its occurrence is not foreseeable (Prosser, 1955). The second stated that the intervening cause would constitute a mitigating factor only when it comprised a voluntary human action (Hart & Honoré, 1959). These hypotheses were assessed in a 2 × 2 design in which the intervening cause varied along the dimensions of foreseeability and voluntariness. In no case was the initial act particularly heinous, causally sufficient to produce the eventual harm, or in violation of a well-defined duty or role responsibility.

Comparison of each cell with a control condition in which no intervening cause occurred showed that judgments of cause, blame, and restitution were reduced when the intervening cause was either voluntary or unforeseeable. Moreover, each hypothesis was supported, as a main effect for both voluntariness and foreseeability was found. Lower ratings were given on all three dependent measures when the intervention was voluntary, as opposed to involuntary, and to a greater degree when the intervention was unforeseeable, as compared with foreseeable. It therefore does appear that ordinary observers do use the notion of intervening causation in making attributions, but only under certain specific conditions. The two investigated thus far, foreseeability and voluntariness, may only define a small subset of those appropriate for its use. Several possible others have been considered in legal writings on the subject, and it remains to determine whether they also affect lay perceivers' judgments. However, there does appear to be at least some direct evidence for suggesting that the omission of such notions in responsibility attribution research is likely to yield a truncated model of how responsibility is determined.

Starting from simple unanswered questions posed by early work on responsibility attribution, our attempt to clarify this process has led through more recent developments in social psychological writings, and ultimately beyond the psychological literature. Throughout, an attempt has been made to show how a reconsideration of the very concept of responsibility, motivated largely by common sense and legal writings, both illuminates previous research and leads to further experimentation. It is not suggested that merely because certain conceptual distinctions can be made, or indeed have been incorporated in law, they will necessarily prove integral to a psychological model of responsibility attribution. However, such an analysis may usefully serve to guide us in constructing an adequate model for future research in this area.

V. Some Suggestions for More Adequate Research

It would have been ideal if at this point we were able to formulate a coherent theory of responsibility attribution. In this respect, however, we must disappoint the reader and admit defeat (at least for the present). Our research, which started simply with an attempt to test the developmental and cumulative nature of Heider's model, has raised many more questions than we can currently answer. Tests of the generality of Heider's model with respect to outcome valence and omissions suggested that legal notions of responsibility attribution might provide us with a more adequate model for attribution processes. This possibility seemed especially promising because both in the law and in legal philosophy distinctions are made between cause, responsibility, and punishment, which, as dependent variables in our first studies, did not seem to be affected in the same way by Heider's levels. Subsequent research suggests that instead of such concepts being regarded as more or less identical, as had been done in previous accident research, an entailment or implicational model might offer a more plausible description of our results. However, the implication of causal attribution by the attribution of responsibility raises all kinds of questions about the commonsense notion of causality. It appeared that the concept of causality used in social psychological attribution theories was not able to answer many ''why'' questions in cases where legal responsibility is involved. In considering such cases, special problems emerged because the relationship between the actor or act and the outcome is often indirect. It is here especially that legal philosophy and the law suggest many relevant research questions for the study of responsibility attribution in everyday life. Obviously the inferred causal relation between ''something in the person" and his action remains an important issue, but an attempt to differentiate further both internal and external causes, as suggested in this contribution, should be a first step in future research. In combination with the study of less direct relationships between actor and outcome this represents a formidable research program, which should not only be of interest to social psychologists but, ultimately, perhaps also to the legal profession and to all of us who are affected by the law.

Although we have tried to present a more adequate conception of responsibility attribution than that used in the social psychological literature to date, it should not be inferred that the parameters influencing this process have been exhausted in the above analysis. Several factors, such as language and social context, have not even been mentioned. To omit them completely would seem to deny their importance, yet to dwell on them at any length is equally inappropriate in the present context because they are likely to affect most attribution processes, and not merely assignment of responsibility. For illustrative purposes two of these factors are considered briefly, their choice being motivated in part by their general neglect in attribution research.

A.   LANGUAGE AND RESPONSIBILITY ATTRIBUTION

Language is possibly the most important of these, and its potential impact on attributed responsibility should not be underestimated. Yet its effects "have not been studied with direct regard to responsibility attributions" (Ross & Di Tecco, 1975, p. 100) and indeed there is little research on the role of language in attribution processes (see Hewstone, 1980). This is rather surprising as Heider (1958, pp. 10–11) clearly recognizes that the naive psychology he sets out to examine is implicit in everyday language. For instance, at the level of word analysis he shows that related transitive verbs (as antonyms of "give") may imply very different sets of relations when considered in terms of the causal source of the action and its direction. In fact Heider sees as one of his primary tasks the construction of a system to represent such relations, an enterprise which shows ordinary language to be one of inference and not pure description. In using language as a tool to analyze common sense, therefore, Heider in effect emphasizes the intimate relationship between language and attribution. An illustration of this point vis-à-vis responsibility attribution is given by Eiser (1975). He notes that the seemingly simple descriptive statement "Nixon is a criminal" in fact "both attributes responsibility for certain actions to Nixon, and implies a negative evaluation of these actions" (p. 236). Although this is a rather crude example, the work of Kanouse (1971) shows just how subtle the influence of language can be.

Kanouse (1971) examined the implicit quantifications involved in making attributions and found that people were more likely to generalize across the sub-

ject of a sentence than across its object in making deductive inferences. However, the reverse was true for inductive inferences. In explaining this phenomenon, Kanouse (1971) points out that persons differ more as actors than as objects
of action and hence such assertions as "Artists detest businessmen" implicitly
"locate the cause primarily with the actor rather than the object" (p. 8). If
correct, this reasoning implies that the statement "Sue passed Professor Zabou's
course" would lead to different attributions from "Professor Zabou passed
Sue," even though they convey the same information (Ross & Di Tecco, 1975).

More directly relevant to the attribution of responsibility rather than causal
attributions is Kanouse's (1971) second major finding as it pertains to the question of intentionality. For example, he notes that given a specific act (e.g., "O
destroys *Readers' Digests*") subjects were more likely to infer intentionality
("Does O want to destroy magazines?") if they were induced to generalize the
original act to a larger object class ("Does O destroy magazines?") than if the act
itself was made intentional ("Does O want to destroy *Readers' Digest*?"). Kanouse
argues that such results reflect differences in the power of the inferences induced
by intermediate questions to explain the initial event. More specifically, it is held
that such general verbs as "destroying" contain more implicit intentionality than
specific action verbs, such as "tearing up," but not vice versa. Therefore, the
precise point at which an intention or explanatory inference is introduced in the
reasoning process has implications for the attributions made. On the basis of this
evidence Kanouse (1971) concludes that the level of generality at which an event
is explained tends to parallel the level at which it is described.

Although there is no direct evidence on language and attribution to substantiate the conclusions drawn on the basis of this microlevel psycholinguistic
analysis, related research shows similar results. For instance, Eiser (Eiser &
Pancer, 1979; Eiser & Ross, 1977) found that subjects who were asked to include
several evaluatively biased words in an otherwise freely written essay tended to
adopt an attitude consistent with the one implied by the words they had been
asked to incorporate. Even the mere presence of evaluatively biased language in
experimental instructions has been sufficient to alter expressed attitudes (Eiser &
Mower White, 1974; Eiser & Osmon, 1978). In a slightly different area, Loftus
(1974) has shown how the word used to refer to a visually presented car collision
affected both estimates of its speed and memory for the event. Subjects who
estimated the car's speed when it "smashed" (as compared with "collided,"
"hit," etc.) were more likely to say that they had seen broken glass (in fact none
was present) when questioned 1 week later.

The implications of such work for understanding attributions of responsibility are manifold. First, the common practice of presenting subjects with written
vignettes requires careful examination. The very fact that linguistic variables
have been overlooked suggests that previous research needs to be carefully
evaluated. To what extent do the results obtained to date represent artifacts of

subtle linguistic differences both between studies and between experimental conditions within a particular investigation? Alternatively, can the data be attributed to the nature of the experimental instruction or to the precise wording of the dependent variable? The indiscriminate use of such conceptually different notions as cause, blame, and punishment for responsibility does not augur well for an overtly linguistic evaluation of responsibility research. Second, it appears that there is no single veridical description of a particular action sequence, as any behavior or event can be described in many ways. Thus, any given verbal account of an event not only contains implicit attributional information as previously argued, but also selects and emphasizes which of the available cues will serve as a basis for inferring responsibility. Third, even where the stimulus material is not verbal, the linguistic structure of the subject's own thought processes concerning responsibility may affect his judgment of the relative contribution of the person and environment to the action–outcome. The relationship between personal and environmental forces constitutes the sine qua non of Heider's levels and its importance has been emphasized repeatedly in this contribution. How subjects cognitively represent stimulus material therefore needs to be directly examined and cannot be assumed a priori as is often done in accident research. An allied problem is to investigate what makes people describe and think about events in a particular way.

These observations do not exhaust all that may be important regarding language and attribution of responsibility. For instance, language may be considered more broadly to include speech variables, and how these may serve as social cues which influence responsibility attribution. Alternatively, one might examine the extent to which the attribution made might influence language usage. However, in the present context it is sufficient to note the close link between language and the attribution process and point out that any complete model of responsibility attribution must incorporate the role of language. However, language itself varies as a function of social context, which is also likely to affect responsibility judgments.

B.   SOCIAL CONTEXT AND ATTRIBUTION OF RESPONSIBILITY

Before we address the issue of social context and responsibility attribution, the expression "social context" needs to be considered briefly. The importance of "context" in making attributions has been explicitly recognized, albeit largely in relation to attribution biases, as has been seen in the research reviewed (see Section I). Situational possibility or relevance is hypothesized as a necessary condition for defensive attributions. In a similar vein, Kelley (1971a) suggests that when the consequences are minimal to the perceiver, only a sufficiently satisfactory attribution is made and not a detailed causal analysis. Ross and Di Tecco (1975) extend this argument, suggesting that "primitive attributions" are the result of a hasty or superficial attributional analysis whatever its source. More recently, the "social" aspects of attributions have also been recognized. In addition to Hamilton's (1978) work on roles, Hewstone and Jaspars (1980) have emphasized that individuals belong to social groups and, to the extent that they are perceived as group members, attributions may not be exclusively interpersonal but may reflect intergroup processes.

Both the contextual and social elements previously emphasized represent important insights with regard to the attribution process, but the logical extension of such work is to "socialize attributional context and contextualize the social nature of attributions." Simply stated, it seems that attributions are necessarily situated in a context, which is often social, while the social nature of the attribution is in turn likely to be context dependent.

The fact that attributions often take place in a social context emphasizes in addition that "attributions of responsibility" may not only be influenced by social factors but that such a judgment is itself a social act with certain consequences. For example, Lloyd-Bostock (1979a, 1979b) argues that the attribution of responsibility for accidents is influenced by the prospect of compensation. More specifically, responsibility is often attributed where there is the greatest likelihood of damages being paid. In fact whether any fault is perceived at all depends, she suggests, on the costs of blaming and prospects of compensation. It is such factors which are held to account for findings such as the low incidence of perceived fault for domestic (9%) as opposed to industrial (40%) or road (64%) accidents.

The extent to which context may influence the use of social (e.g., group membership) as opposed to purely personal (e.g., personality) information in attributing responsibility is equally apparent. For instance, Tajfel and Turner (1979) specifically point out that group membership is less likely to be salient under some conditions (e.g., longstanding friendships) than others (e.g., brief encounters). Even within these constraints, however, particular situations may alter attributions of responsibility. The exact purpose for which one is attributing responsibility, and to whom, may be relevant.

Awareness of the potential importance of social context in attributions questions again the status of most research findings. With few exceptions (e.g., Bulman & Wortman, 1977; Lloyd-Bostock, 1979a), the attributions studied to date are those made in the social context of the psychological experiment. Obviously this raises the usual problems of external validity, but it has also resulted in "attribution of responsibility" being studied as a cognitive process and not as itself a *social* act with all that this implies. Holding someone responsible therefore may depend on shared social representations which determine both the meaning of the behavior judged and the nature of the judgment.

In conclusion, it is suggested that such factors as language and social context are very likely to influence attributions of responsibility. This does not imply that responsibility attributions cannot be usefully investigated without examining these variables or that they are best studied in relation to them. Instead, they are seen as limiting conditions for any hypothesized model of responsibility attribution or as factors that are likely to qualify any account of this process. However, it must be reiterated that the analysis offered here is to be seen not as a general "model" but as an initial step toward a more complete understanding of responsibility attribution.

REFERENCES

Adkins, A. W. *Merit and responsibility: A study in Greek values* London and New York: Oxford University Press (Clarendon), 1960.
Ajzen, I., & Fishbein, M. A Bayesian analysis of attribution process. *Psychological Bulletin,* 1975, **82,** 261–277.
Ajzen, I., & Fishbein, M. Use and misuse of Bayes' theorem in causal attribution: Don't attribute it to Ajzen and Fishbein either. *Psychological Bulletin,* 1978, **85,** 244–246.
Anderson, N. H. Cognitive algebra: Integration theory applied to social attribution. In L. Berkowitz (Ed.), *Advances in experimental social psychology.* Vol. 7. New York: Academic Press, 1974.
Anderson, N. H. Progress in cognitive algebra. In L. Berkowitz (Ed.), *Cognitive theories in social psychology.* New York: Academic Press, 1978.
Arkellin, D., Oakley, T., & Mynatt, C. Effects of controllable versus uncontrollable factors on responsibility attributions. A single-subject approach. *Journal of Personality and Social Psychology,* 1979, **37,** 110–115.
Bradley, G. W. Self-serving biases in the attribution process: A re-examination of the fact or fiction question. *Journal of Personality and Social Psychology,* 1978, **36,** 56–71.
Brewer, M. B. An information-processing approach to attribution of responsibility. *Journal of Experimental Social Psychology,* 1977, **13,** 58–69.
Brickman, P., Ryan, K., & Wortman, C. B. Causal chains: Attribution of responsibility as a function of immediate and prior causes. *Journal of Personality and Social Psychology,* 1975, **32,** 1060–1067.
Bryant, P. B. *Perception and understanding in young children.* New York: Basic Books, 1974.
Bulman, R. J., & Wortman, C. B. Attributions of blame and coping in the "real world": Severe accident victims react to their lot. *Journal of Personality and Social Psychology,* 1977, **35,** 351–363.
Bunge, M. *Causality.* Cambridge, Mass: Harvard University Press, 1959.
Buss, A. R. Causes and reasons in attribution theory: A conceptual critique. *Journal of Personality and Social Psychology,* 1978, **36,** 1311–1321.
Calder, B. J. Endogenous–exogenous versus internal–external attributions: Implications for the development of attribution theory. *Personality and Social Psychology Bulletin,* 1977, **3,** 400–406.
Chaikin, A., & Darley, J. Victim or perpetrator: Defensive attribution of responsibility and the need for order and justice. *Journal of Personality and Social Psychology,* 1973, **25,** 268–275.
Curzon, C. *Criminal law.* (2nd ed.) Plymouth, Eng.: McDonald & Evans, 1977.
Dillehay, R. C., Woods, M., & Raymond, J. S. Moral evaluation of another's action. Paper presented at the meeting of the Southeastern Psychological Association, New Orleans, April 1973.
Eiser, J. R. Attitudes and the use of evaluative language: A two-way process. *Journal for the Theory of Social Behaviour,* 1975, **5,** 235–248.
Eiser, J. R., & Mower White, C. J. The persuasiveness of labels: Attitude change produced through definition of the attitude continuum. *European Journal of Social Psychology,* 1974, **4,** 89–92.

Eiser, J. R., & Osmon, B. E. Linguistic social influence: Attitude change produced by feedback concerning other's use of evaluative language. *European Journal of Social Psychology*, 1978, **8**, 125–128.

Eiser, J. R., & Pancer, S. M. Attitudinal effects of the use of evaluatively biased language. *European Journal of Social Psychology*, 1979, **9**, 39–47.

Eiser, J. R., & Ross, M. A. Partisan language, immediacy and attitude change. *European Journal of Social Psychology*, 1977, **7**, 477–489.

Fincham, F. D. "Oughts" and the augmentation principle. Unpublished manuscript, University of Oxford, 1978.

Fincham, F. D. Outcome valence and situational constraints in the evaluation of intentional acts. Paper presented at the conference of the British Psychological Society, London, December 1979.

Fincham, F. D. Perception and moral evaluation in young children. Manuscript submitted for publication, 1980. (a)

Fincham, F. D. Piagetian theory and the learning disabled: A critical analysis. In S. Modgil & C. Modgil (Eds.), *Piaget at the crossroads*. Slough, Eng.: NFER, 1980, in press. (b)

Fincham, F. D. Responsibility attribution in the culturally deprived. *Journal of Genetic Psychology*, 1980, in press. (c)

Fincham, F. D. A subjective probability approach to attribution of responsibility. Manuscript submitted for publication, 1980. (d)

Fincham, F. D., & Jaspars, J. M. Attribution of responsibility to self and other in children and adults. *Journal of Personality and Social Psychology*, 1979, **37**, 1589–1602.

Fincham, F. D., & Shultz, T. R. Intervening causation and the mitigation of responsibility for harm. *British Journal of Social and Clinical Psychology*, 1980, in press.

Fischhoff, B. Attribution theory and judgment under uncertainty. In S. Harvey, W. Ickes, & R. F. Kidd (Eds.), *New directions in attribution research*. Vol. 1. New York: Erlbaum, 1976.

Fischhoff, B., & Lichtenstein, S. Don't attribute this to Reverend Bayes. *Psychological Bulletin*, 1978, **85**, 239–242.

Fishbein, M., & Ajzen, I. Attribution of responsibility: A theoretical note. *Journal of Experimental Social Psychology*, 1973, **9**, 148–153.

Fishbein, M., & Ajzen, I. *Belief, attitude, intention, and behaviour: An introduction to theory and research*. Reading, Mass: Addison-Wesley, 1975.

Flavell, J. H. The development of inferences about others. In T. Mischel (Ed.), *Understanding other persons*. Oxford: Blackwell, 1974.

Geber, B. A. *Piaget and knowing*. London: Routledge & Kegan Paul, 1977.

Hamilton, V. L. Individual differences in ascriptions of responsibility, guilt, and appropriate punishment. In G. Berment, C. Nemeth, & N. Vidmar (Eds.), *Psychology and the law*. New York: Lexington Books, 1976.

Hamilton, V. L. Who is responsible? Toward a social psychology of responsibility attribution. *Social Psychology*, 1978, **41**, 316–328.

Harré, R. M., & Secord, P. F. *The explanation of social behaviour*. Oxford, Eng.: Blackwell, 1973.

Harris, B. Developmental differences in the attribution of responsibility. *Developmental Psychology*, 1977, **13**, 257–265.

Hart, H. L. A. *Punishment and responsibility*. London and New York: Oxford University Press (Clarendon), 1968.

Hart, H. L. A., & Honoré, A. M. *Causation in the law*. London and New York: Oxford University Press (Clarendon), 1959.

Harvey, M. D., & Rule, B. G. Moral evaluations and judgments of responsibility. *Personality and Social Psychology Bulletin*, 1978, **4**, 583–588.

Heider, F. Social perception and phenomenal causality. *Psychological Review*, 1944, **51**, 358–374.

Heider, F. *The psychology of interpersonal relations*. New York: Wiley, 1958.

Hewstone, M. Attribution processes and the social psychology of language. In J. M. Jaspars, F. D. Fincham, & M. Hewstone (Eds.), *Attribution theory and research*. Vol. 1. New York: Academic Press, 1980, in press.

Hewstone, M., & Jaspars, J. M. Intergroup relations and attribution processes. In H. Tajfel (Ed.), *Social identity, conflict and stereotypes*. London and New York: Cambridge University Press, 1980, in preparation.

Jones, E. E. A conversation with Edward E. Jones and Harold H. Kelley. In J. Harvey, W. Ickes, & R. F. Kidd (Eds.), *New directions in attribution research*. Vol. 2. New York: Erlbaum, 1978.

Jones, E. E., & Davis, K. E. From acts to dispositions, In L. Berkowitz (Ed.), *Advances in experimental social psychology*. Vol. 2. New York: Academic Press, 1965.

Jones, E. E., & McGillis, D. Correspondent inferences and the attribution cube: A comparative reappraisal. In J. Harvey, W. Ickes, & R. F. Kidd (Eds.), *New directions in attribution research*. Vol. 1. New York: Erlbaum, 1976.

Kanouse, D. E. *Language, labeling, and attribution*. Morristown, N.J.: General Learning Press, 1971.

Karniol, R. Children's use of intention cues in evaluating behavior. *Psychological Bulletin*, 1978, **85**, 76–85.

Keasey, C. B. Children's developing awareness and usage of intentionality and motives. In C. B. Keasey (Ed.), *Nebraska Symposium on Motivation*. Vol. 25. Lincoln: University of Nebraska Press, 1977.

Kelley, H. H. Attribution theory in social psychology. In D. Levine (Ed.), *Nebraska Symposium on Motivation*. Vol. 15. Lincoln: University of Nebraska Press, 1967.

Kelley, H. H. *Attribution in social interaction*. Morristown, N.J.: General Learning Press, 1971. (a)

Kelley, H. H. Moral evaluation. *American Psychologist*, 1971, **21**, 293–300. (b)

Kelley, H. H. *Causal schemata and the attribution process*. Morristown, N.J.: General Learning Press, 1972.

Kelley, H. H. The processes of causal attribution. *American Psychologist*, 1973, **28**, 107–128.

Kelley, H. H., & Michela, J. L. Attribution theory and research. *Annual Review of Psychology*, 1980, **31**, in press.

Kohlberg, L. Stage and sequence: The cognitive–developmental approach to socialization. In D. A. Goslin (Ed.), *Handbook of socialisation theory and research*. Chicago: Rand McNally, 1969.

Kruglanski, A. W. The endogenous–exogenous partition in attribution theory. *Psychological Review*, 1975, **82**, 387–406.

Kruglanski, A. W., Schwartz, J. M., Maides, S., & Hamel, I. Z. Covariation, discounting and augmentation: Towards a clarification of attributional principles. *Journal of Personality*, 1978, **46**, 176–189.

Lerner, M. J. Observer's evaluation of a victim: Justice, guilt and veridical perception. *Journal of Personality and Social Psychology*, 1971, **20**, 127–135.

Lerner, M. J., & Miller, D. T. Just world research and the attribution process: Looking back and ahead. *Psychological Bulletin*, 1978, **85**, 1030–1051.

Lickona, T. Research on Piaget's theory of moral development. In T. Lickona (Ed.), *Moral development and behavior*. New York: Holt, 1976.

Lipton, J. P., & Garza, R. T. Responsibility attribution among Mexican-American, black and anglo adolescents and adults. *Journal of Cross-Cultural Psychology*, 1977, **8**, 259–273.

Lloyd-Bostock, S. Common sense morality and accident compensation. In P. Farrington, K. Hawkins, & S. Lloyd-Bostock (Eds.), *Psychology law and legal processes*. New York: Macmillan, 1979. (a)

Lloyd-Bostock, S. M. The ordinary man and the psychology of attributing causes and responsibility. *Modern Law Review*, 1979, **42**, 143–168. (b)

Loftus, E. Reconstruction of automobile destruction: An example of the interaction between language and memory. *Journal of Verbal Learning and Verbal behavior,* 1974, **13,** 585–589.

Lowe, C. A., & Medway, C. A. Effects of valence, severity, and relevance on responsibility and dispositional attribution. *Journal of Personality,* 1976, **44,** 518–538.

Mackie, J. L. *The cement of the universe.* London and New York: Oxford University Press (Clarendon), 1974.

McKillip, J., & Posavac, E. J. Judgments of responsibility for an accident. *Journal of Personality,* 1975, **43,** 248–265.

McMartin, J. A., & Shaw, J. I. An attributional analysis of responsibility for a happy accident: Effects of ability, intention, and effort. *Human Relations,* 1977, **30,** 899–918.

Medway, F. J., & Lowe, C. A. Effects of outcome valence and severity on responsibility attribution. *Psychological Reports,* 1975, **36,** 239–246.

Miller, D. T. What constitutes a self serving attributional bias? A reply to Bradley. *Journal of Personality and Social Psychology,* 1978, **36,** 1221–1223.

Miller, D. T., & Ross, M. Self-serving biases in the attribution of causality. Fact or fiction? *Psychological Bulletin,* 1975, **82,** 213–225.

Nelson, C. A. A cognitive algebra approach to judgments of responsibility, intention, and consequences. Unpublished doctoral dissertation, Kent State University, 1975.

Phares, E. J., & Wilson, K. G. Responsibility attribution: Role of outcome severity, situational ambiguity and internal–external control. *Journal of Personality,* 1972, **40,** 392–406.

Piaget, J. *The moral judgment of the child.* London: Routledge & Kegan Paul, 1932.

Pliner, P., & Cappell, H. Drinking, driving, and the attribution of responsibility. *Journal of Studies on Alcohol,* 1977, **38,** 593–602.

Prosser, W. L. *Handbook on the law of torts.* St. Paul, Minn.: West, 1955.

Raymond, J. S., & Dillehay, R. C. Perceived effort and incidental outcome as determinents of moral judgment in children. Paper presented at the meeting of the Midwestern Psychological Association, Chicago, May 1973.

Reisman, S. R., & Schopler, J. An analysis of attribution process and an application to determinants of responsibility. *Journal of Personality and Social Psychology,* 1973, **25,** 361–368.

Rogers, W. V. H., *Winfield and Jacowicz on tort.* (11th ed.) London: Sweet & Maxwell, 1979.

Ross, M., & Di Tecco, D. An attributional analysis of moral judgments. *Journal of Social Issues,* 1975, **31,** 91–109.

Schopler, J., & Layton, B. D. *Attribution of interpersonal power and influence.* Morristown, N.J.: General Learning Press, 1972.

Schroeder, D. A., & Linder, D. E., Effects of actor's causal role, outcome severity, and knowledge of prior accidents upon attributions of responsibility. *Journal of Experimental Social Psychology,* 1976, **12,** 340–356.

Schultz, L. T., & Dillehay, R. C. Effort and incidental outcome as factors in moral judgment. Paper presented at the meeting of the Southwestern Psychological Association, Fort Worth, April 1970.

Shultz, T. R., Schleifer, M., & Altman, I. Judgments of causation, responsibility and punishment in cases of harm-doing by omission. Unpublished manuscript, McGill University, 1979.

Sedlak, A. Developmental differences in understanding plans and evaluating actors. *Child Development,* 1979, **50,** 536–560.

Shantz, C. U. The development of social cognition. In M. Hetherington (Ed.), *Review of child development research.* Vol. 3. Chicago: University of Chicago Press, 1975.

Shaver, K. G. Defensive attribution: Effects of severity and relevance on the responsibility assigned for an accident. *Journal of Personality and Social Psychology,* 1970, **14,** 101–113.

Shaver, K. G. Intentional ambiguity in the attribution of responsibility: A reply to Fishbein and Ajzen. Unpublished manuscript, The College of William and Mary, 1974.

138   FRANK D. FINCHAM AND JOSEPH M. JASPARS

Shaw, J. I., & McMartin, J. A. Perpetrator or victim: Effects of who suffers in an automobile accident on judgmental strictness. *Social Behavior and Personality,* 1975, **3,** 5-12.

Shaw, J. I., & McMartin, J. A. Personal and situational determinants of attribution of responsibility for an accident. *Human Relations,* 1977, **30,** 95-107.

Shaw, J. I., & Skolnick, P. Attribution of responsibility for a happy accident. *Journal of Personality and Social Psychology,* 1971, **18,** 380-383.

Shaw, M. E., Briscoe, M. E., & Garcia-Esteve, J. A cross-cultural study of attribution of responsibility. *International Journal of Psychology,* 1968, **3,** 51-60.

Shaw, M. E., & Iwawaki, S. Attribution of responsibility by Japanese and Americans as a function of age. *Journal of Cross-Cultural Psychology,* 1972, **3,** 71-81.

Shaw, M. E., & Reitan, H. T. Attribution of responsibility as a basis for sanctioning behaviour. *British Journal of Social and Clinical Psychology,* 1969, **8,** 217-226.

Shaw, M. E., & Schneider, F. W. Intellectual competence as a variable in attribution of responsibility and assignment of sanctions. *Journal of Social Psychology,* 1969, **78,** 31-39. (a)

Shaw, M. E., & Schneider, F. W. Negro-white differences in attribution of responsibility as a function of age. *Psychonomic Science,* 1969, **16,** 289-291. (b)

Shaw, M. E., & Sulzer, J. L. An empirical test of Heider's levels in attribution of responsibility. *Journal of Abnormal and Social Psychology,* 1964, **69,** 39-46.

Slovic, P., & Lichtenstein, S. C. Comparison of Bayesian and regression approaches to the study of information processing in judgment. *Organisational Behavior and Human Performance,* 1971, **6,** 649-744.

Smith, J. C., & Hogan, B. *Criminal Law.* (4th ed.) London: Butterworth, 1978.

Sosis, R. Internal-external control and the perception of responsibility for an accident. *Journal of Personality and Social Psychology,* 1974, **30,** 393-399.

Sulzer, J. L., & Burglass, R. K. Responsibility attribution, empathy, and punitiveness. *Journal of Personality,* 1968, **36,** 272-282.

Tajfel, J., & Turner, J. C. An integrative theory of social conflict. In W. Austin & S. Worchel (Eds.), *The social psychology of intergroup relations.* Belmont, Calif.: Brooks/Cole, 1979.

Tomlinson, P. Moral judgment and moral psychology: Piaget, Kohlberg and beyond. In S. Modgil & C. Modgil (Eds.), *Towards a theory of psychological development.* Slough, Eng.: NFER, 1979.

Vidmar, N., & Crinklaw, L. D. Attributing responsibility for an accident: A methodological and conceptual critique. *Canadian Journal of Behavioural Science,* 1974, **6,** 112-130.

Walster, E. Assignment of responsibility for an accident. *Journal of Personality and Social Psychology,* 1966, **3,** 73-79.

Walster, E. "Second-guessing" important events. *Human Relations,* 1967, **20,** 239-250.

Weary, G. Self-serving attributional biases: Perceptual or response distortions? *Journal of Personality and Social Psychology,* 1979, **37,** 1418-1421.

Weiner, B., Kun, A., & Benesh-Weiner, M. The development of mastery, emotions, and morality from an attributional perspective. Paper presented at the Minnesota Symposium on Child Development, Minneapolis, May 1978.

Weiner, B., & Peter, N. A cognitive-developmental analysis of achievement and moral judgments. *Developmental Psychology,* 1973, **9,** 290-309.

Zuckerman, M. The endogenous-exogenous distinction: A model of attribution or a theory of cognitive motivation? *Personality and Social Psychology Bulletin,* 1977, **3,** 606-611. (a)

Zuckerman, M. On the endogenous-exogenous partition in attribution theory. *Personality and Social Psychology Bulletin,* 1977, **3,** 387-399. (b)

Zuckerman, M. The attribution of success and failure revisited, or: The motivational bias is alive and well in attribution theory. *Journal of Personality,* 1979, **47,** 245-287.

TOWARD A COMPREHENSIVE THEORY OF EMOTION[1]

Howard Leventhal

DEPARTMENT OF PSYCHOLOGY
UNIVERSITY OF WISCONSIN
MADISON, WISCONSIN

[1] Preparation of this chapter was partially supported by funds from a grant by the National Science Foundation (NSF Gs 31450X). I would like to thank Andrea Straus for her indefatigable editorial work and Leonard Berkowitz and Cal Izard for their encouragement.

ADVANCES IN EXPERIMENTAL SOCIAL
PSYCHOLOGY, VOL. 13

I. Introduction

The concept of emotion has played an extraordinarily varied role in behavioral theories. In psychology emotion has been employed to account for the
drive and reinforcement mechanisms involved in learning (Miller, 1951;
Mowrer, 1947; Schlosberg, 1954; Tomkins, 1962) and to explain defense processes (Dollard & Miller, 1950; Freud, 1926/1961), addictions, and attachments
(Solomon & Corbit, 1974). Ethology has used emotion to account for aspects of
natural selection (Darwin, 1872/1904; Eibl-Eibesfeldt, 1970; G. S. Hall, 1914;
McDougall, 1921, 1928), while in anthropological, social, and clinical study
emotion has been a focus for research on expressive behavior and interpersonal
communication (Birdwhistell, 1963; Ekman, Friesen, & Ellsworth, 1972; Frijda,
1969; Izard, 1971; Osgood, 1966; Tomkins & McCarter, 1964; Triandis &
Lambert, 1958). Finally, physiological investigators interested in emotion have
concentrated on studies of autonomic (Cannon, 1927) and central nervous
functions (Gellhorn, 1964, 1968; Lindsley, 1951; MacLean, 1958). The abun-
dance of all of these research perspectives may well be the source of the one thing
upon which various emotion theorists agree: The concept of emotion is poorly
defined and research is fragmented and unintegrated (Hebb, 1949; Izard, 1971;
Plutchik, 1962; P. T. Young, 1967).

The diversity of approaches does not fully explain why the various studies
have failed to complement one another. This incoherence appears to reflect a
more fundamental problem—the need for a frame of reference or theory that
could encompass and integrate the wide range of factors explored by each approach. In the absence of such an integrative framework investigators appear to
be studying diverse phenomena instead of exploring different levels or aspects of
the same problem. Of course, major efforts have been made to overcome this
deficit. Eighty years ago, James (1890/1950, p. 448) despaired that he "should
as lief read verbal descriptions of the shapes of the rocks on a New Hampshire
farm as toil through the literature of emotion again." He sought to lead investigators away from descriptions of expressive, autonomic, and subjective behaviors and have them focus on emotion's adaptive functions and the processes
involved in its creation. Although we may share James' distaste for empiricism
and his desire for an explanatory model, his body feedback hypothesis was too
narrow in conception to deal with the full range of data in emotion research. More
important, although James regarded bodily events as physical stimuli for emotional
experience (James, 1884, p. 188), he failed to provide a psychological model that
could account for the processing and combining of situational and bodily cues into
an emotional experience. James did not say how the situational conditions could
give rise to emotion, or how they might integrate with bodily cues to do so.
James also glossed over the relationship of focal awareness and volitional

mechanisms to the emotion process. As a consequence of these omissions many investigators proceeded to study autonomic events as if they were emotion, giving little attention to situational elicitors. Others paid more attention to situational factors and emotional experience, and still others focused on interpersonal and communicative aspects. Thus, the James hypothesis failed to bring together the separate and unrelated lines of investigation into the expressive, autonomic and subjective reactions called emotion.

The goal of this contribution is to provide a provisional model of emotion that is both comprehensive and unified. The next section focuses on the key questions raised by past theories and research to which the new conceptualization is addressed. The third section undertakes a limited elaboration of the model, drawing upon empirical findings where available and raising questions for future study. In the absence of an integrated data base, the model obviously must be general and suggestive rather than specific and quantitative. It is hoped that this shortcoming does not minimize its integrative and heuristic value.

II.   Past Models of Subjective Emotion

Three types of models form important antecedents to the position I have taken. They are (1) body reaction theory, (2) central neural theory, and (3) cognition–arousal theory. The cognition–arousal position is given greater attention because of the major role it played in the development of the perceptual model I present. I shall emphasize the problems these earlier analyses cannot solve, not to diminish their significance but to make salient the constraints they posed for the formulation of the current perceptual model.

A.   BODY REACTION THEORY

1.   James' theory

Titchener claimed the one novel feature of William James' theory of emotion was his assertion of its novelty (Titchener, 1914). Aristotle, Henle, Lotze, Melebranche, and others had stated the hypothesis before (Titchener's entertaining paper provides a list of predecessors known to James). Therefore, James was but one, although the best remembered, of a line of psychologists and philosophers who rejected the commonsense thesis that the perception of an emotion-provoking object (a bear, tasty food, baby, etc.) leads first to emotional feelings (fear, pleasure, joy, etc.) and then to expressive, autonomic, and overt instrumental action. He argued instead "that the bodily changes followed directly the perception of the exciting fact, and that our feelings of the same changes as they occur is the emotion" (James, 1890/1950, p. 449). James adopted a simple psychophysical parallelism: For every subjective emotional experience there must be a correlated bodily reaction pattern, just as for every visual or auditory sensory experience there must be correlated activity in the nervous system at a particular locus or at a particular rate.

There seem to be two major reasons for James' notion that emotional experience is produced by behavior: (1) Neurophysiological studies had identified only sensory, associative, and motor areas in the brain—there was no "center" for emotion—and (2) the hypothesis was obviously consistent with his own introspective observation. Indeed, body reactions, particularly those that are felt but not directly visible, have a compelling quality that can stimulate lengthy psychological, philosophical, medical, and commonsense speculation regarding their origins and meaning (H. Leventhal, Meyer, & Nerenz, 1980). James' hypothesis had two other virtues as well. It made sense of the everyday observation that emotions are experienced within the perceiver and not as events in the environment, and it provided a clue to the mechanisms responsible for the differentiation of emotional states.

2. Ambiguities in James' theory

However, there were at least five points on which James' hypothesis was unclear.

   a. Defining Responses.   James was quite ambiguous as to the responses that created subjective feeling. His more dramatic statements imply that overt instrumental reactions, as well as covert internal ones, produced subjective feelings: "the more rational statement is that we feel sorry because we cry, angry because we strike, afraid because we tremble..." (James, 1890/1950, p. 450). James, however, did emphasize feedback from internal responses: "If we fancy some strong emotion, and then try to abstract from our consciousness all the feelings of its bodily symptoms, we find we have nothing left behind, no 'mind-stuff' out of which the emotion can be constituted" (p. 451).

   b. Voluntary versus Spontaneous Reactions.   James focused on two basic kinds of response feedback as the source of emotion: expressive facial reactions and autonomic responses. He rejected the hypothesis that facial expression was the source of bodily feedback for emotion because his review of subjective reports by actors from various schools of acting suggested that these responses could be controlled voluntarily. Although he was not consistent on this point, James seems to have believed that nonvoluntary responses provided the most important feedback for emotion. This led him to single out involuntary visceral responses as the key to emotional feelings. In doing this he confounded spontaneity with type of response and failed to carefully evaluate the dual (spontaneous and voluntary) control of the facial expressive system. A consequence of his choice was the plethora of research on the autonomic visceral motor system.

   c. Awareness of Responses.   James was unclear in specifying whether or not people were directly aware of bodily reactions when experiencing an emotion. He first argued that "every one of the bodily changes, whatsoever it be, is felt, acutely or obscurely, the moment it occurs" (James, 1890/1950, p. 451). He then contradicted himself, writing: "If the reader has never paid attention to this matter, he will be both interested and astonished to learn how many different bodily feelings he can detect in himself as characteristic of his various emotional moods" (p. 451). This clearly suggests that one is often unaware of the bodily reactions that give rise to emotion and creates an ambiguity about the meaning of "felt" in the first quotation. One might incorrectly conclude that awareness of a reaction is irrelevant to feeling, but James ruled that out when he said, "It would perhaps be too much to expect him to arrest the tide of any strong gust of passion for the sake of any such curious analysis as this" (p. 451). Attention to responses stems and disrupts the flood of passion.

   d. Stimulus Decoding and Response Selection.   If we accept James' psychophysical hypothesis—that particular responses cause particular feelings —we are next forced to ask how a particular object, for example, a bear, baby, cartoon, or dead body, comes to elicit a particular set of reactions. We may feel happy from the laughter and delight of hugging and kissing the baby, but why do we not kiss and hug the bear? If a cognitive or other selective factor accounts for response selection, does it not also define emotion?

> It is difficult to see how James could deny emotion, as distinguished from a mere feeling of heightened vitality, to any sensory feedback (e.g., hard physical exercise) that involves strong arousal of skeletal and visceral activity; unless, as Dewey points out, the arousing objects were already apprehended as e.g., 'fearful' in which case the emotion has slipped in prior to the reaction. (Angier, 1927, p. 349)

Angier's point was repeated by Arnold (1960, p. 178) and Lazarus (1966). I will return to this argument in discussing cognition–arousal theory.

   e. Feelings and Emotion.   James actually presented two theories of emotion, one for turbulent emotion involving bodily feedback and another for the subtler esthetic emotions or "genuinely *cerebral* forms of pleasure and displeasure" which involved "an absolutely sensational experience, an optical or auricular feeling that is primary, and not due to the repercussion backwards of other sensations elsewhere consecutively aroused" (James, 1890/1950, p. 468). It is of course desirable to integrate both types of experience within a common framework.

3. Critique of Body Reactions Theory

Walter Cannon (1927) presented a well-known five point critique of James' hypothesis that subjective feelings are based on feedback from visceral reactions. Three of the five points are applicable to subjective feelings in a natural setting. They are: (1) The viscera are relatively insensitive and insufficiently supplied with receptors to provide sufficient sensory feedback; (2) the same visceral responses occur for different feeling states, making impossible a functional dependence of subjective feeling quality upon visceral reaction; (3) the latency of many visceral responses greatly exceeds that of the subjective emotional reactions they are supposed to cause (Grossman, 1967; Lehmann, 1914; Nakashima, 1909).

The two remaining points pertain to results of experimental studies: (4) The artificial induction of visceral change, through injection of such pharmacological agents as epinephrine, induced the autonomic and visceral reactions observed during naturally elicited emotion but did not give rise to subjective feeling states (Cantril & Hunt, 1932; Landis & Hunt, 1932; Marañon, 1924); (5) the surgical separation of the viscera from the central nervous system, also occasionally achieved by accident, does not eliminate emotional behavior.

Cannon's critique was not as devastating as he expected and hoped it would be. His fifth point was not fully relevant to James' hypothesis, as expressive behavior may appear following surgical separation of the viscera in animals with or without attendant subjective feelings; we have no way of knowing. His first and second points, that the viscera are insensitive and insufficiently differentiated, are overstated (Grossman, 1967), the viscera being neither quite as insensitive nor as undifferentiated as Cannon thought. The gastrointestinal system proved more sensitive than expected (Boring, 1915a, 1915b), and recent research has found distinct evoked cortical reactions to the stimulation of adjacent areas of the intestinal tract even though the subject is not directly aware of the stimulus events (Adam, 1967, p. 57). Fairly recent data also suggest that the pattern of heart rate, skin temperature and conductance, blood pressure, muscle tension peaks, breathing, etc., differentiate, at the least, between emotions of anger and fear (Ax, 1953; Funkenstein, King, & Drolette, 1957; J. Schachter, 1957) and between hypnotically induced helplessness and insult (Grace & Graham, 1952; Graham, 1962; Graham, Kabler, & Graham, 1962; Graham, Stern, & Winokur, 1960). There is also evidence suggesting particular patterns of electrodermal activity may accompany learned helplessness and depression (Gatchel & Proctor, 1976).

Cannon's third and fourth points, the slowness of visceral reaction and the absence of feeling after artificial induction of visceral activity, raise critical questions respecting the causal significance of these responses for subjective feelings. This issue reappears later on.

B. CENTRAL NEURAL THEORIES

1. Cannon's Theory

Cannon (1927) proposed an alternative model, which argued that feeling states depended upon thalamic or central neural activity. Therefore, ''The peculiar quality of the emotion is added to simple sensation when the thalamic processes are aroused'' (p. 120). In short, ''Thalamic processes are a source of affective experience . . . and the feeling tone of a sensation is the product of thalamic activity'' (p. 118). Muscular feedback did not elicit affect, although Cannon argued it might help sustain it.

Cannon's argument was closely related to his neurological studies of the role of hypothalamic and thalamic centers in emotional expression. He saw a close relationship between expressions and feelings but did not regard the relationship as causal. The signals emanating from the thalamic centers caused both the expressive response and, when they arrived at the cortex, the subjective feeling of emotion. Therefore, the thalamus is not the place where subjective emotional experience happens (see Cannon, 1931; Newman, Perkins, & Wheeler, 1930). He also took careful note of the fact that not all stimuli are capable of activating the emotion centers of the thalamus and suggested that eliciting stimuli may come from both external and internal sources.

Cannon made two additional important points. First, he believed that the feeling and expressive systems were partially independent of one another; the two could function separately even though the thalamic nuclei excited both subjective feeling and expressive reactions. This was so because the expressive and cortical areas receiving thalamic impulses were also influenced by other parts of the brain. Papez (1938) has elaborated on this idea and suggested three separate neural paths:

> One route conducts impulses through the dorsal thalamic and the internal capsule to the corpus striatum. The route represents the ''stream of movement.'' The second conducts impulses from the thalamus through the internal capsule to the lateral cerebral cortex. This route represents the ''stream of thought.'' The third conducts a set of concommitant impulses through the ventral thalamus to the hypothalamus and by way of the mamillary body and the anterior thalamic nuclei to the gyrus cinguil, in the medial role of the cerebral hemisphere. This route represents the ''stream of feeling.'' (Papez, 1938, p. 7)

(See further discussion in Gellhorn, 1964; Grossman, 1967; MacLean, 1958.)

Second, Cannon (1929) believed visceral activity was irrelevant for emotional experience. ''The processes going on in the thoracic and abdominal organs in consequence of sympathetic activity are truly remarkable and various; their value to the organism, however, is not to add richness and flavor to experience, but rather to adapt the internal economy so that in spite of shifts of outer circumstance the evenness of the inner life will not be profoundly disturbed'' (p. 358). Emotions that require exertion, such as fear and anger, have common adrenergic effects which are useful in maintaining internal stability. However, Cannon failed to point out that visceral reactions may summate with other aspects of emotional behavior. For example, visceral activation appears to add to the distress experienced from painful stimulation at specific peripheral body sites (Mountcastle, 1968). It also is conceivable that visceral activation produced by a prior activity may generalize and add to the intensity of a later emotional experience (Zillmann, 1978; Zillmann & Cantor, 1976).

2. Critique of Theory

The central neural theory pointed to ways of constructing more complex models of the relationship between expression and feeling and the neurological pathways and neurochemical changes underlying moods and subjective feeling states. Thus, the main contribution of the model to psychological theory is the proposition that subjective feelings are generated by special centers in the central nervous system. Emotion no longer need be compounded or created by nonemotional processes. The theory had little effect on psychological research, as it was phrased in physiological rather than psychological language. Because Cannon failed to specify the mental structures involved in the elicitation and processing of emotion, he provided no guidance for the subsequent study of environmental events which create feeling, thought, and expressive and instrumental action. Cannon (1927) came very close to specifying such a model, but the main impact of his writing for psychological theories of emotion was its negative, anti-Jamesian influence. He recognized, however, that his criticisms of James were unlikely to deal a fatal blow to a "famous doctrine . . . so strongly fortified by proof and so repeatedly confirmed by experience . . ." (Perry, 1926, quoted in Cannon, 1927, p. 106) unless he provided a clear theoretical alternative.

C. COGNITION-AROUSAL THEORY

Three factors seem to be particularly important for the development of cognition–arousal theory. The first is the failure of the central neural analysis to develop a convincing case for the existence of emotion centers capable of accounting for the diversity of human feeling. The second is the failure of past theories, both body feedback and central neural, to deal with the elicitation of emotion, that is, the problem of stimulus decoding and response selection (Angier, 1927; Gardiner, 1894). The last reason is the conviction (unshaken by Cannon's critique) that autonomic activation was necessary, if insufficient, to create feeling states (Marañon, 1924; Ruckmick, 1936; Russell, 1927/1960; S. Schachter, 1964; S. Schachter & Singer, 1962). As a consequence, numerous authors suggested that subjective emotions were products of bodily arousal combined with the cognition of emotion-eliciting events (e.g., Russell, 1927/1960; Sully, 1902).

Schachter's Theory

S. Schachter's (1964) restatement of this formulation is more explicit than others and more important because of the empirical work it has generated. His position is embodied in the three following propositions.

1. Given a state of physiological arousal for which an individual has no immediate explanation, he will "label" this state and describe his feelings in terms of the cognitions available to him . . . precisely the same state of physiological arousal could be labeled "joy" or "fury" or any of a great diversity of emotional labels, depending on the cognitive aspects of the situation.
2. If the individual has a completely appropriate explanation . . . for his arousal . . . no evaluative needs will arise, and the individual is unlikely to label his feelings in terms of the alternative cognitions available.
3. Given the same cognitive circumstances the individual will react emotionally or describe his feelings as emotions only to the extent that he experience a state of physiological arousal. (p. 53)

The propositions make clear that both arousal and cognition are necessary for emotion, but neither one is sufficient. The arousal component defines an experience as emotional and locates it in the self, but this arousal is presumably a neutral and undifferentiated state. It varies in intensity, not in quality, and supposedly provides only a charge or drive (Hull, 1930, 1932, 1943; Spence, 1958) but does not direct behavior (Zillmann, 1978). For Schachter, however, arousal is not merely a drive stimulus; it is also felt and experienced. Arousal therefore becomes a conscious psychological event and stimulates a need to know, which leads the individual to look outward for the cause of his arousal. The search generates the cognitive component that specifies the quality (anger, fear, joy) of the feeling state. In Schachter's words, a "cognition arising from the immediate situation as interpreted by past experience provides the framework within which one understands and labels his feeling" (S. Schachter, 1964, pp. 50, 51). Mandler (1962) has compared the model to a juke box; both a turntable (arousal) and a record (cognition) are needed to play the tune (specific feeling). It is extremely important to recognize that the cognitive response is the source of the specific feeling quality. If cognition had simply been assigned an eliciting function, with perception or interpretation leading to feeling, the model would not differ from Cannon's.

An important feature of Schachter's restatement of cognition-arousal theory is his introduction of symmetry in the integration of cognition and arousal. Typically, cognition precedes emotion; that is, when the stimulus setting elicits emotion, the cognition precedes arousal and the arousal is naturally linked or attributed to the antecedent cognition. When arousal is induced with a drug, as done in the injection studies (S. Schachter & Singer, 1962; S. Schachter & Wheeler, 1962), the sequence is reversed (see also Sierra, 1921, p. 459). The reversal is theoretically important, since it requires the specification of a number of theoretical details that are left unanswered in James' body arousal theory. Schachter's conception agrees with James' in selecting autonomic reactions as necessary for feeling. It further suggests that the autonomic component of the feeling matrix is involuntary, occurring either spontaneously or by chemical elicitation. The cognitive part is obviously more subject to volitional control. Therefore, emotion has both automatic and voluntary response components. The model also suggests that people are aware of the assembly process; that is, they are aware of their autonomic reactions. Finally, the formulation makes a number of statements about the relationship of emotion to environmental conditions. Environmental perception and interpretation are clearly necessary for emotion and are the source of feeling quality. The model also suggests that the clearer the environment, the clearer the individual's feelings. The model falls back on common sense, however, in responding to the important set of issues regarding why different stimuli arouse different emotions, that is, why we run from the bear and hug the baby. Finally, the model suggests the integration of arousal and cognition is postattentive (occurs after awareness) and multiplicative. If one is completely unaroused or if one confronts a completely benign environment, there can be no emotional experience. A critique of this theoretical position is presented in the following section, which considers in detail the role of arousal and cognition in emotion.

III.   Emotion Is Arousal and Cognition; Emotion Is Emotion

The key issue separating these analyses is whether or not emotion has a separate existence. Central neural theory votes "Yes"; emotion is supposedly a product of specific affective processes in the brain. By contrast, both arousal and cognition–arousal theory vote "No"; for them, emotion is either feedback from bodily reactions or the amalgamation of feedback from bodily reactions with cognition. The "*no*" votes have had the edge in directing research because they point to more readily manipulated and measured factors for the study of emotion. The central neural position appears to expose emotion only to neurophysiological investigation. However, the availability of measures is no assurance that they are related to emotional processes. Cognition–arousal theory, for example, may deal with social influence processes instead of the mechanisms underlying emotion.

As Cannon has noted, it seems difficult, if not impossible, to eradicate the notion of arousal feedback, for it fits our intuitive experience of emotion too well. It is also clear that arousal and cognitive processes are indeed involved with emotion, as they are with all behavior, The issue, however, is whether these processes are the necessary and sufficient mechanisms for defining emotional experience or whether some other mechanism defines emotional experience and arousal and cognition participate with it in the organism's total response to emotion-provoking situations.

This question is addressed in the following section. Because portions of the argument have been presented before (H. Leventhal, 1970, 1974a, 1979), I shall be brief. My goal is to lay the groundwork for the basic issues which need to be solved by a model of emotion and to suggest the kind of model that may have some promise of solving them.

A. IS AROUSAL NECESSARY FOR EMOTION?

Is arousal necessary for emotion? If it is, what is it and how does it operate in the formation of emotional experience?

1. What Is Arousal?

There is no clear way of defining arousal, as the indicators used to measure it are poorly intercorrelated, functionally independent (Lacey, 1967; H. Leventhal, 1970, 1974a; Plutchik & Ax, 1967), and in many instances specific to the individual (Lacey & Lacey, 1958; Malmo, 1975). Cognition–arousal theorists appear to sidestep this issue by focusing on psychological or perceived arousal rather than physiological measures. An advantage of a perceptual definition of arousal is that various psychophysiological measures appear to correlate more highly with perceptual indicators (judgments of arousal) than with one another (Clements, Hafer, & Vermillion, 1976; Godkewitsch, 1972).

2. False Feedback Studies and Arousal

Investigators have adopted a perceptual definition in studies of false feedback, using bogus heart rate sounds (Barefoot & Straub, 1971; Valins, 1966; Valins & Ray, 1967) or fake meter readings (Gerard, 1963; Krisher, Darley, & Darley, 1973) to "vary" subjects' fear level and influence emotionally based judgments. Although some experiments report actual physiological change with false feedback (Stern, Botto, & Herrick, 1972), others do not (Scherwitz, 1973; Valins, 1966), suggesting that arousal is not necessary for emotional experience. Harris and Katkin (1975) argue that false feedback produces emotion-like behavior and judgment, or a learned derivative of primary emotion, but that true primary emotion (James' turbulent emotion?) requires autonomic arousal. However, injection-induced arousal had weak or no effects on indicators of emotion in studies testing cognition–arousal theory (S. Schachter & Singer, 1962), and in studies using expressive behavior as a sign of arousal, verbal reports of affect often correlated negatively with expression. Thus, neither internal arousal nor external expressive change appears to be necessary for emotional experience.

3. Animal Studies and Arousal

Some animal studies suggest that autonomic activation by adrenalin injection does indeed intensify emotional behavior (Singer, 1963), while others find that adrenalin-injected animals show increased levels on such fear behaviors as defecation and choice latency but not on such instrumental measures of fear behavior as choice of a familiar rather than a strange compartment (G. S. Leventhal & Killackey, 1968). The bulk of investigations suggest, however, that arousal is not necessary and has no effects on behavioral measures such as the rate of acquisition and extinction of avoidance response, both of these measures being the closest one may come to a verbal report of fear from a dog or a rat. This conclusion holds whether the procedures involved surgical separation of the autonomic and central nervous systems (Wynne & Solomon, 1955) or chemically induced sympathetic denervation (Van-Toller & Tarpy, 1974). Van-Toller and Tarpy (1974) state "immunosympathectomy reduces the range of an animal's adaptive behavior as does sympathectomy . . . because of the subject's inability to cope with specific physiological stressors . . . this hypothesis does not question the possibility that avoidance may be mediated centrally by fear" (p. 35). Immunosympathectomy can be performed at birth without damaging the animal's ability to acquire avoidance behaviors in a normal environment. In a cold environment, the animal does have difficulty maintaining internal homeostasis and learning avoidance responses (Van-Toller & Tarpy, 1972). It therefore appears that autonomic activity is important for homeostasis but is initially independent of emotional reactions, although life experience may connect the two later on.

4. Studies of Paraplegics

S. Schachter (1964) sought further support for the hypothesis that arousal is necessary for feeling states in Hohman's (1966) fine study of paraplegics. Hohman found that accidental severing of the spinal cord produced sharp reductions in the intensity of emotional experience for these patients, and that the higher the damage on the cord, the greater the elimination of bodily feedback and reduction in emotional feeling. However, the reduction of emotion held only for feelings of sex, aggression, and fear. Paraplegic respondents reported increased grief and sentimentality after their injuries. Can people have stronger feelings in response to injury if they lack one of the two necessary components for emotion?

Before we select from among the possible interpretations of the preceding data, we must take into account one other finding. While paraplegic patients have been found to be devoid of sexual feeling when awake, they report "phantom orgasms" in which they experience all the sensations and erotic tone of sexuality (including, on occasion, ejaculation or bedwetting) during dreams or paradoxical sleep (Money, 1960). When sexual feelings occur without bodily feedback, they will feel abnormal and weak under conditions where bodily feedback typically is available to consciousness, and normal and strong during sleep when the person is unlikely to be aware of body arousal or the lack of it. The complete set of findings suggests that sexual feelings are created by a central neural mechanism and that arousal feedback is integrated with this central feeling response over the organism's life history.

Considering all the evidence reviewed thus far, we can draw the following tentative conclusions. First, bodily activation is important in sustaining adaptive activity but relatively unimportant for generating subjective emotional states. Second, the experience of autonomic activity appears to be conditioned to images and feelings to become part of emotion. Third, an acceptable theory of emotion must provide some mechanism for the joining of arousal and emotion.

B.   IS COGNITION NECESSARY FOR EMOTION?

Does cognition operate in the formation of emotional experience as a label necessary for feeling quality, or is cognition a set of events attached to emotion?

Cognition–arousal theory deserves praise for focusing attention on cognitive processes and rectifying a serious omission in body arousal theory. The term "cognition," however, is used for many things: attentional focus on body cues, emotion, or environment; a need to know; a labeling process that occurs automatically in the forward position; and one that occurs deliberately in the reversed position. It is clear that the word is a topic heading and not an explanatory concept. The following sections make clear that more than one kind of cognition enters into emotional processing.

1.   Which Comes First, Labels or Emotion?

If arousal is neutral and emotional qualities are defined by labels, labeling must precede emotion. According to cognition–arousal theory, neither infants nor children should experience emotion until given social labels for their body states. However, this conjectured sequence of events poses a near insuperable barrier to learning emotion labels. The alternative view, that emotional experience precedes labeling, provides a more reasonable account of the developmental process (H. Leventhal, 1974a, 1979). This latter hypothesis is consistent with MacNamaras' (1972) theoretical analysis of language learning, in which he argues that a great deal of nonverbal conceptual category development precedes and is necessary for the development of language. A variety of empirical data support the argument, including findings that the generalizations among stimuli in young children appear to follow similarities in physical attributes and emotional reactions and that a young child's "labeling" of affect may be inconsistent with socially defined meanings or labels (Bauer, 1976; Woodsworth & Schlosberg, 1954). The hypothesis that emotion precedes social labeling has two important implications: (1) that it is important to distinguish perceptual memories (schemata) from conceptual memories (social labels), and (2) that cognitions are linked to prior emotional states and are not the initial source for the definition of emotion quality.

2. Attention, Clarity of Labels, and Emotion

Cognition–arousal theory states that attention is focused initially on a neutral (nonaffective) body arousal, which becomes emotion after labeling; a relatively clear label is essential for defining the quality of the emotional state.

If the hypothesis is interpreted as reading that emotion appears only after labeling reduces ambiguity and creates the quality of feeling, it conflicts with substantial amounts of data. Clear interpretations of a situation facilitate labeling and therefore should create a greater emotional response, whereas ambiguity should inhibit the production of affect. Instead of serving as a "neutral" preemotional starting point, however, uncertainty and ambiguity both elicit and maintain states of chronic anxiety and depression (Frankenhaeuser, 1975; Janis, 1958; Janis & Leventhal, 1965, 1968; Mason, 1972), as well as increase the stress response to threatened electric shock (Epstein, 1973; Epstein & Roupenian, 1970; Fenz, Kluck, & Bankart, 1969; Weiss, 1970). However, some types of clarification actually decrease the emotional component of an experience; information about the precise sensory features of a stress stimulus (how it will feel on impact) and attention directed to those sensations reduce distress responses to pain (Fuller, Endress, & Johnson, 1978; Johnson, 1973; Johnson, Kirchhoff, & Endress, 1975; Johnson & Leventhal, 1974; Johnson, Morrissey, & Leventhal, 1973; H. Leventhal, Brown, Shacham, & Engquist, 1979; Mills & Krantz, 1979; Sime, 1976; J. F. Wilson, 1977). This reduction of stress does not occur, however, if a threatening interpretation is given to the sensory features (Epstein, 1973; K. R. L. Hall & Stride, 1954; H. Leventhal et al., 1979, Experiment 1; Staub & Kellett, 1972; Teichner, 1965).

Cognition–arousal theory is clearly correct in pointing to the importance of cognitive interpretation. The question is whether the theory specifies the nature of this interpretive process adequately. The data described above show that the interpretation or coding of stimulus inputs has powerful effects on affective arousal, but this is not identical to the assertion that social (verbal?) labeling provides the critical information for defining emotion. Simple verbal assurances alone will not reduce fear. Benign interpretations must be accompanied by perceptual information on how one will experience the sensory features of a stimulus (aching, pins and needles, pulling, etc.) and instructions to attend initially to those responses so as to guide the interpretation (H. Leventhal et al., 1979, Experiment 1).

An interesting example of the stress-reducing properties of clear and concrete information can be found in reports of spontaneous recovery and remission of anxiety neuroses during the London blitz (Stewart, 1950). Confronting the real and cognitively clear threat of the bombing achieved what social therapeutic suggestion could not. In contrast, the ambiguity of unexpected near misses (where the eliciting conditions are not closely observed), or being close enough to disaster to be aware of it but not so close as to clearly see its features, seems critical for the development of neurotic vigilance reactions (Janis, 1951).

In summary, cognition–arousal theory assigns cognition too central a role in emotion when it argues that cognition is necessary and solely responsible for emotional quality. At the same time, this analysis provides too limited a view of the way cognition can be involved with emotion, for cognitions can elicit emotion, enhance it by generating uncertainty, and reduce it by generating clarity, as well as specify ways of coping to eliminate it.

C. IS THE JOINING OF AROUSAL AND COGNITION NECESSARY TO CREATE EMOTION?

It may seem redundant to ask whether the joint action of cognition and arousal represents the core element in creating emotional states, having argued that neither is necessary for emotion. However, there are several issues I have not discussed until now which are best dealt with under this heading. The first of these has to do with the neutrality of arousal. There are differences in the physiological pattern of arousal for different affective states, which implies that arousal creates specific emotions (Ax, 1953; Damaser, Shor, & Orne, 1963; Funkenstein *et al.*, 1957; Grace & Graham, 1952; Graham *et al.*, 1960; J. Schachter, 1957; Sternbach, 1964). However, neither these studies nor earlier injection studies clearly demonstrate that physiological arousal is experienced as emotion, or that different patterns of arousal are experienced as different emotions (Landis & Hunt, 1932; Marañon, 1924; Wenger, Clemens, Darsie, Engel, Estess, & Sonnenschein, 1960) and new evidence suggests otherwise.

1. Is Arousal Neutral?

The hypothesis that emotional states can be altered by attaching neutral arousal to alternative cognitions has been challenged most recently by Maslach (1979a, 1979b) and Marshall and Zimbardo (1979). In discussing the plasticity of emotion, Maslach (1979a) argues that "a state of unexplained arousal is not as affectively neutral as Schachter and Singer had assumed" (p. 577). She maintains that subjects tend to give negative labels to bodily arousal. The more intense this arousal the more likely they will be to assign a negative label. Maslach (1979a, 1979b) believes that her results are particularly troublesome for the cognition–arousal position, as she has found with some degree of consistency that increases in posthypnotically induced arousal lead to increased reports of dysphoric mood regardless of the happy or angry behavior of her experimental confederate. Marshall and Zimbardo (1979) came to a similar conclusion from their attempt to replicate the Schachter and Singer study using injections of epinephrine and a happy stooge (the investigators could not run an angry stooge condition). They found that negative affects were produced by larger doses of the drug despite the presence of the stooge. Marshall and Zimbardo (1979, p. 983) conclude,

> The general picture that emerges ... indicates that epinephrine-related physiological arousal does not provide "emotional plasticity," but rather shows a consistent association with negative affect.... It is somewhat reassuring ... that our true emotions may be more rationally determined and less susceptible to transient or whimsical situational determinants than has been suggested by Schachter and Singer.

A carefully conducted study by Erdmann and Janke (1978) supports both the cognition–arousal position and the final part of Marshall and Zimbardo's statement. Compared to placebo injections, ephedrine injections increased happiness and anger in response to stimuli to those respective emotions, but had no effect on fear reactions to threat of electrical shock. Erdmann and Janke (1978) end their paper by stating, "Regarding Schachter's theory, the results and the conclusions of the present experiment imply that the relationship between emotional and physiological arousal might be less tight and/or less general than the theory proposes" (p. 73).

What can be said from these findings and how can we interpret these investigators' conclusions in the present context? First, I am clearly in accord with Erdmann and Janke since I have already argued that arousal is not essential for emotion. The Marshall and Zimbardo position poses more difficulties. First, in maintaining that arousal generates a negative emotional quality, they question the hypothesis that emotion is a combination of arousal and cognition; for them, cognition is no longer needed. This conclusion is inconsistent with the bulk of their paper. However, Marshall and Zimbardo make an important point when they argue that emotion is "less susceptible to transient or whimsical situational determinants than has been suggested" by cognition–arousal theory. There is reason to doubt that "arbitrary" short-term (situational) cognitions can move emotions about so readily. This does not mean that emotion does not fluctuate, for emotion is a rapidly changing thing. However, the links between emotions and specific images and conditioned stimuli can be stable (Miller, 1951; Solomon & Corbit, 1974). Indeed, it is the linkage of emotion to cognition that lends stability to a system that might otherwise be in constant flux. A change in cognition brings a change in emotion because of the cognition's affect-eliciting properties or its past association with particular emotions. This is not the same as associating a new label with a state of general arousal. Indeed, there is a basic contradiction in Zimbardo's reasoning when he separates arousal and emotion in arguing that arousal is not "plastic," and combines arousal and emotion in arguing for plasticity. The contradiction is readily resolved by differentiating emotion from both cognition and arousal while allowing for the formation of linkages of different strengths between all three of these factors. The most important point is that emotion's connection to cognition stabilizes a system that is otherwise susceptible to rapid fluctuations. Linkages between emotions and objects, people, and tasks are significant because they introduce stable emotional themes (schemata and scripts), attitudes, and object relations into mental life.

How shall we consider the tie between arousal and negative affect? We cannot deal with this issue if we insist emotion is a synthesis of cognition and arousal. However, we have no difficulty with the negative affective quality of arousal if we hypothesize that arousal is a conditioned or an unconditioned stimulus for emotion (Grossman, 1967; H. Leventhal, 1974a, 1979).

The S. Schachter and Singer (1979) response to Marshall and Zimbardo is partially consistent with my resolution of the issue. They comment that very high levels of arousal do not add to affective states, especially to positive ones, as high arousal is in itself a noxious stimulus. It is clear they now see arousal functioning as an unconditioned stimulus. They also make a second and more important point: It was exceptionally difficult to arrange the onset of arousal and the available cognitive cues so that the appropriate understanding of the arousal was established. The difficulty may reflect the care with which people monitor their arousal and reason about its antecedents. This interpretation is consistent with cognition–arousal theory, but there is a simpler explanation. If emotion is perceived automatically, just as we perceive a table or a chair, it is not surprising that subjects have been able to perceive the time order of the events of the study. When specific aspects of the experimental situation evoked a strong emotional reaction, they were able to tell when arousal was separate from these experiences.

There is little reason to assume that most subjects have been sufficiently attuned to, or concerned with, their body states to consciously reason about the antecedents of their emotional feelings. It was more likely to have been directly perceived. Indeed, people do not seem to notice their arousal unless it reaches high levels, nor do they usually make clear conscious attributions of arousal to one of a series of sequential events (Cantor, Zillmann, & Bryant, 1975; Zillmann, 1978; Zillmann, Johnson, & Day, 1974). Zillmann (1978) argues that clear attributions of arousal are made only when an external event is seen as a plausible cause of an existent state of strong (highly noticeable) arousal.

2. What Is Cognition in Cognition–Arousal Theory?

The source of much of the confusion concerning the joining of cognition to arousal lies, I believe, in a misinterpretation of the term "cognition." S. Schachter and Singer (1979) refer to cognitions that automatically become tightly linked to emotional experience and perceptions of danger, attack, support, love etc. They are not necessarily referring to conscious, situationally induced verbal labels—the kind of cognition Marshall and Zimbardo (1979) have in mind. It is not surprising that this confusion arose, for cognition–arousal theory does not distinguish between various forms of cognition. This failure may stem from the fact that it has grown out of social comparison theory (S. Schachter, 1959), which emphasizes social labeling and influence processes.

In light of the above considerations, we can conclude that:

1. Emotion is generated by some third, independent mechanism, and the appearance of emotion does not require the presence of arousal and cognition as understood in cognition–arousal theory.

2. It is important to distinguish perceptual cognition of a situation as threatening, supportive, etc., from social or conceptual cognition; the former seems more important for emotion.

3. Perceptual cognition derives from the outer environment or from inner experiences of arousal and can be tightly conditioned to the affect-generating mechanism. These links provide stability for the affect system.

I have made many of the preceding points in two earlier discussions of misattribution and the false-feedback experiments seeking to test cognition–arousal theory (H. Leventhal, 1974a, 1979; see also Zillmann, 1978). For example, the misattribution experiments claim that associating signs of bodily arousal with a neutral label reduces the subject's tendency to avoid the threat stimulus actually producing the arousal (Dienstbier & Munter, 1971; Nisbett & Schachter, 1966; Ross, Rodin, & Zimbardo, 1969; Younger & Doob, 1978). In these studies information about the sensory features of expected bodily arousal is confounded with the provision of a neutral label for that arousal (misattribution). Calvert-Boyanowski and I (Calvert-Boyanowsky & Leventhal, 1975) found that avoidance behavior was reduced by knowledge about expected body arousal (sweating hands, heart beats, etc.) but not by information about the source of arousal.

The stability of the affect system when emotion is conditioned to specific objects and cues is illustrated by both the misattribution investigations and a host of studies of false feedback. The false-feedback experiments were intended to show that false information about arousal can generate emotional judgments. These investigations indicate that false feedback does not change emotional judgments or responses for subjects who characteristically have strong emotional reactions. For example, false feedback suggesting that fear of a shock is responsible for the arousal produced by a snake does not reduce the fear and avoidance of snakes exhibited by subjects who are truly snake phobic (Bandura, 1969, pp. 435–439; Conger, Conger, & Brehm, 1976), nor does the misattribution of arousal to a pill facilitate sleep for true insomiacs (Bootzin, Herman, & Nicassio, 1976; Kellog & Baron, 1975; Singerman, Borkovec, & Baron, 1976). Even the subject's own behavior, which is usually a strong persuader, failed to influence ratings of electric shocks (escaped shocks rated on severity compared to equally severe shocks that are not escaped) for subjects who are fearful and sensitive to shock (D. Brown, Klemp, & Leventhal, 1975; Klemp & Leventhal, 1974). These earlier findings confirm the S. Schachter and Singer (1979) and Marshall and Zimbardo (1979) observation that it is not easy to deceive strongly emotional subjects. When their history has created clear associations between specific feelings and events, they *know* how they feel. Emotional people seem aware of their feelings but not of the details of their body reactions, and so ignore false information about emotions. On the other hand, there is no evidence that false information induces emotion in those who lack an association between specific emotions and external objects. These "unemotional" persons use false feedback to make judgments or intellectual appraisals, but the information does not induce emotional states (Kerber & Coles, 1978). It seems reasonable to conclude, therefore, that emotion exists as an independent entity. Emotion can be attached to new stimuli where plausible; it can be coped with if one is prepared. Finally, a strong emotion serves as a firm internal anchor to resist an external and "intuitively" implausible influence.

IV.   A Perceptual Motor Theory of Emotion

A.   REQUIREMENTS OF A PERCEPTUAL MOTOR THEORY OF EMOTION

I have briefly analyzed body arousal, central neural, and cognitive–arousal theories to reveal the problems which must be addressed by a complete theory of emotion. This section summarizes these issues and then presents and elaborates a perceptual motor theory of emotion intended to deal with them.

The basic issues our model must handle are:

1. The model must have an independent or primary mechanism that accounts for differences in the quality of emotional experiences.

a. This mechanism must operate early in the organism's life and provide a basis for perceiving similarities and differences in the emotional states associated with different settings and also must allow for the learning of social labels for emotion.

b. The mechanism must retain some degree of independence from situational influence and acquired emotional structures in order for learned feelings to be susceptible to correction.

2. The model must include an emotional memory mechanism to account for the connection of cognition to emotion. These acquired cognitive packages (schemata) must integrate subjective emotions; sets of autonomic, expressive,

and instrumental reactions; and situational memories. This is necessary to handle the S. Schachter and Singer (1962) data and the data on resistance to reattribution by emotional subjects.

    a. These memory packages or schemata should reflect both innate structure and specific environmental experiences.

    b. The schemata should be sensitive to situational variables (such as the behavior of the experimental accomplice in the S. Schachter–Singer studies) and function automatically in generating emotional experience.

    c. The schemata should allow for the development of new and more complex emotional experiences.

    3. The model should point to specific (and different) situational factors for the activation of each of the emotional processing mechanisms indicated in Issues 1 and 2 previously. In particular, each mechanism should suggest particular situational elicitors for specific emotions.

    4. The model must include mechanisms which can shortcircuit or attenuate the processing of emotional responses and lead instead to the processing of veridical or objective perceptual experience.

    5. The model must incorporate such concepts as attention and consciousness and deal with their effects on emotion.

    6. The model must take into account that peoples' understanding of their emotional reactions and their efforts to control these reactions may only be partially correct or appropriate. The key issue here is to understand why people conceptualize their emotions along particular lines.

    The perceptual motor model will be elaborated to demonstrate how it handles these questions. I will offer a more detailed view of the processing mechanisms to further define their mode of functioning. Finally, several issues in respect to the relationships between mechanisms will be discussed. The present analysis treats emotions as unitary and identifiable perceptual experiences; each emotion is discrete and different from every other emotion (Izard, 1971; Leeper, 1970; McDougall, 1928; Tomkins, 1962). This is the fundamental postulate of differential emotion theories in the Darwinian tradition (see Izard, 1977). As Konorski has stated: "From the psychological point of view, the experience of each emotion or drive has all the attributes of unitary perception. . . . pure fear, or pure anger, or pure sorrow are certainly familiar to everyone, nevertheless we are usually afraid of something, angry at someone, sorry because of something, and so on." (Reprinted from *Integrative activity of the brain* by J. Konorski by the University of Chicago Press. Copyright 1967. All rights reserved.) This conception differentiates it from formulations that decompose emotional experience into elements (cognition and arousal) or dimensions, such as pleasantness–unpleasantness (Osgood, 1966; Schlosberg, 1954; Woodsworth & Schlosberg, 1954, Chapter 5). The model presented here makes a sharp distinction between the processes that generate emotion and the experience of emotion (see also Mandler, 1975). The process of generating emotion does not involve experiencing arousal and tying the arousal to explanatory cognitions.

Defining emotion as a subjective perceptual experience eliminates a large number of theoretical and methodological problems. The definition means that we can treat any overt response, whether it be a verbal report, a physiological reaction, or an overt instrumental act, as an indicator of an underlying perceptual experience. The indicator is valid if it generates meaningful relationships under converging experimental operations (Campbell & Fisk, 1959; Garner, Hake, & Eriksen, 1956). This not only legitimates verbal report as an indicator of emotional experience (Mewborn & Rogers, 1979) but also makes clear that physiological reactions, such as heart rate and skin conductance, cannot serve a priori as measures of emotion. The identification of emotion with perception also facilitates the borrowing of concepts and research strategies from more highly developed theories of perception. There are two major approaches that can be useful for the psychological analysis of emotional experience. The first is psychophysical in nature and attempts to uncover the laws relating aspects of emotional experience to various stimulus attributes (J. Gibson, 1950; McClelland, 1955; Vitz, 1966, 1972). The second perspective relies on information-processing theory and attempts to generate models describing the various stages of perceptual processing, the different kinds of events (e.g., stimulus and motor) integrated at these stages, and the rules for integration (Anderson, 1971). The current approach builds primarily on the second type of theory.

B. EXPLICATION OF THE MODEL

The experience of emotion is a product of an underlying constructive process (Neisser, 1967) that is also responsible for overt emotional behavior. One or all of the mechanisms involved can be activated by external stimulus input, but the mechanisms are able to produce emotion without it. As in earlier statements, we have divided the constructive process into two main stages: A perceptual motor stage and a decision action stage (Dewey, 1894, 1895; H. Leventhal, 1970, 1974a, 1979). Emotional experience emerges in the first perceptual motor stage, serving as one of two major sources of information for decision and action. Decision, planning, and action, however, can alter emotional experience. For example, if instrumental actions are closely linked to the perceptual motor processes of stage one, the rapid execution of instrumental volitional actions can short-circuit emotional experience. In contrast, when instrumental action is delayed, particularly under conditions of conflict, one is very likely to experience and express emotion (Dewey, 1894, 1895).

The model also posits a hierarchy of three mechanisms in the perceptual motor system, involving *expressive motor* processing, *schematic* processing, and *conceptual* processing. These three mediational systems act and interact simultaneously in contributing to emotional experience. The expressive motor mechanism is the primary generator of emotion; it can generate subjective feeling in the naive (newborn) in response to elementary stimulus features, such as pitch and contour. The schematic and conceptual systems attach different types of cognitive processes to emotion. The schematic is in some sense the more primary and important; it integrates specific situational perceptions (episodes) with autonomic, subjective, expressive, and instrumental responses in a concrete, patterned, image-like memory system. The conceptual system is more sequential and volitional in nature and corresponds more closely to social labeling processes. We shall examine each of the mechanisms in turn and then discuss their interaction.

C. EXPRESSIVE-MOTOR MECHANISM

A key postulate of our model is that subjective emotional qualities emerge in experience along with the activation of patterned expressive motor reactions. Thus, where James explicitly discounted a special neurological center for generating emotional quality, I hypothesize that motor activity is involved in the generation of feeling quality, defining a basic set of subjective feelings that make up the palette of primary affects. These subjective feelings and expressive responses are then synthesized with specific stimuli to join feeling to eliciting objects and ideas.

This mechanism provides for the basic differentiation of emotional qualities (Issue 1 in Section IV,A) and the early perception of the emotionally based similarities and differences between situations needed to learn socially provided labels for emotion (Issue 1a). The expressive motor mechanism is critical for the individual to retain contact with his or her "true feelings"; it is a source of affective experience that is "felt" even when social learning has distorted the interpretations being given a situation (Issue 1b). It is the basis for the universality of human affective communication, found in the communication of affect across vastly different cultural groups (Issue 1a). Finally, expressive-motor processes are sensitive to specific stimulus events (the expressive reactions of others), which elicit emotional experience (Issue 3) (Öhman & Dimberg, 1978).

Many authors follow Bell (1847) and Darwin (1872/1904) by postulating that distinctive subjective emotional experiences arise from activity in the facial motor system (Ekman *et al.*, 1972; Izard, 1971; Lanzetta, Cartwright-Smith, & Kleck, 1976; H. Leventhal & Sharp, 1965; Tomkins, 1962). Tomkins (1962) has been the strongest advocate of this proposition, along with investigators in ethology (Eibl-Eibesfeldt, 1970). How does facial motor activity affect feelings? One simple hypothesis is that feelings arise from feedback from facial muscle responses.

1. The Facial Feedback Hypothesis

James (1890/1950) believed that a particular feeling would be present whenever a specific pattern of bodily response was produced and absent when the bodily response was missing. In reviewing the role of facial expressions in emotion, he mentioned reports of actors who mimicked expressions of affect without feeling the least bit emotional. Most, if not all, of us can recall at least one occasion on which we have smiled, frowned, or looked guilty to fit the demands of social convention without feeling the appropriate emotion. James (1884) thought that this eliminated the face as the source of emotion, but he also made the following contradictory suggestion, "If we wish to conquer undesirable emotional tendencies in ourselves, we must assiduously, and the first instance, cold-bloodedly go through the outward movements of those contrary dispositions which we prefer to cultivate" (p. 198). James seems to have believed that generating an opposing expression swiftly eliminates an unwanted emotion, but the replacement of the unwanted emotion with the one we wish to cultivate is gradual. For him, therefore, facial expressions can more easily block than create feelings. We will return to this dilemma when we deal with the relationship between deliberate and automatic expressive behavior, but first we will review the evidence related to the feedback hypothesis. This evidence is both neuroanatomical and behavioral. Most of it is indirect rather than direct. Taken together the research findings are consistent with the idea that feedback from the face is the source of subjective emotion, although the research does not test the hypothesis directly.

Tomkins (1962) and Gellhorn (1964) emphasize that facial muscles have extensive neural connections with hypothalamic nuclei which play an important role in generating patterns of expressive, sympathetic, and parasympathetic response. The facial muscle system is also highly differentiated, being composed of 15 symmetrical muscle pairs and the orbicular muscle (see Izard, 1971, pp. 238, 239). Furthermore, facial muscles lack the sheathing common to other striate muscles and can constrict in partial and complex patterns (Tomkins, 1962). Differentiation and hypothalamic connections suggest that the face could serve as an important source of feedback for creating distinctive subjective emotions.

Consistent with this conclusion is evidence showing the face to be extremely sensitive to stimulation (Tomkins, 1962). Newborns are more responsive when stimulated on the face and head than on other parts of the body. Stimulation of both the face and other body regions is more likely to lead to reports of facial than of competing stimuli for both children and adults. Faces also dominate visual fixation, something apparent as early as 5–7 weeks of age (Haith, Bergman, & Moore, 1977), and are the most salient aspect of the human form as drawn by children 3.5–5 years of age (Bower, 1966, 1971; Tomkins, 1962). Finally,

Tomkins (1962) states that resistance to habituation is higher for neuromuscular units of the face than for other neuromuscular units, a condition that would be important for sustaining the alerting and attention-maintaining properties of emotional reactions.

None of the preceding data show the face to be the key source for defining subjective feeling quality, but we would come a step closer to supporting that assumption if there were evidence that facial expressions served as a reliable cues for the judgment of emotional states. During the 1940s and early 1950s it was argued that judges could not make reliable or valid judgments of emotional states from photographs, and that the same emotion could be regularly associated with different patterns of expression, particularly across different cultures (Bruner & Tagiuri, 1954; LaBarre, 1947). However, this argument has been put to rest by Ekman *et al.*'s (1972) thorough and critical review of the expressive judgment literature. Their review supports the following conclusions: Specific situational conditions, such as the stress of childbirth (Leventhal & Sharp, 1965), elicit objectively similar facial motor reactions in many persons. Different parts of the face play a more or less salient role for different feeling states—the top of the face for negative affects and the bottom of the face for positive affects (Coleman, 1949; Hanawalt, 1944; Schwartz, Fair, Salt, Mandel, & Klerman, 1976). Facial expressions can be objectively scored and one can predict a judge's inference of feelings from the scores for the target face (Ekman & Friesen, 1975; Ekman *et al.*, 1972, Chapter 4; Izard, 1971). The objective scoring system will predict the labels given to specific expressions, even when the judgments are made by individuals from cultures different from that of the persons being judged (e.g., Ekman *et al.*, 1972; Izard, 1971). The excellent studies by Ekman and associates, demonstrating that individuals from preliterate bush cultures can accurately infer intended emotional states from photographs of Americans (Ekman & Friesen, 1971) and also produce expressions which can be accurately judged by American students (Ekman *et al.*, 1972), should lay permanently to rest the hypothesis that expressions are entirely a matter of cultural learning.

In sum, we now know that a common set of expressive-motor patterns exists for all people. Individuals from different cultures as well as people within the same culture produce a set of similar expressions to common feeling terms and, therefore, can judge one another's emotions (see also Osgood, 1966; Tomkins & McArter, 1964). Moreover, observers from different cultures can appropriately discriminate and label expressions even when these feelings and expressions are evoked by different situational stimuli, suggesting that they are based on a common core of subjective emotional experience.

Observations of newborns (Brazelton, Koslowski, & Main, 1973; Campos, 1979; Emde, 1979; Sroufe, Waters, & Matas, 1974; Wolff, 1959), premature infants (Peiper, 1963), and children born without sight (Fulcher, 1942; Goodenough, 1932; Eibl-Eibesfeldt, 1970) all support the conclusion that expressive reaction patterns are innate. Studies of blind children indicate that visual experience is unnecessary for the development of appropriate expressive behavior to specific stimuli (Fulcher, 1942; Goodenough, 1932). Indeed, these conclusions seem to hold for children lacking both visual and auditory contact with their environment. Touch alone is sufficient to elicit expected affective expressions, although extensive nervous system dysfunction may minimize the clarity of expression (Eibl-Eibesfeldt, 1970). Finally, as blind children grow older they exhibit a gradual decrease in clarity of expression, suggesting that visual social experience is important for the maintenance of these facial patterns. However, all the evidence so far cited is indirect, as none of the studies cited directly tests for a link between expression and subjective feeling, and it may be premature to conclude that feedback from the face gives rise to feeling.

Two procedures have been used to test the feedback hypothesis directly: direct manipulations of facial expressions and instructions to reveal or hide expressive reactions. Both kinds of investigation assume expressive changes cause (or mediate) subjective feeling.

An early study by Pasquarelli and Bull (1951) directly manipulated facial expressions. While in a hypnotic trance, the subject was instructed to contract specific facial muscles as the experimenter touched them with a pointer. Once the expression was established, the subject was told not to move. He was then instructed to feel an emotion (but not make an expression) that required an expressive-motor pattern either opposite or similar to that in which he had been locked. Unless their expressions changed, none of the subjects felt the suggested emotion if the pattern for this second emotion was opposite to that first molded under hypnosis. This facial pattern blocked the emergence of feeling.

The Pasquarelli and Bull study supported James' suggestion that expressions could block emotions but did not show that expressions could create feelings. Laird (1974) and Izard, Kidd, and Kotsch (undated) have attempted to create feelings using the method of touching specific muscles and instructing subjects to contract them. As in the Pasquarelli and Bull study, in both studies the experimenters avoided using such words as smile or frown, minimizing experimenter demands to report specific emotions. The manipulation of facial pose was crossed with a second variation, exposure to pictures with affective contents that were or were not related to the pose. After the subject was set in a ρose and exposed to a picture, he or she completed a mood adjective check list. The investigations agreed in finding an association between expression and mood. Negative and aggressive moods were accentuated by the manipulated frowns and elated moods were accentuated, although to a lesser degree, by experimentally established smiles.

The second set of experiments attempted to test the same hypothesis by using instructions to achieve expressive change. For example, H. Leventhal and Mace (1970) obtained large differences in expressiveness from groups of grade school children shown a slapstick movie by telling some groups to feel free to laugh during the movie so the experimenters could obtain a good recording of children's laughter and other groups not to laugh so they could obtain a good recording of the film sound track. Lanzetta and Kleck and their associates (Lanzetta *et al.*, 1976) conducted several similar studies where subjects were exposed to a series of electrical shocks of varying intensity and told either to express or to hide their feelings so that an observer would or would not be able to judge the strength of the shock from their expressions. The data from these studies are not always consistent with a simple feedback hypothesis. For example, Leventhal and Mace found substantial sex differences. Female subjects gave more favorable subjective ratings to funny films when their expressive behavior was exaggerated by instructions, whereas the opposite occurred in the case of men. The same results were obtained by several other investigators (Cupchik & Leventhal, 1974; Young & Frye, 1966). The Lanzetta and Kleck studies, in contrast, are fairly consistent in showing direct associations between expressiveness and measures of emotionality. For example, expressions and electrodermal activity are usually lower in the expression-hiding conditions and higher in the expression-showing conditions. Ratings of shock intensity are not as consistently associated, however, with the manipulations of expression.

What do these two sets of studies tell us about expressive behavior and subjective feeling? The first and most substantial finding is that investigators were far better able to alter expressive behavior than reports of subjective feeling. Changes in mood (e.g., Izard *et al.*, undated; Laird, 1974) and ratings of films and cartoons (Cupchik & Leventhal, 1974; H. Leventhal & Cupchik, 1975; H. Leventhal & Mace, 1970) and shocks (Kleck, Vaughan, Cartwright-Smith, Vaughan, Colby, & Lanzetta, 1976; Lanzetta *et al.*, 1976) were very small despite substantial changes in expression. Feelings and judgments seem to be strongly tied to the stimulus of the shock level or film (see also S. Schachter & Wheeler, 1962). Second, it is clear that expressiveness is not always positively associated with subjective feeling. This is seen in the studies of humor conducted by Leventhal and his associates (Cupchik & Leventhal, 1974; H. Leventhal & Cupchik, 1975, 1976; Leventhal & Mace, 1970).

There are at least three arguments that could be made from these findings. First, one might say the studies failed to test the hypothesis that facial feedback is necessary for subjective feeling. Second, one could conclude that the hypothesis is incorrect and that facial feedback and the facial motor system have little or nothing to do with subjective emotion. Third, one might suggest the facial motor system is important for creating feelings but its operation is more complex than a simple feedback model would have us believe. To adequately appraise the feedback hypothesis we should carefully examine the logic of these studies. We can then turn to the alternative feed-forward hypothesis presented in the following section.

We do not have to adopt absurdly rigid standards in order to maintain that the studies just reviewed generally fail to test the hypothesis that feedback from facial motor activity automatically gives rise to subjective emotional experience. In many instances the findings are correlational and we cannot tell which of the two correlated variables, facial expression or feeling, is responsible for change in the other, or whether the change in both factors results from some third variable. For example, Kleck *et al.* (1976) report lower levels of expressiveness and autonomic response and slightly lower levels of judged painfulness of shock when an observer is present than when the observer is absent. This reflects any of the following causal sequences: expressiveness influencing autonomic and subjective reports, autonomic changes influencing expressiveness and subjective reports, reductions in subjective reports influencing expressiveness and autonomic responses, or the situational condition of being observed influencing the impact of shock on all three of the measures. It is no more correct to make a causal interpretation of a correlation between the means of a set of dependent measures across experimental conditions than it is to make a causal interpretation of a correlation between scores across subjects. Yet, Lanzetta and his associates maintain that the positive associations between expression and autonomic indicators across treatments support the feedback hypothesis. There is no logical reason to agree with either this conclusion or with their conclusion that negative correlations for these same measures reflect some other nonfeedback process when obtained in studies of individual differences (Jones, 1950; Lanzetta & Kleck, 1970; Notarius & Levenson, 1979). Although they may be right, neither the logic of their argument nor their evidence is persuasive.

The experiments directly manipulating facial muscle response fare no better in testing the feedback hypothesis since they fail to rule out alternative ways in which expressive change may produce change in mood reports. The investigators posed their experimental subjects by manipulating single muscles and did not ask for smiles and frowns so as to avoid suggesting or demanding emotional reports. Control subjects heard the instructions but did not adopt the poses. The failure of control subjects who heard the instructions to report similar mood changes rules out a direct path from instructions to moods, but it does not rule out other possibilities. For example, it is possible that subjects were reporting mood change in response to the amount of facial muscular change and not to its pattern. The angry and frowning patterns produced the major mood changes in Laird's second study and in the Izard, Kidd, and Kotsch research. It may have been the greater effort required to produce these muscular patterns, and not the pattern of expression per se, that generated dysphoric feelings (Izard, 1978).

Given the equivocal data and the difficulty of establishing adequate tests of the feedback hypothesis, we might expect investigators to conclude it was incorrect (e.g., Tourangeau & Ellsworth, 1979). However, advocates of a hypothesis do not readily accept its demise (Kuhn, 1962). One defense has been that feedback can be produced by invisible expressive reactions, whose brief or micro-expressive changes are sufficient for generating subjective feeling states. E. A. Haggard and Isaacs (1966) recorded close associations between micromomentary facial muscle changes and emotional topics of conversation during psychotherapy; the facial changes were observable only in motion picture films played back in slow motion. Schwartz and his associates have used electromyography to record nonvisible changes in activity at specific muscle sites (corrugator, frontalis, maseter, and depressor) and have identified muscle patterns that distinguish between moods of sadness, anger, happiness, and a typical day's feelings (Schwartz et al., 1976). They also found the happy muscle pattern greatly attenuated in depressed individuals; when the subject's depression improved the happy pattern became clearer (Schwartz, Fair, Mandel, Salt, Mieske, & Klerman, 1978).

However, this line of defense cannot protect the feedback hypothesis against four key problems: (1) The new evidence for the hypothesis is still correlational, and some other factor(s) may mediate the reported associations; (2) substantial changes in expressiveness often fail to relate to associated changes in subjective feelings; (3) the changes observed in microexpressiveness precede changes in subjective reports by days or weeks (Schwartz et al., 1978); and (4) the hypothesis is not consistent with clinical neurological data.

The failure to square with clinical neurological data is a serious blow to the feedback hypothesis. Investigators have typically used clinical reports to examine the relationship between patterned expressive behavior and subjective emotional states (e.g., James, 1890/1950, p. 445). Although the concerns of the practitioner may lead to sketchy and sometimes ambiguous reports, data obtained by clinical neurologists with a clear grasp of the contrasting implications of the Darwinian (1872/1904) and Jamesian theses indicate that: (1) Subjective emotions are present in patients lacking spontaneous facial expression; and (2) subjective emotions are absent in individuals showing extraordinarily intense expressive reactions. The first conclusion is based on data showing that patients completely lacking facial expression can still have a rich subjective life, as in the case of the patient with facial diplegia (absence of expressive motor movement) who comments that "his greatest misfortune (is being) forced to be joyful or sad without making any demonstration of his feelings to his fellow creatures" (Rombert, 1853, cited in S. A. K. Wilson, 1924, p. 315).

Data for the second statement come from the large number of patients who spontaneously and "at the slightest provocation" burst into intense laughter or crying without an appropriate accompanying subjective affect in cases of double hemiplegia, pseudobulbar paralysis, and disseminated sclerosis (S. A. K. Wilson, 1924, p. 300).

The more recent reviews by J. W. Brown (1967, p. 3) and Ironside (1956) reinforce Wilson's observation. It now seems abundantly clear that subjective feelings arise in the absence of overt expressive behavior and fail to arise in its presence. Wilson was sufficiently convinced of these conclusions to adopt Sully's (1902) early version of cognition–arousal theory: "Only when physical and appropriate visceral components are fused can emotion be felt acutely and the latter is less significant than the former" (S. A. K. Wilson, 1929, p. 278).

Given the clinical observations, it seems there is no alternative but to reject a simple feedback hypothesis. Rejecting the feedback hypothesis, however, is not equivalent to denying involvement of expressive-motor mechanisms in the generation of subjective feelings. Abandoning this broader hypothesis would again separate the study of expression and emotional communication from that of subjective feelings. Some kind of motor mechanism is involved in generating emotional experience.

2. The Interactive-Outflow Hypothesis

It is important to remember that the feedback hypothesis was intended primarily to account for the rapid appearance and disappearance of specific subjective feelings and not for the production of longer lasting emotions and mood states. My analysis attempts to account for the same phenomena but avoids the pitfalls of assuming that feelings are a direct product of expression.

The mechanism was suggested by findings from a study in which subjects rated the funniness of cartoons which were viewed and judged either in the presence or in the absence of audience laughter (Cupchik & Leventhal, 1974). Some subjects were asked to monitor their expressive behavior; they then rated these reactions before judging the cartoons. It was predicted and found that the observation and rating of expressive behavior diminished the positive effects of audience laughter on the cartoon ratings; this held true for female subjects only. A similar finding has been reported showing that self-observation (by mirrors) can inhibit the inducement of emotion by suggestion (Scheier, Carver, & Gibbons, 1979).

This prediction regarding the effect of self-monitoring was based on the following assumptions: (1) Subjects' expressive behavior contributes to their feelings; (2) expressive reactions create feelings only when they have been spontaneous or involuntary (H. Leventhal, 1974a); (3) hearing audience laughter intensifies spontaneous laughter; (4) the combination of the stimulus (the cartoon) with the feedback from the exaggerated laughter occurs preattentively; (5) the increased expressiveness adds to the rating of the cartoons only when conditions 2, 3, and 4 are met, that is, when laughter has been intensified, spontaneous, and combined preattentively with the cartoon; and (6) self-monitoring of expression disrupts these conditions by making the laughter voluntary and conscious.

It is, of course, impossible for a single experiment to verify so long a list of assumptions. The results, however, were consistent with these notions, as the subjects' observation of their own expressions eliminated the impact of audience laughter on female participants and upset their ability to differentiate cartoons preselected as good from those preselected as bad. In short, those who monitored their own expressions gradually lost sight of differences in stimulus quality, suggesting that monitoring expressiveness disrupted the integration of the feedback with the stimulus and made the rating task confusing. Responses to the postexperimental questionnaire supported this interpretation. Since self-monitoring also increased expressiveness, it was clear that the reduced ratings of funniness did not occur because self-monitoring inhibited the expression of motor reactions and feelings, as was hypothesized in the Lanzetta *et al.* (1976) studies.

A report in *Nature (London)* confirms the hypothesis that feedback from peripheral stimulation has quite different effects on feeling depending on whether it is generated by voluntary or by involuntary behavior. Weiskrantz, Elliott, and Darlington (1971) exposed subjects to three tickling conditions, one where the bottom of the subject's foot was tickled by a stick moved by the experimenter, another where the stick was moved by the subject, and a third where the subject's hand rested on the experimenter's hand as the latter moved the stick. Reports of felt ticklishness were highest when the experimenter moved the stick, and lower for both of the other conditions, when the subject moved it or the experimenter moved it with the subject's hand carried passively along.

The model suggested by these data is shown in Fig. 1. It was constructed to reflect the following assumptions.

1. There are separate volitional and spontaneous controls in the expressive-motor system. Subjective experience confirms this division of motor activity into spontaneous and volitional acts. Indeed, the term "emotion" is often used to mean external stimulus control in contrast to internal volitional control (Peters, 1970). The neurological literature referred to earlier also confirms the distinction. Individuals who have lost the ability to control their facial expression voluntarily show spontaneous outbursts of expressive activity without experiencing emotion (J. W. Brown, 1967; Ironside, 1956), whereas others possess the ability voluntarily to make expressive reactions but fail to respond spontaneously to outer stimuli (J. W. Brown, 1967; Ironside, 1956).

2. The central nervous system contains all the mechanisms necessary for emotional experience. By moving emotion into the central nervous system, where Cannon (1927) placed it, we need no longer puzzle over inconsistencies between outer expression and inner feeling. This does not deny peripheral feedback access to the central mechanism; it merely asserts that the necessary machinery for emotional experience is centrally located. More specifically, the model postulates that the spatial and temporal patterning of emotional expression

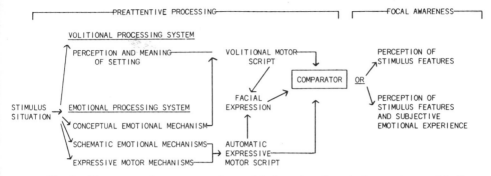

Fig. 1.   The perceptual-motor processing model of emotion. Stage 1 of a two-stage model of the mechanism underlying self-regulation. There are two basic pathways, one creating a representation of the "objective" environment, the other a representation of subjective emotion. Both pathways are hierarchies, but only the hierarchy for emotion is depicted here. The model illustrates the feed-forward mechanism that generates subjective feelings. The representations of the objective environment and of the emotion that are generated by this stage serve as information for planning and action, which is Stage 2.

is centrally programmed and that separate programs exist for both spontaneous and volitional reactions (Geshwind, 1975).

Psychologists have historically given excessive weight to peripheral cueing hypotheses, perhaps because introspection confirms the significance of body cues, such as the bodily upset that follows emotional episodes, for behavior. It is no surprise that an introspectively oriented psychologist such as James placed so much emphasis on peripheral feedback for emotion. The same emphasis is seen in such behavioral concepts as response chaining (Hull, 1943) or response-produced cues (Dollard & Miller, 1950), in part because the fear of mentalistic concepts drove the behaviorists to the periphery. However, Lashley (1951) pointed out long ago that complex serial performances could not be carried out by a regulatory mechanism relying on signals going from center to periphery and back again at every step. The rapid performance of complex reactions patterned in space and time requires that signals be sent to the periphery in an appropriate spatial and temporal order by a central program. These programs encompass the starting and end points of the sequence (Greenwald, 1970).

3. Emotional experience emerges from an interaction of volitional and spontaneous central motor scripts. As already suggested, we feel emotion when the spontaneous motor system overrides the control of the voluntary system. Emotional behavior is typically experienced as under the control of external stimuli. When the volitional system overrides the spontaneous one, in contrast, we experience controlled action. It should come as no surprise, therefore, that volitional actions will be distress reducing even if they do not control outer stimulus

events. Spontaneously provoked emotional reactions that intensify the distress induced by a noxious stimulus are minimized by volitional performance (Geer, Davidson, & Gatchel, 1970; Weiss, 1970).

4. The interaction between the systems may involve a feed-forward mechanism. The basic assumption here is that the automatic system generates a script in response to external stimuli, be it expressive contours or schematically encoded events, and the script then sends a pattern of motor signals (laughter, tears, frowning, etc.) in two different directions. One path leads to the motor controls of the face, the other to a comparator in the volitional motor system—a feed-forward path. The signals sent to the comparator over this feed-forward route are matched to the motor script generated by the voluntary system. If the spatial and temporal features of the two motor systems agree, the comparison will be experienced as a voluntary movement; that is, the information coming from the comparator cannot be distinguished from instructions for an intended movement and is felt as such.

5. The feed-forward comparison process is automatic and preattentive. This point emphasizes that people are unaware of the steps in information processing that lead to the generation of expressive reaction patterns and the comparison of the feed-forward signal with the volitional representation (Mandler, 1975; Nisbett & Wilson, 1977). Usually only the output of the comparison, that is, emotion or willed movement, is conscious. Efforts to control emotion tend to be directed toward those portions of the process of which one is aware, making it difficult to exert volitional control over emotions. Typically, one tries to block out the stimulus that provokes automatic processing or to inhibit the expressive reactions that result from it. Neither alternative directly influences stimulus coding or the comparison of the scripts. Damage to the volitional system can lead to expressive display without emotion (as seen in clinical literature) because either the comparison process can no longer take place or its results are no longer accessible to awareness (J. W. Brown, 1967).

6. Facial feedback can intensify and sustain emotional experience when it arrives at the comparison point. Therefore, feedback can serve the same functions as the feed-forward signal from the automatic processing system, but it is not necessary for emotional experience.

The model (Fig. 1) has several advantages in addition to the obvious one of freeing subjective feeling states from direct ties to peripheral expressive motor activity. One of the most important is the suggestion that volitional performance of automatic expressive actions can, as Cannon (1927) suggested, override automatic control, bringing action under volitional control and eliminating emotion. This is critical in accounting for the humor data generated by Cupchik and Leventhal (1974) and H. Leventhal and Mace (1970), the tickling data of Weiskrantz et al. (1971), and a variety of clinical data suggesting that voluntary performance of emotionally motivated behaviors can remove these acts from emotional control. For example, the deliberate practice of stuttering has been recommended as a procedure for controlling its spontaneous (emotional) generation (Dunlap, 1933). Fear reduction through desensitization (Lang & Lazovik, 1963) and guided participation (Bandura, Blanchard, & Ritter, 1969) also can be interpreted within this framework as both involve voluntary production of behaviors (images, approaching snakes) that are typically controlled by automatic emotional reactions.

The outflow hypothesis is not original; it was borrowed from models developed to account for a problem similar to that previously mentioned: the constancy of visual experience despite changes in retinal image patterns that are generated by eye movements (Gyr, 1972; Von Holst, 1954). Intentional eye movements generate a feed-forward signal which cancels the perception of movement of outer stimuli when the image they cast shifts along the retinal surface. By contrast, externally generated pushes on the eyeball that produce movement not intended by the occulomotor systems produce movement of the retinal image which is seen as movement in the outer world (Holst, 1954).

It is interesting to look at the results of the recent Tourangeau and Ellsworth (1979) study in light of the above model. Their subjects were instructed to contract specific facial muscle areas voluntarily and then were exposed to either a fear-arousing, a sad, or a neutral film. The expressions had no substantial effects on the participants' moods. The investigators argue that "even if the proprioceptive feedback along voluntary and involuntary pathways is recognizably different (facial feedback), the theories sought to predict a generally positive correlation" (p. 1528). From the current perspective, however, we would predict that making a fearful face will reduce feelings of fear. However, there are several reasons why one cannot make predictions for studies such as that by Tourangeau and Ellsworth. First, it is not at all clear that inducing facial expressions on a muscle by muscle basis generates the kind of patterned, central motor template that cancels automatic feedback. Second, we have no idea as to whether the induced facial reactions are within the range that are supposed to generate affective experience. To investigate the problem we need new techniques for separately stimulating spontaneous and voluntary expressive changes independent of the affective changes induced by schematic processes of external stimuli, such as an emotion-provoking film.

D. SCHEMATIC PROCESSING

It is hypothesized that emotional schemata are integrations of separate perceptual codes of the visual, auditory, somesthetic, expressive, and autonomic reactions that are reliably associated with emotional experiences; they are a memory of the emotional experience itself (see Hurvich, 1969, p. 503). Schematic organizations are therefore built upon prior expressive-motor reactions (Issues 2a and 2b, Section IV,A). Schematic processing refers to the combination or coding of new situational inputs with these memories of prior emotional experiences. The reactivation of emotional memories is a critical step in the creation of new emotional experience (Issue 2).

The term "schema" is used, first, to emphasize that we are dealing with an organized representation of other more elementary codes, and second, to emphasize the importance of behavior, particularly expressive-motor behavior, in the formation and organization of these units (Hebb, 1949; Piaget & Inhelder, 1971).

To postulate a schematic memory it is necessary to explain how it functions. Because emotional schemata are perceptual-motor memories, they should exhibit the properties of perceptual memories in general and not require deliberate or conscious thought; they represent a form of automatic, emotional (or affective) recognition (Panagis & Leventhal, 1973; Safer, 1978; Zajonc, 1979). Indeed, there is evidence to suggest that emotional memory schemata are as rapid acting and as sensitive to information as nonemotional representational memory schemata involved in stimulus recognition (see Ericksen, 1958; W. R. Wilson, 1979; Zajonc, 1979. This emotional memory system may well be the main route for the rapid processing of stimulus information and the generation of automatic expressive motor signals that both activate the face and feed forward to be compared to volitional expressive action.

Like other schemata or categories (Broadbent, 1977), emotional schemata act as selective devices, focusing attention on particular stimulus features and generating anticipations about later experience (Issues 4 and 5). Emotionally directed attention is also likely to be long lasting as its expressive and automatic components seem less easily habituated than attention directed by novelty. Therefore, emotion should play a major role in generating the rehearsal of perceptual features of objects (e.g., a lover's face) and lead to the formation of new perceptual memory structures.

By directing attention and facilitating formation of these structures schematic processing plays a central role in the sophistication of development of the emotional life (Issue 2b). This development has several important aspects. One is the formation of specific episodic memories. Indeed, much of emotional memory appears to focus on vivid images, feelings, and expressive, autonomic, and instrumental responses that are highly situationally specific (Issues 2b, 2c, and 3). For example, a given situation can arouse a specific feeling of anger for one person and a fear response for another. Situations with multiple cues can elicit several schemata and lead to sharply contrasting and conflicting emotional experiences, for instance, anger or joy in a setting such as that in the S. Schachter and Singer (1962) study. Perceptual memory can also be general and prototypic (Posner, 1973). This leads to the point that emotional schemata can be expected to play an important role in generalizing emotional experiences. The generalizations will take place along dimensions that are highly characteristic of the set of concrete episodes which originally stimulated that particular class of emotional experiences. Anger and fear may at times generalize along lines of perceived power and status, while depression generalizes along lines of punishment for failure despite effort (Abramson, Seligman, & Teasdale, 1978). These affectively based attributions are automatic and "unreasoned."

Emotional schemata are also important in the development of new emotions. Combinations of the basic emotions of fear, joy, anger, sadness, etc., may be elicited in complex situations and recorded in perceptual schematic memory. Blends of this sort can generate stable new feelings states (Ekman *et al.*, 1972). It is possible to talk, therefore, of automatically elicited emotions such as empathic distress, intimacy, and pride.

One last critical function of emotional schemata is the organization of emotional experience. Emotional schemata combine or integrate situational perception and expressive, autonomic, and instrumental reactions with subjective emotional feeling so that one is aware of an emotion in relation to an eliciting condition. The schemata focus the individual on the object of affective desire or aversion and bathe the perception of the object in a specific emotional feeling. The expressive and autonomic behaviors are relatively nonsalient because the integration of subjective emotion dominates the field of consciousness (Krueger, 1928/1968; Peters, 1970).

Two functions of the organizational aspect of emotional schemata can be distinguished. One is the linking of feeling to objects and situations as emphasized above. In this respect emotional experience is a form of what Polanyi (1968) called tacit knowledge. To help define tacit knowledge Polanyi compares it to the perception of depth in stereoscopic viewing: The viewer uses two monocular views (the particulars) to build a unified experience of a scene in depth. The particulars are necessary to the unified view, but the unified view goes beyond them. Attention to the particulars destroys the integration; the experience of an emotion is greater than the experience of the particulars used to construct it. It is the emotional schemata that integrate the components to create a unified emotional experience.

The other organizational aspect of schematic processing hypothesized by the model is the collative or cumulative nature of emotion. Emotions and their component particulars are combined in an additive (possibly multiplicative) fashion, but they do not seem to average (see Anderson, 1965). This collative property is inherent in the very concept of emotional schemata. Seemingly unrelated events, for example, object perception and expressive behavior, are combined to form a feeling about something. Strengthening any one of these elements, increasing the intensity of spontaneous expression, or heightening autonomic activity, for example, will increase the intensity of the emotional experience (Zillmann, 1978). When a tape of audience laughter was played to female subjects who were judging cartoons, the subjects' laughter became more intense and their judgments more favorable. The increase in the favorability of their judgments was in direct proportion to the increase in their laughter (Cupchik & Leventhal, 1974; H. Leventhal & Cupchik, 1975). Male subjects seemed to make intellectual or reasoned judgments rather than spontaneous emotional judgments and appeared to average the two sources of information—the cartoon and the audience. However, the collative effects seem to occur automatically, while the disruption of this effect can be caused by deliberate thought (averaging) or deliberately ignoring one of the stimuli (Anderson, 1965, 1971).

The fine studies of generalization of arousal conducted by Zillmann and his associates (Zillmann, 1978) also illustrate this collative function. In this research the intensity of arousal from a prior task, such as pedaling an exercise bicycle, added into and strengthened a subsequent but unrelated emotional experience, such as sexual arousal. It is important to note that this cross-situational or cross-emotional addition occurs for active emotions, for example, generalization from vigorous exercise to anger-motivated attacks. Therefore, generalization of arousal from one emotional state to another appears to occur as long as both emotions typically involve extensive autonomic activity and there is a situational cue to action for the second emotional (anger) state (Zillmann, Katcher, & Milavsky, 1972). Zillmann also points out that generalization does not occur when autonomic arousal is so intense that it is clearly perceived to be linked to the prior situation. The subject then knows he or she is shaking and breathing hard from exercise and not anger. As arousal declines to less noticeable levels, it readily adds into the subsequent expression of anger. In summary, Zillmann's studies illustrate that the components of emotions collate automatically unless the organization of the perceptual field (e.g., arousal as part of exercise or emotion) checks the collative efforts.

Emotional memory has the additional function of establishing stable object relationships, that is, positive and negative attitudes, as well as attachments and aversions. Stable object relationships are critical for maintaining a secure social support network and maintaining positive and avoiding negative experiences with specific objects and events. The basic core of the problem of attitude change, which has occupied so much of the energy of social psychologists (McGuire, 1968), is very likely a problem of changing schematic emotional memory. More dramatic examples of emotionally based attitudes are seen in behavior therapy studies of such phenomena as snake phobias (e.g., Lang, 1979). One important aspect of the attitude problem is developing techniques for distinguishing attitude domains in which there is close involvement with emotional memory from those in which there is little involvement of emotional memory. Beliefs or opinions with little emotional involvement are likely to be easy to change and may often be based on inferences from one's own behavior

(Bem, 1972; H. Leventhal, 1974b). The findings encountered in the studies of attribution, that reattribution alters overt behavior but fails to reduce subjective emotional reports, provides further evidence of the stickiness of schematic emotional memory (Calvert-Boyanowsky & Leventhal, 1975). "Resistance" to therapeutic action is also visible in cases of phantom pain, a problem that is discussed in detail in the following section.

1. Behavioral Evidence for Schematic Processing

Evidence for schematic emotional processing varies from the anecdotal to the experimental. The anecdotal examples are, perhaps, more persuasive because of their extraordinary quality. For example, Janis (1958) reported fascinating instances of "unrepression" during the psychoanalytic therapy of a 39-year-old woman who elected minor surgery to remove varicose veins in her legs. The fear associated with the impending surgery led to vivid (dream-like) recall of scenes from childhood, such as seeing a crippled boy while she was looking out a train window and seeing an amputee move himself about on a small wheeled platform. The memory images were linked to the present by fear and threat of injury to the legs.

Other examples of emotional memory range from mild experiences of *déja vu*, where new situations are felt to repeat past experiences of special emotional significance, to the vivid, uncontrollable, and unwanted intrusion into waking life of scenes from previous viewings of upsetting and gory films (Horowitz, 1970). The role of vivid memory images can also be seen in the rich, emotionally laden imagery that is reported upon awakening from paradoxical sleep (D. B. Cohen, 1970; Dement, 1972), including awakening from paradoxical sleep after having been exposed to threat movies (Witkin & Lewis, 1967). The Witkin and Lewis descriptions of experimentally induced dreams strongly suggests that the emotional theme induced by a film is reworked in successive rapid eye movement dream periods, and the imagery is increasingly related to earlier self-relevant experiences as the night goes on.

The behavioral significance of emotional imagery is nicely illustrated in an experimental study by Turner and Layton (1976). They constructed four lists of paired associates, two of neutral words, one high and one low in imagery value, and two of aggressive words, one high and the other low in imagery value. Their subjects learned one of these lists before serving as teachers in a second task, where they delivered shocks whenever a confederate made errors in a learning task. The subjects who learned the words high in aggressive imagery delivered stronger shocks of longer duration when the confederate erred in the learning task. Subjects who learned words high in aggressive meaning but low in imagery delivered the same intensity and duration of shock as did subjects learning neutral words. The imagery value of the words was critical in activating overt aggressive action to situational cues.

Perhaps the most vivid example of the concreteness and specificity of schematic emotional memory is the phenomenon of phantom pain (Melzack, 1971, 1973; Morgenstern, 1970; Simmel, 1962). Following the amputation of a body part (either by surgery or by accident), the individual may come to experience a phantom limb replete with the sensations and pain which were present prior to the loss. The imagery can be exceptionally vivid, and the pain intense. It can be accompanied by subjective distress and anxiety, high levels of autonomic arousal (sweating and heart racing), and complete facial motor displays. It is not clear whether the emotional and autonomic reactions are part of the memory structure or are elicited by the memory pain.

It is necessary to postulate a central memory structure to account for phantom (and other) pain experiences (Engel, 1959; Nathan, 1962) because efforts to explain these experiences on the basis of more peripheral events have been uniformly unsuccessful (e.g., Morgenstern, 1970).

The importance of central memory processes is forcefully emphasized when a phantom, pain and all, is experienced even though surgery occurs several weeks after a spinal cord injury that has destroyed all communication between central and peripheral sensory motor machinery (Cook & Druckemiller, 1952; Li & Elvidge, 1951).

Phantom pain has other properties consistent with the hypothesis of emotional schematic memory. For example, it is far more likely to occur when pain has existed in the body part prior to amputation, and the sensory properties of the pain experience following loss are usually similar if not identical to those experienced beforehand (Melzack, 1973; Morgenstern, 1970; Simmel, 1962). In some cases the pain memory is clearly selected on the basis of its emotional significance. Henderson and Smyth (1948) report such a case. An amputee had sprained an ankle in combat and was then hit by shrapnel in the sprained leg. This latter injury produced severe pain and eventually led to the amputation. However, the soldier attributed his misfortune to the sprain, since it had hampered his movement and was responsible for his wound, and it was the painful sensations of the sprain that appeared in the phantom.

The emotional quality of phantom pain memory is also illustrated by case examples where a phantom that has been dormant for months or years is rearoused by emotionally distressing life experiences (Melzack, 1973). The phantom may reemerge from the feeling of severe upset while discussing life setbacks. Phantoms and phantom pain are also dependent on a reasonably mature memory system; they do not appear in children under 4–6 years of age (Simmel, 1962). It could be that the cognitive imagery system must reach a minimal level of development before a person can establish relatively firm, affectively laden pictorial memories of amputated body parts. Recent data suggest that self-descriptions of 3- to 5-year-olds are less oriented to body image than was previously suspected (Keller, Ford, & Meachem, 1978). In summary, the observations reported all point to the existence of a concrete memory system linking body image with pain experiences and provide good support for the hypothesis of an emotional memory.

The experience of pain is an illustration of the combination of stimulus information (stinging, burning, aching, etc.) with emotion and cannot be understood or treated if it is conceptualized as a sensory system (Beecher, 1959; Melzack & Wall, 1970). For example, most pharmacological treatments of pain attempt to ameliorate emotional distress and have little effect on the sensory signal generated by the noxious stimulus (Beecher, 1946, 1959; Hardy, Wolff, & Goodell, 1952). Both neurological and behavioral data suggest that the emotional component of pain is generated parallel to the informational signals from the noxious stimulus. The emotional reaction does not occur subsequent to a conscious cognitive appraisal of the stimulus. Everhart and I (H. Leventhal & Everhart, 1979) have concluded that the integration of noxious sensations with emotional schemata occurs simultaneously with the coding of the stimulus in terms of perceptual memories based on its physical properties (coldness, pins and needles, etc.).

This hypothesis is consistent with data on the formation of pain memories in dental patients. Nathan (1962) reports an ingenious demonstration by Hutchins and Reynolds in which they applied a nonpainful electrical stimulus to the trigeminal nerve of patients who had had dental work weeks earlier under either nitrous oxide or injections of novocaine. The electrical stimulus to the nerve recreated the pain of having one's teeth drilled for patients who had received nitrous oxide, which works by reducing emotional distress without affecting the sensory signals sent to the brain. The pain had been recorded in memory, therefore, even though the patients had not been conscious of it, and the stimulus reactivated the pain memory. The electrical stimulus did not recreate the pain of drilling for patients who had received novocaine, which blocks the transmission of impulses from the teeth to the central nervous system and therefore prevents the formation of a pain memory.

Using an analysis similar to that just presented, Johnson (1973) reasoned that a noxious stimulus could be experienced as either highly painful or mildly painful, depending on whether or not it was integrated with a schema of pain and distress or integrated in a nonthreatening schema of the sensory features of the stimulus. To encourage an objective sensory schematization, Johnson provided subjects in one of her conditions with detailed information on the sensory features of the stimulus, describing the numbness, aching, pins and needles, and discoloration of the fingers that would be caused by the ischemia induced by a blood pressure cuff. Subjects given the sensory information reported significantly less distress during ischemic stimulation than did control subjects given the description of the experimental procedure. Two additional experiments showed that the difference could not be accounted for by differences in expectations of harm, preexposure fear level, or efforts to distract or turn away from the noxious stimulus. It was concluded that sensory information helped subjects generate an objective schema of the noxious experience which captured the input in preference to coding it in a pain–distress schema.

An alternative interpretation of the Johnson study is that subjects did not become startled or aroused when the stimulus finally impinged on them because they had accurate expectations about how it would feel. Epstein (1973) has suggested that accuracy of expectations alone does not protect a person against distress and disturbance during stimulus impact, although it may aid in coping with the stimulus situation afterward. The first of three studies by H. Leventhal *et al.* (1979) supported the first part of Epstein's suggestion. It compared distress reports during exposure to cold pressor stimulation for four groups of subjects. Subjects were given either sensory information about the cold pressor experience or procedural information about the cold pressor task, and then half of each group received a pain warning. The accuracy hypothesis would predict the lowest levels of distress for subjects given both sensory information and the pain warning since these subjects had more accurate information than the others. The schematization hypothesis, in contrast, would predict a pain warning to facilitate the coding of the noxious input in terms of an emotional pain–distress schema. According to this position, reduction of distress should only occur when sensory information is given without a pain warning so that subjects form a schema of the stimulus features that does not incorporate pain and emotional distress. The results showed distress reduction only in groups given sensory information without a pain warning, and all other groups were virtually identical. Thus, the schematic hypothesis was supported (see also K. R. L. Hall & Stride, 1954; Staub & Kellett, 1972).

Two other features of the data strengthened this interpretation. First, in both the Johnson and the Leventhal *et al.* studies the subjects rated their distress and the intensity of the sensations generated by the stimulus. Ratings of the intensity of sensations showed smaller and usually nonsignificant differences between the sensory informed groups and the control groups. It appears that emotional distress had been extracted from the noxious experience in the sensory informed group (see also Hilgard, 1969; Knox, Morgan, & Hilgard, 1974). Second, in the Leventhal *et al.* study using cold pressor stimuli, the distress and the sensation ratings climbed to approximately equally high levels in all of the groups before group differences appeared. Thus, the lower distress levels for the sensory informed groups occurred because of the very much lower distress ratings in the last half of the cold pressor period. It takes time to form a schema of the noxious stimulus so the reduction of distress does not occur right away.

Experiments 2 and 3 conducted by Shacham (H. Leventhal *et al.*, 1979) further corroborate the schema hypothesis. Subjects asked to analyze and monitor the sensations in the hand immersed in ice water showed substantial declines in felt distress during the second half of the immersion. By contrast, relatively little distress reduction occurred for a control group. If the formation of a nondistress schema leads to the decrease in experienced distress in the latter half of cold pressor trials, it is reasonable to expect that monitoring of the impact site is critical only during the early part of exposure when the stimulus sensations are low in intensity and permit objective scanning and analysis. The data showed that attending to the sensations during the first half of the immersion was as effective as attending throughout and that attending during the second half, after distress was activated, was of no value. Reduction of the emotional response was dependent on early attention to the physical sensations (see also Epstein, Rosenthal, & Szpiler, 1978).

Several new studies suggest clear differences between cognitive strategies, which take in stimulation, and dissociative strategies, which block stimulus information. Shacham (1979) found that instructions to form a clear image of the hand while it was immersed in cold water led to significant reductions in reported pain in comparison to a control condition. Her results were strong, however, only for subjects who obtained high scores on tests of vividness of visual imagery. What was especially interesting was that the pain reduction effects were greatest on the second of the pair of cold pressor trials, even though the subjects generated hand imagery only on the first trial. This is consistent with the assumption that it takes time to build a neutral schema, but that once such a schema is constructed it does not quickly dissipate. By contrast, another group of subjects who were told to think of the ice water as pleasant, so as to block out the noxious experience, showed reduced pain only during the first of the two cold pressor trials, during which they actively tried to block out the distressful stimulus. On the second trial, when they were instructed to do nothing while in the water, this group showed the same level of distress as control subjects and more distress than imagery subjects. Blocking out the noxious experience did not produce lasting distress reduction.

A second pair of studies conducted by Reinhardt (1979) further reinforced the importance of monitoring and coding for distress reduction. In the first of two investigations, 80 subjects were exposed to two cold pressor trials with no one receiving any information at all. Detailed interviews after each trial showed that only 20% of the subjects monitored their hand during exposure. One subgroup of those who did attend to the immersed hand later reported that they had expected the sensations to lessen over time, whereas another group reported they expected the sensations to become more severe. Only those subjects who monitored their hand and who expected the sensations to decrease in severity reported substantially less distress than the others. The second experiment compared three groups instructed to monitor their sensations to a nonmonitoring control. Subjects told to see whether the sensations peaked and declined showed very low ratings of distress, whereas those asked only to monitor were next, and those told to monitor and see whether the sensations became increasingly severe reported the highest levels of distress. Two control groups showed the same level of distress as this last group.

In summary, there is ample evidence that preparing people for a noxious stimulus by giving them sensory information and asking them to monitor their sensations can lead to marked drops in reported distress when these instructions are combined with a benign or neutral stimulus interpretation. Distress is reduced when sensation monitoring begins at low levels of stimulation, but the decrease in felt distress only appears in the latter half of the cold pressor trial (sometimes in a second trial) after a period during which schema formation is presumed to occur. These outcomes seem quite different from those obtained with cognitive strategies, which call for dissociative or reversal thoughts, such as ignoring the stimulus or thinking of it in a positive and pleasant way. The results are also more complex than what would be expected if distress reduction were simply a process of labeling autonomic (or sensory) states. This latter interpretation implies an immediate rather than a delayed effect and probably does not predict carryover to subsequent experiences. The effectiveness of monitoring sensations with benign expectations is undoubtedly dependent on the experience of the stimulus confirming the objective schema. The sensations produced by cold pressor do reach a peak and then diminish because of sensory adaptation. The adaptation checks against the neutral schema and further strengthens this objective schematization because the coded stimulus recruits less emotional response and lowers distress.

Other laboratory studies of distress control are reviewed by H. Leventhal and Everhart (1979) and H. Leventhal and Johnson (1980) discuss a number of studies that have investigated the effects of sensory information and monitoring in clinical settings. The field studies lend further support to the value of sensory information and benign interpretations for distress control. They also suggest that processes of coping and control play a major role in schema formation and distress reduction in clinical settings.

There is evidence suggesting that focusing on or analyzing the perceptual features of stimuli is an effective way of controlling emotional states other than pain. For example, Leyens, Cisneros, and Hossay (1976) found significantly less aggression (in the form of delivering electric shocks) to an insulting partner for subjects who had analyzed the esthetic properties of slides designed to stimulate aggression. Subjects exposed to these same slides without an analytic decentering set delivered substantially more electric shock to their insulting partners. Lazarus and associates found similar reductions in emotional response for subjects instructed to adopt an analytic or intellectualizing set to a stressful movie of a subincision rite by viewing it as though they were students of anthropology (Speisman, Lazarus, Mordkoff, & Davison, 1964). These sets closely resemble those generated by sensory information and attention instructions and contrast with sets aimed at inducing denial, blocking, or avoidance of stimulation (e.g., see Lazarus & Alfert, 1964).

2. Neuropsychological Evidence for Schematic Processing

A vast and growing literature (Harnad & Doty, 1977) strongly suggests differences in function for the left and right hemispheres of the human brain. The left hemisphere appears to dominate for speech and linguistic functions and the right hemisphere seems to dominate for various nonlinguistic skills, including spatial perception. This right hemisphere advantage includes decoding the pictorial and expressive stimuli closely related to emotional experiences. For example, a right hemisphere advantage has been demonstrated for facial recognition (Moscovitch, Scullion, & Christie, 1976) and for recognition of musical tones (Gordon, 1974; Milner, 1962), of emotional sounds such as crying and laughing (Carmon & Nachson, 1973; King & Kimura, 1972), and of emotional tones of voice (M. P. Haggard & Parkinson, 1971; Safer & Leventhal, 1977). Stronger right hemisphere electroencephalogram (EEG) activity has also been recorded during visual imagery (Robbins & McAdam, 1974) and during REM sleep (Goldstein, Stoltzfus, & Gardocki, 1972). These spatial and imaginal functions appear to be closely related to emotion (Grossberg & Wilson, 1968) and to high levels of EEG activity in the right hemisphere during emotional states. For example, high levels of right hemisphere EEG activity have been found during sexual orgasm (H. D. Cohen, Rosen, & Goldstein, 1976) and imagery-induced emotional states (Davidson, Schwartz, Pugash, & Bromfield, 1976).

The sum of the evidence suggests the occurrence of extensive right hemispheric activity involving concrete perceptual imagery in association with emotional states. One could argue that emotional schemata are one form of code used in right hemispheric processing of stimuli. The right hemisphere is especially suited for the formation of emotional schemata as it appears to be well designed to integrate information across modalities; it can integrate perceptual, expressive motor, and autonomic information (Semmes, 1968). Although the final word is yet to be written on the meaning of hemispheric differences (see, e.g., Kinsbourne, 1974), the evidence is consistent with the existence of special memory integrations such as emotional schemata.

E. CONCEPTUAL PROCESSING

Conceptual processing deals with two aspects of emotion. First, it is important for the conclusions we draw about our feelings—our guesses as to what internal events and actions make up emotion as well as the causes and consequences of emotion (Issue 6, Section IV,A). Although these beliefs are based on information gleaned from sensory motor and schematic processing, there is no reason to assume that they accurately reflect the mechanisms, responses, eliciting conditions, or consequences of emotional processing (see Mandler, 1975; Nisbett & Wilson, 1977). The models of emotion considered in this contribution are good illustrations of the difficulty of creating an accurate belief system about affect. However, the incomplete and inaccurate aspects of conceptualizations of emotion are not the important issues. The key issues are to be found in attempting to answer the questions of how people formulate their conceptions, what information they use to do so, and what rules they adopt in making generalizations.

Second, it is hypothesized that conceptual processes are closely related to deliberately controlled, skilled motor performance and to propositional thinking. Conceptual processes can regulate and control expressive motor and schematic processing by controlling attention and voluntary action. The development of conceptual structures that can match schematic and expressive motor mechanisms may be crucial for the integration and control of emotional experience (see Lang, 1979, for a related perspective).

The conceptual system contains a verbal component used for recording and interpreting information about emotional experiences and a performance component underlying the volitional production and control of emotional reactions. Both conceptual codes are generated by abstracting information from specific emotional episodes, both are more flexible than the concrete perceptual memories comprising schematic processing, and both retain information in a sequential format that is useful for the regulation of temporal action sequences. They therefore are useful for reasoning, regulating ongoing sequences of behavior, directing attention to particular events, and generating specific responses to deal with these events.

1. The Verbal Conceptual Component

The terms of the verbal system, for example, fear, anger, joy, or shame, represent specific emotional experiences. The semantic and syntactical features of this conceptual component express the relationship between objects and between objects and feeling. The verbal conceptual system, therefore, is a way of representing and communicating about feelings, but not a representation of the feelings themselves. We recall that we felt a particular way following a specific incident, that we acted on the feeling, and that the acts had specific consequences, and we can talk about how we felt. Communication about feelings seems relatively simple and direct for most laymen, if not for most psychologists (Davitz, 1970), but the verbal conceptual system often seems weak and unable to control emotional processes. A key reason for this is that verbal conceptualizations are based on a small fraction of the features of any one emotional episode. The features on which the abstractions are based are those most salient to attention, and these may not be the stimulus and response features actually controlling emotional behavior. Concrete circumscribed objects and unexpected or particularly vivid features of stimulation are attended to more intently than familiar events and contextual factors so that the former are more likely to be selected out and perceived as the causes of emotion (Bowlby, 1973). For example, one might be startled and frightened by an unexpected sound in a darkened house and attribute one's fear to the sound, failing to recognize that the darkness played an equal role in stimulating the fear reaction. Similarly, being alone may be a critical contextual factor for the arousal of fear and formation of phobias to a wide variety of stimuli (Bowlby, 1973; Bronson, 1968). The "well-documented" fear of strangers also reflects a partial error in causal explanation. Sroufe and Waters (1976) concluded that fear of strangers was readily elicited in 9-month-old infants under laboratory conditions but is seldom seen in the home when the mother is present. In a safe familiar context, strangers provoke positive affective reactions. The perceptual salience of the stranger is greater than that of the context for investigators as well as for children, and the importance of the latter in stimulating fear reactions was slow to be recognized. The schematic and expressive motor systems respond strongly to contextual cues, leading to an inconsistency between the schematic process and the actor's conceptual representation of this process. One consequence is the sense that emotion is provoked from outside and is not under voluntary control. We have elsewhere given a more detailed view of the way in which the schematic system automatically responds to stimuli and searches out episodic memories suggesting specific conclusions about body states; these conclusions are the rules or beliefs that guide voluntary action (H. Leventhal, Nerenz, & Straus, 1980).

A variety of abstract beliefs stand out in the area of pain and distress. For example, subjects in Shacham's (H. Leventhal *et al.*, 1979) and Reinhardt's (1979) studies thought that distraction was helpful in minimizing distress and that attention to the cold water increased discomfort. The data, however, showed the opposite pattern. Subjects in one of Reinhardt's (1979) control groups were told to talk aloud about their experience during the cold pressor. These subjects believed that they had the most effective way of controlling distress, whereas their distress reports were the highest in the study. Finally, in a study which compared sensation monitoring and distraction as strategies for dealing with labor contractions during childbirth, mothers who attended to their contractions were significantly less distressed than those who did not—but it was extremely difficult to persuade mothers to follow the monitoring instructions (Shacham, Boothe, Leventhal, & Leventhal, 1980). When the instructions were strong enough so that mothers did follow them, many reported surprise at their effectiveness.

Another example of a conceptual rule is the belief that the presence of pain and distress always indicates injury. H. Leventhal and Everhart (1979) suggest this belief is based on a history of injury preceding distress. The belief is so powerful that it may lead patients suffering from phantom pain to doubt their sanity (Melzack, 1973). It may also stimulate people to seek and obtain a substantial amount of unnecessary medical care. For example, a survey of medical records found that 60% of the hysterectomies in a sample of women 16–30 years of age were for benign conditions (Ingram, Evans, & Oppenheim, 1965).

2. *Performance Conceptualizations*

Earlier presentations of the perceptual motor model of emotion discussed evidence for performance conceptualizations but did not differentiate them sharply from verbal conceptual processing (H. Leventhal, 1979; H. Leventhal & Everhart, 1979). Performance conceptualizations are nonverbal sequential codes acquired in the volitional, or deliberate, performance of emotional reactions. They are a sequential representation of the perceptual and motor responses that are organized in a spatial or holistic structure in emotional schemata. Performance codes abstract the cues and responses that form the critical junctures or branching points in the automatic schematic codes where a choice is made (see Powers, 1973, for a description of hierarchical control processes). In this way performance conceptualizations exert partial control over schematic and expressive motor processing systems. Individuals develop performance codes by active participation; they thrust themselves into emotional situations, deliberately enact grief, anger, joy, and fear, and practice expressing and generating feeling.

Performance codes play a critical part in emotional life. Their presence means the volitional system can swiftly generate a script for a sequence of voluntary responses to match spontaneous expressive outputs from the schematic system (see Fig. 1). This volitional performance system can anticipate emotional behaviors through self-instruction. The schematic code, by contrast, is more similar to a conditioned response and is situationally governed. The performance system can greatly reduce the impact of emotionally provocative situations by anticipating the automatic processing systems.

Among the studies which point to the existence and operation of emotional performance scripts are findings on the lateralization of cerebral functioning. The data cited earlier suggested that the right hemisphere of the brain played a major role in the automatic processing of emotional schemata. These results, suggesting that emotional codes are located in the right hemisphere, are characteristic for naive or unskilled subjects. However, highly skilled individuals can perform recognition tasks with the left hemisphere as well as they can with the right. Trained musicians, for example, are typically found to be equally proficient in melody recognition (a task with emotional properties) with either left or right hemisphere, and their left hemisphere skills greatly exceed those of nonmusicians (Bever & Chiarello, 1974; Davidson & Schwartz, 1977).

Skilled musicians practice at painstakingly slow rates as well as at normal tempos and, as a result, they construct both voluntary sequential codes and automatic schemata of the same passage. Consequently, there is a sharp contrast in behavior when a skilled performer and a novice make an error in a run of notes. The novice returns to the start of the run to pick up the sequence again, whereas the skilled musician's sequential anticipations permit him or her to correct and continue the piece without interruption.

Practice and skill in generating volitional emotional scripts should have effects for emotional judgments similar to those for the judgment of melodies. Safer (1981) tested this hypothesis in a series of studies in which subjects were exposed to a pair of faces; the first was exposed centrally and the second was flashed to one side of the point of fixation and therefore received by only one side of the brain. Subjects were asked to judge whether the two faces had been the same or were different. In one experiment the subjects were also asked whether the expressions had been the same or different. Safer reasoned that female subjects would be more likely to develop volitional scripts because the female role encourages open expression, performance, and practice of complex emotional reactions (Hoffman, 1977). He found that female subjects were equally accurate in judging emotional expressions in the left and right hemispheres. Their left hemisphere performance greatly exceeded that of male subjects, but accuracy in judging emotional expressions in the right hemisphere was equal for female and male subjects. When the subjects were asked to judge whether or not the second picture had the same pose as the first picture (a pattern judgment), both female and male subjects showed superior skill in the right hemisphere.

The separation of performance and verbal conceptual codes for emotion also receives support from studies of the behavioral control of emotion. For example, both modeling and desensitization procedures are effective in reducing snake phobias, but modeling is even more effective in reducing reported fear and phobic behavior when the observer is encouraged to actively engage in behaviors of looking at, approaching, and touching snakes. Modeling with active participation also appears to produce a longer lasting therapeutic effect, suggesting that active participation helps to develop control of stimulus-elicited emotion or the automatic processing of emotion (Bandura et al., 1969). Lang (1979) has contrasted passive and active imagery in desensitization and found more complete reduction of phobias when the imagery included the participant actively engaging in behavior involving snakes. McKechnie (1975) reports having successfully treated a case of phantom pain by using a desensitization procedure in which the patient imagined himself actively relaxing and using the painful phantom. These findings and others similar to them (see Zillmann, 1978) suggest the value of distinguishing between emotional schematic codes, which automatically connect with perceptual inputs, and conceptual performance codes, which can connect perception with a volitional self-representation that permits control over otherwise automatic affective behavior.

F. RELATIONSHIPS BETWEEN THE PROCESSING SYSTEMS

Postulating a hierarchy of mechanisms for processing emotion raises a variety of interesting questions about the interaction between the processing mechanisms. These questions will focus on such issues as the antecedents of emotional reactions, the conditions giving rise to emotional behavior with or without emotional experience, and the change in emotional experience and behavior with personality development.

1. The Antecedents of Emotional Processing

Each of the systems generating emotional behavior and experience is sensitive to somewhat different cues. Expressive motor processing very early in life appears to be an innate system the functioning of which does not depend on past learning. Processing in this system is initiated by specific stimulus attributes rather than by stimulus identity or meaning (Hebb, 1949). We therefore should be able to represent the stimuli that initiate emotional processing in ways similar to the representations of the stimuli involved in the generation of spatial perception, such as the texture of dimensional cues (E. J. Gibson, 1970; J. Gibson, 1950).

An examination of the literature on emotional response in infants supports the hypothesis that dimensional or gradient cues are important for early expressive behavior. Such stimuli as an object's rate of approach (looming) and lightness and darkness (Bowlby, 1973) are important for provoking startle and withdrawal responses (the beginnings of fear affect) and smiling reactions (Sroufe & Waters, 1976). Features of the expressive responses emitted by adults provide a source of stimulation able to capture the infant's attention and elicit an expressive response. Brazelton et al. (1974) observed head turning and visual search in the neonate to high-pitched vocalizations by an adult. They also found distinctively different motor reactions, such as smooth cycling of arms and legs, when the infant was fixating an adult face as compared to fixating a physical object (see also Condon & Sander, 1974). These stimuli are dimensional; any adult (parent, friend, or stranger) can stimulate the expressive reactions in the infant if his or her speech lies within the range of critical values for the features of pitch and rate. By contrast, particular faces and voices, whose identification requires a categorical process, only become important with development (Kagan, 1970).

Emde (1979) points out that the expressive-motor system exhibits a great deal of spontaneous activity. He cites a substantial amount of evidence suggesting that expressiveness in the newborn is generated largely by internal factors and comes under external stimulus control only gradually. For example, the infant makes available a variety of expressive cues to stimulate expression and feeling in the adult caregiver. The expressive behavior in the caregiver can then evoke expressiveness in the infant. Emotional expression, therefore, is brought under external expressive controls and expression becomes an interactional trait (Emde, 1979). Developmental changes of this sort are obviously of critical importance for the emergence of emotional schemata. However, the concept of schemata may be too limited to deal with the emergence of emotional interaction traits. Interaction traits seem to refer to regularities over time, which are more aptly described by such concepts as emotional scripts (Abelson, 1976; H. Leventhal & Everhart, 1979) rather than emotional schemata. The schemata seem to best describe less temporally expanded emotional events.

It is clear that emotional schemata are likely to be activated by many of the same stimuli that activate expressive motor processing. With repeated exposure to specific emotion-eliciting events, emotional schemata become increasingly complex and the situation must more precisely match the schema to stimulate emotional reactions. For example, as infants first learn to distinguish faces, they smile at strangers and frightening masks as well as at their mothers (Spitz & Wolf, 1946). With increased development they become more discriminating and smile at familiar faces but show fear of strangers when in strange and perhaps "unsafe" environments (Schaffer & Emerson, 1964), whereas they might smile at both in familiar and "safe" environments (Sroufe & Waters, 1976). Developmental data also indicate that children's fears are elicited by vague, phantasy-like events at kindergarten age and only later in sixth grade become more realistic and focused on bodily injury and physical danger (Bauer, 1976).

The continuity between expressive motor and schematic processing is strongly suggested by the Öhman and Dimberg (1978) study of conditioning of skin conductance responses to facial expressions. In this experiment uncomfortable electric shocks served as the unconditioned stimulus for the skin conductance response, while happy, angry, or neutral faces were used as the conditioned stimuli. Although skin conductance was conditioned with equal facility to all three conditioned stimuli, extinction was extremely slow to the stimulus of the angry face! The features of angry caretakers probably have elicited fear reactions in all of us during childhood so that angry faces form a central part of our emotional fear schemata. These schemata and their autonomic and expressive components could be readily activated in later life. As Öhman and Dimberg (1978) suggest, therefore, the organism is prepared to acquire and retain particular emotionally based stimulus response relationships (Seligman, 1970).

It is also clear that contextual cues contribute greatly to schematic emotion by affecting the relative strength or availability of selected schemata. For example, fear schemata are more available than joy schemata in unfamiliar and possibly unsafe environments. Although adults appear to give less emphasis to contextual cues in reporting on the source of their emotional disturbances, moreover, the cues still retain their potency as elicitors of emotional processing (Hebb, 1955).

The development of emotional schemata add at least two other types of antecedents to emotional reactions. First, man and other primates clearly respond emotionally to the disconfirmation of schematic expectations. The violation of schemata is a critical source of affective experiences and reactions. Hebb (1946) suggests this feature of schematic processing can produce emotional reactions to novel events that are general both within and across species. For example, many, although not all, primates form a perceptual schema of the typical configuration of a member of their species. When this is violated, perhaps by exposure to the torsoless head or the anesthetized body of a conspecific, the animal may respond with intense fear. This fear depends on the violation of the schematic expectation of the appearance of a normal animal and does not depend on prior negative experiences with heads or anesthetized animals.

It appears that the development of schemata both narrows and broadens the range of stimuli capable of evoking prolonged and intense emotional reactions. These reactions appear to be based both on the specific meaning of the stimulus and on deviations from expectations. The current situation is constantly compared with schematic expectations and familiar (narrowing) and novel (broadening) stimuli are highly likely to elicit particular emotions.

Conceptual processes, both verbal and performance, are elicited by a variety of situational and social cues. The gracious hostess verbalizes and performs expressions of delight to even the least desirable guest. The competitive Type A executive conceives future situations as a threat to self and marshals his coping resources well before any anticipated threats can materialize; hence, he speaks rapidly, with emphasis, and answers questions before they are completed by the questioner (Scherwitz, Berton, & Leventhal, 1977, 1978). Long-term interests, plans, and self-concerns direct affective responding and coping by bringing individuals into contact with affect-eliciting situations and by generating anticipatory emotional reactions to deal with them. The key to conceptual processing is the system's responsiveness to the symbolic stimuli of verbal information from oneself and others. It can therefore function as an anticipatory device for emotional control.

2. Dynamics of System Interaction

Two types of interaction are discussed here. The first concerns the interaction between automatic processing and volitional processing in the feed-forward system. The second is the influence of conceptual reactions on schematic and expressive motor responses.

a. Feed-Forward Interactions. The most significant interaction in the processing of emotion is the comparison between the automatically elicited feed-forward pattern and the volitional readiness for expressive motor behavior (see Fig. 1). In an earlier section it was hypothesized that a discrepancy between the two signals would lead to an affective experience. If, in contrast, the preexistent volitional motor set matches the feed-forward signal, the experience is of an intended movement rather than an emotion.

Should we assume that one cannot feel emotion in the absence of a feed-forward motor discharge, or is it simply that the feed-forward signal frequently accompanies emotional experience so that it is sufficient, but not necessary, to produce emotion? The latter, weak hypothesis would hold that feeling could be directly experienced from the elicitation of schematic emotional memory as in phantom pain. There is no need to choose between the strong and weak hypotheses at this time, although the weaker version of the hypothesis appears more likely. Emotion may well be directed by the activation of schematic memories alone. Izard's (1979) concept of reafference is consistent with this weaker hypothesis.

A lack of fit between the spontaneous feed-forward signal and an intentional motor set is presumed to generate emotional experience. What is the nature of this discrepancy? Does a volitional set opposite in pose to the spontaneous expression, as was established in the Pasquarelli and Bull (1951) research, create a greater discrepancy and a more intense emotional experience than a neutral volitional set? Do only expressive motor expectations cancel or minimize emotional experience or does a similar mechanism operate for expectations regarding situational perceptions and thought? The feed-forward hypothesis raises a large number of psychological as well as neurological questions.

b. *Verbal Influence on Schematic and Expressive Reaction.* Another critical system interaction is the effects of verbal symbols on the availability of emotional schemata. For example, the repetition of sentences that are affectively positive or negative may intensify schematic imagery and generate affective experience (Parke, Ewall, & Slaby, 1972). It seems, therefore, that the conceptual (symbolic) system can cue and arouse schematic and expressive motor processes. Once the schematic system is activated, it will automatically recruit affect relevant imagery and stimulate still more affective responding. [See Leventhal, Meyer, & Nerenz, 1980, for a model describing such activity in interpretation of symptoms.]

Because verbal responses cannot directly control emotional reactions, the most likely consequences of verbal self-instructions to control emotion would be self-instructions to stimulate opposing imagery and to suppress unwanted expressive reactions and replace them by contrary ones. However, self-instructions to suppress expression may actually increase the discrepancy between volitional and feed-forward motor signals, the so-called "laughter in church" phenomenon where the suppression of expressive reactions intensifies subjective feelings. However, suppression of imagery by blocking inputs through dissociation or thinking positive thoughts can remove unwanted material from conscious awareness by increasing the salience of schemata opposite in emotional sign. The opposing schemata then cancel one another. An example is the reduction of pain and distress by generating positive affective imagery (Barber & Hahn, 1962). Research indicates, however, that the pain and distress return at original levels once the blocking is terminated (see Shacham, 1979).

Self-instructed anticipations can also lead to emotional control by cueing other "heavier" behavioral processes. For example, instructing oneself to monitor stimulus features so that one generates an objective or nonemotional schemata can change the interpretation of the stimulus and shut off emotional reactions (H. Leventhal *et al.*, 1979; Leyens *et al.*, 1976). To be effective, this monitoring must be conducted according to rules intrinsic to schematic operations and not according to the common sense of self-observation. The individual must begin to attend to body sensations at low levels of stimulation, provide a plausible nonthreatening interpretation of the sensory experience, and then allow attention to move elsewhere. Another example of verbal cueing of distress control responses was seen in the study of women in childbirth mentioned earlier (Shacham *et al.*, 1977). In that study, attention to the labor contractions reduced distress during the final period of labor when the mother could affect her experience by timing her pushing and abdominal breathing with the labor contractions. Monitoring helped guide the coping behavior.

G. SYSTEMS INTERACTION AND THE DEVELOPMENT OF EMOTIONAL EXPERIENCE

When the infant expresses emotion does s/he feel emotion? Does the child experience the same fear, anger, joy, grief, and disgust as the adult? Does the adult feel the same fear, anger, and joy if emotion is generated by expressive motor, schematic, or conceptual processes? The model I have presented suggests, and addresses, these and many other such questions. I would like to discuss two: (1) the origin of feeling in infancy and (2) the similarity of feeling when it is activated by different processing systems.

1.   Onset of Feeling in Infancy

The feed-forward outflow portion of our model makes a number of important suggestions about the onset of feeling in the infant. Because it postulates that subjective emotion arises from the interaction of spontaneous and volitional motor control systems, it predicts many forms of spontaneous emotional behavior early in life not to generate subjective emotional states. Early expressive reactions are best viewed as the exercise of motor scripts. They are expressions of emotional states that provide cues to caregivers and are not necessarily accompanied by subjective affect. Subjective affect should first be experienced with the development of the voluntary motor system. The maturation of this system is essential for the comparison of volitional set and feed-forward or feedback signals from spontaneous motor activity. I would speculate that there is some kind of transition period from a phenomenology of excitement experiences (i.e., "everything" is excited) to one of emotional experience in the self. The latter would consist of more specific affective qualities and would be experienced as a state imposed or elicited (nonvoluntary) in the self. It is clear that self-experience and self-concept development play a central role in the formation and governing of volitional activity and one would expect an intimate connection between self-concept, development, and affective experience (Lewis & Brooks, 1978; Lewis & Brooks-Gunn, 1979).

Lewis (e.g., Lewis & Brooks, 1978) and his colleagues have related changes in the self-system to emotional experience and emotional behavior. They suggest the infant responds with emotional states but does not have emotional experiences prior to the development of some level of self-awareness. They also suggest that different emotions will require different degrees of self-awareness. Hoffman (1979) makes a similar suggestion with respect to the emotion of guilt and he posits a sequence spanning a considerable portion of the developmental lifespan.

2. The Similarity of Feelings Activated by Different Processing Systems

Do subjective feelings retain their quality over the lifespan and do they feel the same regardless of the system most heavily involved in their production? Because these questions refer to subjective states they may seem especially difficult to answer. Multidimensional scaling of individual data and other similar cluster techniques may be helpful in resolving them. For these techniques to succeed, however, further articulation of the theory is needed to guide the selection of items for scaling. For example, one would anticipate affective experiences dominated by expressive motor processing to be characterized by a strong sense of motor involvement and somewhat vague ideas about elicitors of affect. Vagueness about the source of feelings occurs because the expressive system is responsive to specific features of stimuli rather than the total objects to which individuals attend. Expressive processing is likely to be responsible for ''mood'' states, that is, just feeling good or just feeling down. Finally, emotion that is expressively processed is likely to be felt as part of the self; it has no specific external cause and contains a strong sense of activity by the self.

Schematic processing should be characterized by a greater amount of imagery and the imagery and the affective state it produces may have an intrusive quality, as though the emotion were imposed on the individual. This would be characteristic of the externally elicited quality of affective episodes early in life and the intrusive quality of the imagery accompanying strong emotions. Affect that is conceptually generated, in contrast, should have a strong quality of being under self-control, since it is generated by the system involved in volitional behaviors.

Continuity in feeling over the lifespan is obviously related to the above issues. Expressive motor processing will dominate emotional experience early in life. As I have already suggested, the earliest emotions may be characterized by expressive behavior without awareness of subjective emotion. As the cognitive system develops, schemata are laid down which include images of state-eliciting conditions along with affective responding, and as volitional behavioral competence grows and the feed-forward system is completed there is a more distinct awareness of self and of emotion in self. With continued growth and development, conceptualizations of affect enter into the picture. I believe there is constancy, however, at the core of basic or primary emotional experiences (Izard, 1977; Tomkins, 1972). Emotions of anger, grief, disgust, fear, shame, joy, interest should retain a common core in experience as they are based on innate motor scripts. The preexistent templates are enriched in acquired mixtures or emotional schemata. However, no matter how we enrich, analyze, or connect affects to cognition, the psychology of emotion depends on a fundamental truth: There must be emotional elements to have emotional experience. Emotions can be attributed to one or another source or process, but emotions are not attributions.

One of the most interesting and potentially problematic aspects of personal growth is the development of elaborate conceptual skills that do not include the basic substantive elements of emotion, in which the motor or schematic forms lack ties to the conceptual system. One example of this is the nonexpressive, overly intellectualized individual who reasons about emotion, seeks social confirmation of emotion, looks for causes of emotion, and is dependent on external cues of self-generated checklists of ideas for making evaluative judgments. It would be unfortunate for the study of emotion to identify such complex reasoning activity with the entire domain of emotion. Cupchik (1972) has attempted to distinguish the judgmental processes characteristic of expressive individuals, who experience emotion, from the attributional, social explanations of nonexpressive individuals, who experience reason. The disagreements about the scientific definition and status of emotion and the contrasting clarity in common language in talking about emotion (Davitz, 1970) is very likely related to the larger number of highly intelligent, reasoning oriented, nonexpressive, and nonemotional persons among academic psychologists.

V.   Emotion and Social Psychology

In a recent honorary address to the American Psychological Association, Zajonc (1979) made a strong plea for the importance of emotion in social psychology. He repeated the argument made by Lang (1969) and by myself (H. Leventhal, 1970, 1974a, 1974b) when he argued that emotion is in many ways prior to and more fundamental than cognition. For example, Zajonc raised the argument used in this and earlier papers (H. Leventhal, 1974a) that emotion plays a key role in organizing or categorizing early experiences as frightening, happy, etc., so that social labels can be attached to them in meaningful ways. He

also argued that emotion is central to the process of evaluation or attitude formation and that how we feel about things is a far more important determinant of our
appraisals than cognitive factors (H. Leventhal, 1974b, p. 125). Although
Zajonc's points are generally in agreement with the present model, it would be
unfortunate if what he called the cognitive imperialism of the past were replaced
by an emotional imperialism of the future. To assign emotion priority (either in
time or in importance) to cognition as a determinant of behavior is to treat
emotional and cognitive processes as unitary events, which they are not.

In an earlier review (H. Leventhal, 1970), I concluded that subjective and
objective processes were parallel and partially independent and that emotionally
provocative situations could give rise to both (a) strong subjective feelings and to
actions to cope with these feelings (fear control processes) and (b) perceptions of
specific dangers and actions to cope with those dangers (danger control processes). I also postulated that both emotional and danger control were dependent
upon prior cognitive encoding (p. 176). This and other elaborations of the
parallel model (e.g., H. Leventhal, 1979; H. Leventhal & Everhart, 1979)
have persuaded me that while cognitive processes may be "external to" or
partially independent of the core emotional process, these two processes become
so intertwined and mutually dependent that their later separation seems artificial
and is sensible only for purposes of theory construction (Dewey, 1894; Mandler,
1975). It is clear that some kind of perceptual process is always active along
with—if not prior to—emotion. It may be a rapid and minimally processed
preattentive perception of a tonal pattern that stimulates an expressive motor
activity or provokes a prototypic schema giving rise to a generalized mood
change. In these cases, it is clear that emotional activity will precede and be
largely independent of complex cognitive reasoning. However, the cognitive
antecedent may also involve a slower, more deeply processed and specific
schematic or conceptual code. In this latter case, emotion would be less independent of cognitive reasoning. In either case, some kind of cognition, broadly
defined, is intimately involved in the generation of emotion. Moreover, regardless of their priority in time, emotional impulses may often be more important as
a determinant of behavior than complex reasoning. Berkowitz (1970) has consistently advanced this position in his discussions of impulsive aggression. He has
also argued that these involuntary reactions are conditioned to and provoked by
situational stimuli (Berkowitz, 1974; Berkowitz & Green, 1967) or what is termed
in this contribution automatic emotional schemata. Although automatic schemata
may be independent of reasoned cognition, they are related to perceptual cognition. Whether the schema is provoked by minimal cues or requires more profound
recognition and processing will vary as a function of the particular schema and the
conditions of exposure (W. R. Wilson, 1979; Zajonc, Markus, & Wilson, 1974).

The problem of the relationship of cognition to emotion should not be
reduced to the issue of who is to rule, but how the pair interact to govern. Given

the complexity of mechanisms subsumed by the two labels, it is not surprising that the interactions can be complex and subtle, creating the perhaps paradoxical and sometimes incorrect impression that we are in fact alternately ruled by our hearts or our heads. This impression may reflect, of course, our limited access to underlying process (Mandler, 1975; Nisbett & Wilson, 1977). The task for the scientific study of emotion is to conceptualize the interaction so as to understand the limitations of our emotional intuition. Moreover, it is not unreasonable to hope that an adequate scientific analysis of emotional processes will advance the education of emotion in our personal lives (Peters, 1970).

It is interesting to stand back a moment and reflect on the origin of the study of emotion. It is obviously linked to the observation of emotional behavior in others. What could be more impressive than a frustrated rage reaction in a child or adult? However, the study of emotion is also linked to observation of events from within. In this regard, it shares many features with the study of illness and the development of lay and scientific theories of disease (H. Leventhal, Meyer, & Nerenz, 1980; H. Leventhal, Nerenz, & Straus, 1980). Shamans, theologians (Bakan, 1968), and psychologists concern themselves with the mind and the body, and with problems of emotions and illness. Individuals seek to understand their emotions and to regulate their emotions and their illnesses. We are all emotion theorists. I hope we will retain emotion in our theorizing.

REFERENCES

Abelson, R. P. Script processing in attitude formation and decision-making. In U. S. Carroll & J. W. Payne (Eds.), *Cognition and social behavior*. Hillsdale, N.J.: Erlbaum, 1976.

Abramson, L. Y., Seligman, M. E. P., & Teasdale, J. D. Learned helplessness in humans: Critique and reformulation. *Journal of Abnormal Psychology*, 1978, **87**, 49–74.

Adam, G. *Interoception and behavior: An experimental study*. Budapest: Hungarian Academy of Sciences, 1967.

Anderson, N. H. Averaging versus adding as a stimulus combination rule in impression formation. *Journal of Experimental Psychology*, 1965, **70**, 394–400.

Anderson, N. H. Integration theory and attitude change. *Psychological Review*, 1971, **78**, 171–206.

Angier, R. P. The conflict theory of emotion. *American Journal of Psychology*, 1927, **34**, 390–401.

Arnold, M. B. *Emotion and personality*. New York: Columbia University Press, 1960. 2 vols.

Ax, A. The physiological differentiation between fear and anger in humans. *Psychosomatic Medicine*, 1953, **15**, 433–442.

Bakan, D. *Disease pain and sacrifice*. Chicago: University of Chicago Press, 1968.

Bandura, A. *Principles of behavior modification*. New York: Holt, 1969.

Bandura, A., Blanchard, E. B., & Ritter, B. Relative efficacy of desensitization and modeling approaches for inducing behavioral, affective and attitudinal changes. *Journal of Personality and Social Psychology*, 1969, **13**, 173–199.

Barber, T. X., & Hahn, K. W. Physiological and subjective responses to pain producing stimulation under hypnotically-suggested and wake-imagined "analgesia." *Journal of Abnormal and Social Psychology*, 1962, **65**, 411–418.

Barefoot, J. C., & Straub, R. B. Opportunity for information search and the effect of false heart-rate feedback. *Journal of Personality and Social Psychology*, 1971, **17**, 154–157.

Bauer, D. H. An exploratory study of developmental changes in children's fears. *Journal of Child Psychology and Psychiatry,* 1976, **17**, 69–74.

Beecher, H. K. Pain in men wounded in battle. *Annals of Surgery,* 1946, **123**, 96–105.

Beecher, H. K. *Measurement of subjective responses.* London and New York: Oxford University Press, 1959.

Bell, C. *The anatomy and philosophy of expression.* (4th ed.) London: Murray, 1847.

Bem, D. J. Self-perception theory. In L. Berkowitz (Ed.), *Advances in experimental social psychology.* Vol. 6. New York: Academic Press, 1972. Pp. 1–62.

Berkowitz, L. The contagion of violence: An S–R mediational analysis of some effects of observed aggression. In W. V. Arnold & M. M. Page (Eds.), *Nebraska Symposium on Motivation.* Vol. 18. Lincoln: University of Nebraska Press, 1970. Pp. 95–135.

Berkowitz, L. Some determinants of impulsive aggression: Role of mediated associations with reinforcement for aggression. *Psychological Review,* 1974, **81**, 165–176.

Berkowitz, L. & Geen, R. G. Stimulus qualities of the target of aggression: A further study. *Journal of Personality and Social Psychology,* 1967, **5**, 364–368.

Bever, T. G., & Chiarello, R. J. Cerebral dominance in musicians and nonmusicians. *Science,* 1974, **185**, 537–539.

Birdwhistell, R. L. The kinesis level in the investigation of the emotions. In P. H. Knapp (Ed.), *Expression of the emotions in man.* New York: International Universities Press, 1963.

Bootzin, R. R., Herman, C. P., & Nicassio, P. The power of suggestion: Another examination of misattribution and insomnia. *Journal of Personality and Social Psychology,* 1976, **34**, 673–679.

Boring, E. G. The sensations of the alimentary canal. *American Journal of Psychology,* 1915, **26**, 1–57. (a)

Boring, E. G. The thermal sensitivity of the stomach. *American Journal of Psychology,* 1915, **26**, 485–494. (b)

Bower, T. G. R. The visual world of infants. *Scientific American,* 1966, **215**, 80–92.

Bower, T. G. R. The object in the world of the infant. *Scientific American,* 1971, **226**, 30–38.

Bowlby, J. *Separation: Anxiety and anger.* New York: Basic Books, 1973.

Brazelton, T. B., Koslowski, B., & Main, M. The origins of reciprocity: The early mother–infant interaction. In M. Lewis & L. A. Rosenblum (Eds.), *The effect of the infant on its caregiver.* New York: Wiley, 1974. Pp. 42–76.

Broadbent, D. E. The hidden preattentive processes. *American Psychologist,* 1977, **32**, 109–118.

Bronson, G. W. The development of fear in man and other animals. *Child Development,* 1968, **39**, 409–431.

Brown, D., Klemp, G. O., & Leventhal, H. Are evaluations inferred directly from overt actions? *Journal of Experimental Social Psychology,* 1975, **11**, 112–126.

Brown, J. W. Physiology and phylogenesis of emotional expression. *Brain Research,* 1967, **5**, 1–14.

Bruner, J. S., & Tagiuri, R. The perception of people. In G. Lindzey (Ed.), *Handbook of social psychology.* Vol 2. Reading, Mass.: Addison-Wesley, 1954. Pp. 634–654.

Calvert-Boyanowsky, J., & Leventhal, H. The role of information in attenuating behavioral responses to stress: A reinterpretation of the misattribution phenomenon. *Journal of Personality and Social Psychology,* 1975, **32**, 214–221.

Campos, J. J., & Stenberg, C. R. Perception, appraisal, and emotion: The onset of social referencing. Paper presented at a seminar on Emotion and Cognition, Social Science Research Council, San Francisco, November 1979.

Campbell, D. T., & Fiske, D. W. Convergent and discriminant validation by the multitrait-multimethod matrix. *Psychological Bulletin,* 1959, **56**, 81–105.

Cannon, W. B. The James–Lange theory of emotions: A critical examination and an alternative theory. *American Journal of Psychology,* 1927, **34**, 106–124.

Cannon, W. B. *Bodily changes in pain, hunger, fear and rage.* New York: Appleton, 1929.

Cannon, W. B. Again the James–Lange and the thalamic theories of emotion. *Psychological Review,* 1931, **38**, 281–295.

Cantor, J. R., Zillmann, D., & Bryand, J. Enhancement of experienced sexual arousal in response to erotic stimuli through misattribution of unrelated residual excitation. *Journal of Personality and Social Psychology,* 1975, **32**, 69–75.

Cantril, H., & Hunt, W. A. Emotional effects produced by the injection of adrenalin. *American Journal of Psychology,* 1932, **44**, 300–307.

Carmon, A., & Nachson, I. Ear asymmetry in perception of emotional nonverbal stimuli. *Acta Psychologica,* 1973, **37**, 351–357.

Clements, P. R., Hafer, M. D., & Vermillion, M. E. Psychometric, diurnal and electrophysiological correlates of activation. *Journal of Personality and Social Psychology,* 1976, **33**, 387–394.

Cohen, D. B. Current research on the frequency of dream recall. *Psychological Bulletin,* 1970, **73**, 433–440.

Cohen, H. D., Rosen, R. C., & Goldstein, L. Electroencephalographic laterality changes during human sexual orgasm. *Archives of Sexual Behavior,* 1976, **5**, 189–199.

Coleman, J. C. Facial expressions of emotion. *Psychological Monographs,* 1949, **63** (1, Whole No. 296).

Condon, W. S., & Sander, L. W. Neonate movement is synchronized with adult speech: Interactional participation and language acquisition. *Science,* 1974, **183**, 99–101.

Conger, J. C., Conger, A. J., & Brehm, S. S. Fear level as a moderator of false feedback effects in snake phobics. *Journal of Consulting and Clinical Psychology,* 1976, **44**, 135–141.

Cook, A. W., & Druckemiller, W. H. Phantom limb pain in paraplegic patients. *International Journal of Neurosurgery,* 1952, **9**, 508–516.

Cupchik, G. Expression and impression: The decoding of nonverbal affect. Unpublished doctoral dissertation, University of Wisconsin, Madison, 1972.

Cupchik, G. C., & Leventhal, H. Consistency between expressive behavior and the evaluation of humorous stimuli: The role of sex and self observation. *Journal of Personality and Social Psychology,* 1974, **30**, 429–442.

Damaser, E. C., Shor, R. E., & Orne, M. T. Physiological effect during hypnotically requested emotions. *Psychosomatic Medicine,* 1963, **25**, 334–343.

Darwin, C. *The expression of the emotions in man and animals.* London: Murray, 1904. (Originally published, 1872.)

Davidson, R. J., & Schwartz, G. E. The influence of musical training on patterns of EEG asymmetry during musical and non-musical self-generation tasks. *Psychophysiology,* 1977, **14**, 58–63.

Davidson, R. J., Schwartz, G. E., Pugash, E., & Bromfield, E. Sex differences in patterns of EEG asymmetry. *Biological Psychology,* 1976, **4**, 119–138.

Davitz, J. R. A dictionary and grammar of emotion. In M. B. Arnold (Ed.), *Feelings and emotion.* New York: Academic Press, 1970, Pp. 251–258.

Dement, W. C. *Some must watch while some must sleep.* Stanford, Calif.: Stanford Alumni Association, 1972.

Dewey, J. The theory of emotion. I. Emotional attitudes. *Psychological Review,* 1894, **1**, 553–569.

Dewey, J. The theory of emotion. II. The significance of emotions. *Psychological Review,* 1895, **2**, 13–32.

Dienstbier, R. A., & Munter, P. O. Cheating as a function of the labeling of natural arousal. *Journal of Personality and Social Psychology,* 1971, **17**, 208–213.

Dollard, J., & Miller, N. E. *Personality and psychotherapy.* New York: McGraw-Hill, 1950.

Dunlap, K. *Habits, their making and unmaking.* New York: Liveright, 1933.

Eibl-Eibesfeldt, I. *Ethology: The biology of behavior.* New York: Holt, 1970.

Ekman, P., & Friesen, W. V. Constants across culture in the face and emotion. *Journal of Personality and Social Psychology,* 1971, **17**, 124–129.

Ekman, P., & Friesen, W. V. *Unmasking the face.* Englewood Cliffs, N.J.: Prentice-Hall, 1975.

Ekman, P., Friesen, W. V., & Ellsworth, P. *Emotion in the human face.* New York: Pergamon, 1972.

Emde, R. N. Levels of meaning for infant emotion: A biosocial view. Paper presented at a seminar on Emotion and Cognition, Social Science Research Council, San Francisco, November 1979.

Engel, G. L. "Psychogenic" pain and the pain-prone patient. *American Journal of Medicine,* 1959, **26**, 899–918.

Epstein, S. Expectancy and magnitude of reaction to a noxious UCs. *Psychophysiology,* 1973, **10**, 100–107.

Epstein, S., Rosenthal, S., & Szpiler, J. The influence of attention upon anticipatory arousal, habituation, and reactivity to a noxious stimulus. *Journal of Research in Personality,* 1978, **12**, 30–40.

Epstein, S., & Roupenian, A. Heart rate and skin conductance during an experimentally induced anxiety: The effect of uncertainty about receiving a noxious stimulus. *Journal of Personality and Social Psychology,* 1970, **16**, 20–28.

Erdmann, G., & Janke, W. Interaction between physiological and cognitive determinants of emotions: Experimental studies on Schachter's theory of emotions. *Biological Psychology,* 1978, **6**, 61–74.

Eriksen, C. W. Unconscious processes. In M. R. Jones (Ed.), *Nebraska Symposium on Motivation.* Vol. 8. Lincoln: University of Nebraska Press, 1958. pp. 169–227.

Fenz, W. D., Kluck, B. L., & Bankart, C. P. The effect of threat and uncertainty on mastery of stress. *Journal of Experimental Psychology,* 1969, **79**, 473–479.

Frankenhaeuser, M. Sympathetic-adrenomedullary activity, behavior and the psychosocial environment. In P. H. Venables & M. J. Christie (Eds.), *Research in psychophysiology.* New York: Wiley, 1975. Pp. 71–94.

Freud, S. *Inhibitions, symptoms and anxiety.* London: Hogarth Press, 1961. (Originally published, 1926.)

Frijda, N. H. Recognition of emotion. In L. Berkowitz (Ed.), *Advances in experimental social psychology.* Vol. 4. New York: Academic Press, 1969. Pp. 167–223.

Fulcher, J. S. "Voluntary" facial expression in blind and seeing children. *Archives of Psychology,* 1942, **272**, 5–49.

Fuller, J. S., Endress, M. P., & Johnson, J. E. The effects of cognitive and behavioral control on coping with an aversive health examination. *Journal of Human Stress,* 1978, **4**(4): 18–25.

Funkenstein, D. H., King, S. H., & Drolette, M. E. *Mastery of stress.* Cambridge, Mass.: Harvard University Press, 1957.

Gardiner, H. N. Review of Professor James' theory of emotion by D. Irons. *Psychological Review,* 1894, **63**, 544–549.

Garner, W. R., Hake, H., & Eriksen, C. W. Operationism and the concept of perception. *Psychological Review,* 1956, **63**, 149–159.

Gatchel, R. J., & Proctor, J. D. Physiological correlates of learned helplessness in man. *Journal of Abnormal Psychology,* 1976, **85**, 27–34.

Geer, J. H., Davidson, G. E., & Gatchel, R. I. Reduction of stress in humans through non-veridical perceived control. *Journal of Personality and Social Psychology,* 1970, **16**, 731–738.

Gellhorn, E. Motion and emotion: The role of proprioception in the physiology and pathology of the emotions. *Psychological Review,* 1964, **71**, 457–472.

Gellhorn, E. Attempt at a synthesis: Contribution to a theory of emotion. In E. Gellhorn (Ed.), *Biological foundations of emotion.* Glenview, Ill.: Scott, Foresman, 1968. Pp. 144–153.

Gerard, H. B. Emotional uncertainty and social comparison. *Journal of Abnormal Social Psychology*, 1963, **66**, 568–573.

Geschwind, N. The apraxias: neural mechanisms of disorders of learned movement. *American Scientist*, 1975, **63**, 188–195.

Gibson, E. J. The development of perception as an adaptive process. *American Scientist*, 1970, **58**, 98–107.

Gibson, J. *The perception of the visual world.* Boston: Houghton, 1950.

Godkewitsch, M. The relationship between arousal potential and funniness of jokes. In J. H. Goldstein & P. E. McGhee (Eds.), *The psychology of humor*. New York: Academic Press, 1972.

Goldstein, L., Stoltzfus, N. W., & Gardocki, J. F. Changes in interhemispheric amplitude relationships in the EEG during sleep. *Physiology and Behavior*, 1972, **8**, 811–815.

Goodenough, F. L. Expression of the emotions in a blind-deaf child. *Journal of Abnormal and Social Psychology*, 1932, **27**, 328–333.

Gordon, H. W. Auditory specialization of the right and left hemispheres. In M. Kinsbourne & W. L. Smith (Eds.), *Hemispheric disconnection and cerebral function*. Springfield, Ill.: Thomas, 1974.

Grace, W. J., & Graham, D. T. Relationship of specific attitudes and emotions to certain bodily diseases. *Psychosomatic Medicine*, 1952, **14**, 243–251.

Graham, D. T. Specific attitudes in initial interviews with patients having different "psychosomatic" diseases. *Psychosomatic Medicine*, 1962, **24**, 257–266.

Graham, D. T., Kabler, J. D., & Graham, F. K. Physiological response to the suggestion to attitudes specific for hives and hypertension. *Psychosomatic Medicine*, 1962, **24**, 159–169.

Graham, D. T., Stern, J. A., & Winokur, G. The concept of a different specific set of physiological changes in each emotion. *Psychiatric Research Reports*, 1960, **12**, 8–15.

Greenwald, A. G. Sensory feedback mechanisms in performance control: With special reference to the ideo-motor mechanism. *Psychological Review*, 1970, **77**, 73–99.

Grossberg, J. M., & Wilson, H. K. Physiological changes accompanying the visualization of fearful and neutral situations. *Journal of Personality and Social Psychology*, 1968, **10**, 124–133.

Grossman, S. P. *Physiological psychology.* New York: Wiley, 1967. Pp. 498–563.

Gyr, J. W. Is a theory of direct visual perception adequate? *Psychological Bulletin*, 1972, **77**, 246–261.

Haggard, E. A., & Isaacs, F. S. Micromomentary facial expressions as indicators of ego mechanisms in psychotherapy. In L. A. Gottschalk & A. A. Auerback (Eds.), *Methods of research in psychotherapy*. New York: Appleton, 1966. Pp. 54–165.

Haggard, M. P., & Parkinson, A. M. Stimulus and task factors as determinants of ear advantages. *Quarterly Journal of Experimental Psychology*, 1971, **23**, 168–177.

Haith, M. M., Bergman, T., & Moore, M. J. Eye contact and face scanning in early infancy. *Science*, 1977, **198**, 853–855.

Hall, G. S. A synthetic study of fear. *American Journal of Psychology*, 1914, **25**, 149–200.

Hall, K. R. L., & Stride, E. The varying response to pain in psychiatric disorders: A study in abnormal psychology. *British Journal of Medical Psychology*, 1954, **27**, 48–60.

Hanawalt, N. G. The role of the upper and the lower parts of the face as the basis for judging facial expressions: II. In posed expressions and "candid camera" pictures. *Journal of General Psychology*, 1944, **31**, 23–36.

Hardy, J. D., Wolff, H. G., & Goodell, H. *Pain sensations and reactions.* Baltimore: Williams & Wilkins, 1952.

Harnad, S., & Doty, R. W. Introductory overview. In S. Harnad, R. W. Doty, L. Goldstein, J. Jaynes, & G. Krauthamer (Eds.), *Lateralization in the nervous system*. New York: Academic Press, 1977.

Harris, V. A., & Katkin, E. S. Primary and secondary emotional behavior: An analysis of the role of autonomic feedback on affect, arousal and attribution. *Psychological Bulletin,* 1975, **82**, 904–916.

Hebb, D. O. On the nature of fear. *Psychological Review,* 1946, **53**, 259–276.

Hebb, D. O. *The organization of behavior.* New York: Wiley, 1949.

Hebb, D. O. The mammal and his environment. *American Journal of Psychiatry,* 1955, **111**, 826–831.

Henderson, W. R., & Smyth, G. E. Phantom limbs. *Journal of Neurology, Neurosurgery and Psychiatry,* 1948, **11**, 88–112.

Hilgard, E. R. Pain as a puzzle for psychology and physiology. *American Psychologist,* 1969, **24**, 103–113.

Hoffman, M. L. Sex differences in empathy and related behaviors. *Psychological Bulletin,* 1977, **84**, 712–722.

Hoffman, M. L. Empathy, guilt and social cognition. Paper presented at the meeting of the Piaget Society, Philadelphia, June 1979.

Hohman, G. W. Some effects of spinal cord lesions on experienced emotional feelings. *Psychophysiology,* 1966, **3**, 143–156.

Horowitz, M. J. *Image formation and cognition.* New York: Appleton, 1970.

Hull, C. L. Knowledge and purpose as habit mechanisms. *Psychological Review,* 1930, **37**, 511–525.

Hull, C. L. The goal gradient hypothesis and maze learning. *Psychological Review,* 1932, **39**, 25–43.

Hull, C. L. *Principles of behavior.* New York: Appleton, 1943.

Hurvich, L. M. Hering and the scientific establishment. *American Psychologist,* 1969, **24**, 497–514.

Ingram, P. W., Evans, G., & Oppenheim, A. N. Right illiac fossa pain in young women. *British Medical Journal,* 1965, **ii**, 149–151.

Ironside, R. Disorders of laughter due to brain lesions. *Brain,* 1956, **79**, 589–609.

Izard, C. E. *The face of emotion.* New York: Appleton, 1971.

Izard, C. E. *Human emotions.* New York: Plenum, 1977.

Izard, C. E. Personal communication, April 11, 1978.

Izard, C. E. Emotions as motivations: An evolutionary–developmental prospective. In R. Dienstbier (Ed.), *Nebraska Symposium on Motivation.* Vol. 27. Lincoln: University of Nebraska. 1979.

Izard, C., Kidd, R. F., & Kotsch, W. E. Facial expression as an activator of the subjective experience of emotion. Mimeo, Vanderbilt University (undated).

James, W. What is an emotion? *Mind,* 1884, **9**, 188–205.

James, W. *The principles of psychology.* Vol. 2. New York: Dover, 1950. Pp. 442–485. (Originally published, 1890.)

Janis, I. L. *Air war and emotional stress.* New York: McGraw-Hill, 1951.

Janis, I. L. *Psychological stress.* New York: Wiley, 1958.

Janis, I. L., & Leventhal, H. Psychological aspects of physical illness and hospital care. In B. Wollman (Ed.), *Handbook of clinical psychology.* New York: McGraw-Hill, 1965.

Janis, I. L., & Leventhal, H. Human reactions to stress. In E. Borgatta & W. Lambert (Eds.), *Handbook of personality theory and research.* Chicago: Rand McNally, 1968. Pp. 1360–1377.

Johnson, J. E. The effects of accurate expectations about sensations on the sensory and distress components of pain. *Journal of Personality and Social Psychology,* 1973, **27**, 261–275.

Johnson, J. E., Kirchhoff, K. T., & Endress, M. P. Altering children's distress behavior during orthopedic cast removal. *Nursing research,* 1975, **11**, 404–410.

Johnson, J. E., & Leventhal, H. Effects of accurate expectations and behavioral instructions on reactions during a noxious medical examination. *Journal of Personality and Social Psychology,* 1974, **29**, 710–718.

Johnson, J. E., Morrissey, J. F., & Leventhal, H. Psychological preparation for an endoscopic examination. *Gastrointestinal Endoscopy,* 1973, **19**, 180–182.

Jones, H. E. The study of patterns of emotional expression. In M. L. Reymert (Ed.), *Feelings and emotions.* New York: McGraw-Hill, 1950. Pp. 161–168.

Kagan, J. Attention and psychological change in the young child. *Science,* 1970, **170**, 826–832.

Keller, A., Ford, L. H., Jr., & Meachem, J. A. Dimensions of self-concept in preschool children. *Developmental Psychology,* 1978, **14**, 483–489.

Kellogg, R., & Baron, R. S. Attribution theory, insomnia and the reverse placebo effect: A reversal of Storms and Nisbett's findings. *Journal of Personality and Social Psychology,* 1975, **32**, 231–236.

Kerber, K. W., & Coles, M. G. N. The role of perceived physiological activity in affective judgments. *Journal of Experimental Social Psychology,* 1978, **14**, 419–433.

King, F. L., & Kimura, D. Left-ear superiority in dichotic perception of vocal nonverbal sounds. *Canadian Journal of Psychology,* 1972, **26**, 111–116.

Kinsbourne, M. Mechanisms of hemispheric interaction in man. In M. Kinsbourne & W. L. Smith (Eds.), *Hemispheric disconnection and cerebral function.* Springfield, Ill.: Thomas, 1974.

Kleck, R. E., Vaughan, R. C., Cartwright-Smith, J., Vaughan, K., Colby, C. Z., & Lanzetta, J. T. Effects of being observed on expressive, subjective and physiological responses to painful stimuli. *Journal of Personality and Social Psychology,* 1976, **34**, 1211–1218.

Klemp, G. O., & Leventhal, H. Self-persuasion and fear reduction from escape behavior. In H. London & R. E. Nisbett (Eds.), *Thought and feeling: Cognitive alteration of feeling states.* Chicago: Aldine, 1974. Pp. 159–173.

Knox, V. J., Morgan, A. H., & Hilgard, E. R. Pain and suffering in ischemia: The paradox of hypnotically suggested anesthesia as contradicted by response from the "hidden observer." *Archives of General Psychiatry,* 1974, **30**, 840–847.

Konorski, J. *Integrative activity of the brain.* Chicago: University of Chicago Press, 1967.

Krisher, H. P., Darley, S. A., & Darley, J. M. Fear provoking recommendations, intentions to take preventive actions, and actual preventive action. *Journal of Personality and Social Psychology,* 1973, **26**, 301–308.

Krueger, F. E. The essence of feeling. In M. Arnold (Ed.), *The nature of emotion: Selected readings.* Baltimore: Penguin Books, 1968. Pp. 97–108. (Originally published, 1928.)

Kuhn, T. *The structure of scientific revolutions.* Chicago: University of Chicago Press, 1962.

LaBarre, W. The cultural basis of emotions and gestures. *Journal of Personality,* 1947, **16**, 49–68.

Lacey, J. I. Somatic response patterning of stress: Some revisions of activation theory. In M. Appley & R. Trumbell (Eds.), *Psychological Stress.* New York: Appleton, 1967.

Lacey, J. I., & Lacey, B. C. Verification and extension of the principle of autonomic response-stereotypy. *American Journal of Psychology,* 1958, **71**, 50–73.

Laird, J. D. Self-attribution of emotion: The effects of expressive behavior on the quality of emotional experience. *Journal of Personality and Social Psychology,* 1974, **29**, 475–486.

Landis, C., & Hunt, W. A. Adrenalin and emotion. *Psychological Review,* 1932, **39**, 467–485.

Lang, P. J. The mechanics of desensitization and the laboratory study of human fear. In C. M. Franks (Ed.), *Assessment and status of the behavior therapies.* New York: McGraw-Hill, 1969. Pp. 160–191.

Lang, P. J. Language, image and emotion. In P. Pliner, K. R. Plankstein, & J. M. Spigel (Eds.), *Perception of emotion in self and others.* Vol. 5. New York: Plenum, 1979.

Lang, P. J., & Lazovik, A. D. Experimental desensitization of a phobia. *Journal of Abnormal and Social Psychology,* 1963, **66**, 519–525.

Lanzetta, J. T., Cartwright-Smith, J., & Kleck, R. E. Effects of nonverbal dissimulation on emotional experience and autonomic arousal. *Journal of Personality and Social Psychology,* 1976, **33**, 354–370.

Lanzetta, J. T., & Kleck, R. E. Encoding and decoding of nonverbal affect in humans. Journal of Personality and Social Psychology, 1970, **16**, 12–19.

Lashley, K. S. *The problem of serial order in behavior.* New York: Wiley, 1951.

Lazarus, R. S. *Psychological stress and the coping process.* New York: McGraw-Hill, 1966.

Lazarus, R. S., & Alfert, E. Short circuiting of threat by experimentally altering cognitive appraisal. *Journal of Abnormal and Social Psychology.* 1964, **69**, 195–205.

Leeper, R. W. The motivational and perceptual properties of emotions as indicating their fundamental character and role. In M. Arnold (Ed.), *Feelings and emotions.* New York: Academic Press, 1970. Pp. 151–158.

Lehmann, A. *Hauptgesetze des menschlichen gefuehlslebens.* Leipzig: Reisland, 1914.

Leventhal, G. S., & Killackey, H. Adrenalin, stimulation, and preference for familiar stimuli. *Journal of Comparative and Physiological Psychology,* 1968, **65**, 152–155.

Leventhal, H. Findings and theory in the study of fear communication. In L. Berkowitz (Ed.), *Advances in experimental social psychology.* Vol. 5. New York: Academic Press, 1970.

Leventhal, H. Emotions: A basic problem for social psychology. In C. Nemeth (Ed.), *Social psychology: Classic and contemporary integrations.* Chicago: Rand McNally, 1974. Pp. 1–51. (a)

Leventhal, H. Attitudes, their nature, growth and change. In C. Nemeth (Ed.), *Social psychology: Classic and contemporary integrations.* Chicago: Rand McNally, 1974. Pp. 52–126. (b)

Leventhal, H. A perceptual–motor processing model of emotion. In P. Pliner, K. Blankenstein, & I. M. Spigel (Eds.), *Perception of emotion in self and others.* Vol. 5. New York: Plenum, 1979.

Leventhal, H., Brown, D., Shacham, S., & Engquist, G. Effect of preparatory information about sensations, threat of pain and attention on cold pressor distress. *Journal of Personality and Social Psychology,* 1979, **37**, 688–714.

Leventhal, H., & Cupchik, G. L. The informational and facilitative effects of an audience. *Journal of Experimental Social Psychology,* 1975, **11**, 363–380.

Leventhal, H., & Cupchik, G. L. A process model of humor judgment. *Journal of Communication,* 1976, **26**, 190–204.

Leventhal, H., & Everhart, D. Emotion, pain and physical illness. In C. Izard (Ed.), *Emotions and psychopathology.* New York: Plenum, 1979.

Leventhal, H., & Johnson, J. E. Laboratory and field experimentation: Development of a theory of self-regulation. In R. Leonard & P. Wooldridge (Eds.), *Behavioral science and nursing theory.* St. Louis: Mosby, 1980, in press.

Leventhal, H., & Mace, W. The effect of laughter on evaluation of a slapstick movie. *Journal of Personality,* 1970, **38**, 16–30.

Leventhal, H., Meyer, D., & Nerenz, D. The common sense representation of illness danger. In S. Rachman (Ed.), *Contributions to medical psychology.* Vol. 2. Oxford: Pergamon, 1980, in press.

Leventhal, H., Nerenz, D., & Straus, A. Self-regulation and the mechanisms for symptom appraisal. In D. Mechanic (Ed.) *Psychological epidemiology.* New York: Watson, 1980, in press.

Leventhal, H., & Sharp, E. Facial expressions as indicators of distress. In S. S. Tomkins & C. E. Izard (Eds.), *Affect, Cognition and Personality.* New York: Springer, 1965. Pp. 296–318.

Lewis, M., & Brooks, J. Self-knowledge and emotional development. In M. Lewis & L. A. Rosenblum (Eds.), *The development of affect.* New York: Plenum, 1978. Pp. 205–206.

Lewis, M., & Brooks-Gunn, J. Toward a theory of social cognition: The development of self. *New Directions for Child Development,* 1979, **4**, 1–19.

Leyens, J., Cisneros, T., & Hossay, J. Decentration as a means for reducing aggression after exposure to violent stimuli. *European Journal of Social Psychology,* 1976, **6**, 459–473.

Li, C. L., & Elvidge, A. R. Observation on phantom limb in a paraplegic patient. *Journal of Neurosurgery,* 1951, **8**, 524–526.

Lindsley, D. B. Emotion. In S. Stevens (Ed.), *Handbook of experimental psychology*. London: Chapman & Hall, 1951. Pp. 473–516.

MacLean, P. D. Contrasting functions of limbic and neocortical systems of the brain and their relevance to psychophysiological aspects of medicine. *American Journal of Medicine, 1958*, **25**, 611–626.

MacNamara, J. Cognitive basis of language learning in infants. *Psychological Review, 1972*, **79**, 1–13.

Malmo, R. B. *On emotions, needs and our archaic brains*. New York: Holt, 1975.

Mandler, G. Emotion. In R. Brown, E. Galanter, E. H. Hess, & G. Mandler (Eds.), *New directions in psychology*. Vol. 1. New York: Holt, 1962. Pp. 267–343.

Mandler, G. *Mind and emotion*. New York: Wiley, 1975.

Marañon, G. Contribution à l'étude de l'action émotive de l'adrenaline. *Revue Française d'Endocrinologie, 1924*, **2**, 301–325.

Marshall, G. D., & Zimbardo, P. G. Affective consequences of inadequately explained physiological arousal. *Journal of Personality and Social Psychology, 1979*, **37**, 970–985.

Maslach, C. The emotional consequence of arousal without reason. In C. E. Izard (Ed.), *Emotions in personality and psychopathology*. New York: Plenum, 1979. Pp. 565–590. (a)

Maslach, C. Negative emotional biasing of unexplained arousal. *Journal of Personality and Social Psychology, 1979*, **37**, 953–969. (b)

Mason, J. W. Organization of psychoendocrine mechanisms: A review and reconsideration of research. In N. S. Greenfield & R. A. Sternbach (Eds.), *Handbook of psychophysiology*. New York: Holt, 1972. Pp. 3–91.

McClelland, D. C. *Studies in motivation*. New York: Appleton, 1955.

McDougall, W. *An introduction to social psychology*. Boston: Luce, 1921.

McDougall, W. Emotion and feelings distinguished. In M. L. Reymert (Ed.), *Feelings and emotion*. Worcester, Mass.: Clark University Press, 1928.

McGuire, W. J. Personality and susceptibility to social influence. In E. Borgatta & W. Lambert (Eds.), *Handbook of personality theory and research*. Chicago: Rand McNally, 1968. Pp. 1130–1188.

McKechnie, R. J. Relief from phantom limb pain by relaxation exercises. *Journal of Behavior Therapy and Experimental Psychiatry, 1975*, **6**, 262–263.

Melzack, R. Phantom limb pain. *Anesthesiology, 1971*, **35**, 409–419.

Melzack, R. *The puzzle of pain*. New York: Basic Books, 1973.

Melzack, R., & Wall, P. D. Psychophysiology of pain. *International Anesthesia Clinics, 1970*, **8**, 3–34.

Mewborn, C. R., & Rogers, R. W. Effects of threatening and reassuring components of fear appeals on physiological and verbal measures of emotion and attitudes. *Journal of Experimental Social Psychology, 1979*, **15**, 242–253.

Miller, N. E. Learnable drives and rewards. In S. S. Stevens (Ed.), *Handbook of experimental psychology*. New York: Wiley, 1951. Pp. 435–472.

Mills, R. T., & Krantz, D. S. Information, choice and reaction to stress: A field experiment in a blood bank with laboratory analogue. *Journal of Personality and Social Psychology, 1979*, **37**, 608–620.

Milner, B. Laterality effects in audition. In V. B. Mountcastle (Ed.), *Interhemispheric relations and cerebral dominance*. Baltimore: Johns Hopkins Press, 1962.

Money, J. Phantom orgasm in dreams of paraplegic men and women. *Archives of General Psychiatry, 1960*, **3**, 373–383.

Morgenstern, F. S. Chronic pain. In O. U. Hill (Ed.), *Modern trends in psychosomatic medicine*. New York: Appleton, 1970. Pp. 225–245.

Moscovitch, M., Scullion, D. & Christie, D. Early versus late stages of processing and their relation to functional hemisphere asymmetries in face recognition. *Journal of Experimental Psychology: Human Perception and Performance*, 1976, **2**, 401–416.

Mountcastle, V. B. Pain and temperature sensibilities. In V. B. Mountcastle (Ed.), *Medical physiology*. Vol. 2. St. Louis: Mosby, 1968. Pp. 1424–1464.

Mowrer, O. H. On the dual nature of learning: A reinterpretation of "conditioning" and "problem solving." *Harvard Educational Review*, 1947, **17**, 102–148.

Nakashima, T. Contributions to the study of the affective processes. *American Journal of Psychology*, 1909, **20**, 157–193.

Nathan, P. W. Pain traces left in central nervous system. In C. A. Keele & R. Smith (Eds.), *The assessment of pain in man and animals*. Edinburgh: Livingston, 1962.

Neisser, U. *Cognitive psychology*. New York: Appleton, 1967.

Newman, E. B., Perkins, E. T., & Wheeler, R. H. Cannon's theory of emotion: A critique. *Psychological Review*, 1930, **37**, 305–326.

Nisbett, R. E., & Schachter, S. Cognitive manipulation of pain. *Journal of Experimental Social Psychology*, 1966, **2**, 227–236.

Nisbett, R. E., & Valins, S. Perceiving the causes of one's own behavior. In E. E. Jones, D. E. Kanouse, H. H. Kelley, R. E. Nisbett, S. Valins, & B. Weiner (Eds.), *Attribution: Perceiving the causes of behavior*. Morristown, N.J.: General Learning Press, 1972. Pp. 63–77.

Nisbett, R. E., & Wilson, T. DeC. Telling more than we can know: Verbal report on mental processes. *Psychological Review*, 1977, **84**, 231–259.

Notarius, C. I., & Levenson, R. W. Expressive tendencies and physiological response to stress. *Journal of Personality and Social Psychology*, 1979, **37**, 1204–1210.

Öhman, A., & Dimberg, V. Facial expressions as conditioned stimuli for electrodermal responses: A case for preparedness? *Journal of Personality and Social Psychology*, 1978, **36,** 1251–1258.

Osgood, C. E. Dimensionality of the semantic space for communication via facial expression. *Scandinavian Journal of Psychology*, 1966, **7**, 1–30.

Panagis, D., & Leventhal, H. Effects of expressive feedback upon judgments of cartoon quality: An investigation of sex differences in the latencies of expressive and cognitive reactions. Mimeo, University of Wisconsin, Madison, 1973.

Papez, J. W. A proposed mechanism of emotion. *Archives of Neurological Psychiatry*, 1938, **38**, 725–743.

Parke, R. D., Ewall, W., & Slaby, R. G. Hostile and helpful verbalizations as regulators of nonverbal aggression. *Journal of Personality and Social Psychology*, 1972, **23**, 243–248.

Pasquarelli, B., & Bull, N. Experimental investigations of the body–mind continuum in affective states. *Journal of Nervous and Mental Disease*, 1951, **113**, 512–521.

Peiper, A. *Cerebral function in infancy and childhood*. New York: Consultants Bureau, 1963.

Peters, R. S. The education of the emotions. In M. B. Arnold (Ed.), *Feelings and emotion: The Loyola symposium*. New York: Academic Press, 1970. Pp. 187–203.

Piaget, J., & Inhelder, B. *Mental imagery in the child: A study of the development of imaginal representation*. London: Routledge & Kegan Paul, 1971.

Plutchik, R. *The emotions: Facts, theories, and a new model*. New York: Random House, 1962.

Plutchik, R., & Ax, A. F. A critique of determinants of emotional state by Schachter and Singer. *Psychophysiology*, 1967, **4**, 79–82.

Polanyi, M. Logic and psychology. *American Psychologist*, 1968, **23**, 27–43.

Posner, M. I. *Cognition: An introduction*. Glenview, Ill.: 1973.

Powers, W. T. Feedback: Beyond behaviorism. *Science*, 1973, **179**, 351–356.

Reinhardt, L. C. Attention and interpretation in control of cold pressor pain distress. Unpublished doctoral dissertation, University of Wisconsin, Madison, 1979.

Robbins, K. L., & McAdam, D. W. Interhemispheric alpha asymmetry and imagery mode. *Brain and Language*, 1974, **1**, 189–193.

Ross, L., Rodin, J., & Zimbardo, P. G. Toward an attribution therapy: The reduction of fear through induced cognitive–emotional misattribution. *Journal of Personality and Social Psychology,* 1969, **12**, 279–288.

Ruckmick, C. A. *The psychology of feeling and emotion.* New York: McGraw-Hill, 1936.

Russell, B. *An outline of philosophy.* New York: Meridian Books, 1960. (Originally published in the U.S., 1927).

Safer, M. A. Sex differences in hemisphere specialization for recognizing facial expressions of emotion. Unpublished doctoral dissertation, University of Wisconsin, Madison, 1978.

Safer, M. A. Sex and hemisphere differences in access to codes for processing emotional expressions and faces. *Journal of Experimental Psychology: General,* in press, 1981.

Safer, M. A., & Leventhal, H. Ear differences in evaluating emotional tones of voice and verbal content. *Journal of Experimental Psychology: Human Perception and Performance,* 1977, **3**, 75–82.

Schachter, J. Pain, fear and anger in hypertensives and normotensives: A psychophysiological study. *Psychosomatic Medicine,* 1957, **19**, 17–29.

Schachter, S. *The psychology of affiliation.* Stanford, Calif.: Stanford University Press, 1959.

Schachter, S. The interaction of cognitive and physiological determinants of emotional state. In L. Berkowitz (Ed.), *Advances in experimental social psychology.* Vol. 1. New York: Academic Press, 1964.

Schachter, S., & Singer, J. E. Cognitive, social, and physiological determinants of emotional state. *Psychological Review,* 1962, **69**, 379–399.

Schachter, S., & Singer, J. E. Comments on the Maslach and Marshall-Zimbardo experiments. *Journal of Personality and Social Psychology.* 1979, **37**, 989–995.

Schachter, S., & Wheeler, L. Epinephrine, chlorpromazine, and amusement. *Journal of Abnormal Social Psychology,* 1962, **65**, 121–128.

Schaffer, H. R., & Emerson, P. E. The development of social attachments in infancy. *Monographs of the Society for Research in Child Development,* 1964, **29** (3, Whole No. 94).

Scheier, M. F., Carver, C. S., & Gibbons, F. X. Self-directed attention, awareness of bodily states and suggestibility. *Journal of Personality and Social Psychology,* 1979, **37**, 1576–1588.

Scherwitz, L. Cognitive and physiological processes involved in perceiving one's own behavior. Unpublished doctoral dissertation, University of Texas, 1973.

Scherwitz, L., Berton, K., & Leventhal, H. Type A assessment and interaction in the behavior pattern interview. *Psychosomatic Medicine,* 1977, **39**, 229–240.

Scherwitz, L., Berton, K. E., & Leventhal, H. Type A behavior, self-involvement and cardiovascular response. *Psychosomatic Medicine,* 1978, **40**, 593–609.

Schlosberg, H. Three dimensions of emotion. *Psychological Review,* 1954, **61**, 81–88.

Schwartz, G. E., Fair, P. L., Mandel, M. R., Salt, P., Mieske, M., & Klerman, G. L. Facial electromyography in the assessment of improvement in depression. *Psychosomatic Medicine,* 1978, **40**, 355–360.

Schwartz, G. E., Fair, P. L., Salt, P., Mandel, M. R., & Klerman, G. L. Facial expressions and imagery in depression: An electromyographic study. *Psychosomatic Medicine,* 1976, **38**, 337–347.

Seligman, M. E. P. On the generality of the laws of learning. *Psychological Review,* 1970, **77**, 406–418.

Semmes, J. Hemispheric specialization: A possible clue to mechanism. *Neuropsychologia,* 1968, **6**, 11–27.

Shacham, S. The effects of imagery monitoring, sensation monitoring and positive suggestion on pain and distress. Unpublished doctoral dissertation, University of Wisconsin, Madison, 1979.

Shacham, S., Boothe, C., Leventhal, H., & Leventhal, E. Use of attention to control distress during childbirth. Unpublished manuscript, University of Wisconsin, Madison, 1977.

Sierra, A. M. Estudio psicológico acerca de la emocion experimental. *Revista de Criminologia Psiquiatria y Medicina Legal,* 1921, **8**, 445–461.

Sime, A. M. Relationship of preoperative fear, type of coping, and information received about surgery to recovery from surgery. *Journal of Personality and Social Psychology,* 1976, **34**, 716–724.

Simmel, M. L. The reality of phantom sensations. *Social Research,* 1962, **29**, 337–356.

Singer, J. E. Sympathetic activation, drugs and fear. *Journal of Comparative and Physiological Psychology,* 1963, **56**, 612–615.

Singerman, K. J., Borkovec, T. D., & Baron, R. S. Failure of a "misattribution therapy" manipulation with a clinically relevant target behavior. *Behavior Therapy,* 1976, **7**, 306–316.

Solomon, R. L., & Corbit, J. D. An opponent-process theory of motivation: 1. Temporal dynamics of affect. *Psychological Review,* 1974, **81**, 119–145.

Speisman, J. C., Lazarus, R. S., Mordkoff, A., & Davison, L. Experimental reduction of stress based on ego-defense theory. *Journal of Abnormal and Social Psychology,* 1964, **68**, 367–380.

Spence, K. A theory of emotionally based drive (D) and its relation to performance in simple learning situation. *American Psychologist,* 1958, **13**, 131–141.

Spitz, R. A., & Wolf, K. M. The smiling response: A contribution to the ontogenesis of social relations. *Genetic Psychology Monographs,* 1946, **34**, 57–125.

Sroufe, L. A., & Waters, E. The ontogenesis of smiling and laughter: A perspective on the organization of development in infancy. *Psychological Review,* 1976, **83**, 173–189.

Sroufe, L. A., Waters, E., & Matas, L. Contextual determinants of infant affective response. In M. Lewis & L. Rosenblum (Eds.), *The origins of behavior.* Vol. 2. New York: Wiley, 1974.

Staub, E., & Kellett, D. S. Increasing pain tolerance by information about aversive stimuli. *Journal of Personality and Social Psychology,* 1972, **21**, 198–203.

Stern, R. M., Botto, R. W., & Herrick, C. D. Behavioral and physiological effects of a false heart rate feedback: A replication and extension. *Psychophysiology,* 1972, **9**, 21–29.

Sternbach, R. The effects of instructional sets on autonomic responsivity. *Psychophysiology,* 1964, **1**, 67–72.

Stewart, I. McD. G. Coronary disease and modern stress. *Lancet,* 1950, **ii**, 867–870.

Sully, J. *An essay on laughter.* London: Longmans, Green, 1902.

Teichner, W. H. Delayed cold-induced vasodilation and behavior. *Journal of Experimental Psychology,* 1965, **69**, 426–432.

Titchener, E. B. An historical note on the James–Lange theory of emotion. *American Journal of Psychology,* 1914, **25**, 425–447.

Tomkins, S. S. *Affect, imagery, consciousness.* Vol. 1. *The positive affects.* New York: Springer, 1962.

Tomkins, S. S., & McCarter, R. What and where are the primary affects? Some evidence for a theory. *Perceptual and Motor Skills,* 1964, **18**, 119–158.

Tourangeau, R., & Ellsworth, P. X. The role of facial response in the experience of emotion. *Journal of Personality and Social Psychology,* 1979, **37**, 1519–1531.

Triandis, H., & Lambert, W. W. A restatement and test of Schlosberg's theory of emotion with two kinds of subjects from Greece. *Journal of Abnormal and Social Psychology,* 1958, **56**, 321–328.

Turner, C. W., & Layton, J. F. Verbal imagery and connotation as memory-induced mediators of aggressive behavior. *Journal of Personality and Social Psychology,* 1976, **33**, 755–763.

Valins, S. Cognitive effects of false heart-rate feedback. *Journal of Personality and Social Psychology*, 1966, **4**, 400–408.

Valins, S., & Ray, A. A. Effects of cognitive desensitization on avoidance behavior. *Journal of Personality and Social Psychology*, 1967, **7**, 345–350.

Van-Toller, C., & Tarpy, R. M. Effect of cold stress on the performance of immunosympathectomized mice. *Physiology and Behavior*, 1972, **8**, 515–517.

Van-Toller, C., & Tarpy, R. M. Immunosympathectomy and avoidance behavior, *Psychological Bulletin*, 1974, **81**, 132–137.

Vitz, P. C. Affect as a function of stimulus variation. *Journal of Experimental Psychology*, 1966, **71**, 74–79.

Vitz, P. C. Preference for tones as a function of frequency and intensity. *Perception & Psychophysics*, 1972, **11**, 84–88.

Von Holst, E. Relations between the central nervous system and the peripheral organs. *British Journal of Animal Behavior*, 1954, **2**, 89–94.

Weiskrantz, L., Elliott, J., & Darlington, C. Preliminary observations on tickling oneself. *Nature (London)*, 1971, **230**, 598–599.

Weiss, J. M. Somatic effects of predictable and unpredictable shock. *Psychosomatic Medicine*, 1970, **22**, 397–408.

Wenger, M. A., Clemens, T. L., Darsie, M., Engel, B. T., Estess, F. M., & Sonnenschein, R. R. Autonomic response patterns during intravenous infusion of epinephrine and nor-epinephrine. *Psychosomatic Medicine*, 1960, **22**, 294–307.

Wilson, J. F. Coping styles influencing the effectiveness of preoperative intervention procedure. Paper presented at the 85th annual convention of the American Psychological Association, San Francisco, August 1977.

Wilson, S. A. K. Some problems in neurology. II. Pathological laughing and crying. *Journal of Neurology and Psychopathology*, 1924, **4**, 299–333.

Wilson, S. A. K. *Modern problems in neurology*. New York: Wood, 1929. Pp. 260–296.

Wilson, W. R. Feeling more than we can know: Exposure effects without learning. *Journal of Personality and Social Psychology*, 1979, **37**, 811–821.

Witkin, H. A., & Lewis, H. B. Presleep experiences and dreams. In H. A. Witkin & H. B. Lewis (Eds.), *Experimental studies of dreaming*. New York: Random House, 1967. Pp. 148–201.

Wolff, P. H. Observations on newborn infants. *Psychosomatic Medicine*, 1959, **21**, 110–118.

Woodsworth, R. S., & Schlosberg, H. *Experimental psychology*. (Rev. ed) New York: Holt, 1954.

Wynne, L. C., & Solomon, R. L. Traumatic avoidance learning: Acquisition and extinction in dogs deprived of normal peripheral autonomic function. *Genetic Psychology Monographs*, 1955, **52**, 241–284.

Young, P. T. Affective arousal: Some implications. *American Psychologist*, 1967, **22**, 32–40.

Young, R. O., & Frye, M. Some are laughing; some are not—why? *Psychological Reports*, 1966, **18**, 747–754.

Younger, J. C., & Doob, A. N. Attribution and aggression: The misattribution of anger. *Journal of Research in Personality*, 1978, **12**, 164–171.

Zajonc, R. B. Feeling and thinking: Preferences need no inferences. Address for the Distinguished Scientific Contribution Award, American Psychological Association, New York, September, 1979.

Zajonc, R. B., Markus, H., & Wilson, S. R. Exposure effects and associative learning. *Journal of Experimental Social Psychology*, 1974, **10**, 248–263.

Zillmann, D. Attribution and misattribution of excitatory reactions. In J. H.. Harvey, W. Ickes, & R. F. Kidd (Eds.), *New directions in attribution research*. Vol. 2. Hillsdale, N.J.: Erlbaum, 1978. Pp. 335–368.

Zillmann, D., & Cantor, J. R. A disposition theory of humour and mirth. In A. J. Chapman & H. C. Foot (Eds.), *Humour and laughter: Theory, research and applications*. New York: Wiley, 1976. Pp. 93–115.

Zillmann, D., Johnson, R. C., & Day, K. D. Attribution of apparent arousal and proficiency of recovery from sympathetic activation affecting excitation transfer to aggressive behavior. *Journal of Experimental and Social Psychology*, 1974, **10**, 503–515.

Zillmann, D., Katcher, A. H., & Milavsky, B. Excitation transfer from physical exercise to subsequent aggressive behavior. *Journal of Experimental Social Psychology*, 1972, **8**, 247–259.

TOWARD A THEORY OF CONVERSION BEHAVIOR

Serge Moscovici

ÉCOLE DES HAUTES ÉTUDES EN SCIENCES
  SOCIALES
GROUPE DE PSYCHOLOGIE SOCIALE
PARIS, FRANCE

Pleasure is none, if not diversified.
JOHN DONNE
Neither is society.

I. Two Types of Social Behavior: Compliance and Conversion

Each time I consider the relations between human beings, I am reminded of Orwell's famous paradox, which, by its refreshing irony, offers a safeguard against the arguments of common sense: All animals are equal, but some animals are more equal than others. What the majority does is good, because there are

ADVANCES IN EXPERIMENTAL SOCIAL
PSYCHOLOGY, VOL. 13

many who do it. The influence of the majority is therefore likely to be great. What the minority does is bad, because there are few who do it. Hence the influence of the minority is likely to be small. In short, the more equal will always win out over the less equal. Such arguments are accepted in daily life, as they are in the scholarly literature. For example, ever since I began studying social influence from the point of view of innovation, I have been asked repeatedly to what extent a minority is more or less influential than a majority and why. This question reflects a legitimate desire to measure the relative importance of innovative and conformist phenomena in society and to evaluate their respective chances of success. However, formulating the question in terms of "more" and "less" implies that the two categories of phenomena operate in the same way, that a majority and a minority exert the same type of influence and produce the same kind of social behavior, the difference being purely quantitative. Starting out from this assumption, one need only compare the changes in public responses in order to reach the expected conclusion: The influence of the majority is stronger than that of a minority. That is at least how it seems on the basis of most of the experimental results (Moscovici, 1976) known until now. All that is very plausible and, unfortunately, hardly surprising.

However, the question bears further investigation, for something real has been left out of account in this formulation. To get to the bottom of the matter, we have to ask "What kind of influence is exerted by a majority or a minority" rather than "How great is this influence?" But can we isolate the symptoms of a difference in kind? We surely can if we take as a starting point:

1. A regularity we have observed, to wit, that private individual responses, after social interaction is completed, often show greater change in the face of a minority influence than they do from a majority influence (Moscovici & Lage, 1976), while public responses frequently display an inverse tendency.

2. The existence of contrary tendencies in the two types of influence. The focus of social interaction, it should be noted, is always on contrasting bipolar pairs—conformity, innovation, nomic, anomic behavior or groups, social control, social change, etc.—and not as variations of degree or complementary aspects of the same form of interaction. This fact has great theoretical bearing, because these fundamental polarities allow us to describe and explain a large range of social behavior.

As far as influence phenomena are concerned, relations between public and private responses often reveal such a polarity. A majority expressing a judgment shared by a social group has an impact on everybody's public response, either because the judgment corresponds to existing norms or because it corresponds to everybody's definition of reality (Deutsch & Gerard, 1955). However, the private response may be quite different. In the former case, resistance is likely to be aroused, a desire to preserve one's own individual response in private. In the latter case, such a resistance may also occur. The resistance arises when the individual's judgment differs from that of the group (Asch, 1956) or when the individual discovers certain aspects of reality that no longer allow him to accept the group judgment as a correct definition of this reality. Such is the case, notably, in scientific, technical communities when new data or predictions that contradict old data or predictions become known. The history of science (Moscovici, 1968) offers ample evidence of such controversies. Last but not least, these resistances manifest themselves in areas where reality is ambiguous or its real structure has not yet been understood.

Conversely, a minority, which by definition expresses a deviant judgment, a judgment contrary to the norms respected by the social group, convinces some members of the group, who may accept its judgment in private. They will be reluctant to do so publicly, however, either for fear of losing face or to avoid the risk of speaking or acting in a deviant fashion in the presence of others. More generally, they are reluctant to transgress a norm that is important in their own eyes and in the eyes of others.

We will see later on how far these very reasonable descriptions correspond to reality. Suffice it to state at this point that they correspond to *compliance* behavior, on the one hand, and to what I have called (Moscovici, 1976) *conversion* behavior, on the other. To put it differently, they correspond to influence exerted to create public but not private acceptance, on the one hand, and influence exerted to create private but not public acceptance, on the other. As a limiting case, one can visualize a purely public compliance without any private acceptance, as illustrated, tragically, by concentration camps, and a private acceptance without public manifestation, as witnessed by secret societies and, during certain epochs, Christian heresies. Reciprocal ignorance is an even more common example. Each member of the group has changed his habits or beliefs but conceals this fact for fear of being categorized as a deviant, without realizing that the other members of the group have changed too, and in the same way as he. It takes an act of courage or special circumstances to have it revealed that they have common habits or beliefs.

Since Festinger's (1953) study, we have acquired a thorough knowledge of compliant behavior. However, we know almost nothing about conversion, which has "received less attention in research... The result is that only a limited picture can be drawn with respect to the psychological factors associated with conversion behavior" (Blake & Mourton, 1961, p. 20). I will therefore try to fill this picture.

II. On Conflict of Influences

There is a difference in kind between majority and minority influence, which can be seen in the asymmetry between compliance and conversion. However, it is not enough to establish this asymmetry. We must understand the underlying processes, sketch the rudiments of a theory, in the hope of grasping the facts that deserve to be taken into consideration and that give one confidence in the value of speculating about them. We know why majority influence mainly, but not exclusively, results in compliance, ever since Festinger (1953) showed how social pressures, the capacity to punish or reward, usually lead to public agreement with the group. Up to a point, moreover, this public agreement will be accompanied by a private acceptance if the individual wishes to be accepted by the group. In this context, liking is a key factor. However, as soon as social pressure relaxes, if the person is not attracted to the group, public agreement will tend to disappear and private acceptance will not take place. These ideas have been verified by Berkowitz (1954), Deutsch and Gerard (1955), Thibaut and Strickland (1956), Raven (1959), in fact, by most scholars who have worked in the field. Their findings are indisputable, and there is no need to come back to them. However, if we wish to understand at the same time compliance and conversion, other assumptions are required. They are as follows.

A.   ASSUMPTION I

Both minorities and majorities always exert influence. What I mean by this is that neither one has any a priori advantage with respect to the other and that each one has a privileged field of action. This results, in our societies, from the separation between private and public life, to the existence of a barrier between the two, and to legal rights guaranteeing respect for this separation. Education, language, and institutions justify this split and prepare us to live, on a psychic level, two lives in one. All our relations with others, particularly with individuals and groups that tend to change our judgments, are subject to this same split and therefore differ depending on whether they impinge on our public or on our private universe. Consequently, it is more acceptable for a majority to reinforce norms or for a minority to transgress them, but it is less acceptable when the reinforcement interferes with personal beliefs or the transgression calls for an outward manifestation. I am not implying that the majority makes no effort to interfere with individual convictions and does not try to control people's private lives—totalitarian governments offer us ample illustration—but this involves resorting to exceptional measures (police, severe questioning, etc.) which in the long run produce a split into an official and a real society, a generalized double talking and double thinking (Zinoviev, 1976). We know, however, that deviant behaviors are tolerated by certain societies at predetermined times (carnivals, holidays, etc.) and are permitted in other societies in the religious, political, and intellectual realm, even if they are attacked and considered undesirable.

Let us assume that people refuse to become conformist in their innermost selves just as they resist becoming deviant with respect to others, and not just with respect to their own selves or those with whom they are intimate. If this amounts to inconsistency, it is an inconsistency that is legitimate and indispensable to the way society operates. We can therefore understand why reactance (Brehm & Mann, 1975) to majority pressure is inevitable whenever it is necessary to keep one's private life intact, or why minority pressures can be tolerated as long as they do not overflow into public life. We are therefore faced with ambivalent attitudes toward a majority and a minority: The views of the latter are not automatically rejected because they are contrary to the norms, nor are the views of the former accepted without resistance because they agree with the norm. Their impact differs not only on the basis of their respective numerical weight but depending on whether they impinge on our public behaviors and beliefs or on our private realm. As a result, just because a minority has no effect on the first set of behaviors and beliefs, it must not be concluded that it has no effect, because it is very likely that its effect will turn up in a second set of behaviors and beliefs. To put it succinctly, if no change can be observed on a direct, outward level, some alteration may well take place on an indirect, latent level. This is a very strong claim, I realize. However, it not only corresponds to observation but has the heuristic advantage of compelling us to examine influence effects in depth, on both levels at once.

B. ASSUMPTION II

All influence attempts, no matter what their origin, create a conflict, either because they aim to introduce too great an inconsistency between private and public behaviors or judgments on the part of individuals or groups, or because they face individuals or groups with totally different behaviors or judgments with respect to something important. We speak of dissonance in one case and of divergence in the other, but either way a conflict is created. It is characterized by the fact that the alternatives are opposites—one affirms what the other one denies. Confronted with such a situation, the individual or group seems to have two main preoccupations: (1) to seem consistent and acceptable, socially, to others and himself; and (2) to make sense out of the confusing physical and social environment in which he is plunged. Obviously, the surer the majority or minority seems to be of what it proposes, the more committed it is to the position it is defending and the less disposed it is to yield on this position, showing it wants no compromise, the more severe such a conflict will be. Thus, accepting or rejecting the opposite term of the proposed alternative will be all the more difficult. It is now more or less recognized that behavioral styles, mainly consistency, reflect this sense of confidence, commitment, refusal of compromise. Hence, things proceed as if only the individual or group would have to make concessions in order to restore consistency and to give a meaning to the social or physical environment; only thus can clear understanding be gained and satisfactory social relations with the source of this influence be established. Therefore, the stronger the consistency at one pole of the social interaction, the greater the conflict at the other pole, and the greater the change required to reduce this conflict.

C. ASSUMPTION III

If it is true that neither a majority nor a minority is necessarily completely followed or entirely rejected, then both the majority and the minority can arouse such a conflict. It is nonetheless true that the center of this conflict, its direction, will be different depending on whether it is aroused by the majority or by the minority. This is true for the following reasons. First of all, it may be assumed that the judgments advanced by the former are accepted rather passively, whereas those emitted by the latter can be accepted only in an active way. An analogy may serve to illustrate this point. Let us compare a majority with a credible source and a minority with a source whose credibility is limited. Bauer (1966) has shown in a very careful analysis that in the field of mass communications, audiences, frequently receive the message rather passively and hardly process the information the message contains. Similarly, Cook (1964) noted that subjects produced more cognitive responses when the source had little credibility and was not mentioned than when it was credible. One might say that credibility presented an obstacle to the processing of information. Falk (1970), in contrast, studied the effect on attitudes of the status of the source as well as its effect on the number of connections made by the audience between the point of view presented by the message and its basic values. Reactions were measured immediately and again 3 and 5 weeks after the communication. The results obtained show that the subjects were more inclined to internalize the message from the source with little credibility than the one from the credible source (Kelman, 1958). One might say, *mutatis mutandis,* that the judgment expressed by a minority is more likely to raise arguments and counterarguments than the one expressed by a majority. The changes induced will, consequently, be stabler and more progressive in the case of a minority.

Now, let us take an individual who is giving an opinion about the properties of an object (its length, color, etc.) and who is confronted with several individuals having an opinion contrary to his own. He will wonder at once "Why do I not see or think like them?" He will not try to solve this dilemma by coming back to the object in question, for in principle the majority response must be correct or legitimate. Are several pairs of eyes not better than one? All he can do is to engage in a *comparison process* to detect a possible flaw in the alternative judgment with which he is faced or to understand why he made a mistake, why his response has so far, without his knowledge, been mistaken. For lack of a satisfactory solution, he is tempted to make concessions, moved by the urge to correct his mistake and be acceptable to others. This compels him to concentrate all his attention on what others say, so as to fit in with their opinions or judgments, especially when they are unanimous. Such a focusing often occurs even if, privately, he has reservations, as Asch (1956) observed by interviewing the subjects who participated in his well-known experiment. Therefore, his responses change during the social interaction. Once the interaction is over and the social pressure removed, however, when the individual is alone in looking at and judging the property of the object, he sees and judges it as he did before, as it is. Sherif's experiments of 1930 seem to prove the opposite, since the change observed in them outlasts the end of the social interaction by far. However, as I have explained elsewhere (Moscovici, 1976), we are dealing here with a variety of opinions expressed by a plurality of individuals; hence there is no common norm or judgment that would dispense them or prevent them from associating their responses each time with the stimulus with which they are presented. In short, there is no clear-cut majority in relation to which a member of the group would consider himself a deviant minority.

When one is faced with a minority, in contrast, its answers are from the start considered deviant and require supplementary verification. Each one wonders: "How can it see what it sees, think what it thinks?" If the minority is insistent, seems very sure of what it proposes, then the individuals belonging to the majority undertake a *validation process,* that is, an examination of the relation between its response and the object or reality just because a single pair of eyes is supposed to see less well than several. One will at the same time examine one's own responses, one's own judgments, in order to confirm and validate them. However, if one looks at the object or the reality in question once one is alone again, one will see and judge it differently, without even being aware of it, just because during the interaction one's main preoccupation was to see what the minority saw, to understand what it understood. It would be an overstatement but not a mistake to say that in the face of a discrepant majority all attention is focused on others, while in the face of a discrepant minority, all attention is focused on reality; that, in the first case, the conflict is primarily a conflict of responses, and in the second case it is a conflict of perceptions. Minorities are most commonly accused of exaggerating (they are making a mountain out of a molehill!), of lacking objectivity, and at first most of their ideas are derided, even in science, as delightful fictions or distorted images of the world as it is. For this reason, the minority point of view is subjected to relentless criticism. However, in the course of these criticisms and discussions, some of the minority's adversaries might be converted, if they do not die beforehand, as Planck once said.

D. ASSUMPTION IV

Every resolution of a conflict of influence, irrespective of its origin, follows a path that corresponds to one of the realms that I have mentioned, the public and the private path. *The more severe the conflict, the more likely it is to follow the more available path, if the other is blocked.* This last assumption is very reasonable and has been repeatedly verified in social and clinical psychology. It is self-evident that it is generally easier and more economical, from a social psychological point of view, to change one's opinion or behavior when one is faced with a "normal" alternative than with a "deviant" one, unless one belongs to a minority with a long-standing record of independence. This was the case, by his own admission, for Freud: "Being Jewish," he declared at a B'nai Brith meeting, "I felt exempt from numerous prejudices limiting the others in the use of their intellectual faculties; as a Jew, I was also ready to join the opposition and to give up any agreement with the compact majority."

Things are far from being that simple. What happens when an external social pressure creates a state of tension, and someone wishes to free himself from it? It all depends on the origin of his tension. In the face of a majority, the best way to lessen this tension is to change one's responses in the public realm; modifying them in the private realm would amount to losing one's self-determination, one's "I" in Mead's (1934/1970) sense, or even to erasing all differences with other people, in short, everything that constitutes one's individuality. In the face of a minority, the converse takes place. The only path for resolving a conflict lies in the private sphere, since it is very difficult to make direct concessions or to change behaviors or judgments in the public sphere. Few people submit to a deviant viewpoint lightheartedly, and they are even less willing to risk becoming deviants in turn, even if they have adopted a deviant point of view.

Although all this may not conform to ethical principles or throw a very happy light on mankind, we can draw some useful conclusions from this analysis. These are that the conflict of influence with a majority is resolved in its presence as long as the social pressure persists, whereas the conflict with the minority is resolved in its absence, when this pressure is relaxed. The more intense the pressure, the greater the effects obtained by the former on the direct, overt level, in short, on the level of the most superficial acceptance, and by the latter on the indirect, latent level, leading on the whole to an acceptance that may be so deep that the subject is not even aware of it.

E. SUMMARY

The four assumptions give us a general picture in which we see that a consistent minority can exert an influence to the same extent as a consistent majority, and that the former will generally have a greater effect on a deeper level, while the latter often has less, or none, at that level. In short, the minority creates a conversion behavior—measured *grosso modo* by the greater change in private than in public responses—and the majority creates a compliant behavior. Irrespective of their current limitations, these assumptions allow us to formulate some interesting and verifiable predictions:

1. Conversion is produced by a minority's consistent behavior.

2. The conversion produced by a minority implies a real change of judgments or opinions, not just an individual's assuming in private a response he has given in public. This is why we are often unaware of the profound modification in our perceptions or our ideas from contact with deviants.

3. The more intense the conflict generated by the minority, the more radical is the conversion. In other words, the more rigid the minority, the less is its direct effect on judgments or opinions, and the greater is its indirect effect on them.

4. At least where perceptions are involved, conversion is more pronounced when the influence source is absent. This conjecture is based on the idea that once a conflict is set in motion, the presence of the deviant minority prevents acceptance of its position, to avoid both losing face and recognizing oneself as deviant.

I shall now present a certain number of facts that substantiate these predictions and make them more plausible. I see no harm in their being considered too speculative even then, as long as their relevance to the question presented here is recognized. It is as impossible to assuage the demands of relentless positivists as it is to appease an avenging deity, and so it will always be.

III. Experimental Studies

> *Here one counsel is valid:*
> *Trust the inadequate and act on it;*
> *then it will become a fact.*
> HELMHOLTZ

A. PRELIMINARY RESULTS

Studies on minority influence have predicted from the very start that the minority's impact on subjects' private responses would be equal to or greater than its impact on their public responses. I know of no experiment where this did not hold and where different results were obtained. It is also evident that the discrepancy between the public and private reactions is more marked where the conflict of influence is sharpest—that is, when a factual judgment is involved—and less marked where a value judgment or preferences are at stake. This is apparent in several experiments, three of which I shall present here.

In one experiment (Moscovici, Lage, & Naffrechoux, 1969), groups of four naive subjects and two experimental confederates were asked to make a series of color perception judgments. The stimulus slides were blue. The subjects were asked to report aloud the name of the simple color they saw and to estimate the light intensity in numerical terms. Of course, on every trial, the confederates said that the slides were green. Upon completing this procedure, the subjects were asked to take part in a second, ostensibly unrelated, experiment concerning the effects of training upon vision. The subjects, tested individually, were exposed to a number of disks in the blue-green zone of the Farnsworth Perception Test. For each disk, the subjects were asked to name the simple color they saw.

The results of this second experiment indicated that the perceptual threshold of subjects who had previously been exposed to the consistent minority shifted. They saw as green disks that are usually perceived as closer to blue. (I shall come back later to this proposition, which requires a stronger foundation). Furthermore, subjects who did not give any "green" responses during the social interaction phase of the experiment were even more likely than those who did join the minority position at least once to call the disks green. The results are satisfactory enough to enable us to conclude that (a) the change in response was stronger in the private than in the public situation; and (b) subjects who felt completely blocked, incapable of adopting the minority judgment in the presence of the others, solved their conflict by adopting the judgment even more, probably without being aware of it, once they were alone. Nothing of the kind was observed when the minority was inconsistent or when the source of influence was a consistent majority (Moscovici & Lage, 1976). This suggests that the consistent majority produced compliance rather than conversion, public without private change.

The experiment by Nemeth and Wachtler (1973) yielded different and more typical results, that is, responses given under social pressure remained the same after this pressure was withdrawn. Subjects, run in small groups, expressed a preference for one of a pair of paintings on each of 19 trials. An experimental confederate consistently expressed a preference for either German or Italian paintings, himself being allegedly German or Italian. Irrespective of his seeming bias or minority position, he exerted a strong influence on the group. A group discussion ensued and, in its wake, the subjects were again asked to state their preferences for each of the 19 pairs of paintings. This time, however, they indicated their choices anonymously in writing instead of giving them aloud. No differences were found between public and private responses, which suggests that subjects had not merely complied but had in fact undergone a real change.

Common to both of these experiments is the fact that they both utilized a direct index, the very same response, to measure the transfer of influence from one situation to another. It was therefore important to see whether this transfer or generalization would occur when more unobtrusive measures were employed, measures associated indirectly with the message received or with the subject matter discussed in the group. An experiment by Wolf (1977) demonstrated that this was in fact the case.

Female subjects, run in groups of four, were led to believe that they were interacting as members of a jury. Their task was to decide upon an amount of compensation to be awarded to the plaintiff in a civil suit. The facts of the case were weighted so as to encourage subjects to award between $20,000 and $30,000. The influence agent, ostensibly one of the group members, advocated the minority position of $3000 throughout their interaction. Three variables were manipulated: the cohesiveness of the group (high or low), the behavioral style of the influence agent (high consistency or low consistency), and the opportunity for rejection of the influence agent from the group (rejection possible or not possible).

The primary dependent measure determined the change in private judgment concerning the compensation award from pre- to postdeliberation. Change in the direction of a decreased award reflected the minority's influence. The results showed that subjects in the high-cohesive conditions reduced their awards to a greater extent than subjects in the low-cohesive conditions. Furthermore, within the high-cohesive conditions, the strongest minority influence was found in the high-consistency/no possibility and the low-consistency/possibility conditions.

Four measures of latent influence examined the cognitive-perceptual effects of the minority influence attempt on subjects' judgments. In an ostensibly unrelated task, the subjects responded anonymously to a series of questions concerning the severity of different prison terms and fines and the usefulness to a plaintiff of different compensation awards. Four measures of latent influence were embedded in the items. On 21-point scales, subjects rated the penalty value of a $3000 and a $20,000 fine and the utility value of a $3000 and a $20,000 compensation award. The questions concerning $3000 measured subjects' perceptions of the critical stimulus value employed in the social influence situation. The questions concerning $20,000 measured the generalization of the effect to a different value. The $20,000 reflected a normative initial judgment in the original influence situation. Subjects whose perceptual codes were influenced by the minority should have viewed the fines as more severe and the awards as more useful than subjects who were not so influenced.

The results of the latent influence measures paralleled those obtained on the judgment-change measure. A major effect for cohesiveness was found on the two utility-value measures. Subjects in high-cohesive conditions perceived both $3000 and $20,000 as more useful to a plaintiff than subjects in low-cohesive conditions. Interactions were revealed on the two penalty-value measures. On both measures, the strongest minority influence was found in the high-cohesive/ high consistency/no possibility and the high-cohesive/low-consistency/ possibility conditions. The latent influence data, then, replicated both the major effect and the more subtle interaction produced on the judgment-change measure. The results of these unobtrusive measures show that subjects' perceptions of the critical stimulus were altered as a function of the influence situation to which they had been exposed and that this effect generalized to a novel but similar stimulus value. Thus, the minority influence attempt succeeded not only in changing subjects' overt responses but in changing the context or cognitive code underlying those responses as well.

The preliminary outcome of these experiments is clear. A consistent minority produces at least as much, if not more, change in private than in public situations. The public–private difference reflects both the intensity of the conflict and the nature of the stimulus around which the influence attempt revolves.

B.   DIRECT AND INDIRECT INFLUENCE

"One cannot break the chains where there are none visible." This statement by Kafka to one of his young admirers is indicative of the kind of incapacity one experiences, unwittingly, when trying to escape from the insistent pressure of a minority. The mere advocacy of a deviant point of view arouses strong feelings in us and binds us by creating an unexpected complexity and ambiguity in a situation that is usually clear and banal. This is enough to stimulate interest, to gain a hearing, and to trigger strongly favorable or adverse reactions.

Any minority that wishes to have an impact must be consistent, but it can be so in two ways. Consistency can be achieved, on the one hand, by speaking and acting in a rigid manner. This unconciliatory behavioral style heightens the threatening and anxiety-producing aspects of the conflict with the majority. A fair behavioral style can be achieved, on the other hand, by consistently manifesting a combination of firmness and flexibility in word and deed, in which the strength of one's own opinions does not preclude taking the opinions and ideas of others into account. This behavioral style provides a way of circumventing the conflict with the minority.

"Rigid" minorities, as a matter of course, block any solution that precludes a wholesale adoption of the deviant position. "Fair" minorities, on the contrary, leave the door open to reciprocal concessions and remove an all-or-nothing character from the adoption of a deviant point of view. The first type of minority creates a more intensive conflict and hence blocks public expression of agreement more completely than the second. It follows that the former will generally produce more conversions, that is, indirect influence, than the latter.

To put it differently, a "fair" minority, exemplified at times by the Socialists, will gain acceptance for the judgments or opinions explicitly contained in its message, whereas a "rigid" minority, such as the extreme left, will on the contrary gain acceptance for judgments or opinions that are implied or derived from the content of its message. A remarkable series of experiments by Mugny (1974) and Papastamou (1979) shed light on the meaning of these suggestions. They were conceived along the same lines as the usual experiments on communication and generally dealt with the topic of pollution. At the same time they presented three special features:

1. The messages were attributed to a minority group or institution.
2. The message style was either "rigid," that is, expressing dogmatic and extreme points of view, or "fair," that is, expressing a consistent point of view but with some "conciliatory" overtones. A slogan of the rigid message, for instance, stated: "Let us close down the factories that do not abide by the rules," whereas the slogan of the fair message expressed its position in these terms: "Let us force the automobile producers to supply their vehicles equipped with antipollution filters."
3. The questionnaire filled out by the subjects before and after reading the message consisted of an equal number of direct and indirect items. The direct items were nearly identical with those contained in the message, whereas the indirect items related to the topic but were not explicitly contained in the message. A change obtained in the latter items would reflect more than a simple adoption of minority positions; it would imply a certain "generalization" produced by connections with or inferences from the opinions upheld in the latter's statement. Conversion is reflected here in the difference between direct and indirect influence. It is the outcome of each person's own deliberation.

Let us now proceed to review this series of experiments, without going into great detail.

At the outset of the first experiment, the subjects responded in the usual fashion to a questionnaire concerning the causes of and responsibilities for pollution. They were subsequently divided up into four groups, each group receiving a message in either a "rigid" or a "fair" style and with either a "dissonant" or a "consonant" content in terms of the general beliefs of the population. (This constituted four communication conditions: rigid–dissonant, rigid–consonant, fair–dissonant, and fair–consonant.) After reading the appropriate text, each subject responded once more to the same questionnaire.

What was observed? Changes in responses to the indirect items were proportionately greater than changes in responses to the direct items, that is, to those actually contained in the message ($F = 5.75$, $p < .005$). However, the details are much more interesting. The minority whose style was fair and whose image was more flexible and less threatening produced an equally great change in responses regardless of the nature of the items. The rigid minority, in contrast, had little influence on responses to the direct items, but its influence was far greater on the responses to the indirect items. The change produced by the rigid minority therefore manifested itself not with respect to the views it upheld but with respect to other, related points. This difference was even more marked when the minority message was dissonant, in other words, when it contrasted sharply with majority beliefs ($F = 4.02$, $p < .05$). The results are self-explanatory.

Wherever a minority exerts a weak pressure and its opinions do not clash head-on with the convictions of the population, the conflict is less intense and the influence effect is direct. However, as soon as the minority's pressure increases and its opinions begin to clash with the subjects' convictions, the influence observed is largely indirect. There is a lesson to be learned here with respect to our measures and the need to determine in advance, in a theoretical manner, which ones are appropriate. Had Mugny been content to use only direct items, the conclusions drawn from this experiment would have been entirely different and would have confirmed the commonsense notion that a fair minority is more effective than a rigid one.

In a second experiment along the same lines, subjects received a communication whose content was either consonant or dissonant with the attitudes of the general population toward foreigners. Some subjects, however, received a message in a consistent style, that is, a consistently structured text, while others received a message in an inconsistent style. The aim of the experiment was to show that only minorities that appear consistent exert true influence. The results showed that this is in fact the case. It was also found that when the content of the communication was consonant with the subjects' opinion, it exerted a greater influence than when it was dissonant. To avoid misunderstanding, I repeat that this applied only in the consistent conditions. Moreover, the consonant communication produced response changes primarily for the direct items, while the dissonant communication produced response changes primarily for items related to but not actually contained in the text ($F = 3.16$, $p < .10$).

The stronger the ideological "opposition," or the greater the resistance to minority pressure, therefore, the stronger the reluctance to accept its message, and the greater the likelihood that its point of view will be accepted in an indirect manner; the contrary occurs when this opposition is less pronounced. This phenomenon is analogous to one that was observed a number of years ago by Schönbar (1945), to wit, that the longer people resist changing their position under conditions of social pressure, the more persistently will they maintain a modified position in the situation that follows.

In a third experiment, the subjects received either a "rigid" or a "fair" message on the topic of pollution. They were advised at the outset that after reading it, they would respond once more to the questionnaire they had just filled out. The authors of the message, they were told, had asked the experimenters to try to find out whether the subjects had been influenced by the message. This instruction was delivered explicitly to produce resistance, to block the process of coming to terms with the minority. It was assumed, additionally, that this blockage would be intensified by the fact that the subjects were asked to cooperate in one way or another with the source and thus identify publicly with a deviant and extreme point of view. In order to verify this assumption, conditions of unilateral and bilateral influence were created. Subjects in the unilateral influence condition were told: "Your responses are of interest to the authors insofar as they want to take your opinions into account in modifying the message."

The prediction was straightforward: Changes with respect to the indirect items would be greater when the message was rigid and the influence bilateral than when the message was fair and the influence unilateral. For lack of an adequate number of subjects, it was possible to complete only three of the four conditions: fair style–unilateral influence, rigid style–unilateral influence, and rigid style–bilateral influence. The results were as predicted: Greater opinion change was found on the indirect than on the direct items ($F = 34.19$, $p < .001$). With respect to the three conditions, it may be noted that the difference between response changes to the direct and the indirect items was practically nil in the first condition (fair style–unilateral influence), that it increased perceptibly in the second condition (rigid style–unilateral influence; $F = 8.06$, $p < .05$), and that it became quite large in the third (rigid style–bilateral influence; $F = 37.81$, $p < .001$). The data, which are presented in Table I, clearly confirm our conjectures: There is in all cases an influence effect.

If the minority is perceived as fair, it produces as great a modification in responses, as much agreement, in short, on items contained in its message as on items that are only related to it. If the minority is perceived as rigid, however, it has less or even no impact on the items reflecting its position and relatively more impact on other items that it does not mention but that are related to its message. The more rigid the minority appears and the more subjects are asked to cooperate with it, the greater this indirect impact. This should not come as a surprise to us. We have observed, over the last several years, how militant minorities and extremists in political and cultural circles have affected our outlook, changed our manner of behaving, dressing, speaking, etc., without at the same time leading most of us to accept their positions or making us act as they would wish.

The greater the conflict produced by the minority, by virtue of its rigidity or consistency, therefore, the greater the extent to which the change taking place will be the outcome of the subjects' own inference. This outcome is far less

TABLE I

MEAN CHANGES OF OPINION WITH RESPECT TO POLLUTION[a]

Condition	Direct items	Indirect items
Fair–unilateral	+.491	+.738
Rigid–unilateral	+.194	+.831
Rigid–bilateral	−.081	+1.300

[a] Responses were scored on a 7-point scale. An analysis of covariance yielded essentially the same results. + means positive influence.

affected by the specific content of the message than by the global view that this content expresses. Consequently, a seeming lack of influence at any given moment may be misleading. What has been left out of account is the fact that while the persons may have refused to comply publicly and to identify themselves as deviants, they may have been privately converted to the thinking of the minority.

C. CONFLICT AND CONVERSION BEHAVIOR

All experiments of this kind demonstrate that minority influence is greater on indirect items than on the direct items contained in the message, and that this applies even more to rigid than to flexible messages. It would follow logically that if this difference in impact results from a conflict between the opinions held by the source and those of the audience, it should be more marked if the deviant character of the source is highlighted and its pressure increases. The simplest way to create such a situation is to strengthen the minority numerically: If several deviants express the same point of view, it becomes much more difficult to reject it by attributing it to "subjective" factors; hence one must concede that something "objective" must also be involved. In this case the conflict between two judgments of fact rather than two judgments of value. In a first experiment based on exactly the same principle as the ones I have just described, Papastamou (1979) has created two conditions: In one condition the subjects read a text that expresses minority positions on pollution, while in another condition they read the two halves of this text, in slightly revised form, but with the first half of the text attributed to minority group X and the second half to minority group Y. The order in which the text segments are presented as well as the attribution to group X and Y is of course neutralized. As was the case in the previous experiments, the message style is either rigid or fair, so that the following communication situations arise: a "fair" source–a "rigid" source–two "fair" sources–two "rigid" sources. On the basis of what we have found out so far, we expect the indirect influence to be greater both in the situation where the source is perceived as rigid and where the two sources are similar. The results support these conjectures. It can be noted, first of all, that while the two messages from the two flexible sources do not exert more influence than one message from a single flexible source, two messages stemming from two rigid sources exert significantly more influence (F 1/68 = 5.709, $p < .05$) than a message from a single rigid source. However, as was to be expected, this influence is not identical on the direct and the indirect items. It is first of all far lower for the former than for the latter (F 1/68 = 44.186, $p < .0005$). In addition, on closer inspection it becomes apparent that the difference between the situations with a single source and with two minority sources is not at all significant for the direct items; it becomes significant only for the indirect items (F 1/68 = 4.151, $p < .05$). In other words, by increasing the intensity of the conflict by means of attributing the message to two sources instead of a single source, a significantly higher conversion rate is obtained than would otherwise be the case.

In a second experiment, which was analogous to the previous one, the subjects were asked to read two texts attributed to different groups expressing minority opinions on the pollution problem. Before reading their texts, however, they were faced with an introductory page in their booklet informing them that in the following section there would be two notorious minority groups expressing their stands with respect to this problem. The relation between these groups was not presented in the same way in all the situations, however. In one situation, as a matter of fact, the groups in question are said to be in a minority position within the general framework of the antipollution campaign, but coordinating their efforts to fight efficiently against pollution. In the other situation, it is stated that these groups are competing for influence, each one trying to outstrip the other in its campaign against existing pollution. Therefore, there are minorities appearing to be cooperative, on the one hand, and minorities appearing to be competitive, on the other. In addition, they are either flexible and fair or rigid and extremist. It might have been reasonable to expect that cooperative minorities, generally speaking, would have greater influence than competitive minorities and that their direct influence would be greater. Nevertheless, in keeping with the points I have just presented, this is not the case. On the whole, the relation between the minorities seems to have no impact, since no difference between the cooperative and the competitive situation can be observed. However, the nature of the message makes a difference, because rigid minorities have greater influence than flexible minorities (F $1/68 = 4.222$, $p < .05$). The customary effect does not manifest itself here; in fact, it is reversed. It therefore seems that when there are two minority sources, a firm position has a greater payoff, while flexibility is more productive for a single source. This conclusion must be qualified, however. A breakdown of the effect of the message style on the cooperative and the competitive level reveals the following: Although the two styles have a more or less equal impact for the competitive situation, the same is not true where the two minorities are supposed to cooperate. There a rigid message produces a much stronger impact than a flexible message (F $1/68 = 6.183$, $p < .01$). Let us now compare the responses to the direct and the indirect items (Table II). The nature of the message makes no difference as far as the direct items are concerned. For the indirect items, however, the rigid minorities have a greater positive influence than the flexible minorities. In the light of these results, as a whole, one may say that cooperative relations between minorities, especially rigid minorities, emphasize their deviant character. If they thereby have an impact on the audience, this impact manifests itself more strongly on the indirect than on the direct level, that is, by conversion rather than by compliance.

TABLE II

MEAN CHANGES OF OPINION ON DIRECT ITEMS
AND ON INDIRECT ITEMS[a]

Minority source		Direct items	Indirect items
Fair	In cooperation	−.316	+.203
	In competition	+.028	+.250
Rigid	In cooperation	−.014	+.250
	In competition	+.083	+.556

[a] + means positive influence from influence source. Responses were scored on a 7-point scale.

D.   MINORITY INFLUENCE, MAJORITY INFLUENCE, AND COMPLIANCE

Minorities are not the only ones to seek and secure conversions. It is probable, though, that they are the ones who most often produce such an effect. To compare their influence with majority influence, I carried out the following experiment in collaboration with Mugny and Papastamou. Although it was similar to the previous experiments in that the communication dealt with pollution and the message read by the subjects were either "rigid" or "fair," it differed from the others in two important respects:

(a). The same messages were attributed either to a majority source or to a minority source.

(b). The effectiveness of the messages was measured immediately after and after a certain period of time had elapsed, as was done in the experiments on the "sleeper" effect.

The experimental procedure consists of three phases. During a first phase (pretest), the subjects responded to a 20-item questionnaire by circling the number expressing the extent of their agreement or disagreement with each statement. The second phase, the actual experimental phase, took place a week later. The subjects were informed of the positions attributed either to a majority or to a minority group, depending on the conditions, and they read a text on the pollution problem. There are altogether four conditions: rigid–majority, fair–majority, rigid–minority, fair–minority. Right after the perusal of the text, the subjects answered the usual opinion questionnaire. Three weeks later, during the third phase, the subjects once more filled out the questionnaire on pollution problems. They then answered a series of complementary questions intended to measure how accurately they remembered the exact nature of the influence source and the opinions it had expressed. In this case the subjects were Swiss adolescents, about 15 years of age and living in a suburb of Geneva. Like many young people in Europe, they were personally concerned about ecological questions, so one can say that the content of the messages mattered to them.

What were their responses right after reading the text? The results we obtained show that, irrespective of the nature of the source or of the message, there is practically no influence. However, slight as this influence is, a significant difference appears: The subjects let themselves be influenced a little more on the direct than on the indirect items (F $1/80 = 4.876$, $p < .05$). There was, therefore, a slight compliance effect that was reinforced by our instruction. The results obtained 3 weeks later present a different picture. To begin with, the minority appeared somewhat more influential than the majority (F $1/80 = 3.85$, $p < .10$). As expected, the influence exerted was not the same for the two groups (Table III). On the direct items, the majority and the minority did in fact have a similar effect. On the indirect items, conversely, the majority obtained a negative effect, the subjects returning to the opinion that they held prior to reading the messages, whereas the minority obtained a positive effect, the subjects accepting the point of view upheld in the message to a greater extent at the later time than immediately after having read it (F $1/80 = 7.88$, $p < .01$).

That is not all. The message style does seem to play a certain role. The breakdown of the interaction between the source factor and the style factor of the message provides us with interesting results. With respect to the majority, it made no difference, on the whole, whether the style was rigid or fair, whereas it made a difference with respect to the minority. The fair minority actually lost some of its influence on both the direct and the indirect items, although less, on the whole, than the fair majority. The rigid minority, on the contrary, lost much of its influence on the direct items but gained considerable influence on the indirect items ($F = 5.36$, $p < .05$). This was the minority that won the greatest acceptance for its point of view by the audience 3 weeks later, on opinions that it had not explicitly advocated.

Before I draw any conclusions from this experiment, I would like to mention some other interesting results. When the subjects were asked about the source of the messages after completing the questionnaire 3 weeks later, they recalled the identity of the minority source more accurately than that of the

TABLE III

MEAN CHANGES OF OPINION BETWEEN THE
PRETEST AND THE SECOND POSTTEST[a]

Influence source		Direct items	Indirect items
Majority	Fair	+.167	−.268
	Rigid	+.179	−.310
Minority	Fair	+.155	+.071
	Rigid	+.048	+.440

[a] + means positive influence.

majority source (30 out of 41 as against 13 out of 41). Irrespective of its rigid or fair style, it seems, the minority had a stronger impact than the majority. Similarly, subjects confronted by the minority remembered the content of the message more accurately than those confronted by the majority ($F = 17.434$, $p < .001$). The message style seems to have a slight effect in that, on the whole, people remember "fair" messages less clearly than "rigid" messages ($F = 3.015$, $p < .10$).

The conclusions of this experiment were very clear indications that a majority produces compliance, which disappears over time, whereas a minority produces conversions—indirect conversions, that is—especially if it is rigid. Curiously enough, the "rhetoric," in other words, the behavioral style, is relevant only for the latter and not the former. The question arises why the identity and the content of a majority message are more easily forgotten than those of a minority. There is one plausible explanation: The majority message is treated more passively than the minority message. Whatever the validity of this explanation, the fact remains that there is no clear-cut relationship between accuracy of recall of the source and the opinion change observed. Thus, subjects confronted with a deviant source remember it equally well whether it is rigid or fair, and yet they do react differently in each case. One finding persistently runs through all these results: These effects obtained by a minority have a specific character and are not, as a rule, obtained by a majority.

This experiment has some implications for the body of research on the "sleeper effect." As is well known, this effect consists of a delayed message influence on the opinions of an audience. This delayed influence is explained by dissociating the source from the message: Once the source is forgotten, the content alone continues to act on individuals' opinions. In our experiment, it was rather the opposite that was observed: The delayed influence went hand in hand with a greater recall of the source. If that is the case, the usual explanation could not be applicable. The "sleeper effect" seems to occur, moreover, only when the source is deviant, even extremely deviant. When this source is conformist, it is more likely to cause a resumption of the individuals' original opinion. It would be more accurate to say: The sleeper effect is associated with a deviant or minority message. Among the minority messages, moreover, those whose content people are more likely to have forgotten are the ones that are the most effective. Actually, subjects confronted with rigid minority remember its exact opinions less accurately than subjects confronted with a fair minority ($F = 7.58$, $p < .05$); and yet those subjects show the greatest change. In short, to the extent that forgetfulness plays a part at all, the opposite of what has been asserted takes place, since it affects the content rather than the source of the message.

How can the results we have obtained be reconciled with those hitherto obtained? There is no clear-cut answer to this question. I would only like to make these observations as a contribution to a possible future discussion.

The sleeper effect was demonstrated, not surprisingly, in earlier studies with a typically counterattitudinal message, that is, a message clashing with the norms and beliefs of the audience. The delayed attitude change was explained by saying that once the identity of the source, which had interfered with the acceptance of the content, had been erased from memory, its opinions could be accepted because the content could now be judged on its own merit. A negative message, however, may have two meanings, depending on the context: On the one hand, it is in opposition to something and, on the other hand, it is deviant in relation to something. It is conceivable that in the earlier experiments it had its impact not so much because of its association with a negative source as because of its expressing a deviant position that upset some widely held beliefs or attitudes, in other words, because it was counternormative and not because it was counterattitudinal. The reason we have obtained such striking effects is that we have, on the one hand, emphasized this counternormative aspect by associating it with a minority and, on the other hand, deemphasized it by associating it with a majority. It is likely that the contradictory results and contradictions of the "sleeper effect" analyzed by Gillig and Greenwald (1974) are attributable to the fact that these two aspects of the message have not until now been distinguished and that experimenters have failed to control this variable, although individuals sometimes react to one aspect and sometimes to the other. If this is the case, it follows that a large part of the attitude change attributed hitherto to the "pro" and "con" character of the message, to the positive or negative content of the communication, could be attributed to its deviant or nondeviant meaning. This calls for a reevaluation of an entire body of generally accepted data and ideas that would benefit from being viewed in a new light. Even dissonance theory might be reevaluated in order to determine whether dissonance results from opposition between two opinions, opposition between a deviant and a nondeviant opinion (Nuttin, 1975), or opposition between a deviant behavior that one is obliged to assume publicly and the norms and beliefs to which one privately subscribes.

Another question now arises. In our experiment, the majority failed to obtain conversion, but why did it fail to obtain compliance? Was this because of the message content or because of some other factor? If it was caused by the content, then the results obtained by us and the conclusions drawn from them are valueless. However, it is much more likely that we failed to obtain compliance because one of the causes of this behavior was missing, to wit, the existence of an external compulsion, that is, social control. Papastamou (1979) confirmed this supposition. His experiment used the same kind of materials involving the struggle against pollution, but he attributed it to a majority source. This experiment consisted of three phases. In the first phase, the subjects gave individual answers to the pollution questionnaire as well as to some supplementary questions. Ten days later, the second phase took place. At this point a majority communication was read and the subjects were asked to draw up their own arguments justifying their stand on the pollution problem. At the same time the subjects were informed that the group that had drawn up the message asked in exchange to be acquainted with the opinions of part of the persons involved, and to be given their names and addresses so as to be able to contact the various people for a later discussion. This introduced the notion of social control. The experimenters then pretended to draw lots in order to respond to this request. They thereby created four conditions:

(a) In the individual control condition, the subjects were informed that they were among those whose names and replies would be communicated to the authors of the texts they were about to read.

(b) In the collective control condition, the subjects were informed that they were among those whose discussion group and replies of their group would be communicated to the authors of the text they were about to read.

(c) In the individual noncontrol condition, the subjects were informed that they were among those whose replies would be communicated to the authors of the text, but nothing else.

(d) In the collective noncontrol condition, the subjects were informed that they were among those whose names and replies would not be communicated to the authors of the text they were about to read and that only the numbers of the discussion groups would be given to these authors.

In a third phase, which followed immediately, the subjects once more answered individually the pollution questionnaire and some complementary questions. The results show that the majority source has a strong influence and that this influence bears more strongly on the direct than on the indirect items ($F = 20.77$, $p < .001$). In contrast to the changes in response produced by a minority, changes in response produced by a majority are limited to the opinions advocated by the majority; there is no impact at all on the items when inferences would have to be drawn from its messages. This connotes a passive acceptance. What are the effects of external compulsion? It can be observed that where social control is "weak," the degree of influence is the same in the individual and in the collective conditions. In contrast, where it is "strong," the majority exerts considerable influence in the collective control condition and very little influence in the individual control condition ($F = 6.55$, $p < .05$). In other words, an isolated individual tends to offer resistance, while individuals explicitly belonging to a group tend to conform. If one takes into account the fact that the response changes occur only for the direct items and that they are more pronounced for subjects belonging to a group, it follows that compliance takes place and that it is maximized where external compulsion is maximized. This agrees with Festinger's (1953) and Deutsch and Gerard's (1955) hypotheses. Additional results confirm our conclusion. In the postexperimental questionnaire, the subjects' compliance in a potential discussion with the authors of the message is measured by asking them whether they would try to reach a consensus. As was to be expected, the subjects in the control conditions assert that they would want such a consensus ($F = 3.66$, $p < .10$) and this desire is stronger in the collective control than in the individual control condition ($F = 4.03$, $p < .05$). Furthermore, as I mentioned at the beginning of this study, such a control on the individual is bound to provoke resistance, as results show. In his experiment, Papastamou proceeded to analyze the arguments written by the subjects to justify their stand, categorizing the arguments as either "majority" or "minority" with respect to their content on the pollution struggle. The score shows that the subjects in the individual control condition produce more minority arguments than the subjects in the collective control condition ($F = 2.842$, $p < .10$) and those in the weak social control conditions ($F = 3.942$, $p < .05$). In short, they not only refuse to adopt majority opinions but even start adopting minority opinions and thus become deviants. The results obtained seem to me to display great coherence. Majority influence in combination with social control, even weak social control, leads to compliance, which is maximized when there is strong collective control and minimized when there is strong individual control. The absence of this compliance in the previous experiment therefore makes sense and the interpretations concerning conversion and the "sleeper effect" remain plausible.

These results taken as a whole refine our understanding of minority influence. As predicted, fair minorities have their strongest impact on the specific responses of individuals belonging to the majority. Rigid minorities seem to have their greatest impact on the cognitive code underlying these responses. In this sense one may say that the former have a direct effect and the latter an indirect one.

IV. Verbal Responses and/or Perceptual Changes

One of the few books referring to conversion behavior defined it as follows: "Conversion is a change process in which a person gives up one ordered view of the world and one philosophical perspective for another" (Zimbardo, Ebbesen, & Maslach, 1977, p. 182). What is notable in this definition is the stress it places on the global character of changes in perception and knowledge. At first glance, we obtained such changes in the Moscovici *et al.* (1969) experiment, described in Section III,A, in which most of the subjects said that the slides were blue, although they had started to see them as green. These results seem to indicate a generalization of the verbal response from the social to the individual level. The subjects who heard the novel and strange "green" response to all of the slides in the first phase of the experiment, having been reluctant to adopt it in the presence of others, might have employed it as their own response in the second phase without their perception of the color having been truly modified. That would mean that what we observed was a manifest conversion, of which each individual was more or less aware. A latent conversion certainly occurred, however, at least partially, a modification which escaped the subjects' consciousness and was manifested by a perceptual modification. Verbal change without perceptual change or verbal change with perceptual change, that is our question. In order to confirm this second intriguing possibility—and prediction of the theory—we (Moscovici & Personnaz, 1978) conducted the following experiment.

As was the case in our previous research, the subjects were shown a series of blue slides, which a confederate consistently designated as being green. However, instead of using a color test to measure the perceptual modification following the social interaction, we used the chromatic afterimage. As we know, if one fixates on a white screen after having fixated on a color for several seconds, one perceives its complementary color. In our case, this would be yellow–orange for the blue slides and red–purple for the green. Several series of observations suggest that afterimages result from peripheral processes of the visual apparatus, but these processes are not yet well understood. From what is already known, it may be assumed that if (a) subjects simply modify their verbal responses, the afterimage perceived following the blue slide would be found in the yellow–orange zone of the spectrum; (b) subjects really changed their perceptual code, even without changing their verbal responses, the afterimage perceived would be the complementary color of green, which is closer to red–purple.

Let us return to the details of the experiment. The material was the same as that used in the previous experiments, i.e., blue slides. The subjects were invited to participate, in pairs, in an experiment on color perception. The pairs of course consisted of a naive subject and a confederate. The experiment consisted of four phases. The first phase comprised five trials; the answers were private. The subjects and the confederate wrote down their judgment of (a) the color of the slide and (b) the color of the afterimage on a 9-point scale ranging from yellow (1) to purple (9). The experimenter then collected the response sheets and informed the subjects that he had the results previously obtained with respect to the color of slides in other studies, in which a large number of people had participated. He then handed the subjects a sheet on which the percentage of persons having seen the color of the slide as green was marked:

1. Majority source condition
   a. 18.2% saw the color as it was indicated by the naive subject
   b. 81.8% saw the color as it was indicated by the confederate.
2. Minority source condition
   a. 81.8% saw the color as it was indicated by the naive subject
   b. 18.2% saw the color as it was indicated by the confederate.

Prior to the interaction, therefore, each subject knew, depending upon the condition, whether the confederate's response was deviant or not. Over the course of the next 15 trials, the judgments were made publicly and related solely to the color of the slide. The confederate was the first to respond orally on each trial. Her judgment remained consistent in that she always responded "green." This response was different from the one given by the subject in the first phase of the experiment. After this second social-interaction phase there followed a third phase of 15 trials during which the subject and the confederate noted their judgment in private with respect to (a) the color of the slide and (b) the color of the afterimage, perceived by fixating on the white screen after the slide was removed. At the end of this phase, the confederate said that she had an urgent appointment and left the room. Alone now, the naive subject responded privately to another five trials by reporting both the color of the slide and the complementary color. At the end of this fourth phase, each subject was interviewed about the experiment and debriefed.

What were the results observed during the interaction? The number of green responses given by the subjects during the social interaction (second phase) was about 5% and did not vary significantly according to whether the confederate was presented as expressing a majority or a minority judgment. The perceptual modification was measured by the change in the individual's judgment of the complementary color before and after the social interaction.

In order to take into account the fact that the phases involved differing numbers of trials, the subjects' chromatic afterimage scores were standardized across conditions, separately for each phase, prior to analysis. It should be noted that in Table IV a movement toward a higher score indicates a shift toward the complementary color of green (red–purple), while movement toward a lower

TABLE IV

Color Perception of the Aftereffect Following
Slide Presentation

	Influence source present		Influence source absent; scores after interaction
Influence source	Scores before interaction	Scores after interaction	
Minority ($n = 18$)	m = 5.47 s = 1.16	m = 6.17 s = 1.18	m = 6.22 s = .95
Majority ($n = 18$)	m = 5.90 s = .99	m = 5.56 s = 1.41	m = 5.54 s = 1.42
Control group ($n = 10$)	m = 5.70 s = 1.06	m = 5.45 s = .95	m = 5.45 s = 1.56

score indicates a shift toward the complementary color of blue (yellow–orange). The data were analyzed by means of a 3 (Conditions) × 3 (Phase) unweighted means analysis of variance, with repeated measures on the Phase factor. The analysis yielded a significant Conditions × Phase interaction ($F = 2.58$, $p < .05$). Inspection of the means indicates that the subjects' judgment in the minority influence condition shifted toward the complement of green from the pre- to the postinteraction situations. A series of a priori comparisons revealed that this shift was significant from the first to the third phase, with $t(102) = 2.17$ and $p < .05$, and that it became even greater when the influence source was absent, with $t(102) = 2.49$ and $p < .02$. No such effect was obtained in the other conditions. In fact, there was a tendency for majority influence subjects to shift in the opposite direction, that is, toward the complement of blue, from the first to the fourth phase, $t(102) = 1.75$, $p < .10$.

A consistent minority obviously produced a change in perceptual responses, and this change was even more pronounced when the minority was no longer present, a phenomenon we observed in an earlier study (Moscovici & Neve, 1971). The consistent majority, in contrast, failed to produce such a change or, if it did produce any change, it was in the opposite direction. A replication of this experiment by a student experimenter led to the same results.

Carrying the analysis of this phenomenon one step further, Doms (1978) raised the question whether the effect should be attributed to the fact that the two individuals symbolized a majority and a minority, respectively, or whether it should be ascribed to the simultaneous physical presence of two individuals, one of whom said green and the other, blue. In other words, was the effect truly produced by the deviant character of the green response or simply by the conflict in responses, the former being contrary to or different from the latter? Doms settled this question by placing a naive subject in the presence of a confeder ate who was identified neither with a majority nor with a minority. In other respects, the experiment was carried out in a manner identical to the previous one. In this critical condition, no influence effects were produced with respect to the chromatic afterimage. Conversion behavior therefore takes place only if the influence source has a social meaning, which the mere simultaneous presence of two individuals fails to provide.

These studies demonstrate, surprisingly enough, the existence of a much greater latent and apparently subconscious change than the one that takes place on the manifest and conscious level, that is to say, a conversion phenomenon. They confirm Mead's observation:

> There is, then, a process by means of which the individual in interaction with others inevitably becomes like them in doing the same thing, without that process appearing in what we term consciousness: we become conscious of the process when we definitely take the attitude of others, and this situation must be distinguished from the previous one. (Mead, 1934/1970, p. 193)

I know that many people would be tempted to dismiss the afterimage effect by saying that it is a sort of cognitive generalization. However, this would be both a trivializing and a purely "verbal" explanation, given the facts (a) that the response to the stimulus and the response to the afterimage were different (green–blue in the first case, a mark on a scale in the second); (b) that only the response to the stimulus was given in public, the response to the afterimage remaining private, so that the subject never heard the words yellow, orange, purple, etc., uttered; (c) that the subject was not aware of the relationship that existed between a color and its complement; and (d) that even if the conflict had actually been produced on the verbal level, it was resolved on a level that must be characterized as perceptual.

I realize that this conclusion is hard to believe, since I myself experienced the same difficulties until I was forced to reconcile myself with the evidence. This actually makes it all the more interesting, if not as a final result, then as a starting point for a series of studies in a little-explored field, which could benefit from the use of even more rigorous experimental procedures. Nevertheless, a mystery remains: How can one see a color whose name one fails to give and give the name of a color one no longer sees? This antinomy undermines our belief that verbal changes are easy to produce, while perceptual changes are indeed exceptional. When people say: "This is only verbal," they have in mind a malleable and labile behavior. When they say: "This is not only verbal," they have in mind a firm and stable behavior. The behaviorist's equivalent of Hamlet's "Words, words, words," is likely to lead to error. In fact, the currently accepted behavioral hierarchy in terms of proneness to change may be reversed. There is reason to believe that whatever belongs to the verbal realm is under permanent social control and is therefore more rigid and more resistant to change than anything of a nonverbal nature; and that makes the latter less susceptible to the surveillance of others as well as to that of one's own consciousness. In line with the proposed interpretation, we can observe every day how contagious intonations, gestures, emotions, etc., may be. To come back to our experiment, it shows us that although minorities may have only a weak impact on the verbal level, on the perceptual level their impact is strong indeed. They transform the way the majority of individuals perceives an object and are thereby unwittingly turned into deviants, in short, are converted to a different way of seeing.

V.   Final Observations

There is a visible convergence between the elements of the proposed theory and the experimental illustrations of conversion behavior. I am reluctant to say that the theory has been verified, knowing full well how heedlessly this word, which assumes the weight of authority, is bandied about, as though what mattered were not the interest of what was verified but rather the fact of its having been verified. Before closing this contribution, however, I should like to add some supplementary remarks.

I imagine that all of the observed effects can be explained in some other manner. Contrary to general belief, it rarely happens that one really eliminates all alternative interpretations, without engaging in scholasticism. I do feel compelled to point out two factors that cannot serve as starting points for these alternative theories, namely, competence and attraction. It has been said (Festinger, 1953) that if one disregards external pressures, the greater a person's attraction toward the source of influence, the more he or she will come to accept privately the responses given in public. This may well hold for compliance, but conversion cannot be a sheer effect of attraction or competence. We know from several studies (Moscovici, 1976) that minorities tend to be disliked. Therefore, liking the source cannot account for one's accepting deviant positions, unless one likes what one can dislike, which is not exceptional. Neither does the competence of the minority account for the influence it exerts, because minorities are generally regarded as relatively incompetent. In fact, the problem is to understand why competence and attraction do not play the role in the case of minority influence that they do in the case of majority influence.

If one were to take a simplified view of things, as often happens despite all our precautions, one might be tempted to say from the preceding experiments that minority influence alone results in private or latent change, that majority influence does not have such effects. That would be contrary to observation. Studies have shown that the opinions of individuals can remain close to those of the group, following interaction with it (Allen, 1965, Doms, 1978, Hardy, 1957). Moreover, history teaches us that religions and political parties try to control private beliefs as well as public expression and that they succeed. I therefore do not mean to imply in the least that there is an exclusive link between minority influence and conversion behavior, on the one hand, and majority influence and compliance on the other. On the basis of the theoretical reasons I have explained, however, which seem to be confirmed by a considerable number of experiments, an asymmetry does exist. Actually, in a conformity situation compliance seems to be the rule and conversion the exception, whereas in an innovation situation the opposite holds. This in itself is a remarkable social fact. It authorizes us in any case to say that while there is no exclusive association between the nature of a source and the effect it produces, nevertheless there does exist a privileged association, which is not without significance. Consequently it is logical to relate majority influence more closely with compliance and minority influence more closely with conversion and to treat them as if they expressed independent ways of interacting and behaving in society, each corresponding to specific psychological processes.

We must also address the problem of how a deviant response that is accepted privately, in a latent manner, is transformed into a public and outward response. To put it differently, what induces a person (or group) to become aware of and express openly what he accepts in his innermost self? Having established that conformity produces compliance, open, and public change, researchers have studied how this change becomes individual and private, in short, *internalized* (Kelman, 1958). All theories of attitude change have tried to explain this phenomenon, primarily dissonance theory. To the extent that innovation produces conversion, we are faced with the opposite phenomenon, that of *externalization*. This may amount to asking what incites an individual to behave freely, to transgress the norms in which he no longer believes, to defy the prejudices of his society, and to say simply what he sees, even if it belies the fact, for example, say green when the object is blue or vice versa.

Last, but not least, I believe that the ideas and facts presented here are deeply and nontrivially related to what is usually called social learning. An overview of research in this area (Bandura & Walters, 1967) shows that interest has been limited exclusively to the way children imitate acceptable models. This is ultimately considered the aim of a good education. However, all one needs to do is to leave the classrooms and go to the play areas, the street, or the athletic fields to see how children are attracted to and taught by the "bad examples," the deviant personalities and peers. Surrepticiously and unintentionally, they acquire ways of talking, thinking, and behaving against which adults often contend without much success. The more adults fight against them, moreover, the greater the resistance they arouse in their children, accelerating the very learning they seek to prevent. The acquisition of anomic responses and the conversion to the many minicountercultures prevailing in each school and district are forms of social learning that deserves to be attentively studied. We should know more about how this happens and what mechanisms are at work, if not for practical reasons, then at least to understand better our psychological makeup.

I would be tempted to draw the conclusion at the end of this contribution that minorities are more influential than majorities in the usual sense of the term, since they produce more genuine change. This conclusion is paradoxical, contrary to everyday experience and solid common sense. Taken as a starting point, such a paradox, as is true of every paradox, can be a fruitful way of looking at phenomena.

REFERENCES

Allen, V. L. Situational factors in conformity. In L. Berkowitz (Ed.), *Advances in experimental social psychology*. Vol. 2. New York: Academic Press, 1965.

Allen, V. L. Social support for non-conformity. In L. Berkowitz (Ed.), *Advances in experimental social psychology*. Vol. 8. New York: Academic Press, 1975.

Asch, S. E. Studies of independence and conformity: A minority of one against a unanimous majority. *Psychological Monographs*, 1956, **70**(9, Whole No. 416).

238 SERGE MOSCOVICI

Bandura, A., & Walters, R. H. *Social learning and personality development*. New York: Holt, 1967.
Bauer, R. Source effects and persuasibility: A new look. In D. E. Cox (Ed.), *Risk taking and consumer behavior*. Cambridge, Mass.: Harvard University Press, 1966.
Berkowitz, L. Group standards, cohesiveness and productivity. *Human Relations*, 1954, **7**, 509–519.
Blake, R., & Mouton, J. Conformity, resistance and conversion. In A. Berg & B. Bass (Eds.), *Conformity and deviation*. New York: Harper, 1961,
Bovard, E. W. Social norms and the individual. *Journal of Abnormal and Social Psychology*, 1948, **43**, 62–69.
Brehm, J. W., & Mann, M. Effect of importance of freedom and attraction to group members on influence produced by group pressure. *Journal of Personality and Social Psychology*, 1975, **31**, 816–24.
Cook, T. Competence, counterarguing, attitude change. *Journal of Personality*, 1964, **3**, 342–359.
Cooper, J., Darley, J. M., & Henderson, J. E. On the effectiveness of deviant and conventional appearing communicators: A field experiment. *Journal of Personality and Social Psychology*, 1974, **29**, 752–757.
Deutsch, M., & Gerard, H. B. A study of normative and informational social influences upon individual judgment. *Journal of Abnormal and Social Psychology*, 1955, **51**, 629–636.
Doms, M. Résultats de la réplication de l'expérience sur l'effet consécutif. Mimeo, Louvain, 1978.
Eagly, A. H., Wood, W., & Chaiken, S. Causal inferences about communicators and their effect on opinion change. *Journal of Personality and Social Psychology*, 1978, **36**, 424–435.
Falk, D. The effects on attitude change of manipulating antecedents of Kelman's internalization process. Unpublished master's thesis, Northwestern University, 1970.
Festinger, L. An analysis of compliant behavior. In M. Sherif & M. O. Wilson (Eds.), *Group relations at the cross roads*. New York: Harper, 1953.
Gillig, P., & Greenwad, A. Is it time to lay the sleeper effect to rest? *Journal of Personality and Social Psychology*, 1974, **22**, 132–139.
Goethals, G. R. An attributional analysis of some social influence phenomena. In J. H. Harvey, W. J. Ickes, & R. F. Kidd (Eds.), *New directions in attributional research*. Vol. 1. Hillsdale, N.J.: Erlbaum, 1976.
Hardy, K. R. Determinants of conformity and attitude change. *Journal of Abnormal and Social Psychology*, 1957, **54**, 289–294.
Kelman, H. C. Compliance, identification and internalization. *Journal of Conflict Resolution*, 1958, **2**, 51–60.
Leibovitch, N. B., & Paolera, M. B. Recherche sur la perception de la couleur et de la post-image en relation avec des images significatives. *Annales Médico-Psychologiques*, 1970, **1**, 735–741.
Mead, G. H. *Mind, self, and society*. (C. W. Morris, Ed.) Chicago: University of Chicago Press, 1970. (Originally published, 1934.)
Moscovici, S. *Essai sur l'histoire humaine de la nature*. Paris: Flammarion, 1968.
Moscovici, S. *Social influence and social change*. New York: Academic Press, 1976.
Moscovici, S., & Lage, E. Studies in social influence III: Majority versus minority influence in a group. *European Journal of Social Psychology*, 1976, **6**, 149–174.
Moscovici, S., Lage, E., & Naffrechoux, M. Influence of a consistent minority on the responses of a majority in a color perception task. *Sociometry*, 1969, **32**, 365–379.
Moscovici, S., & Nemeth, C. Social influence II: Minority influence. In C. Nemeth (Ed.), *Social psychology: Classic and contemporary integrations*. Chicago: Rand McNally, 1974.
Moscovici, S., & Neve, P. Studies in social influence: I. Those who are absent are in the right: Convergence and polarization of answers in the course of social interaction. *European Journal of Social Psychology*, 1971, **1**, 201–213.

Moscovici, S., & Personnaz, B. Studies in social influence V: Minority influence and conversion behavior in a perceptual task. *Journal of Experimental Social Psychology*, 1980, **16**, 270–282.

Mugny, G. Négociation et influence minoritaire. Unpublished dissertation, Geneva, 1974.

Mugny, G. Bedeutung der Konsistenz bei der Beeinflussung durch eine konkordante oder diskordante minderheitliche Kommunikation bei sozialen Beurteilungsobjekten. *Zeitschrift für Sozialpsychologie*, 1975, **6**, 324–332.

Mugny, G., & Papastamou, S. Pour une nouvelle approche de l'influence minoritaire: Les déterminants psychosociaux des stratégies d'influence minoritaires. *Bulletin de Psychologie*, 1976–1977, **328**, 573–579.

Nemeth, C., & Wachtler, J. Consistency and modification of judgment. *Journal of Experimental Social Psychology*, 1973, **9**, 65–79.

Nuttin, J. M. *The illusion of attitude change: Towards a response contagion theory of persuasion.* New York: Academic Press, 1975.

Papastamou, S. Stratégies d'influence minoritaires et majoritaires. Unpublished dissertation, Geneva, 1979.

Raven, B. H. Social influence on opinions and the communication of related content. *Journal of Abnormal and Social Psychology*, 1959, **58**, 119–128.

Schachter, S., & Hall, R. Group derived restraints and audience persuasion. *Human Relations*, 1952, **5**, 397–406.

Schönbar, R. A. *The interaction of observer-pairs in judging visual extent and movement. Archives of Psychology*, 1945, **4**.

Thibaut, J., & Strickland, L. M. Psychological set and social conformity. *Journal of Personality*, 1956, **25**, 115–129.

White, C. W., & Montgomery, D. A. Memory colors in afterimages: a bicentennial demonstration. *Perception & Psychophysics*, 1976.

Wolf, S. Behavioral style of the deviate and group cohesiveness as sources of minority influence. Mimeo, 1977.

Zimbardo, P. G., Ebbesen, B. E., & Maslach, C. *Influencing attitudes and changing behavior.* Reading, Mass.: Addison-Wesley, 1977.

Zinoviev, *Hauteurs béantes.* Lausanne: Age d'Homme, 1976.

THE ROLE OF INFORMATION RETRIEVAL AND CONDITIONAL INFERENCE PROCESSES IN BELIEF FORMATION AND CHANGE[1]

Robert S. Wyer, Jr. and Jon Hartwick

DEPARTMENT OF PSYCHOLOGY
UNIVERSITY OF ILLINOIS AT
URBANA-CHAMPAIGN
CHAMPAIGN, ILLINOIS

[1]This contribution and the research described in it were supported by National Science Foundation Grants GS-2291, GS-29241, SOC73-05684, and BNS 76-24001 to the first author and a Canada Council Doctoral Fellowship to the second author. Appreciation is extended to the many students and colleagues who have contributed to this research and the conceptualization underlying it: Marilyn Henninger, Ron Hinkle, Nancy Rosen, Daniel Romer, and Lee Goldberg.

ADVANCES IN EXPERIMENTAL SOCIAL
PSYCHOLOGY, VOL. 13

When someone is asked to judge a person, object, or event, he is apt to search memory for information relevant to this judgment. He then construes the implications of the retrieved information, integrates them to arrive at a single value, and finally reports this value in a language he believes the recipient will understand. Although this simple description is almost self-evident, it immediately raises several questions, the answers to which are less readily apparent.

One set of questions concerns the amount and type of information a person retrieves from memory to use in making a judgment. A person is unlikely to conduct an exhaustive search of long-term memory for all information relevant to the judgment at hand. Instead, he will retrieve only a relatively small subset of the stored information that happens to be easily accessible. This subset of retrieved information along with its implications will then be treated as representative of all relevant information. A similar tendency, the "availability heuristic," has been described by Tversky and Kahneman (1973). The amount of information retrieved is likely to depend on the importance of the judgment to be made and the time available for making it. Moreover, the specific information that is retrieved first may depend in part upon the manner in which the information is organized in memory (cf. Collins & Loftus, 1975; Wyer & Carlston, 1979; Wyer & Srull, 1980a, 1980b). In addition, it may depend upon such factors as the recency with which the information has been used in the past (Collins & Loftus, 1975) and the amount of thought that has previously gone into processing it (Craik, 1977).

The type of information retrieved also depends on the type of judgment to be made and the nature of the object to be judged. For example, a person is likely to retrieve different information about an acquaintance if he is asked to evaluate her as a potential graduate student than if he is asked to evaluate her as a potential date. However, more general differences may exist as well. Suppose someone is asked to evaluate the validity of a target proposition (e.g., the statement that marijuana will soon be legalized). In making such a judgment, the person is apt to retrieve beliefs in other propositions that, if true, have implications for the validity of the target (e.g., beliefs that marijuana is harmless, that its use is becoming increasingly widespread, that the tobacco industry has a strong lobby against legalization). However, suppose the person were asked instead to judge the desirability of the event described in the proposition (e.g., the desirability of legalizing marijuana). In this case, the person may not search memory for "antecedents," or factors that facilitate or interfere with the occurrence of the event. Instead, he may search for possible desirable and undesirable consequences of the event (i.e., the possibilities that the cost of marijuana will decrease, that fewer young people will become alcoholics, that the use of hard drugs will increase).

A related set of questions concerns the manner in which the implications of information are combined to arrive at a single judgment. The answers here also depend on the type of information to be combined and the type of judgment to be made. A variety of inference processes have been postulated to underlie judgments. These include syllogistic (McGuire, 1960; Wyer, 1975c), pseudological (Abelson & Rosenberg, 1958; Heider, 1958), probabilistic (Slovic & Lichtenstein, 1971; Trope, 1974), algebraic (N. H. Anderson, 1974; Fishbein, 1965), and configural (Abelson, 1976; Wyer, 1973a) processes. It seems likely that each process is invoked under some conditions. Unfortunately, few attempts have been made to circumscribe these conditions.

Although the questions just noted are easy to ask, their answers are likely to be complex and hard to find. In this contribution, we will attempt to identify a few of the considerations that underlie the formation of and change in beliefs about oneself and one's environment. In this discussion, we will focus on the role of conditional inference processes (e.g., inferences concerning the validity of one proposition given the validity or invalidity of others) in the acquisition and the change of beliefs. As previously implied, these processes are undoubtedly only one of several types of reasoning that may underlie social judgments. However, the conditions under which they are likely to occur are sufficiently diverse that this will not be a major restriction upon our considerations.

In the pages that follow, we first try to provide both an intuitive feel for the sort of inference process we postulate to underlie judgments and some evidence for a formal descriptive model of this process. We then turn to a consideration of several factors that affect the availability and use of information to make inferences of the sort to which this model is relevant. Finally, we consider applications of the proposed conceptualization to inferences in several content domains and identify further questions made salient by the approach we have taken.

I. A Model of Conditional Inference

A. GENERAL CONSIDERATIONS

Conditional inferences play a central role in social judgment both in and outside of the laboratory. Many decisions we make, and many conclusions we draw on the basis of information we receive, involve these inferences. For example, we may decide to go to a particular restaurant because we are told that (a) a friend likes the restaurant and we believe that (b) if this friend likes a restaurant, it is usually a very good place to eat. Or, we may conclude that marijuana should be legalized because we learn that (a) marijuana is psychologically and physically harmless and we believe that (b) if it is harmless, it should be freely accessible. Similarly, we may infer that a person is likely to be honest on the basis of (a) information that the person has returned a lost wallet to its owner and (b) the belief that if a person returns lost property, he is typically honest.

Conditional inference processes may be particularly important when a person is asked to evaluate the validity of a proposition. When this occurs, he is likely to activate a search of memory for information relevant to this proposition. If the person has recently stated his belief in the statement to be evaluated, he may simply retrieve this prior judgment and repeat it in the present situation. When a prior judgment has not been made, however, or if this judgment is not readily accessible, the person will search his memory for another belief or piece of factual information that has implications for the proposition being evaluated. While the person may not completely ignore the possibility that other relevant information exists as well, these other considerations may be lumped into a somewhat diffuse estimate of what implications this other information would have if the retrieved information were false. For example, suppose a person is asked his belief in the proposition that marijuana should eventually be legalized. If he has not recently thought about this statement and cannot recall a previously formed belief that it is true, the person may search his memory for other propositions and beliefs in these propositions that have implications for its validity. When a proposition (e.g., that marijuana is harmless) is encountered and recognized as having such implications, this proposition may be used as a premise to infer the validity of the target proposition (the conclusion); that is, the person may make a conditional inference of the likelihood that the conclusion is true given that the premise is true (i.e., infer the likelihood that marijuana should be legalized if it is harmless) on the basis of other information stored in his memory. In addition, the person may also make a conditional inference of the likelihood that the conclusion is true even if the premise is false (i.e., infer the likelihood that marijuana should be legalized if it is not harmless). The implications of these two conditional inferences will then be combined (in a manner to be shortly outlined) in order to arrive at an estimate of the validity of the target proposition.

This conceptualization implicitly assumes that when a person is asked to report his belief in a target proposition, he typically does not engage in an exhaustive search of memory for information bearing on it. Rather, he searches only until he encounters a piece of information (i.e., another proposition) that he considers relevant, and bases his judgment primarily on (a) the implications of its being true and (b) the implications of its being false, without taking into account other information that may also bear on the validity of the target proposition.[2] This process implies that the person's reported belief in a target proposition may be influenced greatly by factors that affect which of several alternative pieces of

[2] When a judgment is particularly important, when there are situational pressures to be accurate, or when there is ample time to make the judgment, several pieces of information may be retrieved. In such cases, the judge may construe the implications of each piece of information separately in the manner outlined previously, and may then arrive at an overall judgment that represents some composite of these implications. Even here, however, the judge is unlikely to consider all of the relevant information that is potentially available to him.

information he happens to retrieve in his search of memory. Later sections of this chapter are devoted to a consideration of certain of these factors.

The preceding description of conditional inference processes may be formalized by applying the model of social cognition proposed initially by McGuire (1960) and more recently extended by Wyer (1974a, 1975; Wyer & Carlston, 1979). According to this model, one's belief in a target proposition B, defined in units of probability, is represented as a function of one's beliefs associated with a second proposition A, according to the equation

$$P_B = P_A P_{B/A} + P_{A'} P_{B/A'} \qquad (1)$$

where P_B is the belief in B, P_A and $P_{A'}$ ($= 1 - P_A$) are beliefs that A is and is not true, respectively, and $P_{B/A}$ and $P_{B/A'}$ are conditional beliefs that B is true *if* A is and is not true, respectively. The conditional beliefs, $P_{B/A}$ and $P_{B/A'}$, are formed as a result of the two conditional inferences mentioned earlier (i.e., inferences that the target proposition is true given the premise is true and that the target proposition is true given the premise is false).

As pointed out elsewhere (Wyer, 1975), the cognitive processes described by this equation are somewhat ambiguous. For example, the two products comprising the right side of the equation can be conceptualized as the beliefs in the validity of two mutually exclusive sets of premises ("A; if A, then B" and "not A; if not A, then B"), each of which implies the conclusion B. Based on this observation, Wyer and Carlston (1979), following McGuire (1960), assumed that inferring the validity of the conclusion B, subjects first construed the implication of each set of premises for B separately on the basis of syllogistic reasoning, and then summed the two implications to arrive at an overall judgment. However, it may be equally reasonable to assume that the process underlying this judgment is algebraic; that is, subjects may first infer the likelihood that B is true given that A is and is not true (i.e., $P_{B/A}$ and $P_{B/A'}$), and then may subjectively average these conditional beliefs, assigning a weight to each that is proportional to their beliefs that A is and is not true (P_A and $P_{A'}$, respectively).

Equation (1) theoretically provides an exact description of the relation between a person's belief in a proposition and his belief in other propositions that are brought to bear on it. Thus, it is capable of predicting the magnitude of change in one belief (i.e., P_B) produced by a given change in others (e.g., P_A). Moreover, if the equation is generally valid, quantitative discrepancies between beliefs in B and implications of beliefs in the premises may indicate a temporary inconsistency between the person's beliefs in the set of propositions. Alternatively, they may indicate the extent to which the beliefs associated with a given proposition A have been used as a basis for inferring the likelihood of B. (In other words, the equation should be more accurate if proposition A has been used to infer the likelihood of B than if it has not.)

Equation (1) and its derivatives have in fact been used effectively to investigate a variety of theoretical and empirical questions concerning social inference and cognitive organization, including belief and opinion change (Wyer, 1970, 1975a; Wyer & Polsky, 1972), impression formation (Wyer, 1973a, 1973b), the relation between interpersonal similarity and interpersonal attraction (Wyer, 1972), the relation between beliefs and attitudes (Wyer, 1973a), the elimination of inconsistencies among beliefs (Henninger & Wyer, 1976; Rosen & Wyer, 1972; Wyer, 1974b), and the manner in which the implications of previously formed beliefs combine with the implications of new information to affect inferences (Wyer, 1976). Certain of these applications will be noted later in this contribution. Before we embark on this discussion, however, it may be worthwhile to present a few rigorous tests of the validity of the formulation in describing the processes to which it theoretically pertains.

B. EMPIRICAL EVIDENCE

Three general criteria have been used to evaluate the validity of Eq. (1) as a description of the way people use their beliefs to make inferences. One is whether information that bears directly on the validity of propositions comprising the two sets of premises combines functionally to affect beliefs in the conclusion in the manner implied by Eq. (1). A second criterion is whether the equation provides a quantitatively accurate description of these inference processes. The third criterion is whether beliefs that are not related in the manner implied by Eq. (1) are in fact perceived by subjects to be inconsistent as they personally define it. The studies in the following sections bear on these issues.

1. Validity in Describing Conditional Inferences

The value of the above formulation lies in its ability to characterize a person's organization of beliefs about familiar issues and events of concern and in his use of previously acquired beliefs as an informational basis for subsequent ones. However, in evaluating the validity of the model as a description of conditional inference processes, it seemed advisable to use materials pertaining to issues about which persons had no preconceptions, thus requiring them to rely only upon the information presented in the experimental setting. In addition, the methodology employed for evaluating the functional relations among model components (N. H. Anderson, 1970) requires that values of these components be manipulated independently. For these reasons, abstract stimulus materials were used. Specifically, subjects were presented sets of information about the frequency with which persons had a hypothetical gene (identified by a letter of the alphabet), the frequency with which persons with the gene had a given attribute (also denoted by letter), and the frequency with which persons without the gene had this attribute. These frequencies, which were described using the adverbs "usually," "sometimes," and "rarely," were expected to convey high, moderate, and low probabilities of the relations described, respectively. Each set of statements was of the form:

Persons usually (sometimes, rarely) have gene A.

Persons with A usually (sometimes, rarely) have attribute B.

Persons without A usually (sometimes, rarely) have attribute B.

In all, 27 sets of three statements were constructed to convey all possible combinations of P_A (the likelihood that a person has A), $P_{B/A}$ (the likelihood that a person has B if he has A), and $P_{B/A'}$ (the likelihood that a person has B if he does not have A). Subjects read each set of statements and then estimated the likelihood that a particular person (described by first name) had attribute B (P_B), followed by each of the three component probabilities to which the information directly pertained. Here, as in most other studies to be reported, judgments were made along a scale from 0 (not at all likely) to 10 (extremely likely) and were divided by 10 prior to analyses to convert them to units of probability.[3]

Two criteria may be used to evaluate the validity of Eq. (1) in describing inferences. First, if the equation is a valid description of the manner in which information bearing upon beliefs in the premises combines to affect beliefs in the conclusion, the informational manipulations of P_A and $P_{B/A}$ should have multiplicative effects upon estimates of P_B; specifically, estimates of P_B should increase with $P_{B/A}$, but the magnitude of this increase should be greater when P_A is high than when it is low. Inferences of P_B should also increase with $P_{B/A'}$; however, in this case, the effect should be greater when P_A is low ($P_{A'}$ is high) than when it is high. Data in Figs. 1b and c support these predictions.[4] Statistical analyses corroborated this interpretation (for details, see Wyer, 1975b).[5,6]

A second criterion for evaluating the validity of Eq. (1) is quantitative. If a subject's estimates of the four components of the equation are in units of probability,

---

[3]Judgments in a few studies have employed a 21-point scale ranging from 0 (not at all likely) to 100 (extremely likely) in steps of five. Estimates using this scale are divided by 100 to convert them to units of probability. No discernable differences have been noticed between results obtained with either of these scales.

[4]Note that when the value of one conditional belief (e.g., $P_{B/A}$) is zero, this does not necessarily mean that P_B is zero, because the other conditional belief may contribute to judgments. Therefore, the fact that the curves in Fig. 1b and c cross at a point at which the conditional belief is nonzero is expected.

[5]If P_A combines multiplicatively with $P_{B/A}$ and $P_{B/A'}$, the two interactions described in Fig. 1, b and c, should each be concentrated in a single degree of freedom corresponding to the linear × linear component, and the residual after this component is eliminated, should be zero (for an elaboration of the basis for this prediction, see N. H. Anderson, 1970). The bilinear component was significant ($p < .05$) in each case and accounted for over 96% of the total sums of squares associated with the interaction, whereas the residual was nonsignificant in each case ($p > .20$) and accounted for less than 4% of the total sums of squares.

[6]In addition to these predicted effects, a small but significant interaction of $P_{B/A}$ and $P_{B/A'}$ occurred. This interaction, which is shown in Fig. 1d, appears caused by a significant deviant point. Because the interaction has not been replicated in subsequent studies (Wyer, 1976, 1977), it should probably not be taken as a serious disconfirmation of the model.

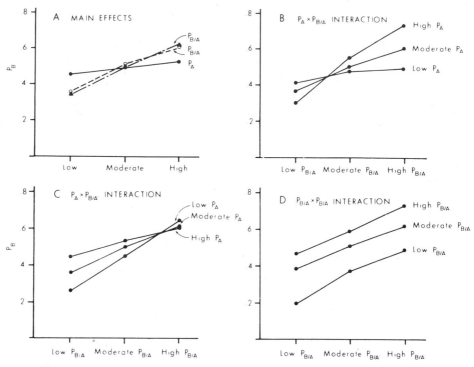

Fig. 1. Main effects (A) and interactions (B–D) pertaining to P_B as a function of P_A, $P_{B/A}$, and $P_{B/A'}$. Reprinted from Wyer (1975b, p. 97). Copyright 1975 by The American Psychological Association. Reprinted by permission.

his actual estimate of P_B should be numerically equal to the value predicted on the basis of the expression on the right side of the equation. To explore this possibility, predicted values of P_B were calculated for each subject separately for each of the 27 sets of stimulus statements, assuming that $P_{A'} = 1 - P_A$.[7] Mean obtained values are plotted in Fig. 2 as a function of mean predicted values. If the model were perfectly accurate, each of the 27 points would fall on the 45° line shown. In fact, the standard error of the difference between mean obtained and mean predicted values[8] (σ_e) was .047, or less than half a scale unit.[9]

[7]In fact, subjects' estimates of P_A and $P_{A'}$ typically sum to a value slightly greater than 1 (i.e., 1.1); however, this discrepancy, which decreases when subjects report these beliefs a second time (Rosen & Wyer, 1972), is not sufficiently great to offset the practical advantage of generating predictions of P_B on the basis of three rather than four other beliefs.

[8]Specifically,
$$\sigma e = [(O_i - E_i)/n]^{\frac{1}{2}}$$
where O_i and E_i are the observed and predicted values of P_B for the ith stimulus. Note that E_i is the exact value of the expression on the right side of Eq. (1), based upon subjects' actual numerical judgments of P_A, $P_{B/A}$, and $P_{B/A'}$ and does not involve the introduction of best-fitting slope and intercept parameters estimated through curve-fitting procedures.

[9]Jacknifing procedures (Mostellel & Turkey, 1968) indicated that the slope and intercept of the

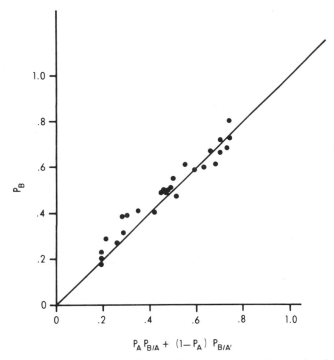

Fig. 2.   Mean obtained estimates of P_B as a function of predicted values based upon Eq. (1). Reprinted from Wyer (1975b, p. 98). Copyright 1975 by The American Psychological Association. Reprinted by permission.

2. Validity as an Index of Belief Inconsistency

An important consideration in evaluating the extent to which Eq. (1) provides a psychologically valid description of cognitive functioning is whether beliefs that are not related in the manner implied by this equation are regarded by subjects as being inconsistent. If this is not the case, the assumption that the equation describes the manner in which persons actively combine information in a way they believe follows from the "premises" that are salient to them would be suspect.

Perceptions of the inconsistency (Inc) of a set of conditionally related beliefs of the sort to which the equation pertains should be a function of the absolute difference between predicted and obtained values of P_B, based on Eq. (1); that is,

$$\text{Inc} = |P_B - [(P_A P_{B/A} + (1 - P_A)P_{B/A'}]| \qquad (2)$$

To test this hypothesis, 36 sets of four statements each were constructed. Each set of statements was the same; specifically: (a) A person belongs to group

---

best-fitting function relating predicted to obtained values of P_B (.89 and .07, respectively) did not differ reliably from their theoretical values of 1 and 0 ($p > .30$).

A, (b) If a person belongs to A, he has attribute B, (c) If a person does *not* belong to A, he has attribute B, and (d) A person has attribute B. Each statement in a given set was followed by an 11-point scale from 0 (not at all likely) to 10 (extremely likely), and a value along each scale was circled to represent a hypothetical subject's belief in the statement. The values assigned to the four statements in each set, divided by 10, were assumed to correspond directly to P_A, $P_{B/A}$, $P_{B/A'}$, and P_B, respectively. The 36 stimulus sets enabled the values of the four beliefs to be manipulated systematically over two levels of P_A (.2 and .8), two levels of P_B (.3 and .7), and three levels of each of the two conditional beliefs (.2, .5, and .8). In each case, judges were asked to assume that a hypothetical subject had reported the four beliefs in the set and then to estimate the inconsistency of these beliefs along an 11-point (0–10) scale.

If Eq. (2) is valid, the inconsistency of beliefs predicted by it should be highly related to subjects' actual estimates of their inconsistency. Mean estimates of inconsistency for the 36 test items were in fact correlated .935 ($p < .01$) with the predicted values based on Eq. (2). This evidence, along with other statistical analyses reported in more detail elsewhere (Henninger & Wyer, 1976, Experiment 1),[10] support our contention that persons regard sets of beliefs that are not related in the manner implied by this equation as inconsistent.

3. A Simulation of Belief Change Processes

If the proposed formulation is valid, people should not only infer their belief in a conclusion B from their belief in A and its implications but also should change their belief in the conclusion if, for some reason, their belief in A is altered. This change can also be described quantitatively. That is, suppose new information is presented that produces a change in beliefs in a premise A. If A is salient to the person at the time he subsequently reports his belief in B, the change in the latter belief would be predictable from the equation

$$\Delta P_B = \Delta[(P_A P_{B/A} + P_{A'} P_{B/A'}] \tag{3}$$

If the information affects only P_A, leaving its implications (reflected in the conditional beliefs $P_{B/A}$ and $P_{B/A'}$ unchanged), and if $P_{A'} = 1 - P_A$, the equation simplifies:

$$\Delta P_B = \Delta P_A (P_{B/A} - P_{B/A'}) \tag{4}$$

The latter equation is useful in conceptualizing the conditions under which one's belief in B is affected by a change in his belief in A. The magnitude of change in

---

[10]In the design employed, variation in subjects' judgments of inconsistency should theoretically be concentrated in only eight of the 35 degrees of freedom associated with various combinations of values of the four beliefs comprising Eq. (4). In fact, these eight degrees of freedom accounted for 93.4% of the total predictable sums of squares, with the remaining 27 degrees of freedom accounting for only 6.6%.

P_B produced by a given change in P_A is a direct function of the difference between the two conditional beliefs that B is true if A is and is not true. This difference is conceptually equivalent to the relevance of beliefs in A to beliefs in B.

Although we will discuss belief change processes in more detail later in this contribution, a more direct test of the above conceptualization may be worth noting briefly here. The study (Wyer, 1970) was analogous to a traditional study of belief change and involved inferences about the sort of events that might occur in everyday life. However, the persons and events involved were fictitious, so that beliefs would be based primarily upon information provided in the experiment, and so the particular beliefs brought to bear on the conclusion B could be controlled and manipulated.

Specifically, information about each of nine hypothetical situations was constructed. Each situation pertained directly or indirectly to a different set of propositions A and B (e.g., "There will be a riot at State University" and "University President Smythe will be fired"). The information about each situation was presented in two paragraphs. The first paragraph established subjects' "initial beliefs"; that is, it conveyed a low value of P_A (in our example, a low likelihood that there would be a riot at State University) and implied one of nine possible combinations of $P_{B/A}$ (high, moderate, or low) and $P_{B/A'}$ (high, moderate, or low). However, the conclusion to be inferred (B) was not mentioned. The second paragraph contained information that increased the likelihood that A was true while leaving the two conditional beliefs relatively unchanged. After reading each paragraph, subjects reported their belief that B was true (P_B) followed by their beliefs corresponding to other components of Eq. (1) (P_A, $P_{B/A}$, and $P_{B/A'}$). Mean obtained values of P_B after reading each paragraph, and also the change in P_B after reading the second paragraph, are plotted as a function of mean predicted values in Fig. 3. These data show a remarkably close quantitative fit of the model; the standard error of the difference between mean obtained and mean predicted values of P_B was .035, and of ΔP_B was .051 (about a half a scale unit).

4. An Alternative Interpretation

While the fit of Eqs. (1) and (2) to the data previously described seems to provide nice support for the qualitative and quantitative accuracy of these equations in describing inference phenomena and is consistent with our assumptions concerning the processes underlying them, an alternative interpretation is worth noting; that is, it is conceivable that subjects do not arrive at a compromise between the two conditional beliefs in making a judgment, but rather rely upon only one. In other words, if they believe that the premise A is more apt to be true than false (i.e., if P_A is greater than .5), they may base their inference on their perception of the likelihood that B is true if A is true, ignoring entirely the possibility that B may be true if A is not true. However, if they believe that A is

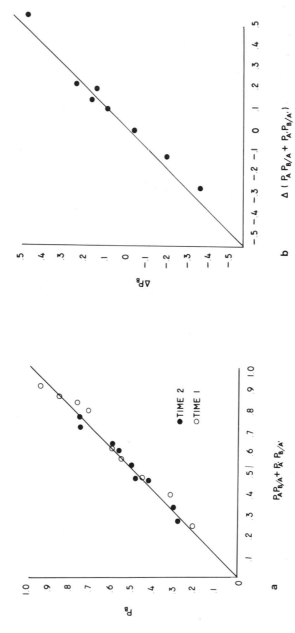

Fig. 3. (a) Mean ratings of P_B after subjects read the first and second paragraphs (times 1 and 2, respectively), and (b) mean change in P_B from time 1 to time 2, as a function of predicted values based upon Eqs. (1) and (3), respectively. Reprinted from Wyer (1970, p. 564). Copyright 1970 by The American Psychological Association. Reprinted by permission.

not likely to be true, they may base their inference on their belief that B would be true if A is not true, ignoring the implications of A's being true.

While this possibility a priori seems plausible, it seems unlikely that if this is what subjects are doing, the quantitative accuracy of Eqs. (1) and (2) would be as high as that shown in Figs. 2 and 3. In fact, application of a one-component model of the form $P_B = P_A P_{B/A}$ has been shown elsewhere (Wyer, 1970; Wyer & Goldberg, 1970) to produce very poor quantitative predictions both of beliefs in B and changes in these beliefs as a result of changes in beliefs in A. A second indication that both conditional beliefs contribute to judgments simultaneously is suggested by the data in Figs. 1b and c; that is, if the alternative interpretation just noted were correct, $P_{B/A}$ would have no effect on judgments of P_B when P_A is low. Similarly, $P_{B/A'}$ would have no effect on these judgments when P_A is high. In fact, these effects are slightly positive, as implied by Eq. (1). Thus, it seems reasonable to conclude that of the two alternative interpretations, the one we have proposed is the more consistent with the data available.

5. Summary

The studies described in this section provide support for the validity of Eq. (1) as a description of cognitive functioning under conditions in which all relevant beliefs are newly formed on the basis of information provided in the immediate situation. Further, people regard beliefs that are *not* related in this manner as inconsistent. It seems reasonable to suppose that previously acquired beliefs which are retrieved from memory to bear on an inference will be used in a similar manner.

6. Limitations on Generalizability

We are not stating that the model we have proposed applies to all types of inferences and in all situations. As noted earlier, conditional inference processes are certainly not the only processes underlying social judgments. The question is when these processes are most likely to occur. One factor to consider is whether the propositions being judged are evaluative or nonevaluative. For example, a person who is asked whether the frequency of getting married will decrease over the next several years may seek and retrieve "premises" that, if valid, imply that the proposition is or is not true. However, a person who is asked whether the frequency of getting married should decrease (or, alternatively, to estimate the desirability of getting married) may seek and retrieve possible consequences of this event (i.e., "conclusions") and combine their evaluative implications algebraically (cf. N. H. Anderson, 1974; Fishbein, 1965). Conditional inference processes would therefore be more likely to occur in the first case than in the second.

Nevertheless, the processes implied by Eq. (1) seems likely to occur in a wide variety of inference situations both in and outside of the laboratory. In these situations, the question becomes what factors affect the accessibility and use of particular sets of previously acquired beliefs as bases for reporting other beliefs. The next two sections are concerned with this question.

II. Determinants of Information Accessibility: Recency

A person who is asked to report his belief in a proposition is unlikely to perform an exhaustive search of memory for all relevant information bearing on this belief. Tversky and Kahneman (1973) postulate that people base their judgments on only a sample of information that is most easily accessible, assuming that the implications of this information is representative of the "population." If this is the case, it implies that subjects' reported beliefs are likely to vary over time and situation, depending on what information is most readily available to them at the time.

To understand what factors affect the accessibility of belief-relevant information, and therefore the likelihood that this information is used to infer one's beliefs, it is useful to view the idea conveyed by a proposition as a complex concept. To this extent, its retrieval for use in making inferences should be governed by factors similar to those that govern the retrieval and use of concepts of the sort typically investigated in research on long-term memory. Two major factors have been postulated to affect the accessibility of previously acquired information and concepts related to it. First, the likelihood of invoking a concept when making a response is a function of the recency with which the concept has been employed in the past (Collins & Loftus, 1975; Wyer & Srull, 1979). Second, the recall of information may be a function of the amount of processing it has received in the past (Craik & Lockhart, 1972). This processing may have occurred when the concept was first interpreted and encoded, or possibly at a later time after the person has thought further about it. The effects of both factors on the processing of social stimulus information have been assumed implicitly in several areas of social psychological research and have been investigated either directly or indirectly in a variety of studies of a sort we will indicate presently. Let us therefore turn to a consideration of these factors and some of the research bearing on their relation to the issues of concern in this contribution, beginning first with the effect of recency.

A.   GENERAL CONSIDERATIONS

Several formulations of memory, pertaining both directly to social cognition (Wyer & Carlston, 1979; Wyer & Srull, 1980b) and more generally (J. R. Anderson & Bower, 1973; Collins & Loftus, 1975), imply that once a concept has been activated for use in processing information, the likelihood that it is accessed later on for use in processing subsequent information is increased. The precise mechanisms postulated to underlie these "priming" effects vary over theories. For example, Collins and Loftus (1975) and Wyer and Carlston (1979) conceptualize memory as a network of concepts connected to one another by pathways. Further, they assume that a concept is activated when excitation, transmitted to it from other concepts along these pathways, exceeds a certain threshold. After a concept has been activated, some residual excitation will remain at the location of the concept in memory. Consequently, less additional excitation is required to reactivate it in the future, making it more accessible. When a concept is not being used, the amount of excitation left at its location will gradually decay over time. It follows that the amount of excitation remaining at the location of a concept in memory, and therefore its likelihood of being activated in the future, is a positive function of how recently it has been activated in the past.

A quite different conceptualization of memory has been postulated by Wyer and Srull (1980b). They liken long-term memory to a set of storage bins, each containing information bearing upon a person, object, or event. Information contained in these bins is hypothetically stored in the order in which it is deposited and is subsequently drawn from the bins from the top down. Therefore, the more recently deposited information is retrieved first and, if relevant, is used as a basis for judgment. After a piece of stored information has been retrieved for use in interpreting new information or arriving at a judgment, it is returned to the top of the bin from which it was drawn, and therefore is most likely to be accessed for use in later judgments to which information in the bin is relevant. For example, a person who is asked to report his belief in the proposition that marijuana is harmless may draw information bearing on the proposition from a bin containing information about marijuana and, after responding to these demands, may return the information, along with the belief he has reported, to the top of this bin. If the person is subsequently asked whether marijuana will be legalized and searches the "marijuana" bin for information relevant to this judgment, the belief that marijuana is harmless is most apt to be retrieved and used as a basis for this later judgment. The judgment may therefore be different than it would have been if some other proposition (e.g., "The tobacco industry has a strong lobby against marijuana legalization") had been recently considered and therefore was on top of the "marijuana" bin at the time the judgment was made.

A detailed discussion of these and other formulations that predict recency effects on the use of previously acquired concepts is beyond the scope of this contribution (for a discussion of several current approaches in the area of social cognition that have implications for this matter, see Hastie, Ostrom, Ebbesen, Wyer, Hamilton, & Carlston, 1980). Instead, we will summarize below a variety of empirical and theoretical issues to which the general hypothesis is relevant, pointing out their additional implications for the use of information when making conditional inferences.

B.   THE EFFECTS OF PRIOR JUDGMENTS ON SUBSEQUENT INFERENCES

When a person searches memory for information relevant to a judgment, he may often retrieve a previous judgment that has implications for the present one. To the extent that this prior judgment is the most recently acquired or processed cognition about the object or concept being considered, it may be used independently of the information upon which it originally has been based.

This possibility is of particular interest when the original information and the initial judgment have different implications. To see this, suppose a subject is given information that one person has helped another out during an examination and then is asked whether the person is kind. In making his judgment, the subject is likely to reason that helping someone out is a kind act, and that if the person manifested this behavior, he is kind. However, suppose that after making this judgment, the subject is asked whether the person is honest. If the subject were to retrieve the original behavioral information, he would likely conclude that the person is dishonest, because helping someone out on an examination is a dishonest act. However, if he retrieves his prior judgment of the person as kind, he may infer that the person is honest, based on his assumption that favorable attributes are apt to be associated (Rosenberg & Sedlak, 1972) and that therefore if a person is kind, he is also likely to be honest.

A study supporting this line of reasoning was performed by Carlston (1977; see also Wyer & Carlston, 1979). Specifically, subjects first read a series of behaviors implying that a target person was either (a) both kind and dishonest or (b) both unkind and honest. Then, they rated the target person with respect to one of the two attributes to which the behaviors were directly relevant (i.e., either kindness or honesty). Finally, after either a short delay or a period of several days, subjects judged the target again, but this time along the other attribute dimension as well as other evaluative scales. As expected, the target person was judged more favorably along these dimensions when the evaluative implications of the interpolated judgment were favorable (e.g., when the information presented implied kindness and dishonesty and the interpolated judgment was of the target's kindness) than when its implications were unfavorable. Therefore, subjects tended to use their initial judgments rather than the original behavior information as bases for their final ones. Furthermore, this tendency appeared to increase with the time interval between subjects' initial judgments and their final ones; in other words, the initial judgments had relatively more influence, and the original behavioral information relatively less influence, as time went on. Supplementary data showed that (a) subjects recalled their interpolated judgments accurately and (b) the favorableness of the behavioral information recalled was unrelated to the favorableness of their final judgments. These data lend further support to our interpretation.

An alternative interpretation of these effects should be noted. It is conceivable that an individual's own judgments or reactions are more memorable than is the external stimuli upon which these judgments are based. This possibility has anecdotal support in the fact that we are often able to recall our subjective feelings about a person or event without being able to recall the things that produced these reactions (i.e., "I don't remember what he said in his talk, but I remember that I didn't like it"). To this extent, the greater effects of subjects' interpolated judgments obtained by Carlston may not have been a result of their recency per se. The relative merits of these two possible interpretations are worthy of investigation.

C. THE SOCRATIC EFFECT: A REINTERPRETATION

While conditional inference processes were not investigated directly in Carlston's study, the effects obtained may have implicitly involved such processes. More direct evidence that subjects may use their recent judgments as bases for later ones in the manner implied by Eq. (1) comes from research on the "Socratic effect," or the tendency for related cognitions, once made salient, to become more consistent over time (cf. Henninger & Wyer, 1976; McGuire, 1960; Rosen & Wyer, 1972; Wyer, 1974b). In this research, subjects are typically asked to report their beliefs in several sets of conditionally related propositions of the sort to which Eq. (1) is relevant. Propositions comprising each set, which concern contemporary issues and concepts familiar to subjects, are typically distributed randomly throughout the questionnaire. In some cases, therefore, propositions occupying the position of the conclusion B follow the propositions serving as premises (propositions of the form "A," "if A, then B," etc.), whereas in other cases they precede these premises. Subjects who are asked to report their belief in B will presumably search memory for other salient concepts or beliefs that have implications for it. If a subject has recently reported his belief in A, this belief is likely to be retrieved and used as a basis for his judgment of B. As a result, his belief in the conclusion should be inferred in the manner implied by Eq. (1), and the set of beliefs associated with A and B should appear consistent as defined by Eq. (2). However, suppose a subject is asked to evaluate the conclusion before the premises. In this case, the subject may often retrieve concepts other than A to use as a basis for his judgment. Moreover, in his subsequent evaluation of A, he is unlikely to consider his belief in B (a proposition implied by A) but will retrieve beliefs that, if true, have implications for A. As a consequence, the sets of beliefs reported in this latter condition are likely to be inconsistent as defined by Eq. (2). Data reported by Henninger (1975; see also Henninger & Wyer, 1976, Experiment 2) are in accord with this analysis. In this study, the order in which conditionally related beliefs were reported was systematically varied, and the inconsistency of these beliefs, as defined by Eq. (2), was investigated as a function of this order. As expected, the inconsistency of beliefs was less when the proposition corresponding to the premise A preceded the conclusion B than when this order was reversed.

If the above analysis is correct, it suggests a reinterpretation of the Socratic effect, as evidenced by an increase in the consistency of conditionally related beliefs over repeated administrations of the questionnaire. This effect has often been attributed to a general process of cognitive reorganization that is stimulated by the desire to eliminate inconsistencies among beliefs that become salient as a result of initially reporting them (McGuire, 1960; Rosen & Wyer, 1972; Wyer, 1974b). In other words, if subjects in the course of completing the belief questionnaire the first time are made aware of an inconsistency in their beliefs, as defined by Eq. (2), they may perform cognitive work during the period between sessions to modify one or more of these beliefs in a way that will reduce the inconsistency. This tendency may indeed exist. However, inconsistency reduction may also be partly a by-product of subjects' greater tendency to use the particular premise denoted A to infer the validity of the conclusion B when these beliefs are reported a second time. That is, when subjects report their beliefs in B in the first session, premise A may not yet have been evaluated. In this case, the likelihood that A is spontaneously retrieved and used as a basis for evaluating this conclusion may be low, as noted above. However, when subjects report their beliefs during the second session, the premise A, having been considered in the first session, is more likely to be recalled and used to evaluate the conclusion. This may be true regardless of the order in which the propositions occur in the questionnaire. As a result, the beliefs should appear generally consistent in the second session, as results typically indicate.

An implication of this analysis is that a reduction in inconsistency over sessions should be most likely when subjects judge the conclusion before they judge premises in the first session of the experiment. When they judge the conclusion after premises in the first session, inconsistency should be low initially and therefore should not be appreciably less in the second session. Henninger's results support this prediction. That is, the reduction in inconsistency over experimental sessions was greater when B preceded A in the initial questionnaire than when A preceded B. Moreover, these differences were primarily a result of differences in the inconsistency of beliefs reported during the first session; the inconsistency of beliefs reported in the second session was generally low and was similar regardless of the order in which beliefs were reported.

Not all of a set of conditionally related beliefs needs to be explicitly called to subjects' attention in order for A to be retrieved for use in evaluating B. In a second study (Henninger & Wyer, 1976, Experiment 3), the number and type of related beliefs reported in the first session of the experiment were varied. In some cases, therefore, only beliefs in premise A were reported during the first session; in other cases, only beliefs in the conclusion B were reported; in yet other cases, beliefs in both A and B were reported, and in still other instances, neither belief was reported in the first session. Subjects who reported their beliefs in A during the first session exhibited less inconsistency among the beliefs they reported later on than did subjects who did not initially report beliefs in A. Presumably, reporting one's belief in A in the first session increased its retrievability and therefore the likelihood that it would be used to infer the validity of B during the second session. In contrast, whether or not beliefs in the conclusion were reported during the first session did not affect the inconsistency of beliefs reported during the second. These results in combination support our general assumption that subjects use premises as a basis for inferring the validity of conclusions but do not use conclusions as a basis for inferring the validity of premises.

Although not formally applying Eq. (1), studies in other paradigms have similar implications. An experiment by Salancik and Calder (1974) is particularly provocative. Subjects reported the frequency with which they engaged in a series of behaviors related to religiousness (going to church, praying, etc.) either before or after they reported their personal religiousness and their belief in the desirability of being religious. In addition, they reported various demographic characteristics associated with religion (the religiousness of their upbringing, the religiousness of friends, etc.). When subjects are asked to estimate their personal religiousness and their belief in the favorableness of being religious, they may search memory for aspects of their background and experience that have implications for these judgments, and the beliefs they report will depend upon the information they retrieve. If they have previously reported the frequency of engaging in certain religious behaviors, these particular behaviors and the cognitions associated with them are likely to be retrieved and their implications used as a basis for judging their religiousness. However, if they have not been asked to report these specific behaviors, the likelihood of retrieving them spontaneously is less. The reported frequencies of manifesting these religious behaviors should therefore be more highly correlated with self-judgments of religiousness when these behaviors are considered before self-judgments are made than when they are considered afterwards. This was in fact the case. When attitudes were assessed after behaviors were reported, they were correlated over .90 with behavioral indices and less than .14 with demographic characteristics. However, when attitudes were assessed before reporting behaviors, they were correlated only .75 with the behavioral measure, and over .47 with demographic variables. This suggests that subjects not only tended to sample a different (although overlapping) subset of their past behavior to use as a basis for their judgments when the specific set described in the questionnaire items was not salient to them but also tended to use nonbehavioral information to a greater extent under these conditions.

D.   EFFECTS OF BELIEF ACCESSIBILITY ON CHANGES IN RELATED BELIEFS

The preceding studies provide evidence that a subject's beliefs in a given proposition are formed on the basis of the previously acquired information retrieved from memory. Other research and theory cited implies that the specific information a subject retrieves is determined by the recency with which it has been used in the past. In combination, these considerations suggest that a subject's beliefs in a proposition will be influenced to a greater extent by recently processed information rather than by other information less accessible from memory. (A common example of this phenomenon may be the tendency for public opinion ratings of Presidential performance to bounce up and down as a function of the most recent week's headlines.) Furthermore, it should be possible to manipulate a subject's beliefs in a proposition by varying the type and implications of other beliefs they report before considering this proposition. These systematic differences are often hard to detect using the procedures employed in the Socratic effect research described earlier unless individual differences in the beliefs in premises are taken into account. However, a study by Wyer and Henninger (1978) is suggestive. In this experiment, sets of conditionally related propositions were constructed so that in all cases, the premise A had positive implications for the conclusion B (i.e., B was believed more likely to be true if A was true than if A was not true). In such instances, making A more accessible to the subject by asking him to report his belief in it is likely to increase beliefs in B that are reported later on. Results bear out this possibility. That is, beliefs in conclusions were significantly more positive in the second session of the experiment (when beliefs in all premises and their implications had previously been reported) than in the first (when beliefs in conclusions were often reported before beliefs in premises.

A more provocative demonstration of these general effects has been reported by Salancik (1974). Here, students near the end of a course were asked to complete a series of open-ended statements about their classroom behavior. In one condition, each sentence was completed following the phrase "in order to" (i.e., "I raise my hand in class in order to . . ."), and in the other condition, it was completed following the phrase "because I" ("I raise my hand in class because I . . ."). Salancik reasoned that responding to the first set of statements would predispose students to think of extrinsic reasons for their behavior (i.e., ". . . in order to get a good grade"), whereas responding to the second set would predispose them to think of intrinsic reasons (i.e., ". . . because I want to understand what is going on"). Upon completing the questionnaire, students were asked how much they had enjoyed the course. These ratings were subsequently correlated with final course grades (an extrinsic factor). As expected, this correlation was much higher among subjects in the first condition (for whom extrinsic considerations were presumably more accessible at the time they evaluated the course) then among subjects in the second condition (for whom intrinsic factors were more accessible).

The considerations outlined above have more general implications for a conceptualization of belief and opinion change processes. Specifically, they suggest that the influence of belief change techniques may often be interpreted in terms of their effectiveness in making accessible previously acquired information with implications for the beliefs to be modified, as well as in terms of the new information that they provide. Two bodies of literature are of particular relevance to these considerations, each of which is worth noting briefly.

1. Role-Playing Effects on Self-Judgments

We have postulated that subjects do not conduct an exhaustive search of memory in making a judgment but tend to use whatever relevant information is most easily accessible. This assumption also underlies the self-perception formulation proposed by Bem (1967, 1972). Specifically, suppose a person has recently engaged in a behavior that has implications for his self-judgment. If the person is subsequently asked to make this judgment, he is likely to retrieve and use this behavior as a basis for his inference instead of equally relevant information that was acquired before engaging in this behavior. This prior information is likely to be sought and retrieved only if the more recent behavioral information is considered irrelevant to the self-judgment or if its implications are unclear.

Perhaps the most compelling demonstration of this possibility is provided in a study by Bem and McConnell (1970). Subjects initially reported their beliefs in a proposition and then, 1 week later, were asked to write an essay advocating a position contrary to these beliefs. Some subjects were given a choice as to whether or not they would write this essay and others were not given this choice. After writing the essay, some subjects in each choice condition reported their belief in the proposition a second time and others were asked to recall the position they had reported the week before. Subjects under free-choice conditions should perceive their behavior to have positive implications for their beliefs in the position advocated, whereas subjects under forced-choice conditions should regard their behavior as an unreliable index of their beliefs, leading them to search further for belief-relevant information. Consistent with this hypothesis, subjects reported their beliefs to be more in favor of the position advocated under free-choice than under forced-choice conditions. More intriguing, however, is the finding that subjects also recalled their prebehavior beliefs as more consistent with the position they advocated under free-choice than under forced-choice conditions. Indeed, the average error in recalling their prebehavior beliefs was virtually identical in both magnitude and direction to the apparent change in beliefs manifested by the first group of subjects. This suggests that subjects who had recently engaged in a belief-relevant behavior used this behavior not only as information about their current beliefs, but also as information about what their beliefs must have been before engaging in the behavior, without searching for other information that was equally or more relevant to their judgments.

2. Communication and Persuasion

The preceding examples concern the effects of recent behavioral information on beliefs and attitudes. However, similar considerations arise in the case of information from other sources. In many instances, a persuasive message may contain unfamiliar factual information that has implications for beliefs in the target proposition. However, in some cases, a communication may simply consist of assertions that the recipient already believes to be true with high probability. (For example, a communication that supports the proposition that abortion should be freely available to all may assert that a woman should have freedom of choice over whether she has children, thus reminding the recipient of his previously formed belief that this is true. In contrast, a communication that opposes abortion may assert that taking a life is immoral, thus directing the recipient's attention to his previously formed belief in this proposition instead.) When the recipient is later asked to report his opinion, he will be more apt to retrieve these recently processed cognitions than others and to use their implications as a basis for his judgment, thus leading to a reported belief that is consistent with the position advocated in the message.

The basic assumption underlying this analysis is that the belief-relevant cognitions stimulated by a communication, rather than the context of the communication itself, provide the material upon which recipients' subsequent judgments are based. This point was compellingly made by Greenwald (1968), who notes that surprisingly little evidence exists for a relation between the influence of a persuasive communication and the recall of the specific contents of this communication. Greenwald argues that reading or listening to a communication may stimulate a variety of thoughts associated with the issue being discussed. Although these thoughts may in some cases be simply an encoding or interpretation of the communication content, they may also include additional concepts and beliefs that are relevant to the issue at hand, including arguments both supporting and opposing the validity of the assertions made in the communication, opinions held by oneself and others, and other previously acquired cognitions that, although not directly related to communication content, nevertheless bear on the issue being discussed. These mediating cognitions, and not the communication content per se, may provide the basis for subsequent judgments of propositions to which these cognitions are relevant. Several studies reported by Greenwald (1968) are consistent with this hypothesis.

One implication of this line of reasoning is that if a person is distracted or otherwise prevented from generating these mediating cognitions at the time the communication is received, the content of the communication may have more effect. Research on distraction effects (for a review and theoretical analysis, see Wyer, 1974a) supports this possibility. For example, Festinger and Maccoby (1964) found that when fraternity members were distracted by an entertaining movie while they listened to a communication attacking fraternities, they changed their opinions about fraternities to a greater extent than those who received the same message without being distracted. Presumably in the absence of distraction, fraternity members generated counterarguments and other opinion-relevant cognitions while the communication was presented, the implications of which were favorable toward fraternities. These cognitions, and not the original communication content, were then used as a basis for the subsequent beliefs they reported. Distracted subjects, in contrast, may not have been able to generate these cognitions. Therefore, only the direct encodings of the communication content and its implications may have been retrieved and used as a basis for their reported beliefs.

Persons who are not initially opposed to the position advocated in a communication are of course unlikely to generate counterarguments while receiving it, regardless of whether they are distracted or not. Therefore, they should be likely to use the encoded implications of the message content as bases for their later judgments in both cases. Consistent with this hypothesis, nonfraternity members in Festinger and Maccoby's study were equally influenced by the antifraternity message under both distraction and no distraction conditions.

E. EFFECTS OF PRIOR USE OF CONCEPTS ON THE INTERPRETATION OF
    BELIEF-RELEVANT MATERIAL

The previous discussion has focused on the extent to which recently used cognitions are likely to be retrieved and used to infer the validity of related propositions. An additional consideration concerns the effect of recently used concepts on the interpretation of new information a person receives. The implications of the new information for subsequent judgments obviously depends upon the way this information is interpreted. For example, by altering the way a piece of information is initially perceived, recently used concepts may have an indirect effect on future judgments. To borrow an example from Higgins, Rholes, and Jones (1977), suppose a person is asked to infer the likeableness of someone who is described as being well aware of his ability to do things well. The implications of the information for likeableness may depend upon whether it is interpreted as conveying that the target is self-confident (a desirable attribute) or conceited (an undesirable quality). Which interpretation is made may in turn be a function of how recently one or the other of these concepts ("self-confident" or "conceited") was used in the past.

These "priming" effects and their influence on social judgment have been demonstrated in studies by Srull and Wyer (1979) and by Higgins et al. (1977). In the Srull and Wyer study, subjects were initially required to take a "personality test." In this task, they were presented sets of four words and asked in each case to underline which three would make a sentence. In some cases (e.g., "boy the hit girl"), the possible sentences constructed from the words conveyed hostility, whereas in other cases (e.g., "pack box the paint"), the sentences were irrelevant to this trait. The number of hostility-related items contained in the questionnaire was systematically varied over four levels (6, 18, 24, or 48 items).

Then, either immediately, 1 hour, or 1 day after completing the task, subjects as part of a different experiment (run by a different experimenter) read a story describing the behavior of a hypothetical person in various situations under instructions to form an impression of the person described. The behaviors (e.g., not paying the rent until the landlord painted his apartment) were typically ambiguous; that is, they could be interpreted as either hostile or not hostile. In forming an impression of the person, subjects were expected to retrieve concepts from memory relevant for interpreting the person's behavior. If recently used concepts relevant to the interpretation are most likely to be retrieved, subjects should encode the behavior as hostile when a larger number of hostility-related concepts have been ''primed'' as a result of completing the sentence-construction task. Moreover, this tendency should decrease as the delay between the sentence-construction task and the presentation of the stimulus information decreases.

After receiving the behavioral descriptions of the target person, subjects were asked to evaluate the target person along both dimensions directly related to hostility and dimensions that were evaluative but unrelated to hostility. Fig. 4a, provides support for the hypotheses outlined above; that is, judgments of the target's hostility were a positive function of the number of hostility-related items

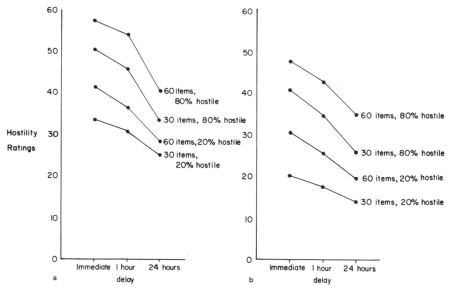

Fig. 4. Mean ratings of target person along (a) dimensions related to hostility and (b) dimensions unrelated to hostility as a function of number of priming items, percentage of hostile priming items, and delay.

in the priming task. Although the effect of priming decreased with the time interval between task and presentation of the stimulus paragraph, it was still evident even 24 hours after the concepts had initially been primed. A demand compliance interpretation of the data seems unlikely in light of postexperimental questioning indicating that no subject under any condition identified the two tasks (which were presented along with several others over the course of two experimental sessions) as related to one another.

Finally, the direct effects of priming on judgments of the target person's hostility generalized to judgments along other evaluative dimensions that were not denotatively related to hostility. However, these effects, shown in Fig. 4b, were not as strong as the effects on hostility judgments. This suggests that while subjects may have generalized the evaluative implications of their hostility judgments, once formed, to other characteristics of the target person, the priming effect resulted principally from the descriptive implications of the priming for the interpretation of the behavioral information and was not simply a generalized evaluative set that affected judgments of the target independently of the encoding.

Evidence supporting this conclusion was obtained in two other studies by Srull and Wyer (see Wyer & Srull, 1980b) and by Higgins, Rholes, and Jones (1977). In the first study, a paradigm similar to that already described was used except that the stimulus information about the target person was presented before rather than after the task designed to prime hostility. In this case, the pattern of results shown in Fig. 4 completely disappeared; that is, neither the number of hostility-related priming items nor delay interval had any effect on judgments of the target, regardless of whether this delay was between the presentation of the stimulus information and the priming task or between the priming task and the judgments of the target. These data suggest strongly that effects reported in the first study were mediated by the effects of priming on the interpretation of the stimulus information at the time this information was presented, and did not affect judgments directly. In the study by Higgins *et al.* (1977) a somewhat different paradigm was used. Here, subjects in the course of an initial color-naming task were exposed to one of two sets of trait terms. Both sets could potentially be used to encode the same behavior. However, one set (adventurous, self-confident, independent, and persistent) had favorable connotations and the other set (reckless, conceited, aloof, and stubborn) had unfavorable connotations. After engaging in the priming task, subjects read a paragraph about a target person describing behaviors that could be encoded using either set of trait terms (e.g., as wanting to cross the Atlantic in a sailboat, as being well-aware of his ability to do things well, etc.). A few minutes later, subjects were asked to evaluate the target person. According to the reasoning outlined, the evaluations should be based upon the traits assigned to the target on the basis of his behavior, and these traits should in turn be a function of the terms made accessible as a result of the priming task. As expected, subjects evaluated the target person more positively under favorable priming than under unfavorable priming conditions. Furthermore, this difference was greater when the priming words were appropriate for encoding the target's behavior than when they were inappropriate.

An additional aspect of this experiment is also worth noting. Subjects returned 2 weeks later and were required to make their evaluations once more. All of the priming effects were found to be greater at this time than they were at first. This finding, which was corroborated in a later study by Srull and Wyer (see Wyer & Srull, 1980a) and is consistent with the implications of results obtained by Carlston (1977) in a study described earlier, provides further insight into the dynamics of recency effects; that is, the effect of making a concept salient on the tendency to use it to interpret new information decreases with the time interval between the prior use of the concept and the information to be interpreted. However, once the concept has been used, the likelihood that subsequent judgments are based upon it increases over time. Similar results, obtained by Carlston (1977), were discussed earlier. Perhaps when judgments are made immediately after the original stimulus information is presented, this information as well as the abstract encoding of it is retrieved, and thus both in combination are brought to bear on inference. However, with the passage of time, the original information gets "lost," and only the encoding and its implications are retrieved for use in inferences, leading the encoding to have proportionately greater effect. Possible cognitive mechanisms underlying this effect are outlined by Wyer and Srull (1980b).

F. EFFECTS OF PRIMING ON BEHAVIOR TOWARD ACTUAL PERSONS

While the previously discussed research concerns the effect on the judgment of hypothetical persons of making a concept accessible, similar effects may occur on behavior toward actual people. A study by Berkowitz and Alioto (1973) is worth considering. In this study, subjects first viewed a tape of a sporting event (e.g., a boxing match or a football game) under either instructions that it was a grudge match or instructions that it was a routine encounter. As would be expected, subjects who were told that the event was a grudge match judged the behavior observed to be more aggressive than did other subjects. Moreover, the former subjects were subsequently more apt to shock another person who had provoked them. While other interpretations of this finding are possible, it seems reasonable to speculate that the subjects who were told that the sporting event was a grudge match interpreted the behavior they saw as hostile. Subsequently, they used the salient hostility-related concepts to interpret the confederate's shocking behavior, leading them to deliver more shocks to this confederate in return.

III. Determinants of Information Accessibility: Amount of Processing

The recency with which a piece of information has been used is only one of several factors that may affect the likelihood it is retrieved for use in making a judgment. Craik and Lockhart (1972; see also Craik, 1977) hypothesize that information is better recalled when it is processed more "deeply" or extensively. If this is true, the recall of belief-relevant information may be partly a function of the amount of cognitive work involved in interpreting it and identifying its implications. This activity may take place either at the time the information is first received or later on.

This possibility has important implications in the context of the formulation proposed here. Specifically, it suggests that the likelihood of retrieving any particular proposition for use in evaluating others will be a function of the amount of cognitive work expended on this proposition in the past. Several factors may affect the amount of processing, four of which will be discussed here: the plausibility of the proposition, the strength of its implications for other related propositions, the inconsistency between beliefs in this proposition and other beliefs, and situational factors that lead one to think carefully about the objects or concepts to which these beliefs pertain.

A. PLAUSIBILITY AND STRENGTH OF IMPLICATIONS

A person who is called upon to evaluate a proposition presumably searches memory for information that has implications for its validity. However, the search is apt to be less extensive if the proposition is highly plausible, or intuitively likely to be true, than if it is less so. Indeed, one reason that propositions are plausible is simply that abundant information implying their validity is stored in memory, and that some of this information is quickly and easily retrievable for use in evaluating them. In addition, the ideas conveyed by relatively implausible propositions (e.g., "Edward Kennedy is a close friend of Richard Nixon") may be more unfamiliar or deviant from expectancies than plausible ones (e.g., "Men often suffer heart attacks while shoveling snow") and so may be more thought provoking. For these reasons, the evaluation of relatively implausible propositions may involve more cognitive activity than the evaluation of plausible ones. As a result, implausible propositions may be more readily recalled.

For similar reasons, the likelihood that one proposition is brought to bear on a second may also depend on the strength and clarity of its implications for the second proposition; that is, a person who is explicitly asked to consider the implications of one proposition for a second may engage in more cognitive work to construe these implications when they are weak or unclear.

Preliminary data collected by Wyer and Henninger (1978) bear on the considerations just raised. Subjects in this study reported their beliefs in a set of randomly ordered propositions of the sort to which Eq. (1) theoretically pertains. Sets were selected such that the plausibility of the premise denoted A (operationalized in terms of the strength of the normative belief in A) and the strength or clarity of A's implications for the conclusion B (i.e., inferred from the magnitude of the belief that B is true given that A is true) were manipulated independently. (In all cases, however, A had positive implications for B; that is, B was believed more likely to be true if A was true than if it was not true.) An example of a pair of propositions (A and B) representing each combination of these variables may be helpful:

1. High plausibility, strong implications: (A) Vast oil resources lie under the frozen earth of Antarctica. (B) The settlement of Antarctica will be vastly accelerated in the next few years.

2. High plausibility, weak implications: (A) Men frequently suffer heart attacks while shoveling snow. (B) Exercise is bad for the heart.

3. Low plausibility, strong implications: (A) The all-volunteer Army is accepting an increasing number of mentally retarded recruits. (B) The overall level of intelligence of Army personnel will decline in the coming years.

4. Low plausibility, weak implications: (A) Edward Kennedy is a good friend of Richard Nixon. (B) Edward Kennedy made illegal contributions to Nixon's presidential campaign fund.

Subjects were required to complete the belief questionnaire and then to return for a second session 1 week later. At this time, they attempted to recall as many of the propositions in the questionnaire as possible and then completed the questionnaire a second time.

The mean probability of recalling each proposition is shown in Table I as a function of A's plausibility and implications for B. Both A and B were recalled well when A's plausibility was low. This tendency was particularly pronounced when A's implications for the validity of B were weak. Under these circumstances, not only A but also propositions related to it were thought about more extensively.[11] When A's plausibility was high, however, the recall of the conclusion was generally poor, as expected. Furthermore, the recall of A itself was appreciable only when its implications for beliefs in the conclusion were strong. This suggests that reporting beliefs in a plausible premise does not stimulate

---

[11]The higher recall of B when A's plausibility was low than when it was high might be attributed to the fact that B was also less plausible in the former conditions and so to a direct effect of plausibility. However, beliefs in B were only slightly lower when A was low in plausibility ($M = .34$) than when it was high ($M = .37$); this difference is not of sufficient magnitude to account for the substantial difference in recall obtained in Table I. Moreover, although beliefs in B were lower on the average ($M = .36$) than beliefs in A ($M = .50$), B was recalled slightly less well ($M = .26$) than A ($M = .32$). This also argues against the interpretation that recall differences result simply from a general tendency for statements to be recalled better when beliefs in them are low.

TABLE I

MEAN PROBABILITY OF RECALLING PROPOSITIONS A AND B AS A FUNCTION OF A'S
PLAUSIBILITY AND A'S IMPLICATIONS FOR B

	High plausibility	Low plausibility
Recall of A		
Strong implications for B	.19	.21
Weak implications for B	.06	.36
Recall of B		
Strong implications for B	.07	.20
Weak implications for B	.10	.32

thinking about the conclusion upon which it bears but does increase thinking about the premise itself when its implications for other reported beliefs are strong.

A better indication of the extent to which one proposition has been thought about in relation to another is the extent to which the recall of one proposition in a set is facilitated by recall of the second. The reasoning outlined above implies that this facilitation should be greater when A's plausibility is low, or when A's implications for the validity of B are weak, than under other conditions. This is in fact the case. The probability of recalling the premise A of a set given that B was and was not recalled, and also the probability of recalling B given that A was and was not recalled, are shown in Table II as a function of A's plausibility and the

TABLE II

CONDITIONAL PROBABILITIES OF RECALL OF A AND B,
GIVEN RECALL OR NONRECALL OF THE OTHER PROPOSITION

Beliefs recalled before completing questionnaire in Session 2	Probability of recalling B			Probability of Recalling A		
	Given that A was recalled	Given that A was not recalled	Difference	Given that B was recalled	Given that B was not recalled	Difference
High plausibility, strong implications	.133	.061	.072	.333	.176	.157
High plausibility, weak implications	.800	.053	.747	.500	.014	.486
Low plausibility, strong implications	.706	.063	.643	.750	.078	.672
Low plausibility, weak implications	.690	.118	.572	.769	.166	.603

strength of its implications for B. A facilitating effect of recalling one proposition on recall of the other is reflected by a positive difference between the conditional probabilities of recalling the second given that the first is and is not recalled. Table II indicates that this difference is much greater when either A is implausible or its implications for B are weak than when neither of these conditions exists. These results are therefore consistent with expectations and with the general interpretation given to the data in Table I.

Effects on Reported Beliefs

The previous considerations imply that if beliefs in a set of conditionally related propositions have been reported at one time, the subsequent recall and use of a premise A as a basis for inferring the validity of a conclusion B may be more likely if A is implausible than if A is plausible. Moreover, this tendency may be greater when the implications of A for B are unclear. The effects of these factors on beliefs in the conclusion are difficult to predict, however. This is because the conditions that lead A to be retrieved more readily (that is, low P_A and low $P_{B/A}$) and so to be used more frequently as a basis for beliefs in B are also those in which the magnitude of change in B produced by taking A into account is less (see Eq. 1). However, correlational analyses provide indirect evidence of the effects predicted on the basis of differences in recall probability. Because the premises used in the Wyer and Henninger (1978) study all had positive implications for beliefs in the conclusions, subjects should typically increase their beliefs in a conclusion more to the extent they have thought more about the implications of the premises for that conclusion. Moreover, this cognitive activity should also lead to better recall of the conclusion. Therefore, to the extent that thinking about the implications of the premise for the conclusion mediates changes in beliefs in the conclusion as well as recall of this conclusion, there should be a positive correlation between the recall of the conclusion B and increases in beliefs in it. In fact, when premise A's plausibility was low, this correlation was significantly positive and was somewhat greater when A's implications for the conclusion B were weak ($r = .403$) than when they were strong ($r = .302$). However, when A's plausibility was high, these correlations were negligible ($r = -.064$ and .021, respectively). These data suggest that when the plausibility of a premise was at a level that stimulated subjects to retrieve it from memory and think about its implications, they did in fact increase their beliefs in the conclusion more to the extent that they thought about it more (as evidenced by the greater recall of this proposition). However, when the plausibility of the premise was high, and so subjects tended to think less about its implications, whatever cognitive activity led them to recall the conclusion did not systematically affect their beliefs in this proposition.

The data just described seem sufficient to conclude that the cognitive activity required to evaluate implausible propositions makes these propositions more easily accessible and so makes them more likely to be invoked in the future as a basis for other beliefs. It is important to note, however, that these effects may occur only if the subject has the possible implications of these propositions called to his attention (e.g., by being asked to evalute them). If subjects in the first session of the Wyer and Henninger (1978) study had not been explicitly asked to evalute conditional propositions (i.e., "if A, then B"), they might not have recognized the possible relation of A to B, particularly when A's implications were weak or unclear. In such an event, the effects of A's plausibility on recall of B would not occur.

B. EFFECTS OF INCONSISTENCY

McGuire (1960) postulated that when someone becomes aware of inconsistencies among his cognitions, he will engage in cognitive activity to eliminate them. If this is the case, and if the recall of these cognitions is a function of the amount of this activity, there should be a positive relation between the initial inconsistency of cognitions and recall of propositions to which these cognitions pertain. Moreover, if the reduction of inconsistencies, like the recall of propositions, is a reflection of the expenditure of cognitive energy, there should be a positive relation between the recall of propositions and the decrease in inconsistency of beliefs associated with them.

This possibility was also investigated in the Wyer and Henninger (1978) study. Specifically, the correlation between (a) the initial inconsistency of the beliefs associated with a premise A and a conclusion B (as defined by Eq. 2) and (b) the recall of propositions to which the beliefs pertained was computed at all combinations of plausibility and implication strength. This correlation was more positive when A was implausible but had clear implications for B (mean $r = .343$) than when one or the other (or both) of these conditions was not met (mean $r = -.110$). This suggests that the cognitive activity resulting from an awareness of belief inconsistency increases when the premise is relatively implausible but has clear implications for beliefs in the conclusion. Presumably this activity is directed in part toward decreasing the inconsistency between the two beliefs. In fact, reduction of inconsistency over experimental sessions was positively correlated with recall of beliefs when the premises had strong implications for the validity of the conclusions (mean $r = .222$). However, this relation was negligible (mean $r = -.027$) when these implications were weak. Although these correlational differences are too low to be taken as definitive without replication, they again suggest that a premise's implications for the conclusion must be clear in order for the inconsistency of beliefs in these propositions to be manifested and subsequently reduced.

C. GENERAL EFFECTS OF THOUGHT ON REPORTED BELIEFS

We have argued that in many instances, a person who is called upon to evaluate a proposition (i.e., a conclusion) may use only the first relevant information he retrieves as a basis for his judgment instead of searching for other previously acquired information (propositions or sets of premises) that may also be relevant. However, this is obviously not always the case. Certainly on matters of considerable personal importance (getting married, taking a new job, etc.), people may weight the implications of several pieces of new or previously acquired information. Moreover, there may be situational demands to think carefully about a judgment or about the object being judged. Presumably, as persons think more about an object, they bring more previously acquired beliefs and concepts to bear on it. Their judgments may therefore change relative to conditions in which less information is retrieved.

The effect of thought about an object on judgments of the object depends upon the implications of the additional information retrieved. Each piece of retrieved information may serve as a premise that has positive or negative implications for the judgment to be made (one's belief in a conclusion). If the implications of these additional propositions are similar to those of the first information considered, they may increase the judge's confidence in his initial opinion. This should lead to a more extreme judgment than would result from considering less information. However, if the implications of the additional propositions differ from those of the original information, they may weaken the initial opinion and result in a less extreme judgment.

Some evidence bearing indirectly on these considerations has been obtained in a series of studies by Tesser (for a summary, see Tesser, 1978). In these studies, subjects first rate a series of stimuli (persons described by personality adjectives, pictures of football plays, etc.) along an evaluative dimension. Based on these initial judgments, a target stimulus is selected that has received either a moderately favorable or moderately unfavorable rating (e.g., either +3 or −3 along a scale from +5 to −5). Subjects then either are asked to spend time thinking about the target stimulus or are distracted from doing so by performing an interpolated task. The target, along with other stimuli, is then reevaluated. Relative to distraction conditions, ratings typically become more extreme as a result of thought. Moreover, the magnitude of this "polarization" effect increases with the amount of time spent thinking about the stimulus.

In accounting for this phenomenon, Tesser postulates that people who judge a stimulus often invoke previously formed "schemata" that serve as bases for their evaluations. Unfortunately, Tesser does not indicate the nature of a schema. However, it may suffice for present purposes to assume that a schema simply consists of a set of attributes believed to be possessed by some prototypic object. (For a more rigorous conceptualization of schemata about persons, see Wyer &

Carlston, 1979.) These attributes may be used to decide whether a particular object is a member of the category defined by the schema. If the object is assigned to this category, the schema may then be used to infer other attributes of the object that have not been mentioned in the original information but are typically possessed by category members.

Given these assumptions, Tesser's results can be explained. To give a concrete example, suppose a subject is first asked to estimate his liking for a target person on the basis of information that the person is intelligent. In doing so, the subject may focus primarily on the implication of this attribute alone, and may make a judgment on the basis of a conditional inference process similar to that described earlier (e.g., the subject may infer that "if someone is intelligent, (s)he is probably likeable" and conclude that "the target is probably likeable"). However, now suppose that the subject is asked to think more carefully about the stimulus. In this case, he is more apt to invoke a prototypic schema of the type of stimulus described, or in this case, of an "intelligent person." In general, there are two ways in which this schema could have an effect. First, the subject may attempt to identify additional features of the stimulus information that confirm his assumption that the target is actually of the type to which this schema pertains. Second, the subject may infer the target to have attributes that are not specified in the original information but are typical of objects in the schema category. In either case, the additional attributes are likely to be evaluatively similar to the original ones (Rosenberg & Sedlak, 1972). If the subject is now asked to reevaluate the stimulus and considers the implications of these additional attributes as well as the original ones, his judgments of the stimulus may become more extreme than they were initially. (For evidence that judgments increase in extremity with the number of evaluatively similar attributes on which they are based, see N. H. Anderson, 1965; Fishbein & Hunter, 1964.)

This interpretation implies that the polarization effect should occur only if the subject does in fact have a prototypic schema to use in evaluating the stimulus. If such a schema does not exist, thought should not lead additional attributes to be generated, and so the polarization effect should be attenuated. Two studies by Tesser and Leone (1977) provide indirect support for this line of reasoning. In their first study, subjects were initially presented sets of trait adjectives. In one condition they were asked to evaluate a single person described by the adjectives in each set, and in a second condition they were asked to evaluate a group of persons each described by a different one of the adjectives. They then either were told to think about a particular one of the stimuli or were distracted from doing so. Tesser and Leone assumed that subjects would have prototypic schemata for evaluating individual persons but not for evaluating groups. Polarization effects would then be expected to occur only when individuals were judged. Consistent with this hypothesis, ratings of individuals became relatively more extreme following thought, whereas ratings of groups did not.

In a second study, subjects were initially asked to evaluate either a series of football plays or a series of women's fashions and then were asked to rerate a particular one of the stimuli after having either thought about it or not. Male subjects were expected to have prototypic schemata for evaluating football plays but not women's fashions, whereas female subjects were expected to have schemata for evaluating fashions but not football plays. Consistent with implications of this assumption, males increased the extremity of their ratings of football plays following thought, whereas their ratings of women's fashions were unaffected. Likewise, female subjects increased the extremity of their ratings of women's fashions but not those of football plays.

A Note of Caution

Although the phenomenon reported by Tesser is provocative, some caution should be taken in interpreting it and evaluating its generality. For one thing, there are other, somewhat more mundane interpretations of the results. For example, people who are asked to give a spontaneous reaction to a stimulus without much thought may not report a judgment as extreme as they feel may be justified because apprehension over appearing foolish if future events should prove them wrong. However, if further thought does not alter their initial reaction, they may become more confident of the validity of their initial reaction and so more inclined to report a judgment consistent with it. To this extent, the results obtained by Tesser and his colleagues may not indicate that thought increases the polarization of subjective judgments of a stimulus. Instead, they may reflect a "cautiousness" about reporting these judgments in the absence of thought.

In terms of the formulation proposed in this contribution, it is unclear why thought should always increase polarization of an opinion rather than decrease it. McGuire (1960) postulates that thought typically increases the consistency of related cognitions, as evidenced by the Socratic effect discussed earlier. However, this increased consistency may be attained through either an increase or a decrease in beliefs in a conclusion, depending upon whether the implications of retrieved beliefs in "premises" are more or less extreme than the initial belief in the conclusion. Our formulation therefore suggests that if subjects are equated in terms of their initial judgments, thought should lead to increased variability in these judgments relative to distraction conditions, and that this increased variability should occur primarily when subjects do, in fact, have previously formed beliefs that they can bring to bear on the judgments they make. Graphs reported in Tesser and Leone (1977) appear to support this contention. We would also predict polarization effects to occur only when there is a tendency to retrieve information with extreme implications. The effects obtained by Tesser may therefore not generalize to other stimulus domains and experimental conditions in which thought is likely to lead information with less extreme implications to be accessed.

D. SUMMARY AND CONCLUSIONS

The results reported in Section III are generally consistent with the hypothesis that if information is processed extensively at one time, either in order to respond to it or as a result of instructions to think about it, this information may be more likely to be recalled in the future and brought to bear on judgments to which it is relevant. Additional research is necessary to tie down several interpretive and empirical ambiguities associated with the results obtained to date, and to demonstrate more directly the mediating link between the particular information recalled as a result of extensive processing and the judgments that are theoretically affected by it. However, the research conducted so far provides some useful leads in coming to grips with these phenomena.

IV.   Additional Considerations

In the preceding sections, we have focused on factors that affect the retrieval of information to use in making conditional inferences about one's social environment. In this discussion, we have neglected many factors that should be considered in developing a general understanding of social inference phenomena. Moreover, additional considerations also arise when the conceptualization we have proposed is applied in certain content domains. A few of these issues are particularly worth noting. They concern (a) the integration of new and previously acquired information bearing on a conclusion, (b) the role of nonlogical factors in social inference, and (c) the application of the conditional inference formulation to person perception and interpersonal attraction phenomena.

A. THE INTEGRATION OF NEW INFORMATION AND PREVIOUSLY
ACQUIRED BELIEFS

In our discussion, we have considered the effects on judgments of either previously acquired information retrieved from memory or the effects of new information to which previously formed beliefs are irrelevant, but not both simultaneously. In many instances, however, a person may receive new information with implications that are inconsistent with those of information readily accessible from memory. In such cases, the person must somehow integrate the implications of the new information with those of the information retrieved from memory in order to draw a conclusion based upon the two sets of implications in combination.

The manner in which this integration is accomplished is not entirely clear. The nature of this ambiguity can be conveyed with a rather mundane example. Suppose a person receives information that (a) newborn babies rarely cry, that (b) if newborn babies cry, they are usually loved by their parents, and that (c) if newborn babies do not cry, they are rarely loved by their parents. Then, the person is asked the likelihood that a particular baby, John, would be loved by his parents. If the person attends only to the information presented, he may reason that because John is unlikely to cry, and because if John does not cry he is not apt to be loved by his parents, it follows that John is unlikely to be loved by his parents. However, suppose the person believes that in reality, newborn babies are very likely to cry but are typically loved by their parents regardless of whether they cry or not. This set of a priori beliefs implies that John is apt to be loved by his parents. If these a priori beliefs affect the person's inferences, therefore, his belief in the conclusion should be greater than the value implied by the information given. However, there may be two reasons for this. First, the person may simply ignore the implications of the new information and rely solely on his previously formed beliefs. Second, he may use the information but interpret its implications as being more consistent with his previously formed beliefs than is actually the case.

These possibilities were explored by Wyer (1976). In this study, stimulus materials consisted of eight sets of three propositions of the form "A"; "if A, then B"; "if not A, then B" (e.g., "Surgeons perform their operations carelessly"; "Surgeons who perform their operations carelessly are competent"; "Surgeons who do not perform their operations carelessly are competent"). The strengths of a priori beliefs in each of the three propositions varied systematically over the eight sets. [For example, the combination of a prior beliefs in the above set of propositions were denoted low P_A, low $P_{B/A}$, and high $P_{B/A'}$, as defined in Eq. (1).] Stimulus statements were then constructed on the basis of these sets that varied systematically in their implications for these beliefs. This was done by inserting the words "usually" or "rarely" into the original propositions (e.g., "Surgeons usually (rarely) perform their operations carelessly," etc.). The overall design therefore permitted subjects' a priori beliefs in each type of proposition and the implications of the information presented for the validity of this proposition to be varied independently. The result was a 2^6 design.

Subjects read each set of stimulus information under instructions to assume that the statements presented were definitely true and then inferred the validity of both the conclusion to which the information was relevant (e.g., the likelihood that surgeons are competent, or P_B) and the premises bearing on it.

Despite instructions to treat the stimulus information presented as definitely true, subjects' estimates of the validity of each premise were affected not only by this information but also by their a priori beliefs. Moreover, these effects were independent. This suggests that subjects interpreted the stimulus information differently, depending on their a priori beliefs; for example, their interpretation of the frequencies implied by the adverbs "usually" and "rarely" may have depended on their previously formed beliefs that the relation described was likely to hold in reality.

In addition, subjects' estimates of the validity of the conclusion B were generally affected, by both their a priori beliefs in the premises and the implications of the information presented, in the manner implied by Eq. (1). For example, a priori beliefs that B was true if A was true ($P_{B/A}$) and the implications of the information presented for this proposition both had greater effect on judgments that B was true when a priori beliefs in A (P_A) were high than when they were low and also had greater effect when the information presented implied a high value of P_A than when it implied a low value. Analogous effects occurred in analyses involving the likelihood that B was true if A was not true.

In combination, these results suggest that when subjects are asked to evaluate a conclusion on the basis of new information, they not only may use this information but also may retrieve previously formed beliefs in the validity of propositions to which the information pertains. The implications of these beliefs are then combined with those of the new information when evaluating the conclusion. Moreover, this may occur even when subjects are explicitly instructed to ignore their prior beliefs when processing the new information. It may be a mistake to generalize these results to situations in which subjects' a priori beliefs are unlikely to be easily accessible. In the study described above, all stimulus information concerned propositions about events or relations that were generally recognized as true or false without an exhaustive search of memory. Whether previously acquired beliefs are automatically retrieved and integrated with new information when these beliefs are less easily accessible is unclear, as suggested in earlier sections of this contribution.

Further insight into the processes underlying the integration of new information with previously formed beliefs was gained from an analysis of the difference between obtained and predicted beliefs in conclusions (based on Eq. 1) as a function of the experimental variables. One particularly interesting hypothesis was suggested. Specifically, when persons consider the implications of their conditional beliefs that B is true given that A is or is not true, they appear to give greater weight to whichever source of evidence (the new information or their a priori beliefs) implies that the proposition they are using as a basis for their inference is more likely to be true. For example, if their a priori belief that A is true is greater than the value implied by the information presented, they weight this belief more when considering the likelihood that B is true if A is true, but weight the new information presented more when considering the likelihood that B is true if A is not true.

This conceptualization should be treated with some caution pending a more direct investigation of its validity. However, these preliminary data demonstrate the potential heuristic value of the proposed formulation in diagnosing conditional inference processes. Moreover, they suggest a framework for subsequent research designed to investigate the conditions in which subjects are more or less apt to retrieve and use previously acquired information as well as new information. For example, subjects who are simply asked to read a persuasive communication bearing on the premises of a set of conditionally related propositions may be more apt to retrieve previously formed beliefs when they are more easily accessible, and the influence of such beliefs may be greater under these conditions than in the study just described.

B. NONLOGICAL FACTORS IN SOCIAL INFERENCE

The inferences that people make are obviously not always of the sort that we have described thus far. Moreover, the reasoning that underlies their inferences may often not be of the sort one would expect on the basis of known principles of formal logic. This fact was recognized by McGuire (1960) in his initial conceptualization of the role of syllogistic reasoning in social cognition, and its implications have been explored by Wyer (1977) in an analysis of nonlogical factors underlying social inference. This research seems to indicate that people tend to treat propositions as equivalent in meaning, based upon their similarity with respect to such physical characteristics as their form and the objects they describe. For example, if people are told that X is Y, they are also likely to conclude that Y is X, that not-X is not Y, and that not-Y is not X.

This possibility has important implications, for it suggests that the information retrieved from memory to evaluate a conclusion of the form ''X is Y'' does not necessarily consist of beliefs in premises that have direct implications for this proposition but may also concern premises that have implications for other propositions that are incorrectly assumed to be equivalent to it in meaning. For example, estimates of the likelihood that businessmen are conservative may be based upon previously acquired beliefs in premises that, if true, imply this conclusion. However, they may also be based on beliefs in premises that imply that conservatives are businessmen, or that nonbusinessmen are not conservative. Evidence that subjects do draw such nonlogical conclusions from premises of the form to which Eq. (1) pertains has been obtained by Wyer (1977). Moreover, the nature of these inferences can be predicted from knowledge of the contributions of nonlogical factors, such as similarity of the propositions in form and content to the proposition that logically follows from the premises presented. Further investigation of these matters is desirable.

C. SOCIAL EVALUATION PROCESSES

The issues raised in this contribution, and the framework we have proposed for conceptualizing them, are relevant to social inference processes in a variety of domains. However, some special considerations arise in applying these notions to social perception and interpersonal attraction. The final section of this chapter therefore is devoted to these considerations.

When a person is asked to estimate his liking for another, he may search memory for attributes of the person that have implications for this judgment. The attributes retrieved may often be those that have been most recently applied to the person in the past or have most recently been used to encode the person's behavior. The process of using these attributes to infer liking may involve conditional reasoning; that is, having accessed the characteristic honest, a subject may base his judgment that a target person is likable on his inferences that (a) a person is likable if he is honest, and (b) a person is likable if he is not honest, weighting these inferences by beliefs that the target is and is not honest, respectively. For example, suppose a judge who is asked to evaluate a target person O retrieves attribute X and uses this as a basis for his judgment of the person. The inference process should theoretically be described by the equation:

$$P_L = P_X P_{L/X} + P_{X'} P_{L/X'} \tag{5}$$

where P_L is the belief that he would like the person, P_X and $P_{X'}$ ($= 1 - P_X$) are beliefs that the person does and does not have X, and $P_{L/X}$ and $P_{L/X'}$ are conditional beliefs that a person would be liked if he did and did not possess X, respectively.

In applying this equation, however, some additional considerations arise. First, many attributes of a person have implications for liking, and these implications, considered in isolation, may not all be the same. Therefore, if a judge who is asked to evaluate someone retrieves a single trait of the person to use in evaluating him, this evaluation will be consistent with the implications of the trait (as defined by Eq. 5) but may be inconsistent with the implications of other traits of the person. Evaluations of this person may vary over time, however, depending on which trait is retrieved. The piece of "information" a judge retrieves, however, may not always consist of a single trait. Rather, it may be a "schema," or cluster of traits and personal characteristics (Cantor & Mischel, 1977; Wyer & Carlston, 1979; Wyer & Srull, 1980b). If this is true, predictions of liking, although consistent with implications of the schema, may be somewhat inaccurate when considering any particular trait contained in this cluster.

Two studies, each with a somewhat different focus, bear indirectly on certain of the general questions just raised. Each is worth reviewing briefly.

1.   Liking for Hypothetical Persons

If a subject reads a paragraph about a person's behavior in a given situation (e.g., that he has returned a lost wallet), he is likely to encode the behavior in terms of a general trait to which the behavior is directly relevant (e.g., as "honest"). If the subject is then asked if he would like the person, he may retrieve the trait and use it as a basis for his judgment. Suppose, however, that after making this judgment, the subject is asked to infer other traits of the target person. The subject may infer these traits on the basis of the original information presented as well. However, because these traits were not considered at the time liking for the target was estimated, this estimate should be more inconsistent with the implications of these latter traits than with those of the trait most directly implied by the stimulus information.

These general predictions were supported in a study by Wyer (1973b). The procedure was analogous to that used in the simulated study of belief and opinion change described previously (Wyer, 1970). Subjects read sets of two paragraphs describing a hypothetical person's behavior. The behavior described in one paragraph implied a high degree of a given attribute X (i.e., a high value of P_X), whereas that described in the second implied a low degree of the attribute (a low value of P_X). (For example, in one case, where the attribute was "honesty," the target person was described in one paragraph as finding and returning a lost wallet containing a large sum of money, and in the other paragraph as stealing an examination from a professor's office.) After reading each paragraph, judges first reported their beliefs that they would like the person if they were actually to meet him (P_L), followed by their beliefs that he had the specific attribute to which the behavior in the paragraph pertained (P_X) and their beliefs that he had each of two standard attributes, intelligence and sarcasm. Finally, they estimated the various conditional beliefs that the person would be liked if he did and did not have these various attributes. Consistent with the general conceptualization previously described, predictions of liking based upon beliefs associated with the attribute to which the stimulus information pertained (X) were more accurate than those based on beliefs associated with the standard traits that were not directly implied by this information and were inferred after liking was estimated.

2. Inferences about Real Persons

The processes postulated to underlie the effects described above should also be involved when subjects estimate their liking for real persons on the basis of limited information about them. To investigate this possibility, subjects run in pairs were first asked to describe themselves to one another with respect to a characteristic expected to be relevant to liking (e.g., recreational interests, socioeconomic background, attitude toward communism, etc.). Each subject in the pair described a different characteristic. The subject then reported his initial beliefs that he would like the other, that the other was similar to him with respect to the characteristic he had personally described, and the conditional beliefs that he would like the other if they were or were not similar with respect to this characteristic. After making these ratings and performing an interpolated task, each subject received bogus feedback to the effect that the other perceived them to be either very similar or very dissimilar with respect to the target characteristic, thus increasing or decreasing the subject's own belief in their similarity. New ratings of the other person were then obtained.

Beliefs in liking were predicted from beliefs about similarity on the basis of the equation:

$$P_L = P_{Sim}P_{L/Sim} + (1 - P_{Sim})P_{L/Sim'} \qquad (6)$$

where P_L is either the subject's belief that he would like the other or his belief that the other would like him, P_{Sim} is the subject's belief that he and O were similar with respect to the characteristic to which feedback pertained, and $P_{L/Sim}$ and $P_{L/Sim'}$ are conditional beliefs associated with the implications of this similarity for the judgment.

It would seem likely that before they received feedback information about their similarity to one another, subjects' predictions of their liking for the other would be based on criteria other than similarity with respect to the particular characteristic they had discussed. As expected on the basis of this reasoning, the subjects' predictions of liking were unsystematically related to beliefs about their similarity. In contrast, following feedback, subjects' liking estimates were affected by this information and its implications in a manner implied by Eq. (6). These results are therefore consistent with the general notion that subjects retrieve different attributes to use as a basis for their judgments, depending upon which are more salient, and that the accuracy of the proposed formulation in predicting these judgments on the basis of beliefs about a particular attribute varies accordingly.

V. Concluding Remarks

In this contribution we have attempted to provide a general conceptualization of the role of conditional inference processes in social inference, and of the conditions in which previously acquired information is accessed for use in making these inferences. Whereas the research applying the specific information proposed here has already been extensive, much more work is required to circumscribe the conditions in which the processes implied by this formulation are invalid, as well as to pinpoint more precisely the amount and type of information that are involved in these processes. However, if the formulation is valid, it provides a means of diagnosing the conditions in which particular pieces of information are used as a basis for forming beliefs about one's social environment and suggests a framework for exploring more rigorously some of the questions raised in this contribution.

REFERENCES

Abelson, R. P. Script processing in attitude formation and decision-making. In J. S. Carroll & J. W. Payne (Eds.), *Cognition and social behavior*. Hillsdale, N.J.: Erlbaum, 1976.

Abelson, R. P., & Rosenberg, M. J. Symbolic psycho-logic: A model of attitudinal cognition. *Behavioral Science*, 1958, **3**, 1–13.

Anderson, J. R., and Bower, G. H. *Human associative memory.* Washington, D.C.: Winston, 1973.

Anderson, N. H. Averaging versus adding as a stimulus-combination rule in impression formation. *Journal of Experimental Psychology,* 1965, **70,** 394–400.

Anderson, N. H. Functional measurement and psychophysical judgment. *Psychological Review,* 1970, **77,** 153–170.

Anderson, N. H. Cognitive algebra: Integration theory applied to social attribution. In L. Berkowitz (Ed.), *Advances in experimental social psychology.* Vol. 7. New York: Academic Press, 1974.

Bem, D. J. Self-perception: An alternative interpretation of cognitive dissonance phenomena. *Psychological Review,* 1967, **74,** 183–200.

Bem, D. J. Self-perception theory. In L. Berkowitz (Ed.), *Advances in experimental social psychology.* Vol. 6. New York: Academic Press, 1972.

Bem, D. J., & McConnell, H. K. Testing the self-perception explanation of dissonance phenomena: On the salience of premanipulation attitudes. *Journal of Personality and Social Psychology,* 1970, **14,** 23–31.

Berkowitz, L., & Aliote, J. T. The meaning of an observed event as a determinant of its aggressive consequences. *Journal of Personality and Social Psychology,* 1973, **28,** 206–217.

Cantor, N., & Mischel, W. Traits as prototypes: Effects on recognition memory. *Journal of Personality and Social Psychology,* 1977, **35,** 38–48.

Carlston, D. The effects of interpolated encoding on the recall of behavior and judgments based on it. Unpublished doctoral dissertation, University of Illinois, 1977.

Collins, A. M., & Loftus, E. F. A spreading-activation theory of semantic processing. *Psychological Review,* 1975, **82,** 407–428.

Craik, F. I. M. Depth of processing in recall and recognition. In S. Dornic (Ed.), *Attention and performance VI.* Hillsdale, N.J.: Erlbaum, 1977.

Craik, F. I. M., & Lockhart, R. S. Levels of processing: A framework for memory research. *Journal of Verbal Learning and Verbal Behavior,* 1972, **11,** 671–684.

Festinger, L., & Maccoby, E. On resistance to persuasive communications. *Journal of Abnormal and Social Psychology,* 1964, **68,** 359–366.

Fishbein, M. A consideration of beliefs, attitudes and their relationships. In I. Steiner & M. Fishbein (Eds.), *Contemporary studies in social psychology.* New York: Holt, 1965. Pp. 107–120.

Fishbein, M., & Hunter, R. Summation versus balance in attitude organization and change. *Journal of Abnormal and Social Psychology,* 1964, **69,** 505–510.

Greenwald, A. G. Cognitive learning, cognitive response to persuasion and attitude change. In A. Greenwald, T. Brock, & T. M. Ostrom (Eds.), *Psychological foundations of attitudes.* New York: Academic Press, 1968.

Hastie, R., Ostrom, T., Ebbesen, E., Wyer, R., Hamilton, D., & Carlston, D. (Eds.), *Cognitive bases of impression formation and person memory.* Hillsdale, N.J.: Erlbaum, 1980.

Heider, F. *The psychology of interpersonal relations.* New York: Wiley, 1958.

Henninger, M. The reexamination of the "Socratic effect": Will artifact be its hemlock? Unpublished master's thesis, University of Illinois, 1975.

Henninger, M., & Wyer, R. S. The recognition and elimination of inconsistencies among syllogistically related beliefs: Some new light on the "Socratic effect." *Journal of Personality and Social Psychology,* 1976, **34,** 680–693.

Higgins, E. T., Rholes, W. S., & Jones, C. R. Category accessibility and impression formation. *Journal of Experimental Social Psychology,* 1977, **13,** 141–154.

McGuire, W. J. A syllogistic analysis of cognitive relationships. In M. J. Rosenberg, C. I. Houland, W. J. McGuire, R. P. Abelson, & J. W. Brehm (Eds.), *Attitude organization and change: An analysis of consistency among attitude components.* New Haven, Conn.: Yale University Press, 1960.

Mosteller, F., & Tukey, J. W. Data analysis, including statistics. In G. Lindzey & E. Aronson (Eds.), *Handbook of social psychology*. Vol. 2. Reading, Mass.: Addison-Wesley, 1968.

Rosen, N. A., & Wyer, R. S. Some further evidence for the "socratic effect" using a subjective probability model of cognitive functioning. *Journal of Personality and Social Psychology*, 1972, **24**, 420–424.

Rosenberg, S., & Sedlak, A. Structural representations of implicit personality theory. In L. Berkowitz (Ed.), *Advances in experimental social psychology*, Vol. 6. New York: Academic Press.

Salancik, J. R., & Calder, B. J. A nonpredispositional information analysis of attitude expressions. Unpublished manuscript, University of Illinois at Urbana-Champaign, 1974.

Salancik, J. R. Inference of one's attitude from behavior recalled under linguistically-manipulated cognitive sets. *Journal of Experimental Social Psychology*, 1974, **10**, 415–427.

Slovic, P., & Lichtenstein, S. Comparison of Bayesian and regression approaches to the study of human information processing in judgment. *Organizational Behavior and Human Performance*, 1971, **6**, 649–744.

Srull, T. K., & Wyer, R. S. The role of category accessibility in the interpretation of information about persons: Some determinants and implications. *Journal of Personality and Social Psychology*, 1979, **37**, 1660–1672.

Tesser, A. Self-generated attitude change. In L. Berkowitz (Ed.), *Advances in experimental social psychology*, Vol. 11. New York: Academic Press, 1978.

Tesser, A., & Leone, C. Cognitive schemas and thought as determinants of attitude change. *Journal of Experimental Social Psychology*, 1977, **13**, 340–356.

Trope, Y. Inferential processes in the forced compliance situation: A Bayesian analysis. *Journal of Experimental Social Psychology*, 1974, **10**, 1–16.

Tversky, A., & Kahneman, D. Availability: A heuristic for judging frequency and probability. *Cognitive Psychology*, 1973, **5**, 207–232.

Wyer, R. S. The quantitative prediction of belief and opinion change: A further test of a subjective probability model. *Journal of Personality and Social Psychology*, 1970, **16**, 559–571.

Wyer, R. S. Test of a subjective probability model of social evaluation processes. *Journal of Personality and Social Psychology*, 1972, **22**, 279–286.

Wyer, R. S. Category ratings as "subjective expected values": Implications for attitude formation and change. *Psychological Review*, 1973, **80**, 446–467. (a)

Wyer, R. S. Further test of a subjective probability model of social inference. *Journal of Research in Personality*, 1973, **7**, 237–253. (b)

Wyer, R. S. *Cognitive organization and change: An information-processing approach*. Potomac, Md.: Erlbaum, 1974. (a)

Wyer, R. S. Some implications of the "Socratic effect" for alternative models of cognitive consistency. *Journal of Personality*, 1974, **42**, 399–419. (b)

Wyer, R. S. Direct and indirect effects of essay writing and information about other persons' opinions upon beliefs in logically related propositions. *Journal of Personality and Social Psychology*, 1975, **31**, 55–63. (a)

Wyer, R. S. Functional measurement analysis of a subjective probability model of cognitive functioning. *Journal of Personality and Social Psychology*, 1975, **31**, 94–100. (b)

Wyer, R. S. The role of probabilistic and syllogistic reasoning in cognitive organization and social inference. In M. Kaplan & S. Schwartz (Eds.), *Human judgment and decision processes*. New York: Academic Press, 1975. (c)

Wyer, R. S. Effects of previously formed beliefs on syllogistic inference processes. *Journal of Personality and Social Psychology*, 1976, **33**, 307–316.

Wyer, R. S. The role of logical and nonlogical factors in making inferences about category membership. *Journal of Experimental Social Psychology*, 1977, **13**, 577–595.

Wyer, R. S., & Carlston, D. *Social cognition, inference and attribution*. Hillsdale, N.J.: Erlbaum, 1979.

Wyer, R. S., & Henninger, M. The effects of reporting beliefs on the recall of belief-related propositions. Unpublished manuscript, University of Illinois at Urbana-Champaign, 1978.

Wyer, R. S., & Polsky, H. Test of a subjective probability model for predicting receptiveness to alternative explanations of individual behavior. *Journal of Research in Personality*, 1972, **6**, 220–229.

Wyer, R. S., & Srull, T. K. Category accessibility: Some theoretical and empirical issues concerning the processing of social stimulus information. In E. T. Higgins, C. P. Herman, and M. P. Zanna (Eds.) *Social cognition: The Ontario Symposium on Personality and Social Psychology*. Hillsdale, N.J.: Erlbaum, 1980. (a)

Wyer, R. S., & Srull, T. K. The processing of social stimulus information: A conceptual integration. In R. Hastie, T. Ostrom, E. Ebbesen, R. Wyer, D. Hamilton, & D. Carlston (Eds.), *Cognitive bases of impression formation and person memory*. Hillsdale, N.J.: Erlbaum, 1980. (b)

INDEX

Performance (*cont.*)
  social comparison processes and, 29–30
  social uses of equation for, 11–17
  theory of self-esteem and, 32–34
Personality, excuses and, 22–25
Persuasion, communication and, 261–263
Plausibility, strength of implications and, 267–271
Power, performance attribution equation and, 5–8
Priming, effects on behavior, 266
Probability, subjective, attribution of responsibility and, 123–126
Punishment, entailment model of, 125–127

R

Reasons, attribution of responsibility and, 114–116
Recency, information accessibility and, 254
  effects of belief accessibility on changes in beliefs and, 259–263
  effects of priming on behavior and, 266
  effects of prior judgments on subsequent inferences and, 256–257
  effects of prior use of concepts on interpretation of material and, 263–266
  general considerations, 254–255
  Socratic effect and, 257–259
Response(s)
  emotional, in James' theory, 142–143
  verbal, conversion behavior and, 231–235
Responsibility, attribution of, 82
  accident research and defensive attribution and, 85–90
  attribution theory and, 82–85
  commonsense notions of responsibility and, 95–96
  developmental studies, 90–93
  entailment model and, 125–127
  Heider's levels and, 117–123
  intervening causes and, 127–129
  language and, 130–132
  quantitative models and, 106–113
  relationship to attribution theory and research, 104–106
  relevant legal concepts, 101–104
  responsibility in legal philosophy and, 96–101
  social context and, 132–134

subjective probabilities and, 123–125
theories for assigning responsibility, 113–116
Rewards, intrinsic motivation and, 67–68
  factors in rewardee, 68–69
  factors in rewarder, 70
  factors in situation, 69–70
Role(s), responsibility and, 113–114
Role playing, effects on self-judgments, 261

S

Salience, intrinsic motivation and, 48–50
  rewards and, 69–70
Schematic processing, emotion and, 171–181
Schools, intrinsic motivation and perceived competence in, 70
  descriptive information on school children and, 74
  impact of teacher characteristics and, 71–73
  motivational subsystems and, 73–74
Self-determination, intrinsic motivation and, 41–42, 58–61
Self-esteem
  performance and, 17–18
    excuses and accounts for poor performance and, 18
    excuses, interests, and personality and, 22–25
    excuses in the long term and, 21–22
    short-term excuses for a single poor performance and, 18–21
  theory of, performance and, 32–34
Social context, attribution of responsibility and, 132–134
Socratic effect, 257–259
Stimulus decoding, response selection and, 143

T

Task
  difficulty of, performance attribution equation and, 8–9
  intrinsic motivation and, 50–53
Teacher characteristics, perceived competence in school and, 71–73

V

Validity
  in conditional inferences, 246–248
  as index of belief inconsistency, 249–250

CONTENTS OF OTHER VOLUMES